PRINCIPLES OF LAW

LAW AND PHILOSOPHY LIBRARY

Managing Editors

ALAN MABE, *Department of Philosophy, Florida State University,
Tallahasse, Florida 32306, U.S.A.*

MICHAEL D. BAYLES, *Department of Philosophy, Florida State
University, Tallahassee, Florida 32306, U.S.A.*

AULIS AARNIO, *Dept. of Civil Law, University of Helsinki,
Vvorikatv 5c, SF-00100 Helsinki, Finland*

Editorial Advisory Board

RALF DREIER, *Lehrstuhl für Allgemeine Rechtstheorie, Juristisches
Seminar der Georg-August Universität*
GEORGE P. FLETCHER, *School of Law, Columbia University*
ERNESTO GARZÓN VALDÉS, *Institut für Politikwissenschaft,
Johannes Gutenberg Universität Mainz*
HYMAN GROSS, *Corpus Christi College, Cambridge University*
JOHN KLEINIG, *Department of Law, Police Science and Criminal
Justice Administration, John Jay College of Criminal Justice, City
University of New York*
NICOLA LACEY, *New College, Oxford University*
NEIL MacCORMICK, *Centre for Criminology and the Social and
Philosophical Study of Law, Faculty of Law, University of
Edinburgh*
ALEKSANDER PECZENIK, *Juridiska Institutionen, University of
Lund*
ROBERT S. SUMMERS, *Cornell University*
ALICE ERH-SOON TAY, *Faculty of Law, University of Sydney*
ERNEST J. WEINRIB, *Faculty of Law, University of Toronto*
CARL WELLMAN, *Dept. of Philosophy, Washington University*

MICHAEL D. BAYLES
Dept. of Philosophy, Florida State University

PRINCIPLES
OF LAW

A Normative Analysis

D. REIDEL PUBLISHING COMPANY

A MEMBER OF THE KLUWER ACADEMIC PUBLISHERS GROUP

DORDRECHT / BOSTON / LANCASTER / TOKYO

Library of Congress Cataloging-in-Publication Data

Bayles, Michael D.
  Principles of law.

  (Law and philosophy library)
  Bibliography: p.
  Includes index.
  1. Jurisprudence. 2. Law – Philosophy.
  I. Title. II. Series.
  K230.B425P75   1987   340.'1   87–4542
  ISBN 90–277–2412–1
  ISBN 90–277–2413–X (pbk.)

Published by D. Reidel Publishing Company,
P.O. Box 17, 3300 AA Dordrecht, Holland.

Sold and distributed in the U.S.A. and Canada
by Kluwer Academic Publishers,
101 Philip Drive, Assinippi Park, Norwell, MA 02061, U.S.A.

In all other countries, sold and distributed
by Kluwer Academic Publishers Group,
P.O. Box 322, 3300 AH Dordrecht, Holland.

All Rights Reserved
© 1987 by D. Reidel Publishing Company, Dordrecht, Holland
No part of the material protected by this copyright notice may be reproduced or
utilized in any form or by any means, electronic or mechanical,
including photocopying, recording or by any information storage and
retrieval system, without written permission from the copyright owner

Printed in The Netherlands

340.1
B358p

To the memory of my grandparents:
Howard and Lois Widger, Ross and Zola Bayles

CONTENTS

ANALYTICAL TABLE OF CONTENTS

EDITORIAL PREFACE

During the last half of the twentieth century, legal philosophy (or legal theory or jurisprudence) has grown significantly. It is no longer the domain of a few isolated scholars in law and philosophy. Hundreds of scholars from diverse fields attend international meetings on the subject. In some universities, large lecture courses of five hundred students or more study it.

The primary aim of the Law and Philosophy Library is to present some of the best original work on legal philosophy from both the Anglo-American and European traditions. Not only does it help make some of the best work available to an international audience, but it also encourages increased awareness of, and interaction between, the two major traditions. The primary focus is on full-length scholarly monographs, althouogh some eidted volumes of original papers are also included. The Library editors are assisted by an Editorial Advisory Board of internationally renowned scholars.

Legal philosophy should not be considered a narrowly circumscribed field. Insights into law and legal institutions can come from diverse disciplines on a wide range of topics. Among the relevant disciplines or perspectives contributing to legal philosophy, besides law and philosophy, are anthropology, economics, political science, and sociology. Among the topics included in legal philosophy are theories of law; the concepts of law and legal institutions; legal reasoning and adjudication; epistemological issues of evidence and procedure; law and justice, economics, politics, or morality; legal ethics; and theories of legal fields such as criminal law, contracts, and property.

ALAN MABE
MICHAEL BAYLES

PREFACE

During the 1970s, the economic analysis of law became the dominant mode of analysis in jurisprudence, at least in American law schools. However, as its critics always recognized and some of its foremost proponents came to realize, it rests on normative assumptions – that efficiency or wealth maximization should be the sole aim of the law. Normative analyses of the law tend to be either abstract considerations of principles for all legal systems or extremely detailed considerations of particular problems. In recent years, some normative analyses of particular legal fields, specifically, contract and criminal law, have appeared. Nonetheless, there is no systematic normative analysis of the law at an intermediate level.

This book attempts to help fill this gap. It presents a unified normative analysis of procedural, property, contract, tort, and criminal law. The unity resides more in the methodology than in principles spanning these fields. The central question is what principles rational persons would accept for judges to use in deciding cases in a modern, industrialized common-law society in which they expected to live. This method is used to develop principles for the fields considered. The restriction to fields of traditional judge-made law is important; a frequent theme is the limits the institution of adjudication imposes on acceptable principles. Obviously, even with the restriction of fields, many important topics had to be omitted, and the discussion of those included is much briefer than one finds in law review articles. The point is as much to frame the issues and to illustrate the method of analysis as to reach fully defended conclusions on particular points.

The book is primarily intended for legal philosophers without an extensive background in law and law school students. Legal philosophers and law students interested in jurisprudence should find it a useful first approach to various topics that can be followed with more detailed study. Law students should also find the systematic normative presentation of fields usually studied in the first year a help in grasping an overview of these fields of law. Many standard cases from law school texts are discussed or cited. However, on the recommendation of several friends and acquaintances, the book is written to be accessible to as wide an audience as possible. Consequently, I have presented informal definitions of legal terms and background information about the extant law. Although a glossary is not included, when technical terms are first used they are in single quotes and references to informal defintions can be found in the index. Thus, philosophy students and others with little legal background may find it a useful introduction to the law as well as the normative problems in the various fields.

A major problem exists in discussing the extant law, even if only as a general background for normative analysis. There is no single body of extant common law. Besides the differences between the United States, Canada, England, Australia, and New Zealand, significant differences exist among the various jurisdictions within the United States and Canada. In general, I have emphasized what appears to be the majority view in the United States, although attention is given to major English cases. The chapter on procedure focuses almost exclusively on U.S. federal procedure. However, as explained further in the introduction, I have eschewed assuming a federal system or U.S. constitutional law so that the analysis will be widely applicable.

In some ways, work on this book spans at least a decade. During the 1974-75 academic year, I was a Liberal Arts Fellow at Harvard Law School, which was made possible by an American Council of Learned Societies study fellowship. But it was not until discussions with others at the Council for Philosophical Studies Institute on Law and Ethics during the summer of 1977 that I became fully conscious of the need for normative analysis of the basic legal fields. At that time, I had no thought of providing one myself. While Director of the Westminster Institute for Ethics and Human Values in London, Canada, I was director of projects on the philosophy or jurisprudence of tort, contract, and labor law. What I learned from the persons involved in these projects gave me some hope that I could write this book. However, it took the confidence and encouragement of Joel Feinberg to keep me from abandoning the project, although I still have misgivings about the audacity of presuming to write a book of this scope.

This book would not have been possible without the 1984-85 academic year for concentrated work at the National Humanities Center. Besides the kindness and efficiency of the Center staff, I must thank the J. N. Pew, Jr., Charitable Trust for its generosity in funding my fellowship at the Center and the University of Florida for granting me research leave. Several persons read and commented on early drafts of one or more

chapters, and I appreciate their time and efforts. They are Lawrence
Alexander, Richard Bronaugh, David Ellins, Barbara Levenbook, and
Nancy Margolis. Conrad Johnson and Paul Horton reviewed the penul-
timate version and provided both encouragement and criticism. In par-
ticular, Paul Horton's detailed comments saved me at least one egregious
mistake and made the final version much better, although I am confident
Paul would think it better had I followed more of his advice. I thank
David Ellins, my research assistant at Westminster Institute during
1983-84, Rebecca Sutton of the National Humanities Center staff, and
Eric Baker my research assistant at the University of Florida during the
Spring 1986, for invaluable bibliographic and library assistance. Dr.
Joseph Greic and Garratt Maass provided Yoeman Service in
proofreading.

Excerpts of sections 1.1, 1.2, and 1.4 as well as the bulk of 2.0–2.1
and 4.0–4.2.4 have previously appeared in slightly different form as
"Legally Enforceable Commitments," *Law and Philosophy* **4** (1985):
311-42; and "Principles for Legal Procedure," *Law and Philosophy* **5**
(1986): 33-57. An early version of sections 6.0-6.2.4 was presented to the
Canadian Section, International Association for Philosophy of Law and
Social Philosophy, Guelph, Ontario, June 1984. Finally, a version of section 3.4.4 was presented to the Florida Philosophical Association, Ocala,
Florida, November 1985.

LIST OF ABBREVIATIONS

Legal materials—cases and statutes—are generally cited following *A Uniform System of Citation* Thirteenth Edition. However, I deviate in a few instances and include a couple of other items below for those unfamiliar with legal citations. 'See' indicates that full information is in the list of Works Cited.

A.B.A.	See American Bar Association.
A.P.A.	See American Psychiatric Association.
Fed. R. Civ. P.	*Federal Rules of Civil Procedure* (as amended through February 26, 1983).
Fed. R. Evid.	*Federal Rules of Evidence* (1975).
G.B.R.C.	See Great Britain, Royal Commission on Civil Liability and Compensation for Personal Injury.
L.R.C.C.	See Law Reform Commission of Canada.
M.P.C.	*Model Penal Code.* See American Law Institute.
N.C.I.D.	See National Commission on the Insanity Defense.
N.Z.R.C.	See New Zealand, Royal Commission of Inquiry.
Prosser and Keeton	See Keeton, W. Page et al.
Rest. Contracts	*Restatement (First) of Contracts* (1933).
Rest. Property	*Restatement (First) of Property* (1936).
Rest. 2d Contracts	*Restatement (Second) of Contracts* (1979).
Rest. 2d Judgments	*Restatement (Second) of Judgments* (1980).
Rest. 2d Property	*Restatement (Second) of Property: Landlord and Tenant* (1977).
Rest. 2d Torts	*Restatement (Second) of Torts* (1965 for secs. 1-503; 1976 for secs. 504-707A; 1979 for secs. 708-).
U.C.C.	*Uniform Commercial Code* (1978).
U.C.C.C.	*Uniform Consumer Credit Code* (1974).

CHAPTER 1

INTRODUCTION:
A FRAMEWORK FOR ANALYSIS

INTRODUCTION

1.0.   Law is studied in various ways for many different purposes. The most common purposes are descriptive and predictive. Practicing lawyers study the law to obtain legal rules and principles describing the law and enabling them to predict what courts will decide and to persuade courts to so decide. Another purpose is to explain the law, especially as a sociological or economic phenomenon. Some philosophers study law to determine the conceptual elements of legal systems and to distinguish law from other institutions and practices. But the law can also be studied to determine what legal principles and rules are justifiable or desirable. This normative purpose is the dominant perspective of this book. However, because adequate normative analysis cannot occur in a vacuum, a secondary purpose is to describe the extant common law. The combination of normative principles and description will also provide a rational systematization of the law.

A NORMATIVE APPROACH

1.1.   The purpose of this book is to determine justifiable legal principles for a contemporary common-law society. Obviously, one volume is not sufficient to analyze all the principles of a plausible legal system for contemporary society. To have a possible task, two limitations are necessary. First, only five fields are considered: procedural, property, contract, tort, and criminal law. These fields form the foundation of common-law systems and are the chief subjects for beginning students. Second, within these five fields, some subtopics are omitted, and many complexities and details are not examined. Volumes can be and have been written about each of these fields. The focus here is on the basic principles outlining and systematizing them.

   Although much is lost in specificity, the compensation is breadth of analysis. Current legal philosophy leaves a gap between discussion of

1

specific issues and discussion of abstract features of all legal systems. Although some recent work has considered the substantive elements of particular fields, especially contract and criminal law, the gap remains. There are also problems of coordination between legal fields, which detailed normative analyses of specific fields often ignore. For example, if an analysis of contract law consigns cases of misrepresentation to tort law, then one needs to be sure that the analysis of tort law adequately handles them. Finally, outlines and hornbooks for specific fields do not fill this gap. The outlines are confined to a description of extant law, and although hornbooks sometimes provide normative justification as well as descripition, the focus is often on specific rules so that the forest is not seen for the trees.

The normative purpose has important implications for the types of arguments that are appropriate. That a principle was adopted by courts does not imply that it is justifiable. Cases and precedents are considered primarily to illustrate problems and suggest arguments and secondarily to describe extant law. It is no argument against the normative views put forth here that they do not account for as many precedents as other views. The normative issue is whether the principles embodied in precedents are justifiable; if they are not, then at least on the merits there are reasons for overruling them, although judges have other reasons for following precedents (2.3.9). Moreover, it is no objection that the principles are not part of any extant legal system; the argument is that they should be. It is conceivable that the whole thrust of a field of law is unjustified. Socialists condemn much of property law, and plausible arguments can be given for replacing the common-law tort system with comprehensive no-fault accident insurance (5.5). These issues are generally beyond the scope of this book, which, except for a brief discussion of tort law (5.5), is restricted to what courts should do when confronted by parties to a dispute. Although legal decisions can sometimes lead to rather sweeping changes, as explained below (1.4), courts do not have the power simply to institute a comprehensive no-fault accident insurance scheme. This limitation to what courts can and should do is a crucial restriction on the principles and traditional common law.

The secondary descriptive purpose is chiefly limited to providing a context for understanding the normative principles and their justifications and implications and showing how they systematize the law. For the most part, the differences in extant law between common-law countries and between jurisdictions within a country are not important at the level of analysis undertaken. Sometimes the differences are useful as illustrating the difference between justifiable principles and others. Generally, the description focuses on the majority view in American jurisdictions, with secondary emphasis on England and Canada. In discussing procedural law, the description is almost exclusively of American federal procedure.

The reasons why a principle is in law, and those why it should be, need not be the same. Causal or historical explanations of the law do not necessarily provide normative justifications of it. One can have a perfectly good explanation of why a court or legislature adopted a law, but the law be quite unjustifiable. Similarly, there may be perfectly good justifications for legal principles but they not be the reasons the principles were incorporated into the law. Even though the arguments given here often support extant principles, because the purpose is normative and not explanatory, the reasons may not be those given when they were incorporated into the law or even those usually given now. It is no objection that the reasons for, or causes of, incorporation of a principle are different from those given here. Of course, the reasons historically given for legal principles are sometimes also adequate justifications, and there can also be justifications for legal principles that have not been adopted but should be.

Finally, no attempt is made to predict the course of the law, what courts will in fact decide. Nor is it a valid objection to the normative views here that courts are not likely to, or certainly will not, accept principles advocated. Of course, reasons courts have for not doing so might be good grounds for rejecting the principles. Contrarily, the arguments here should provide courts good reasons to adopt the principles and might be used to persuade them to do so.

If appeals to what courts have done or will do or to the explanations for their decisions do not count against the proposed principles, then obviously the principles cannot be defended on these grounds either. Because justifying differs from describing, explaining, and predicting, substantive reasons must be given to show that the principles are justifiable. That is, what in law schools are called policy arguments or arguments of principle are generally appropriate. These types of arguments are often used for reform, and they can be presented to courts (or legislatures) in support of principles. Much disagreement exists about what constitutes an appropriate substantive argument. The disagreement is not simply over the soundness of such arguments, or even what can serve as premises, but the very form of appropriate arguments.

Justification is of something to someone in certain circumstances (Bayles 1986, 60). The preceding discussion has indicated roughly the something, namely, principles for courts to use in the five fields. This will be made more precise (1.4). In doing so, assumptions about the nature of courts and the judicial system are also made more explicit. Before doing this, we consider to whom the justification is to be given and the circumstances.

RATIONAL PERSONS

1.2. Principles are to be justified to rational persons who expect to live in a society in which the principles are used by courts to decide cases (Brandt 1985, 169; Brandt 1979, 10-16; Bayles 1978, 51-54). A rational person uses logical reasoning and all relevant available information in acquiring desires and values, deciding what to do, and accepting legal principles. Logical reasoning is not restricted to deductive logic but also includes inductive logic or scientific method. A rational person considers arguments for and against principles, accepting the sound arguments and rejecting the unsound ones.

All relevant available information is all pertinent information that a person in the situation can obtain. First, it is information, not knowledge, that a rational person has. People are rational if they use the best information available, even if it later turns out to be incorrect; indeed, it would be irrational to use information that, on the basis of presently available evidence, appeared incorrect, even if it were later found to be correct. Second, information is available if it is publicly ascertainable. Available information includes publicly available scientific information (the best scientific views at the time) as well as factual information justified by evidence accessible to the public. The information available thus varies over time.

The most difficult concept to elucidate is that of relevance. A causal concept of relevance is that information is relevant if it would make a difference to a person's tendency to choose an action or to find something attractive (Brandt 1979, 14). Although there are some questions for which no better concept is available, for present purposes a more precise concept can be used. Information is relevant to the acceptability of a legal principle if it indicates that the principle's use by courts has or lacks some normative characteristic, such as fairness, or that the probable consequences of such use would be good or bad. The first element, that a principle's use has or lacks some normative characteristic, is designed to capture considerations independent of the consequences of decisions based on it. The second element pertains to the consequences of decisions based on a principle. Besides the effects on the parties to the case, it includes effects on others and the likelihood of principles being used correctly by courts. For example, a principle might be too vague or complex for courts usually to use it correctly. Both elements require a prior normative basis for evaluating characteristics or consequences. In effect, information is relevant if, in legal terminology, it indicates something about the nature or consequences of the principle.

As the discussion of relevance makes clear, some normative basis must be used in determining what legal principles are justifiable or acceptable. This normative basis need not be a moral or legal one; it could simply be, for example, desires for wealth and security. Rational persons would not have irrational desires, those that one would not acquire if one had all relevant available information and used logic. (It is here that the causal concept of relevance is most appropriate.) However, rational persons might have different desires. For example, some rational people might like and desire tapioca and others not. Neither group obviously fails to use logic or relevant available information.

Much legal analysis and justification, especially in tort law, is in terms of people's interests. There is little reason to believe that these interests or desires (the difference is not important here) are irrational. Certain basic desires are assumed to be rational: those for bodily and mental integrity (including life), prestige or reputation, wealth, and security. The dispute about the rationality of these desires usually concerns their extent – how much wealth – not having them at all.

One might question the appropriateness of justification to rational persons. After all, no actual person is fully rational; each of us has some irrational desires and on occasion acts foolishly. So why should a justification to rational persons be relevant to actual human beings who are at best usually rational? There are three answers to this question. First, when ordinary people justify conduct and principles, they are trying to decide what the rational thing is – what a fully rational person would want, accept, or do. Ordinary people do take justifications to be unsound if they are shown to rest on incorrect information, involve invalid reasoning, or rest on irrational desires. Second, rational persons choosing legal principles for a society would recognize that ordinary people are not fully rational. They would not ignore irrational desires, although they might be less concerned to fulfill them than rational ones. Indeed, taking freedom as a value partly allows for irrational desires and conduct based on them. Third, the rational desires assumed above are quite general ones that almost everyone has. Consequently, the arguments appeal to everyone, or almost everyone, and indicate rational legal principles relevant to fulfilling these desires. At this level of generality, the differences between persons' desires (whether or not rational) are not usually important.

However, differences in peoples' circumstances can be important. Specifying their circumstances includes specifying the type of society in which they expect to live. Appropriate legal principles can vary depending on social conditions. For example, a principle restricting liability for contractual damages to the foreseeable consequences of breach might be necessary for a contemporary commercial society but not a traditional noncommercial one. For legal principles, detailed knowledge is not always necessary; legal rules often specify that the customs and practices of an activity be followed. This analysis assumes that the society is an industrialized Western one. The usual background assumption is North American society – the United States and Canada.

Still, a person's position in such a society could make a difference, particularly which party to a case one might be. It is assumed that rational persons could be either party to a dispute or legal case. This assumption is implicit in the very question being asked, for it concerns the acceptability of legal principles for a society in which one expects to live. Often one cannot assume that one will be a plaintiff or defendant. In tort, one either might have carelessly injured another or have been so injured. In contract cases, many principles can be used by plaintiff or defendant. The requirement that the principles be those for a legal system does not impose equal probability of being either party. One might, for example, have good reasons to believe that one is extremely unlikely to be a defendant in a criminal case.

This possibility requires using the general probability of being one party or another. By 'general probability' is simply meant 'that for the whole society – the number of different persons who will be plaintiff or defendant divided by the total population'. This precludes using factors that affect the probability of subpopulations being one party or the other. Thus, if one-half of one percent of the total population are ever criminal defendants but two percent of the black population, then one must assume that one has a one in two hundred chance of being a criminal defendant, not a one in fifty or no chance. This restriction to general probability is a limitation on rationality, for a fully rational person would use all available information. The justification for this limited restriction on information is to provide for equality or fairness in the methodology. Resort to the general probability of being a particular party is limited to those cases in which it is clear that a significantly smaller percentage of the population is likely to be in the role of one party than the other.

In arguing for a legal principle, one must then consider its acceptability from both parties' points of view (see also Richards 1979, 1414-15, 1436). This type of argument is rather common in courts. An example is the following argument by Judge Turnage for the rule that rejection of a purchased option does not terminate the right to accept later unless the other party has materially changed position.

> This rule fully protects the rights of both parties. It extends to the optionor the protection he requires in the event a rejection of the option is communicated to him and he thereafter changes his position in reliance thereon to his detriment. At the same time it protects the right of the option holder to have the opportunity to exercise his option for the full period for which he paid, absent the material change in position. (*Ryder v. Wescoat*, 535 S.W.2d 269 (Mo. Ct. App. 1976).)

This argument shows that it is a reasonable rule whichever party one might be. One has no reason to think that people are more likely to have written than purchased an option. In other situations, however, there might be reason to think that people are more likely to be one party than another. In that case, one must assess the advantages and disadvantages to a party by the probability of being in that position.

Throughout this book the question concerns what legal principles a rational person in these circumstances would accept for courts to use. However, for stylistic reasons, the arguments are addressed to the reader as such a rational person.

VALUES

1.3.   Besides desires for wealth, reputation, and so on, rational persons also have values such as those for freedom, privacy, responsibility, and equality of opportunity. Such values are often relevant to the evaluation of the nature and consequences of legal principles. Three of them are especially important for legal principles and have often been recognized in the traditional common law. Freedom, responsibility, and equality are each centrally related to respect for one as a rational person. If people are denied freedom to act without a justification based on principles they could rationally accept, they are not respected as rational persons. Also, rational persons are responsible agents. To fail to treat people as responsible agents when they are is to fail to accord them respect. One might even contend that people are denied respect if they are held legally liable when they are not responsible, because they are then treated as mere instruments for the well-being of others. Whether this connection is justifiable, rational persons would not accept being held liable when they were not responsible unless there were good reasons based on principles they could accept for doing so. Finally, rational persons should receive equal opportunities. To treat persons unequally without justification is to fail to accord them equal respect. Other arguments can be given for these values. The point here is merely to suggest why rational persons would hold them, not to argue for them in detail. Their justification is a complex and difficult matter that cannot be pursued here. Most of them have been justified elsewhere (Bayles 1978), but a brief analysis is appropriate.

To be free is to be free from some limit to doing something (see Bayles 1978, 71-78). For example, if Abbott has rented an automobile, she is free from liability for theft in using it. Sometimes laws increase freedom by enabling one to act in ways one could not otherwise act. The law of contract enables one to make and receive enforceable future commitments. Whether laws increase or decrease freedom depends on assumptions about a baseline condition. For example, if one's baseline is a condition of no laws, a so-called state of nature, laws concerning legal capacity to own property or contract enable one to do things and increase freedom. If one's baseline assumption includes laws of ownership and contract, then laws about legal capacity prevent some people from owning property and contracting and decrease freedom. Thus, asking whether laws or fields of law increase or decrease freedom is an unanswerable question until a baseline is specified.

Even then, there are many difficulties in answering. Laws that confer rights might be thought to increase freedom. However, each right has a correlative legal consequence for another person (see 3.2.0). If one person gains freedom by receiving an enforceable claim, then someone else loses freedom by having a duty to respect that claim. Consequently, there is always a reciprocal gain and loss of freedom. Whether recognition of a right is desirable or good depends on how one evaluates the freedom gained and lost. Nonetheless, if one assumes certain common preferences, one can evaluate legal fields, principles, and rules by how they reflect a concern for the freedoms most people prefer.

It only makes sense to talk of freedom to do things that human beings can do. One is not unfree to leap tall buildings in a single bound, for human beings do not have that capacity. Limits can be roughly classified as external or internal. External limits are conditions outside the person, such as threat of punishment or physical constraint. External limits often operate by making an action less desirable. For example, legal liability for smashing another's automobile does not make one physically incapable of doing it, but it does make it a less desirable course of action. Internal limits prevent one making a rational choice. Thus, mental illness or intoxication can prevent one making rational choices. Some factors fall on the borderline between external and internal limits. For example, ignorance can prevent one making a rational choice. If one's ignorance is due to another's deliberately misleading statements, then the limit can be classified as external. If it is due to one's own failure to obtain information, it can be classified as internal – a result of one's lack of effort.

There are several senses of 'responsible' (Hart 1968, 211-30). The one most frequent in the law is 'liability-responsibility'. In this sense, to be responsible is to be held accountable or liable for one's conduct or an occurrence. We shall use 'liable' for this sense. A second sense is 'capacity-responsibility'. One is responsible in this sense if one has the capacity reasonably to choose whether to do something or to bring something about and to do so. This is the type of responsibility mentally abnormal persons and children often lack. A third sense is 'causal-responsibility'. In this sense, a person or event is responsible for some state of affairs if it caused it.

One's interest is in being respected as a responsible person. But there are several senses of 'a responsible person'. In one sense, a responsible person is one who normally fulfills duties and obligations. In another sense, a responsible person is one who is responsible in one or more of the above senses of 'responsible'. Both of these senses are involved in being respected or treated as a responsible person. If a person cannot normally be counted on to fulfill duties and obligations, we do not respect him or her. However, our primary focus here is on being respected as a responsible person in the other sense.

Several normative considerations are involved. One way to fail to recognize someone as a responsible person is to impute a lack of capacity-responsibility when he or she has it. We often impute lack of capacity-responsibility by prohibiting people from engaging in activities. For example, we do not allow children to use firearms, because they lack the capacity to handle them safely. One can also fail to respect persons as having capacity-responsibility by failing to hold them liable for conduct. Normally, if one has capacity-responsibility and causal-responsibility for some consequence, one should be liable. If causal-responsibility is clear, then failure to hold a person liable implies the person lacks capacity-responsibility. Thus, generally one is not respected as a rational person if one is not allowed to act as others are or is not held liable.

As noted above, rational persons rarely have good reasons to be treated as liable when they are not responsible. We can now make this point more explicit. Without a justification based on acceptable principles, one could not accept being liable if one lacked capacity-responsibility or causal-responsibility. Situations are imaginable in which one might want to be liable even though one lacked capacity-responsibility. Word of one's incapacity, though temporary, might frustrate rational plans and projects that one had before and will have after the incapacity. Nevertheless, because these situations are rare, one would not want legal principles to ignore lack of capacity-responsibility or causal-responsibility. Thus, for legal principles to recognize responsibility as a value, they should permit people with capacity-responsibility to act and impose liability when they are also causally responsible for harms, but not impose liability on people who lack causal- or capacity-responsibility for harms.

Equality does not require the same treatment for all persons. Treatment as an equal, not equal treatment is the value (Dworkin 1977, 227). What recognition of rational persons as equals involves is much controverted, and we cannot here analyze the many problems involved. For present purposes, we can use two criteria for equality and fairness. The first criterion is the extent to which burdens are distributed fairly. A fair distribution is an equal one unless there are good reasons for an alternative distribution. Thus, individuals should not be singled out for no acceptable reason to bear burdens. However, equal distributions also violate equality and fairness if there are good reasons to treat people differently. In the legal context, the primary reasons for differences in treatment are differences in liability or culpability. For example, punishing the innocent equally with the guilty violates equality and fairness. The second criterion is the extent to which people have equal opportunities. If one person is given opportunities another is not, then they are not treated as equals. For example, there is not equal respect if one party is permitted to present evidence and the other is not. Of course, these two criteria are related, because imposing unfair burdens on individuals denies them equality of opportunity. This also points out that differences in opportunities can be justifiable. A person who has been convicted of a crime and incarcerated does not have equal opportunities with a person who has not. In general, the presumption for distribution of burdens and opportunities is equality; departures from this equality must be justified by acceptable principles.

Legal Principles

1.4. Legal principles are what is to be justified. Principles and rules can be distinguished (Dworkin 1977, 22-28; Bayles 1978, 42-44). On the one hand, rules apply in an all-or-nothing way; if they apply to a situation, they determine its evaluation. For example, a law requiring two witnesses to a will not in the handwriting of the deceased is a rule. If a will has only one witness, it is invalid. In contrast, when principles apply, they do not necessarily determine an evaluation. It may be a principle that people should be free to dispose of their property by 'devise' (a will) as they wish. It does not necessarily follow that a freely made will should be upheld, because a contrary principle, for example, that a person should make adequate provision for children, might also apply. On the other hand, because principles do not apply in an all-or-nothing way and can conflict, principles have a 'weight'. That is, conflicting principles must be weighed or balanced against one another, and some have more weight than others. Because rules apply in an all-or-nothing fashion, they do not have to be weighed or balanced against one another.

Some scholars reject this distinction between principles and rules, contending that principles differ from rules only by being more general (Raz 1972). On this view, both rules and principles have weight and can be balanced against one another. These are the essential features of the legal principles to be discussed. Moreover, principles can have different degrees of generality. Thus, a principle about freedom to dispose of property by devise is less general than one about freedom to dispose of property generally – by gift, sale, or devise. A principle can be supported by another more general one. Indeed, in the following, general principles justified at the beginning of a chapter are often used to justify more specific ones later in the chapter. Whether they are distinguished by the two characteristics above or only by specificity, rules are usually justifed by principles.

In short, principles present good- or bad-making characteristics that can be weighed or balanced against one another. They are usually used to

evaluate more specific principles or rules, although they can be used directly to evaluate particular actions or decisions. However, in common-law
systems, judicial decisions establish rules (precedents), and it is best to
conceive of principles as applying to the rules of decisions. The principles
of law are stated using 'should': for example, "Involuntary transfers of
property should be prohibited." This does not imply that involuntary transfers are always bad or wrong; involuntary transfers to pay court judgments
are not wrong. It does imply that in the absence of contrary considerations
(based on other principles), they should be prohibited; that is, there is a
good reason to prohibit them.

One must also distingish *legal* principles from nonlegal ones. Legal
principles are those to be used by judges in rendering decisions or by those
who develop legislation to be applied by judges. Thus, it is important to
indicate the role and powers of judges without prejudging questions of
substance or procedure. The following discussion distinguishes the roles of
courts and judges from other government organizations, especially legislatures, and indicates other features of the judicial system that are or are not
assumed. The institutional limits on adjudication have important implications for the principles that can be justified in the fields we consider.

Courts are generally limited to deciding actual cases or issues initiated
by one of the parties. The United States Constitution limits federal courts
to cases and controversies (art. III, § 2; see also Mermin 1973, 174-76,
179-80, 184-85; Wright 1983, 53-59). This restriction does not prohibit
'declaratory judgments' when disputes arise concerning a matter of law
likely to be involved in an actual controversy. But it does prohibit advisory
opinions in which some person or group simply wants an answer to a legal
question. Not all common-law courts are so restricted. Some, such as the
Canadian Supreme Court, can take issues referred to them by government
bodies, such as the legislature. This method is rarely used, especially in the
fields considered here. We shall assume that courts are limited to cases
brought to them by the parties in dispute. This limitation to particular
disputes significantly limits the scope of solutions that courts can provide.

Courts must render decisions applicable to the parties in the case. Of
course, the decision can be that no claim has been stated for which relief
can be granted, but that is to render a decision. Courts cannot simply
decline to decide because an issue is too complex. Appellate courts can
often refuse to take cases, but then the lower court decisions stand. The
U.S. Supreme Court can decide that a matter is a political question for
Congress rather than the Court, but again that is quite rare and does not

apply in the fields being considered (see *Baker v. Carr*, 369 U.S. 186 (1962)). Moreover, when courts give a final decision, it is legally binding on the parties. Of course, collecting a judgment for damages is sometimes harder than getting a favorable judicial decision, but this fact is not central to most of the issues considered in this book. It is assumed that a court decision will be carried out, but this assumption is relaxed where it is likely to be false and have significant implications for an acceptable principle.

Courts have limited investigative powers. At best, they can investigate matters relating to the specific case before them. They do not have the power to conduct a general investigation into, for example, business practices in an industry. In the common-law system, the burden of amassing and presenting evidence rests with the parties. Since the advent of the 'Brandeis brief', at least in the United States, lawyers can and do provide available relevant social information, but courts cannot undertake general social investigations of the sort made by legislative committees and commissions of inquiry. In civil-law countries, courts are more actively involved in amassing and presenting evidence, especially in criminal law cases, but they still do not have the powers of legislatures; they are limited to the case at hand. The assumption made here about the investigative powers of courts thus leaves open the difference between common and civil-law courts. That issue is partly discussed in considering the adversary system (2.2). Any bias, however, is towards the common-law system.

Courts do not always use principles correctly. Were one to assume that they did, different principles or rules might be accepted. For example, assuming a perfect court, a 'statute of limitations' might simply say that a case cannot be brought if, due to lapse of time, it would be unfair to allow it. In practice, such a rule would probably be unworkable for the courts. Some bright lines are needed for courts as much as potential litigants. Thus, a better rule is one that forbids bringing a case, say, more than three years after the basis for the claim arose.

Two further assumptions are made about the legal system in which courts operate. First, it is assumed to be a unitary rather than federal system. The fundamental question concerns the substantive justifiability of principles, and the reasons for and against them should be the same in either federal or state courts. Concern over federalist issues would simply complicate the discussion. Moreover, the division of powers in a federalist system tends to distort the fields of law. In Canada, because the federal government has the power to make criminal law, there is a tendency to include matters in criminal law so as to have federal jurisdiction and uniform laws. In the United States, the federal government lacks general criminal jurisdiction, and there is therefore a tendency to use the federal power to control interstate commerce to address matters that might better be addressed in other fields. Any conclusions based on one assumption of the division of powers might well be irrelevant to a system with a different division.

Second, and for similar reasons, no constitutional requirements are assumed. Any such assumptions would render the discussion irrelevant for systems without those requirements. As the general question is what the principles should be, assuming constitutional principles might beg the question. For example, England uses preventive detention of criminals, but the U.S. Constitution arguably forbids as broad a use of preventive detention as in England and other countries. However, the broader use of preventive detention might be the most justifiable principle. In short, assuming constitutional principles would limit the range of legal principles that might be considered and thus might exclude what in fact are the most justifiable principles. However, some of the matters discussed do relate to constitutional questions. Some principles might well be embedded in a constitution, if they are not already, or used to interpret constitutional provisions. Nonetheless, some common-law countries have managed without specific constitutional provisions, merely treating some principles as fundamental to the common law. Thus, constitutional cases are discussed, but only for the light they shed on particular principles, not because principles must conform to some given constitution.

It is now possible to formulate our question more precisely: What are the central principles that rational persons would accept on their merits for courts to use to decide procedural, property, contract, tort, and criminal issues in an industrialized Western society in which these persons expected to live? Before addressing this question, it is useful to examine briefly the elements of a legal case. These elements provide a set of subtopics in each substantive field for which principles are needed. In turn, these subtopics help organize consideration of the fields.

ELEMENTS OF A LEGAL CASE

1.5. Although there are differences between them, cases in property, contract, tort, and criminal law all involve three main elements. (1) The defendant had a legal duty to the plaintiff. (There is no reason to distinguish between legal obligations and duties, and the two terms are used interchangeably in this book.) (2) The defendant violated that duty. (3) A certain legal response is appropriate. Unless plaintiffs or prosecutors can establish each of these elements, they will lose. These three elements thus provide subtopics in each substantive field of law. The central principles specify what is involved in each of these elements. An additional subtopic in each field concerns its specific aims; these aims provide the most general principles in each field and are often involved in the justification of other principles.

The task of establishing that the defendant had a legal duty to the plaintiff varies among the legal fields. In property law, duties derive from property rights. Thus, to establish a duty, one usually has to establish the plaintiff's rights to property and derive the duty from that. The duties vary significantly depending on the form of property in question (kind of thing and ownership of it). Consequently, it is important to consider the forms of property before considering more specific rights and limits to them. Although more and more duties in contract law are being implied by law, by and large they stem from the contract, so a prior question is whether or not a contract exists, which involves issues of how contracts are formed. Duties in tort law are generally based on precedents and principles. When statutory duties are the basis of tort actions, they are usually not written directly for that purpose but another, for example, a statute or ordinance requiring people to clear the snow from sidewalks in front of their property. Nowadays in criminal law, crimes are specified in statutes. Few common law crimes remain as such; most jurisdictions have abolished them all. But whether a duty stems from statutory enactment, general principles, property rights, or a contract, whether or not the defendant had a duty is an essential element of cases in all the substantive fields.

Establishing that a defendant is liable for violating a duty involves two steps. First, one must show that an act or omission of the defendant was contrary to a duty. In some of the fields, such as criminal law, this is often a major source of dispute; the defendant contends "I didn't do it" – did not do the act contrary to duty. In other fields, such as contract, this aspect is rarely contested. The supplier clearly did or did not deliver two tons of steel. It does become an issue when the performance must be measured by some standard, such as completion of a house to specifications or whether delivered goods were satisfactory. Second, a defendant is not liable for an act or omission contrary to a duty if he or she has a valid defense. What constitutes a defense varies from field to field. Because establishing that the defendant performed or failed to perform an act is an empirical question for each case, our focus is on what defenses are acceptable.

Establishing the appropriateness of a legal response also often involves two steps. First, one must show what type of response is appropriate – payment of damages, 'specific performance' (4.4.4), 'injunction' (5.4.2), or punishment. Second, for damages and punishment, which are the more common responses, one must also indicate what amount is appropriate. Consequently, principles are needed to indicate when different types of response are appropriate and to provide guidance in determining the amount of damages or punishment.

It might be thought that a fourth element should be added, namely, causation. However, causation is not always an element in the fields being considered. For example, it is not an issue in property law cases involving the interpretation of a deed or will. Nor is it relevant in many contract cases. It is not even relevant in all of criminal law. Some crimes do not involve bringing about a harm independent of the criminal act; the wrong or harm is in the act itself, for example, rape. Moreover, where causation is especially prominent in criminal and tort law, it can pertain to the second or third element. In 'resultant-harm crimes' where the harm is independent of the act, if a defendant did not cause the harm, then he or she did not violate a duty (see Gross 1979, 124-27; Fletcher 1978, 388-90). The amount of harm actually caused can also be relevant to the duty violated and the appropriate amount of punishment. If the victim dies, assault and battery are converted to homicide carrying a greater punishment. Similarly in tort law, while causation is usually relevant to whether or not the defendant violated a duty, it is also important in determining amounts of damages. It is thus best to treat causation as a part of the issues of violation or response rather than as an independent element.

Consequently, in each substantive field, principles are needed for the following subtopics: aims, duties, defenses, and responses. In property, principles are also needed for the kinds of property and its acquisition and disposal. In contract, additional principles are needed concerning contract formation. Of course, these principles can also be relevant for tort and criminal law cases, for example, to determine whether someone had a property interest that was wrongfully taken.

Before considering the substantive fields, procedural law is examined. Substance and procedure are usually said to be closely connected, and one of the aims of procedural law, but not its sole aim, is to increase the likelihood that court decisions will conform to substantive principles. Still, procedure has more of an effect on substance and outcome than vice versa. The available substantive principles are limited by judical power and legal procedures for enforcement. Procedural law is common across all the civil or private law fields, and even criminal procedure is not vastly different. Thus, it is probably preferable to consider procedural law before considering the substantive fields. When the justifiable central principles for the subtopics in each of the substantive fields are added to procedural principles, a systematic outline of an important part of a justifiable legal system is established.

CHAPTER 2

PROCEDURAL LAW

Introduction

2.0.   In the previous chapter (1.4), we distinguished courts from legislatures by the necessity for courts to render decisions applicable to the particular parties in actual cases and controversies and by courts' limited investigative powers. In examining procedural law, further distinctions need to be made between adjudication and other methods of resolving controversies. A prominent conception of adjudication defines it by the form of participation of the parties – "presenting proofs and reasoned arguments" (Fuller 1978, 364). However, this definition tends to beg questions about the best type of procedure, biasing it in favor of an adversary system. A more neutral conception must be a more formal one.

Most features distinguishing adjudication from other forms of dispute resolution are implicit in the conception of courts deciding controversies between particular parties (see Golding 1975, 108-12; Golding 1978, 101-02). (1) There is a particular dispute. (2) Particular parties are involved; the dispute is not between large, amorphous groups such as environmentalists and industry. (3) A third party is involved. (4) A hearing is held in which information concerning the dispute is presented. (5) The third party "settles" the controversy by rendering a decision. (6) This decision is based on principles and rules – those of the substantive law – with reference to the information presented at the hearing.

These features clearly distinguish adjudication from mediation and negotiation. In the latter, no third party is involved; the dispute is settled directly by agreement between the parties or their representatives. In mediation, although a third party is involved, the third party does not render a decision; instead, as in negotiation, the parties agree to a settlement.

The above features do not clearly distinguish adjudication from arbitration. One might suggest that arbitration differs from adjudication by its reliance on private rules created by private agreement of the parties rather than public rules (Golding 1978, 101). However, courts regularly enforce contracts, most terms of which result from agreement of the parties; and arbitrators use public rules in interpreting agreements. Alternatively, one

18

might suggest that the difference is that adjudicators are publicly appointed but arbitrators are chosen by the parties. Although this is usually the case, some arbitrators are appointed by the government, and one can at least conceive of a private court system in which the parties choose the court and judge. The difference between the private and public status of decision-makers is primarily a matter of authority or jurisdiction, not the essence of adjudication. Consequently, no clear and sharp distinction exists between adjudication and arbitration; at most, there is a continuum with privately chosen third parties deciding on the basis of private rules at one end and publicly appointed third parties deciding on the basis of public rules at the other end.

Aims

2.1.0. *Introduction.* Legal philosophers are inclined to seek one aim for a field of law and to build their entire account around it. An advantage of this approach is that it provides a unity to the field. However, human beings, and courts composed of them, are not such single-minded machines. People can and usually do have more than one purpose for their activities or institutions and reconcile or balance them when they conflict. Consequently, these single aim or purpose theories fail to capture all of what courts do and one might rationally want them to do.

Two general purposes are inherent in the above concept of adjudication – resolving disputes and finding the "truth." That courts render decisions in cases and controversies implies that one purpose is the resolution of disputes. If judicial decisions were not intended to resolve disputes, but, say, only to indicate support for one side or the other, there would be little reason to litigate. One must be clear about the sense in which a dispute is resolved. Even after final judgment, losing parties can still think they were right, and enmity can still exist between the parties. Courts do not necessarily resolve disputes at the psychological level, only at the practical level, and even there they are not always successful. If Abramowitz claims Baxter owes him $5,439 and the court finds for him, then he is entitled to use state power to collect. Usually, but not always, Baxter will pay. The difficulty ex-spouses have in collecting spousal and child support indicates that court decisions do not always result in a practical settlement.

The purpose of ascertaining truth is less obviously inherent in the concept of adjudication. Adjudicators are to decide disputes by the application of rules and principles. Even assuming that the rules and principles are correct, a dispute will not be properly decided in accordance with them unless the "truth" or correct facts are determined. The truth needs to be found not for its own sake but to apply the rules and principles to the dispute correctly. The particular aims of the rules and principles – justice, economic efficiency, public policy – make no difference. If the situation is not accurately understood and described, then the aims cannot be rationally served by the decision either as a resolution of the particular case or as a guide in others (Summers 1978, 123). To the extent courts formulate rules for practical guidance, they need to be based on accurate information about the situations to which they are to apply, otherwise they might prescribe impractical and even harmful conduct.

Of course, judicial decision making is not a simple application of rules and principles to facts. First, finding facts is not a straightforward descriptive process. Facts must be classified for the application of rules and do not come neatly labeled (Hart 1983, 63). Second, many so-called factual questions are matters of evaluation (Atiyah 1983, 34-36). Determining whether someone was negligent, reasonable, or insane requires judgment and evaluation. Third, even when the facts are clear, it is not always clear what the rules and principles imply. Is a child on a railroad tie extending over a public river on railroad property or not (*Hynes v. New York Cent. R.R. Co.*, 231 N.Y. 229, 131 N.E. 898 (1921))? Nonetheless, there are core factual matters that one needs to get correct – that the child was on the tie, that the tie was fastened to railroad property, and so on.

The purposes of dispute resolution and ascertainment of the truth do not provide usable criteria for evaluating legal procedure; they are too general. Dispute resolution is a purpose of the whole of law, substantive as well as procedural. Unlike pure science, the law does not aim at the truth, the whole truth, and nothing but the truth. That would be too expensive and often irrelevant to the purpose of dispute resolution. Yet, disputes could be resolved without any concern for the truth. Arbitrary fiats or flips of a coin could be used practically to resolve many disputes. Consequently, more specific aims are needed to evaluate legal procedures.

2.1.1. *Economic costs.* Although in this section we focus on economic analysis of procedure, it is merely a specific instance of 'single value instrumentalism'. That is, the underlying concept is to design legal procedures as a means to maximize a single value or end. The economic approach seeks to maximize wealth or economic efficiency. Like any other instrument, legal procedure is viewed as an expense incurred in achieving an end, so the aim is to minimize the expense. The costs of incorrect decisions are called error costs, and those of making the decisions direct costs. The short statement of the aim is to minimize the sum of error and direct costs (Posner 1973, 399-400; Posner 1977, 429; Tullock 1980, 5-6). If we let 'EC' stand for error costs and 'DC' for direct costs, it can be written as follows:

Minimize Sum (EC + DC)

One does not aim to minimize either cost alone but the sum of the two. If one tried to minimize only direct costs, error costs might become exorbitant. Similarly, at some point the increase in direct costs to achieve accuracy is greater than the savings in reduced error costs.

A homey analogy might help one understand the view. In grocery shopping, one aims to achieve the most value for the least expense. An error cost occurs when one purchases an item at one store, say, a can of beans, when it could have been purchased for less at another. The direct costs are those of obtaining information about prices at various grocery stores and of transportation to and from them. One could drive from store to store with one's shopping list and price the various items, and then return to the stores buying the items at the lowest price. However, the investment of time and automobile expenses would probably make the total cost greater than simply purchasing all the items at one store. Many shoppers take an intermediate approach. They determine which store generally has the lowest prices for frequently bought staples. They also subscribe to the local newspaper and read the food advertisements for specials. When they go shopping, they do most of their shopping at the low priced store but stop at others nearby to purchase specials. Although some items purchased could have been obtained for less elsewhere, the combined cost of groceries, transportation, and newspaper is less than on any alternative. The economic approach recommends the same general method for evaluating legal procedure.

Legal error costs arise when an incorrect decision is made. The defendant is in fact either guilty or innocent. (Criminal terminology is used for ease of expression; for civil cases one can substitute 'liable' and 'not liable' for 'guilty' and 'innocent'.) There are thus four possible outcomes. The court can convict a guilty person (CG), convict an innocent person (CI), not convict a guilty person ($\sim$CG), or not convict an innocent person ($\sim$CI). Two of these decisions – CI and $\sim$CG – are incorrect, and two – CG and

~ CI – are correct. If the aim of the substantive law is economic efficiency, then each incorrect decision results in an inefficient use of resources and is an inappropriate expense. For example, if a company whose negligence causes an accident is mistakenly found not liable, then economic deterrence will not be achieved; insufficient resources will be spent on safety and the cost of accidents will increase. Moreover, because courts might make such incorrect decisions, some potential defendants will fail to invest in safety equipment, and some potential plaintiffs with good cases will not bother to sue (Tullock 1980, 6-7). A very rough estimate is that U.S. courts make incorrect decisions in about one-eighth of cases (Tullock 1980, 31). In criminal cases, conviction of innocent persons is probably much lower, but still significant – from 1 to 5 percent of cases ("When Nightmare" 1984, 45). The errors of false convictions are likely balanced by many more errors of false acquitals.

Direct costs are those of running the legal system. These include the public costs for judges' salaries, juries, courthouses, and so on, and the private costs of the parties in hiring lawyers, obtaining expert testimony, and so forth. In general, as private costs increase fewer cases are taken to court and public costs decrease, although many other factors influence decisions to go to trial, such as the amount at stake and the estimated chances of winning. The direct costs of settling out of court or plea bargaining are significantly less than trials. Consequently, an increase in settlements decreases direct costs. Most economic analysts assume that increased settlements increase error costs (Posner 1973, 442). This assumption appears well founded, because a settlement of a civil case is usually incorrect. Suppose the total damages in a tort case are $10,000. A settlement will almost always be between zero and the maximum a losing defendant can expect to pay. However, either the defendant should pay $10,000 or nothing, so the settlement involves the defendant paying less or more than he or she ought. (This argument does not apply under comparative fault (see 5.3.3) if the plaintiff's negligence is in dispute, for then the defendant's proper liability might be near the settlement.)

The U. S. Supreme Court appears to have adopted a variation of the economic cost approach to determine due process requirements for administrative decisions. Although the Court is concerned to minimize costs, it has not restricted them to the single value of economic costs. The Court has specified that in evaluating procedures one should balance the private interest, the chances of error, and the government's interest (*Mathews v. Eldridge*, 424 U.S. 319, 335 (1976)). If errors too often favor of the government, then the cost to the private interest will outweigh the government's gain. If the errors too frequently favor private parties, then the government's costs will outweigh the private gain. So balancing amounts to cost minimizing. To decide between two administrative procedures, one calculates the costs of each and then uses the one with the lowest total costs.

Two objections are commonly made against the economic approach. First, many people claim that one cannot place a dollar value on the concerns of plaintiffs. The loss of life or limb, it is said, cannot be adequately valued in monetary terms. However, this objection goes as much to substantive law as to procedural law. It applies more to the calculation of monetary damages for tort losses than it does to procedural law. In 5.4.1, we consider how courts do and should calculate monetary damages for such losses. Criminal cases might be a better basis for the objection. Nonetheless, an economic analyst can reply that crime costs money. It can be given a monetary value by considering its actual costs (for example, amount stolen) and the costs of deterring it. Even those plaintiffs in defamation actions who want vindication more than damages indicate how much vindication is worth to them by how much they are willing to spend to obtain it.

The second objection is that the economic approach or any other single value analysis omits important values. One can reasonably be concerned about the fairness as well as as total cost of legal procedures. A process might be less expensive than another but unacceptable because distinctly less fair. Other values that might be omitted from an economic annalysis are dignity and participation. However, an economic analyst can reply that, as in the case of vindication in defamation cases, one need only place a dollar value on concerns for fairness or dignity and the theory can accommodate them. Here, however, the response is not adequate. In the previous objection, the concern was with outcomes. The economic approach is concerned only with the costs of outcomes – producing them and their being incorrect. Concerns for fairness and dignity are not necessarily aspects of outcomes (error costs) or costs of the procedure (direct costs). Fairness is not necessarily the same as the minimization of error (Tullock 1980, 124). We return to this issue below (2.1.3).

The economic approach does at least indicate one important factor to be taken into account in evaluating legal procedure. One has no reason to increase economic costs without good reasons. In short, all else being equal, anyone concerned with wealth has a good reason to prefer lower to higher economic costs, whether they be direct or error costs. *(2-1) The principle of economic costs: one should minimize the economic costs of legal procedures.*

2.1.2. Moral costs. Another approach to legal procedure emphasizes that values other than economic costs are involved in evaluating outcomes. The moral cost approach of Ronald Dworkin (1985, ch. 3) is an instance of 'multi-value instrumentalism', that is, an approach that evaluates procedures by seeking to maximize several values of outcomes. Dworkin contends that utilitarian (including economic) approaches to procedure ignore rights. He focuses on criminal cases in which he claims there is a right not to be convicted if innocent (cf. the principle of innocence (6-1) in 6.1.1). A utilitarian single value instrumentalism looks at what Dworkin calls the "bare harm" inflicted by mistaken decisions; it considers how much suffering actually results from mistaken decisions. Dworkin contends that convicted innocent persons might not suffer any more bare harm than results from failing to convict guilty persons. Consequently, there need be no greater reason to avoid convicting the innocent than not convicting the guilty. This gives inadequate weight to a right not to be convicted if innocent (or the principle of innocence).

Economic analysts do argue that there is a greater cost in convicting innocent persons than in failing to convict guilty ones (Posner 1973, 410-15). This then supports the higher burden of proof required for criminal than civil liability. One reason for lower error costs in failing to convict the guilty than convicting the innocent is that failure to convict one guilty person will probably not have much of an effect on the law's deterrence (see 6.1.1), and an increased crime rate is the chief error cost. Nonetheless, the fewer guilty persons convicted, the greater the punishment has to be to maintain an effective deterrent. Thus, as the burden of proof requirement is raised, the amount of punishment also needs to be raised to maintain an equal deterrence. It is not clear that innocent persons benefit from a lower chance of a greater punishment (Tullock 1980, 82).

The moral cost approach implies that there are at least two types of error costs. Consider the two possible mistaken decisions, convicting the innocent (CI) and not convicting the guilty ($\sim$CG). The first is worse than the second, regardless of the bare or economic harm involved in the two, because it infringes the right not to be convicted if innocent (the principle of innocence). Such violations of rights are moral harms or costs. Moral harm can also occur in civil cases. If one party has a right that might be infringed by an incorrect decision and the other party does not, then procedures should be biased against infringing that right and causing moral harm. Often in civil cases a mistake in either direction involves equal moral harm. For example, whether a deserving tort plaintiff is denied recovery or an "innocent" tort defendant is made to pay damages, moral harm is involved. But in some civil cases, moral harm is perhaps greater on one side than another; for example, suffering an uncompensated defamation rather than paying damages for a truthful libel (Dworkin 1985, 89).

The moral cost approach adds another determinant to the economic approach's analysis of error costs. Besides the economic or bare harm costs of error, there are also moral costs. Thus, the aim of legal procedure can be stated as mimimizing the sum of the economic and moral error costs and the direct costs. If we here let 'EC' stand for the economic or bare harm error costs and 'MC' for the moral error costs, then the moral harm view merely adds another term to the economic approach's formula:

$$\text{Minimize Sum (EC + MC + DC)}$$

Moreover, according to Dworkin, moral cost is an objective and constant factor across cases of the same type (Dworkin 1985, 81, 87). That is, moral harm is the same whenever the same right is infringed, so moral costs are a constant factor for each type of case.

Moral costs can make a significant difference in the procedures that are justified, because they attach to some errors but not to others. Consider the following diagram of possible decision outcomes.

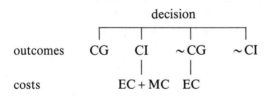

Since there are greater costs in CI than in ~CG, one should bias the procedural system to avoid CI errors. That is, ~CG errors are preferable to CI errors. This effect can be obtained by shifting the burden of proof to make conviction more difficult. In the example of defamation above, the burden would be shifted the other way, making it easier to establish liability; that is, placing the burden of proof of the truth of the statements on the defendant. If, however, one recognizes a right of freedom of speech in the defendant, then such a shift would be inappropriate (*Philadelphia Newspapers, Inc. v. Hepps,* 106 S. Ct. 1558 (1986) (private figure plaintiff in defamation action against media on matter of public concern has burden of proving falsity of statement).

One has good reason to add moral costs to economic costs if one has good reason to prefer one type of error over another. To do so, one need not accept Dworkin's notion of rights being involved. Indeed, we arrive at basically the same position as Dworkin regarding the aim of avoiding punishment of innocent persons, the principle of innocence, without invoking rights (see 6.1.1). Consequently, CI is a less desirable outcome than $\sim$CG, so there is a reason to prefer $\sim$CG errors to CI errors. The same result occurs whenever a principle of substantive law is based on something other than economic efficiency. Moral costs are simply the costs of failure to achieve aims other than economic efficiency, such as not enforcing unconscionable contract terms (see principle (4-12) in 4.3.2) or providing compensation in tort (principle (5-3) in 5.1.3). *(2-2) The Principle of moral costs: one should minimize the moral costs of legal procedures.*

The moral cost approach does not differ from the economic approach as significantly as might appear. First, some economic analysts have recognized that the substantive law might have aims other than economic efficiency (Posner 1973, 401). If the failure to achieve a substantive aim can be evaluated in monetary terms, the same cost minimizing approach can be used. Second, one cannot plausibly maintain that no monetary value can be placed on moral costs, because the moral cost approach requires balancing monetary error and direct costs with moral costs. Even if a price cannot be directtly placed on moral costs, an indirect pricing occurs. One need only consider how much one is willing to pay in economic costs to avoid moral costs, the cost of increased crime and punishment resulting from placing the burden of proof on the prosecution is the price of the moral harm in punishing the innocent. Third, the moral cost approach is still an instrumentalist one. Legal procedure is simply a means to achieving proper outcomes.

The similarity of the approaches can be seen by considering *Santosky v. Kramer* (455 U.S. 745 (1982)). This case involved the burden of persuasion a state must carry in proceedings to terminate parental rights permanently. The U.S. Supreme Court used the method of analysis it developed in

Mathews v. Eldridge (424 U.S. 319 (1976)) which we used to illustrate the economic cost approach and which Dworkin thinks might be a utilitarian approach (Dworkin 1985, 99-100). However, in *Santosky* the Court considered the fundamental liberty interest of parents as specially weighing against errors of wrongly terminating rights. Thus, it required clear and convincing proof rather than a mere preponderance of the evidence (see 2.3.7 for the difference). This appears to be a moral cost approach, the Court saying that the moral harm in wrongly depriving persons of parental rights makes these errors worse than those of failing to terminate rights.

However, one can challenge the application of the moral cost approach in *Santosky* as well as Dworkin's apparent application of it to a case in which a woman had been falsely accused of child abuse by an anonomous informer (Dworkin 1985, 75, 94-96; *D v. National Society for the Prevention of Cruelty to Children*, 1978 A.C. 171). Both the *Santosky* majority and Dworkin emphasize the rights of the parents (to custody of children or not to be falsely accused). Both seem to ignore the rights of children not to be abused. The *Santosky* majority clearly does so; Dworkin is ambiguous about the matter (Dworkin 1985, 76). In both cases, it is important to look past the procedural form to the substance, past the nominal parties of state or society to the children whose interests are involved. Once that is done, there are equally strong substantive principles on both sides. There is no reason to prefer one type of error to another.

The instrumentalism of the economic and moral cost approaches has a significant implication for legal procedure. One can evaluate procedures as leading to correct and incorrect outcomes (consider error costs) only if outcomes are either correct or incorrect. The economic approach is assured of outcomes being correct or incorrect, if the aim of substantive law is economic efficiency. An outcome either is or is not economically efficient. Similarly, one of Dworkin's major theses is that legal cases always have a right answer (Dworkin 1985, ch. 5). But if they are wrong and there are no correct answers, there are no error costs. If there are no error costs, both the economic and moral cost approaches presribe minimizing direct costs. Consequently, one should not have a hearing with the presentation of information but merely flip a coin or otherwise inexpensively render a decision to settle the dispute.

One must distinguish some or a few cases not having a correct answer from there never being correct answers for certain types of cases. The dire implications above result only if cases of a certain type never, or almost never, have correct answers. If only a few cases of some type fail to have correct answers, then one might design legal procedures on instrumental grounds for the usual cases with correct answers. Nonetheless, the amount of direct costs one should rationally bear to avoid error costs should be reduced by some amount to account for cases without correct decisions.

Another implication of instrumentalist approaches and our first two principles deserves notice. Substance and procedure are closely related. The more significant the substantive issues, whether economically or morally, the greater the error costs. A mistaken judgment in a case involving $500 does not impose the error costs a similar mistake in a case involving $500,000 does. Similarly, moral costs vary with the substantive principle involved or the amount of moral harm. Contrary to Dworkin, the moral harm of imprisoning an innocent person for five years is greater than that of imprisoning an innocent person for five months; his mistake is to focus on a right not to be convicted if innocent rather than a right not to be punished if innocent. Even then, convicting an innocent person of child abuse might be a greater moral harm than convicting an innocent person of speeding. Consequently, fewer direct costs are justified in cases involving less significant substantive matters. This reasoning suppoorts less expensive and less elaborate procedures for smaller matters – small claims courts, traffic violations, and so on.

Contrarily, procedure can affect substance. First, the direct costs might so clearly outweigh any error costs that it would be foolish to allow certain claims to be heard. A standard legal principle is that the law does not concern itself with trivial matters. Second, the ability of courts (third parties) to determine certain matters accurately might be so low that they might as well be ignored. This might occur, for example, if objective evidence is unavailable either because the issue concerns a complicated state of mind or the incident occurred so long ago that most evidence has been destroyed.

Because they are instrumentalist approaches concerned with the costs of avoiding errors, the economic and moral cost approaches focus on truth finding. If there is no truth to be found, there is no reason for legal procedure. They are concerned with dispute resolution only in that decisions give correct answers to disputes. One can view the next approach as adding a concern with resolving disputes at the psychological as well as practical level.

2.1.3. *Process benefits*. Another approach to legal procedure is to consider values or benefits of procedures independent of their effect on the accuracy of outcomes (see Summers 1974; Mashaw 1981). As noted at the end of 2.1.1, there might be values such as fairness, dignity, and participation served by legal procedures even though they do not increase the accuracy of decisions. One might describe this approach as an 'inherent process value' approach. However, the concept of inherent value can be misleading. It might suggest that the values are independent of the effects of a process. This is not the case, or at least, need not be the case. The moral and economic error costs are the result of incorrect decisions. The inherent values served are simply independent of decision outcomes. Put another way, the causal chain from procedure to economic and moral error costs goes through the decision rendered, while the causal chain from procedures to process values or benefits does not go through the decision. Process values are logically in the position of direct costs, which are also independent of the decision. They are satisfactions derived from the process itself (see Frankel 1980, 6).

The process values served by legal procedure can be viewed as benefits corresponding to direct costs. Both the economic and moral cost approaches view legal procedures as expenses to be borne only if they contribute to reducing error costs. However, one might prefer one procedure to another even if both have the same direct costs and are equally effective in producing a desired outcome, have the same error costs. An analogy illustrates the point. Suppose one wants to lose ten pounds. Further suppose one can do so equally well by a daily exercise program of either calisthenics or tennis. One might prefer tennis to calisthenics, even if tennis costs more. One might consider tennis to have other benefits than mere weight loss. Similarly, one might prefer one type of legal procedure to another, even though they are equally accurate.

An instrumentalist might contend that these alleged benefits can be included in direct costs. For example, if calisthenics are less desirable than tennis, one can consider how much more one would be willing to pay for tennis than calisthenics. One can then add that amount to the direct costs of calisthenics so that they have a higher cost. However, this approach has a conceptual problem. The greater direct costs of calisthenics are calculated by comparison with another program. To obtain the full costs of a procedure or calisthenics by this approach, one would have to conceptualize a perfect procedure or weight loss program and determine costs of others in comparison to it, but it is not clear that one can conceptualize a perfect legal procedure or weight loss program.

Alternatively, an instrumentalist might contend that one can noncomparatively calculate the costs of procedures. One can ask what outcome benefits one would have to receive to engage in a procedure or calisthenics. (How much would one have to be paid to do calisthenics?) But this shows the defect; the instrumentalist is trying to convert the benefits of one activity into the costs of another. One might not have to receive any outcome benefits to play tennis. Some people find it worthwhile in itself. There are costs – time, rackets, and so on – but there are benefits or satisfactions in the playing that outweigh these costs. Both benefits and costs occur in tennis, and perhaps in calisthenics. The same can be true of legal procedure. The instrumentalists might be correct to claim that in legal procedure, unlike tennis, the costs are always greater than the benefits, but that can only be a conclusion of weighing or balancing the costs and benefits. It is more perspicuous to consider them as separate items than to use a conclusory sum. Simply speaking of direct costs can lead one to overlook the benefits and thus exaggerate total costs.

The argument so far shows that one might perceive benefits or values in legal procedures independent of outcomes. Moreover, these benefits should be kept distinct from direct costs. Consequently, the formula for evaluating legal procedures needs to have another term added to indicate process benefits. If we let 'PB' stand for process benefits, the formula can be represented as follows:

$$\text{Minimize Sum (EC + MC + DC – PB)}$$

Process benefits are subtracted rather than added, because the other terms are costs.

This approach avoids one possible problem of instrumentalism, namely, the implication that if there is no correct outcome, then the least expensive procedure should be used. Process benefits might offset significant direct costs, so a fairly complex and expensive procedure might still be justified. Of course, if 'least expensive' is confusingly taken to mean 'the net of direct costs and process benefits', then one should use the least expensive procedure. The process benefits approach retains the instrumentalist implication that substance can affect procedure, because error costs are still relevant whenever they exist.

We have not yet established that there are any process values or the basis on which they can be determined, only that if there are such values, evaluation of legal procedure should explicitly take them into account. A basis for process values exists in the inherent purpose of dispute resolution. As we have seen, instrumentalist approaches focus on truth finding, ignoring dispute resolution except as it results from correct decisions. Process benefits contribute to both psychological and practical dispute resolution. Features of legal procedure can contribute to dispute resolution without contributing to accuracy. Without claiming completeness, a number of process benefits and principles can be identified on these grounds (see also Summers 1974, 20-27).

(2-3) The principle of peacefulness: procedures should be peaceful. This principle is one of the foundations of a legal system. Without legal procedures for resolving disputes, they are likely to result in violence and blood feuds. For the same reasons people rationally desire the criminal law to prevent violence, they also want peaceful procedures. This principle is especially important in limiting self-help.

(2-4) The principle of voluntariness: people should be able voluntarily to have their disputes legally resolved. This principle must be carefully restricted. It states that one should be able, if one chooses, to have disputes legally settled. It does not imply that if one party does not want a legal resolution, that party can veto such a procedure. Instead, the principle applies primarily to plaintiffs in civil cases. Defendants, whether civil or criminal, should not be able to block legal proceedings by failing to consent to them. This principle contributes to dispute resolution by enabling aggrieved parties to obtain an authoritative settlement. It thus also contributes to peace. An alternative would be to have state agents bring all cases. This would involve great public expense or else many disputes that could be legally resolved would not be. Not all disputes are open to legal resolution. For a variety of reasons, such as the direct costs of processing a trivial claim, courts should not undertake to resolve some disputes. Many of these limitations are part of the substantive law.

(2-5) The principle of participation: parties should be able to participate meaningfully in the legal resolution of disputes. This principle is evidenced in the common notion of having one's day in court. If one cannot participate, then one is denied one's day in court. The principle contributes to dispute resolution, because parties that have been able to participate are more likely to accept a decision; although they might not agree with the decision, they are more likely to comply with it. Trials *in absentia* and *ex parte* hearings (without the defendant or other party) violate this principle and are used sparingly. One value underlying the principle is participation in decisions that significantly affect one's life. One reasonably desires to at

least be heard, to have one's say, before decisions affecting one are made. Being permitted to participate also evidences others' respect, that one is to be considered seriously.

(2-6) The principle of fairness: procedures should be fair – treat the parties equally (see also Dworkin 1985, 84-85, 88; Tullock 1980, 124). Fairness here essentially means equality of treatment in the procedures. Given an equal chance of being plaintiff or defendant, one would not want the procedures biased toward one side or another, except as that can be justified by considerations acceptable from both perspectives. For example, we saw in the previous section that the burden of proof can justifiably be weighted due to substantive aims. Parties are less likely to accept decisions as resolving their dispute, either psychologically or practically, if they think the procedures used to arrive at them were unfair. Several sub-principles help spell out fairness (cf. Golding 1975, 122-23). (1) The dispute settler should be neutral. People should not be judges in their own cases; a judge or jury should not be biased (28 U.S.C. § 455 (1982); *SCA Services v. Morgan,* 557 F.2d 110 (7th Cir. 1977)). (2) At the hearing, the information of both sides should be presented. (3) Each party should at least be aware of the information presented by the other and have an opportunity to respond to it. The principle of fairness only specifies that the parties have an equal opportunity to participate; the principle of participation provides a reason for significant participation.

(2-7) The principle of intelligibility: procedures should be intelligible to the parties. Generally, rationality increases intelligibility (Summers 1974, 26). Consequently, the more rational the procedures for ascertaining the truth and arriving at decisions, the more rational parties will assent to the outcomes. That is, if people can understand the process and the reasons for a decision, they are more likely to accept it as settling their dispute. It follows that decisions should be articulated in terms of rational rules and principles and information developed at a hearing or trial.

(2-8) The principle of timeliness: procedures should provide timely decisions. Timeliness is a mean between the extremes of haste and dilatoriness. Persons do not rationally want decisions made without adequate time to gather information and reflect on its significance. In part, this concern pertains to outcomes; hasty decisions are more likely to be incorrect. However, the concern the other way, to avoid dilatoriness, is not. People do not want to wait longer than necessary for resolutions of their disputes. Delay in dispute resolution encourages people to take matters into their own hands. The saying that "Justice delayed is justice denied" is not correct substantively, for a delayed decision can be substantively correct.

Nonetheless, delay prevents people planning and living their lives. An instrumentalist approach to delay is likely to ignore this aspect, concentrating only on its effects on settlements and economic costs (Posner 1973, 420-21).

(2-9) The principle of repose: a final resolution of a dispute should be made. Disputes are not resolved if they can be reopened. If appeals are always possible, if the same issues can be raised in another case, then the dispute is not settled. If people invoke legal procedures to settle disputes, then there must be a point at which they are finally settled, otherwise there is no point in invoking legal procedures.

The inherent purposes of legal procedure are truth finding and dispute resolution. Obviously, people want to achieve these purposes at as little cost as possible. The purpose of truth finding primarily involves the avoidance of economic and moral error costs. The purpose of dispute resolution involves process benefits making a practical resolution more likely. These elements must be considered in a framework of trying to keep the direct costs of legal procedure as low as reasonably possible. The general normative aim, then, is to minimize the sum of economic and moral error costs and direct costs less process benefits.

Finally, one important aspect of legal cases should be noted, namely, they are minus sum interactions; that is, there is less value after a case than before (see 4.0). This point is implicit in the assumption that error and direct costs are greater than process benefits. Although individual plaintiffs can gain from legal cases by obtaining damages and other remedies, overall, legal cases are a net loss. Consequently, from a social perspective or that of potentially being either plaintiff or defendant, lawsuits are to be avoided. The justification of a legal system and procedures must be one of lesser evils, that legal resolution of disputes is preferable to blood feuds, rampant crime and violence, and so on.

THE ADVERSARY SYSTEM

2.2. A major distinction in legal procedure is between the 'adversarial system' of common law and the 'inquisitorial system' of civil law. The central issue here is whether one is preferable to the other on the basis of the principles for evaluating legal procedure. To consider this issue, at least the major differences between the two systems need to be noted.

Traditionally, the two types of system have been distinguished by the use of precedent and the roles of judges and parties (Frankel 1980, 13-14). In adversarial systems, parties marshal and present evidence with judges in a passive role, whereas in inquisitorial systems, especially in criminal cases, judges are more active in structuring cases, calling evidence, and so on. In adversarial systems, written decisions constitute precedents for future cases. Similar cases are to be decided in accordance with preceeding ones. In inquisitorial systems, cases do not constitute precedents but are decided by general statutory principles applied to each case.

This traditional view, while generally correct, does not perhaps depict the differences in a way most conducive to normative evaluation. Another account distinguishes them as centralized hierarchical systems (inquisitorial) and decentralized systems (adversarial) (Damaška 1979). In inquisitorial systems, professional judges decide cases, but lower level court findings of both law and fact are reviewed by higher level ones (Abraham 1975, 258). Because of the great amount of higher level review, decisions are very much alike; judges know that their decisions will be overturned if they do not conform to accepted rules. Certainty is promoted at the cost of ignoring differences between cases. In decentralized adversarial systems, trial judges have much greater authority, because appeals are less frequent and rarely include findings of fact. With less appellate review, judges have more scope to tailor decisions to particular circumstances. However, this leaves more room for abuse of discretion. The fundamental normative difference is between certainty and individualized justice.

One cannot, in these general terms, make a rational choice between the two kinds of systems. Both certainty of outcome and individualized justice are rational aims. In the abstract, there is no reason to prefer one of the values over the other. Nonetheless, one can make some direct evaluations of adversarial systems. One can consider the extent to which an adversarial system is likely to satisfy the principles for evaluating procedures. As there are important differences between adversarial systems, in this chapter the focus is on legal procedure in the United States, for in some ways, it is more adversarial than other systems. Indeed, the focus is primarily on procedure in U.S. federal courts.

To evaluate the adversarial approach, one must specify what adversarial features one is considering. The central features used here are party control and prosecution of cases by partisans (Frankel 1980, 13; Golding 1978, 106; Simon 1978, 36). Parties are responsible for bringing cases, formulating the issues, and presenting the evidence and arguments. These partisans do not pretend to be neutral investigators. Criminal prosecutors are said to seek justice, not convictions, but in reality they seek convictions. In court, they do their best to present the case for conviction; they rarely think they have won when justice is done if that means the defendant is found not guilty.

One factor to consider is the efficacy of the adversarial process for truth finding and reducing economic and moral error costs. Many proponents of the adversarial method claim it is effective at truth finding. Direct empirical testing of this claim is not feasible, for one would need an independent and reliable finding of facts to determine the accuracy of the adversarial process. The central claim in behalf of the adversarial method's truth finding is that parties have an incentive to discover and produce evidence in their favor and to dispute that in favor of the other party. The open competition is likely to produce the truth.

One psychological study indicated that client oriented adversarial attorneys were inclined to seek evidence more thoroughly when most of the evidence was unfavorable to their client than were nonclient oriented attorneys (those seeing their function as investigators for the court) (Thibaut and Walker 1975, 38). However, as client oriented attorneys present only the favorable evidence, there will be a skewing of the evidence presented. Side A, which the evidence supports, will present, say, five items, while side B will also present five items. Since of the total evidence perhaps only twenty-five percent supports side B, the decisionmaker is then presented with a skewed sample.

The adversarial trial as a truth finding mechanism is not without critics (for example, Frankel 1977, 182-87). To begin with, many resources are spent by a party trying to mislead the court (Tullock 1980, 96). One party's claim is incorrect, yet all that party's efforts are bent toward supporting the claim and getting the court to reject the truthful claim of the other party. Moreover, many aspects of the adversarial process obscure rather than promote the truth. Lawyers often try to discredit witnesses whom they know are telling the truth, and many criminal lawyers put their clients on the stand even when they know the clients are committing perjury.

In addition, wealthier parties such as large corporations have many advantages over poorer parties (Galanter 1979; Gorsky 1978). The richer parties that have many similar cases – landlords, banks, and so on – can play long-run strategies. For example, they can wear down opponents by endless delays and drive up expenses by costly discovery to discourage parties from going to trial and other perhaps deserving parties from even suing. Poorer parties often cannot afford to pay for investigators, expert testimony, lawyers' time, and so on. Many possible witnesses are reluctant

to come forward – "Don't get involved!" – because of the possible harass-
ment and humiliation in cross examination, time lost from work, and so
forth.

Consequently, one cannot conclude that the adversarial process, at least
as it has been practiced in the United States, is the best one for discovering
the truth. Indeed, so far as determining factual matters, it is probably pretty
poor. As a prominent trial judge has remarked, "[W]e have allowed
ourselves too often to sacrifice truth to other values that are inferior, or
even illusory" (Frankel 1980, 12). Various modifications in the adversarial
process might increase its truth finding capacity. However, the central
difficulty is that partisans are to find and present the information; to the
extent this element is reduced, so is the adversarial nature of the process.
Still, the truth that courts seek to discover is not purely factual. Questions
of negligence, sanity, reasonableness of conduct, and others are not purely
factual questions. To the extent this is so, the adversarial process might be
better than appears. The question is less finding distinct facts – was the
money paid? – than the construction to put on them. Here competing
interpretations and evaluations are possible, and adversarial presentations
of views are often helpful (Frankel 1980, 9). Before making such decisions,
one wants to hear the strongest possible arguments on both sides.

The difficulties of poorer parties in marshaling and presenting information stems from an inequality outside the legal context. This independent inequality of wealth and so on is exacerbated by parties paying most
of the direct costs of legal cases. Although the justice system (including
criminal prosecution and prisons) costs the public a considerable amount
of money, only a small percentage of government budgets in developed
countries are allocated to it. For example, the cost of the U.S. federal court
system is one billion dollars ("Courts" 1985, 49), which is little more than
one-tenth of one percent of the total federal budget. If one includes the cost
of law enforcement forces, it is a larger percentage. Much of the cost for
noncriminal law could be reduced by simplifying the substantive law and,
where they have not been, adopting simple no-fault principles for accidents
(5.5.2). The traditional adversarial process probably involves greater direct
costs than a less adversarial process, because of the inefficient direction of
resources by parties both prior to and at trial (Tullock 1980, 97).

Finally, the adversarial process must be evaluated by its ability to provide process benefits. An important study concluded that adversarial adjudication produces more satisfaction with the decision, especially when it
is unfavorable, than inquisitorial adjudication (Thibaut and Walker 1975,

74, 80, 91). This suggests that process benefits of the adversarial system aid in psychological dispute resolution. The principles of peacefulness, voluntariness, and intelligibility are not especially relevant. Continental inquisitorial systems also provide peaceful, voluntary, and as intelligible resolutions of disputes. Nothing in the adversarial process is likely to make it better than an inquisitorial process at promoting these process values.

In some respects, the adversarial process hinders peaceful resolution of disputes. Lawyers, trained to be partisan advocates to promote the interests of their clients, often exacerbate discord and tensions (Frankel 1980, 114). This was (and is) notoriously true in fault-based divorce. Couples are often parting amicably with a reasonable division of assets until they meet with their lawyers. Many lawyers create antagonism and enmity by encouraging their clients to seek a larger division of the assets, at the same time running up their fees. The adversarial process is an especially poor method for resolving disputes between parties who must continue to deal with each other after the dispute – between employers/employees, landlords/tenants, spouses, neighbors, and others.

Nor are timeliness and repose necessarily better fostered by an adversarial than an inquisitorial system. One might argue that repose is better served by an adversarial system, because appeals are more frequent in inquisitorial systems. However, repose is attained in them, often more quickly than in adversarial ones. The adversary process leaves more scope for one party to delay the process. Again, the differences need not be inherent in the systems. One can imagine inquisitorial systems that do not permit as many appeals as is common, and adversarial ones that are more timely than those that currently exist. Indeed, most adversarial systems are more timely than those in the United States, and even there the time to repose varies greatly between jurisdictions and types of cases.

Participation and fairness are the two process benefits that many advocates of the adversarial process think especially support it. At the beginning of this chapter (2.0), we rejected the characterization of adjudication as party participation by presenting proofs and reasoned arguments, because it biased the concept in favor of an adversarial system. A central argument for an adversarial system based on that concept is that if judges are responsible for investigating and presenting the evidence, they will find it difficult to maintain a neutral position (Fuller 1978, 382-83). The judge must take first one side and then another. Early on the judge needs a theory or framework in which to understand the case and organize the facts. Adopting a theory will bias a judge towards one party or the other. Moreover, one psychological study claims to support this thesis (Thibaut and Walker 1975, 49). However, the bias set up in this study was not exactly that of the argument. Instead of a bias from needing a theory to organize the case, it was from having observed similar cases with decisions adverse to a particular party.

One can further strengthen the argument by adding the benefits of participation. People desire to present their own positions, their sides of the story, as they see them. Only by doing so will they feel that their concerns have been presented fairly. Indeed, a major psychological study of procedural justice concluded that party control is the best predictor of people's perception of the fairness of and preference for procedures (Thibaut and Walker 1975, 121). This clearly links participation and perceived fairness, and party control is a defining characteristic of adversarial adjudication.

While these are significant reasons that one can rationally accept, they are not overwhelming arguments for the adversarial process. The possible slant of a judge in existing inquisitorial systems is moderated by the investigating judge in a criminal case not being the trial judge, the ability of parties to argue for their positions at trial, and the likelihood of review by an appellate court. However, the separate inquiries might add to the direct costs. They might also delay achieving repose, although that need not be, and generally is not, the case. Moreover, one can easily overemphasize the satisfaction of parties with their participation (see Simon 1978, 94-99). Many parties are only concerned with the outcome – will they receive money or have to pay. People who receive a decision they believe to be correct are as satisfied with one procedure as another (Thibaut and Walker 1975, 91). Nor do parties get to have their say; as they see it, their lawyers incant mumbo jumbo irrelevant to their complaint. Moreover, the psychological study did not consider a situation in which one party was at a significant disadvantage due to wealth and so forth, yet as noted above, such a situation is not unusual. Nevertheless, if a decentralized system with significant trial court powers is preferred, these are good reasons not to give judges the control in acquisition and presentation of information possessed by judges in inquisitorial systems.

The arguments for the preferability of an adversarial system over an inquisitorial system perhaps reflect the biases of those trained in adversarial systems almost as much as arguments that would persuade a rational person. A noted scholar of comparative judicial processes has concluded that the French inquisitorial system for criminal law is at least as effective as the adversarial system (Abraham 1975, 102). Nonetheless, an adversarial system is a plausible system for trials. There are good reasons to modify some of the excesses of the adversarial process as it has existed, and the tendency of procedural law has been to do so. Extensive pretrial discovery has virtually eliminated the element of surprise (see 2.3.5). For example, in *Smith v. Ford Motor Co.* (626 F.2d 784 (10th Cir. 1980)), a jury verdict was reversed, because the plaintiff had only indicated that an expert would testify as to the medical treatment and prognosis of the plaintiff's injury, not its cause. Of course, as in this case, discovery can delay reaching repose. More liberal pleadings, class actions, and various other techniques have also helped eliminate some of the disadvantages of the adversarial system. Particular features of adversarial systems must be evaluated by the principles developed earlier in this chapter. We sketch some central features of an acceptable adversarial legal procedure.

ELEMENTS OF PROCEDURE

2.3.0. *Introduction.* Procedural law is as complex and as important as substantive law. Having a valid substantive claim or defense is of little value if one cannot invoke the processes of the law to enforce it, for example, because the procedure is too expensive to make it worthwhile or because rules of procedure or evidence prevent one obtaining or presenting evidence necessary to support one's position. Such situations consitute errors and impose economic and moral costs. Even if one can do so, other features of legal procedure can fail to provide process benefits.

2.3.1. *Jurisdiction.* The first question of procedure is: "Who can be sued where?" This question can arise even in unitary systems if courts have limited territorial jurisdiction. Suppose Cheek, a resident of New York, is involved in an automobile accident on Interstate highway 75 in Ohio with Dawkins, a resident of Ontario, Canada, heading for a winter vacation in Florida. In which courts should Cheek be permitted to sue Dawkins – New York where Cheek lives, Ohio where the accident occurred, Florida where Dawkins is at present, Ontario where Dawkins lives, or anywhere else? We can assume that Ohio law is applicable wherever the case is brought. Considerations of direct costs generally rule out places other than New York, Ohio, Florida, and Ontario, because both parties would have to travel to, say, Hawaii, should suit be filed there. Direct costs do not clearly decide between the other locations. One might think that they would exclude Ohio because neither party lives there, but since Ohio law is to be applied, the familiarity of Ohio courts and lawyers with the applicable law might decrease costs enough to offset the travel expenses.

The principle of voluntariness is of value here. When we introduced it (2.1.3), we noted that it primarily applies to plaintiffs choosing to sue. One could not justly allow defendants simply to refuse to be sued. Nonetheless, it has an important application for jurisdiction over defendants. The substantive law makes persons or parties liable for their conduct and its effects. Consequently, they should be legally liable wherever they go or carry on activities. In effect, one voluntarily accepts liability wherever one carries on activities. Thus, it seems, Cheek should be able to sue Dawkins in Ohio since Dawkins was carrying on activities there (driving) from which the claim arises. However, Dawkins is no longer in Ohio or carrying on activities there.

Suppose Cheek decides to sue Dawkins in Florida. Should Dawkins be allowed to argue successfully that while she is liable in Florida for her activities there, the accident occurred in Ohio and thus is none of Florida's business? Dawkins could give a similar argument should Cheek sue her in Ontario. If people can avoid liability for conduct or activities by simply leaving the territorial jurisdiction, then the law will not be effectively enforced and there will be great error costs. Thus, liability for past conduct should follow Dawkins wherever she goes.

Suppose Cheek decides to sue Dawkins in New York, because his lawyer is there and he will not have to travel. Might not Dawkins reasonably claim that she is not in New York, that the accident did not occur there, that she does not carry on any activity in New York, and in fact she has never been there. When she goes to Niagara Falls, she always stays on the Canadian side. Here Dawkins has a good argument that she has never explicitly or implicitly voluntarily agreed to be sued in New York (see *Kulko v. Superior Court*, 436 U.S. 84 (1978)). No voluntary conduct by Dawkins has indicated a willingness to be sued in New York.

Three factors are involved in deciding where Dawkins can be sued – where she is, where the interaction that is the subject of the lawsuit occurred, and where Dawkins carries on activities. First, suppose the only factor is that the defendant is there. But this is not a realistic possibility; one cannot have the person without activity of some sort, although that activity need not be related to the interaction in dispute.

Second, consider activity alone. It is reasonable for Cheek to be able to sue Dawkins in Ontario, even if Dawkins is still vacationing in Florida.

After all, Dawkins lives there, and it is her primary place of activity. Viewing oneself as possible plaintiff or defendant, one would find the benefits of being able to sue people where they live to outweigh the disadvantages of being sued while one is temporarily away. Of course, other localities might be preferable from a plaintiff's perspective, but acceptance of jurisdiction at the defendant's primary place of residence does not foreclose other possibilities. As a defendant, one can have little objection to jurisdiction at one's primary place of residence.

Suppose Dawkins owns one third of a hardware store in Pennsylvania that she inherited from her maternal grandfather. Is that sufficient activity so that viewing the matter from the perspectives of plaintiff and defendant it is acceptable for Cheek to sue her there? No answer appears evident. In the past, U.S. law permitted Dawkins to be sued in Pennsylvania for an amount not to exceed the value of her property there (*Pennoyer v. Neff*, 95 U.S. 714 (1877)). But Dawkins's hardware store has nothing to do with the interaction between she and Cheek. Extension of this doctrine could make Dawkins subject to suit almost anywhere. Suppose she had bought some stock in a New York corporation on the Toronto exchange. Should that then enable Cheek to sue her in New York (to the value of the stock) despite our earlier conclusion that it would be inappropriate for Dawkins to be liable to suit there (see *Shaffer v. Heitner*, 433 U.S. 186 (1977))? If the interaction arose out of a person's property in a jurisdiction, for example, negligence in the Pennsylvania hardware store, then one ought to be able to sue in that jurisdiction. If the interaction is unrelated to the activity, then the activity should be substantial before a person can be sued in the jurisdiction. The relevant principles are those of voluntariness and fairness – has the defendant voluntarily undertaken sufficient activity in the jurisdiction so that making him or her subject to suit would not be unfair? The burden of being subject to suit in such a jurisdiction is not unfair if it is no greater than that in other permissible jurisdictions, or the extra burden is small in proportion to the total burden or the extra burden the plaintiff would have to bear to sue elsewhere.

Finally, is the interaction alone sufficient for jurisdiction? In our original hypothetical, neither party is in, normally resides within, or carries on significant activity in Ohio, so there is no benefit to allowing suit there. As a plaintiff, one would have to sue at a distance, so one might as well do it in Ontario or Florida. Matters are different, however, if Cheek were to live in Ohio. Then the advantages to Cheek offset the disadvantages to Dawkins, so given that one might be either party, one has no reason to reject this possibility. We thus have a fourth, subordinate, factor that tips the scales of interaction alone, namely, the location or residence of the plaintiff in the same jurisdiction.

We have, then, a set of instances supporting jurisdiction. *(2-10) The principle of jurisdiction: persons should be capable of being sued (a) where they are or normally reside; (b) where they conduct ongoing activity if (i) the event or transaction in question occurred there and was related to the activity or (ii) the activity is so extensive that defense there would not be an unfair burden; and (c) where the event or transaction occurred if the plaintiff resides there.*

These conditions generally apply to corporations as well as individuals. A corporation's location is that of its headquarters or incorporation. However, a business need not have as great a proportion of its activity in an area as an individual for jurisdiction to attach (b, ii). Otherwise, corporations can manipulate practices so as not to do business in certain states. For example, in *International Shoe Co. v. Washington* (326 U.S. 310 (1945)), the company made all contracts at its headquarters and shipped f.o.b. so that goods belonged to buyers as soon as they were shipped. However, because it employed a number of persons soliciting sales and residing in the state of Washington, the Supreme Court held it was subject to Washington's jurisdiction for payment of unemployment compensation contributions. Of course, here the subject of suit arose directly from the activities in Washington, namely, employment of salespersons, even though they were paid from St. Louis.

In the extreme, a corporation might be sued in a state in which it never did business. Consider *Gray v. American Radiator & Standard Sanitary Corp.* (22 Ill. 2d 432, 176 N.E.2d 761 (1961)). Gray sued American Radiator in tort for a water heater that exploded, including Titan Valve which made the valve responsible for the explosion as a second defendant. American Radiator also filed a 'cross-claim' against Titan (claim of one defendant against another). Titan objected that it was an Ohio corporation, did no business in Illinois, and had sold the valve to American Standard in Pennsylvania. Nonetheless, the court held that Titan could be sued in Illinois, since that was where the tortious event (explosion) occurred. This case meets our condition (c) provided 'event' refers to the occurrence of harm rather than negligent conduct, which occurred at the site of manufacture. Considerations of direct costs also support making Titan liable for suit in Illinois. Were it not brought into the case and American lost, American should then be able to sue Titan in Ohio or Pennsylvania. If American were

not able to do so, then error costs would be significant, for the manufacturer of the defective product could not be sued.

Nonetheless, one might have a different view of the matter were Alpha
company, a retail store, to sell a television to Ewing in New York, he then
move to Illinois, and sue Alpha in Illinois on a contract warranty even
though Alpha did business only in New York and New Jersey. Assuming
the interaction at issue is the sale, this hypothetical does not meet the
principle of jurisdiction. In part, the question is assignment of risk of
litigation costs. Either the purchaser must take the risk of the expense of
suing in New York should the purchaser move, or the company must bear
the cost of defending anywhere a purchaser might move. The latter would
increase the price for all consumers.

Some judgment must be used about the national character of the company and the foreseeability of the product being used in various places. For
example, automobiles might be treated differently from television sets. In
World-Wide Volkswagen Corp. v. Woodson (444 U.S. 286 (1980)), the
plaintiffs bought a car in New York, and while moving to Arizona were
involved in a collision in Oklahoma. They sued the manufacturer and
importer, as well as the regional distributor and retailer, in products
liability. The Court majority held that Oklahoma did not have jurisdiction
over the regional distributor and retailer, because they did not conduct
business in Oklahoma. The dissents generally argued that because automobiles are designed for travel, the regional distributor and retailer should
expect their products to be used in Oklahoma. By this reasoning, however,
retailers of television sets can expect purchasers to move, so one might
have all retailers of moveable products liable nationwide.

For us, the question is whether condition (c) should apply. The accident
occurred in Oklahoma and the plaintiffs were there when they filed suit,
but they did not normally reside there. We developed condition (c) on the
assumption that the defendant committed an act in the jurisdiction – was
the driver of the other car – but expanded it to include a tortious event
causing harm even if the act making it tortious did not occur there. Were
the suit based on a contract warranty, then one might claim the interaction
was the sale, which occurred in New York rather than Oklahoma. Indeed,
the sale is the only activity by the retailer and regional distributor. Our
principle of products liability (5-10 in 5.2.3) is designed to exclude from
liability sellers who do not manufacture or modify a product, so we would
not even hold the regional distributor or retailer liable under substantive
law. Moreover, unlike *American Radiator*, should the retailer and regional

distributor be excluded from the case and the plaintiffs win, the manufacturer would not have a claim against them. Indeed, it is puzzling why the plaintiffs pursued inclusion of the retailer and regional distributor. Consequently, retailers should not be subject to suit under (c) but only under conditions (a) and (b). Note that (b)(ii) will leave national retailers such as Sears and K-Mart liable to suit almost anywhere.

2.3.2. *Notice.* The problem of notice often arises with lawsuits in jurisdictions in which the defendant does not reside. The principle of participation supports notice. If defendants do not know they are being sued, then they cannot participate. *(2-11) The principle of notice: defendants should personally receive a statement of the complaint with adequate time to prepare a reply and make an appearance.* Preferably, a written notice is handed directly to a defendant. However, modifications of this ideal notice are acceptable for special situations to keep direct costs reasonable or to avoid errors. These situations can be divided into those in which the form of notice can be varied and those in which notice itself can be dispensed with.

Cases of the first sort primarily arise when the defendant cannot be located. First, the defendant might not be in the jurisdiction but indirectly conduct activity there. Usually there is a manager who can be notified. Alternatively, notice might be given by mail (Fed. R. Civ. P. 4(c)(2)(C)(ii)). Newspaper notices should not be accepted unless there is no better way – no manager or address can be found. If parties can reasonably be served personal notice, notice by newspaper is not acceptable (*Mullane v. Central Hanover Bank & Trust Co.*, 339 U.S. 306 (1950)). Moreover, given the importance of notice, one attempt at personal service is not adequate (*Greene v. Lindsey*, 456 U.S. 444 (1982)).

The primary situation for possibly dispensing with notice arises when the defendant might act in such a way as to make the suit pointless. The issue at stake is an *ex parte* hearing. Perhaps the most common situation involves repossession of goods when time payments are not made, sometimes because of a dispute over the product. As we argue that good faith purchasers should be entitled to keep property (principle (3-11) in 3.3.1), it is especially important for persons with a security interest to be able to prevent purchasers selling the secured property before trial. Yet, in some cases, defendants have a legitimate defense. To allow their property to be taken or tied up even briefly without a chance to be heard is a great imposition.

The U.S. Supreme Court has beaten a tortuous path through this issue without any clear principle discernible. In *Fuentes v. Shevin* (407 U.S. 67 (1972)), it struck down a Florida law permitting repossession on the basis of a defendant's complaint and bond for the value of the property but without any hearing. Yet, in *Mitchell v. W. T. Grant Co.* (416 U.S. 600 (1974)), it upheld a similar Louisiana law. The court distinguished *Fuentes* on the grounds that it did not require the participation of a judge, did not specify a quick hearing on the merits of the case, and did not require any significant showing of facts. But this is cutting it very thin, especially since outside of New Orleans the Lousiana law did not require a judge's involvement. In other cases involving garnishment of wages or bank accounts, the Court has required a hearing (*Sniadach v. Family Finance Corp.*, 395 U.S. 337 (1969); *North Georgia Finishing, Inc. v. Di-Chem, Inc.*, 419 U.S. 601 (1975)).

The interest in notice and an opportunity to be heard is so fundamental that it should be abridged only for the most serious reasons and with all possible protection of the defendant's interests. Thus, plaintiffs should be required to make a plausible showing that they will win on the merits, that there is reason to believe that their interests will be seriously jeopardized if preliminary *ex parte* action is not taken, and whenever appropriate to post bond sufficient to compensate the defendant for any loss. Moreover, defendants should have an opportunity to recover goods or monies by posting a bond to protect the plaintiff. Finally, a speedy hearing on the merits should be assured. If all these conditions are met, then one could accept preliminary action without notice.

Finally, one should be able voluntarily to waive notice or specify how it is to be made. However, any such waiver should meet the substantive rules of contract. Because notice is so fundamental, it should be waivable only if it is done knowingly and is to the benefit of both parties (see principle of required conditions (4-12) in 4.3.2). This could occur, for example, when two corporations negotiate a settlement with lawyers representing each (*D. H. Overmyer Co. v. Frick Co.*, 405 U.S. 174 (1972)). It is not likely that the conditions could be met in consumer contracts (*Swarb v. Lennox*, 405 U.S. 191 (1972)). The manner in which notice is to be provided could similarly be waived. In *National Equipment Rental, Ltd. v. Szukhent* (375 U.S. 311 (1964)), the U.S. Supreme Court went too far in upholding a standard form contract that appointed a third party with no connection to the defendants to accept notice and did not even require the defendants to be promptly informed of receipt of a summons. Like other crucial clauses in standard form consumer contracts, such a term should be explicitly brought to the attention of purchasers, and they should be given an opportunity to substitute an alternative person to receive notice.

2.3.3. *Legal representation*. The right to legal counsel only came to be recognized over a long period of time. Today, no one challenges the right of persons to have counsel if they want and can obtain one, except in a few small claims courts from which lawyers are excluded. There are several reasons why one would want to be permitted counsel. The first and most obvious one is for their expert knowledge. Laws are not readily available to the average citizen, who does not know where to begin to look for statutory rules, let alone relevant precedents. Even should laypersons be able to find the authoritative texts, they probably could not understand the technical legal terminology. If the parties in an adversary system are ignorant of the law, errors are likely to result.

Second, the use of lawyers can reduce direct costs. Lawyers can marshal facts and present them in an appropriate manner according to court procedure. One can imagine that trials would take much longer if laypersons presented their own cases, which increases public costs even if private costs are reduced. During the past decade or so, several people have complained of the incompetence of U.S. trial lawyers. Incompetence by trial lawyers not only causes errors, but also often makes the trial process longer, increasing direct costs. In England, trial lawyers – barristers – constitute a separate and specially trained branch of the bar, so the problem is not likely to be acute. Moreover, the expert advice of lawyers about the chances of winning at trial might encourage settlements and thus decrease direct costs.

Third, some process benefits result from the use of lawyers. Even though it is vicarious, clients represented by counsel usually have more effective participation in the trial process. Fairness is also served by counsel. If only one side has legal representation, then that party can probably take advantage of the other's ignorance of even fair procedural rules. Legal counsel can also make cases more intelligible to parties, because they can explain what is happening and why, although they often fail to do so to the extent they could or should.

Being permitted legal representation, although a major improvement from the time this was not allowed, is not sufficient. Many people cannot afford legal counsel. The formal freedom to retain counsel is of little value if one cannot afford to do so. Moreover, the practical availability of counsel can make a signficant difference in one's access to courts and "justice." Two general methods of handling fees can be noted for their effect on access to courts. In England and Canada, the winning party normally recovers lawyers' fees. The effect of this practice, however, is probably to discourage litigation. Although indigent persons can recover legal fees should they win, since they cannot pay the opposing party's fees should they lose, they cannot afford to sue. An American practice in some cases is to permit plaintiffs' legal fees to be contingent on winning. As a result, indigent persons, say, in negligence personal injury cases, can sue and pay lawyers from the damages if they recover. (Pain and suffering awards are possibly inflated by juries to help cover legal fees.) Although this permits greater access to the courts, successful plaintiffs are not compensated for all their losses (unless awards were inflated to allow for the fees).

During the twentieth century, legal aid programs to provide counsel for the poor have developed or greatly expanded. One can view publicly provided lawyers as a type of insurance. The insurance rationale has been recognized by unions that have provided their members legal counsel (*Mine Workers v. Illinois Bar Ass'n*, 389 U.S. 217 (1967)) or bargained for prepaid legal services as a fringe benefit. Even the American Bar Association finally came to recognize its legitimacy. Its application to provision of legal services to the poor is still not fully recognized. Even if one can afford counsel, one might pay for a public system in case one might become poor; bankruptcy is not unknown. (John DeLorean, the automobile entrepreneur, conducted a public campaign for donations to help pay his expenses in defending against criminal charges.) The insurance rationale might even support a system to provide legal services to everyone for certain problems, such as a national legal service (Frankel 1980, 124-26) or a draft of lawyers for a period of service (Bayles 1981, 47-50). We limit our consideration to provision of counsel to those who cannot afford to pay.

The wisdom of insurance depends on the expectable loss that one might incur. It is not worthwhile to insure an ordinary pair of socks alone, because recovery for their loss does not justify the administrative cost of insurance. A similar consideration applies to public provision of legal counsel. The greater the possible loss, the more worthwhile insurance for legal counsel. The loss need not be solely economic but also moral, as in being punished when innocent. *(2-12) The principle of legal assistance: persons should be allowed legal counsel, and persons who cannot afford to pay should be provided legal counsel at public expense for important legal problems.*

The central question about this principle concerns what legal problems are important enough to warrant provision of counsel at public expense. Imprisonment represents a major loss for almost everyone, so public provision of legal counsel in criminal cases is appropriate (*Gideon v. Wainwright*, 372 U.S. 335 (1963); *Argersinger v. Hamlin*, 407 U.S. 25 (1972)). It is also often appropriate in cases involving the deprivation of other fundamental civil rights, such as equal employment opportunities (*Bradshaw v. Zoological Soc'y*, 662 F.2d 1301 (9th Cir. 1981)) or parental rights (*Lassiter v. Department of Social Serv.*, 452 U.S. 18 (1981)). In the fields of private law that we consider, the case for public provision of counsel is more complicated. The possible economic losses tend to increase with the wealth of parties, but more wealthy parties can afford private counsel. However, the personal significance of potential losses is not necessarily proportionate to wealth. For example, the eviction of a poor tenant from a $200 a month apartment can have a greater impact on the person than the eviction of a middle income person from a $700 a month apartment. Thus, publicly provided legal counsel for such problems as landlord/tenant disputes and conditional sales contracts for household items and automobiles can be quite significant. It is probably not important for estate matters and purchase of real estate, because if property of much value is at stake, people can afford to pay legal fees.

Probably the most disputable area concerns personal injury tort actions. If our recommendation to institute a national accident insurance program were followed (see 5.5.2), the problem would be largely obviated, although as with workers' compensation, lawyers might be needed to represent people before agencies administering the plan. In the absence of such a plan, many people argue that the contingent fee system provides access. However, as noted above, it might not adequately compensate winning plaintiffs. Moreover, those with the largest claims tend to be undercompensated. Consequently, one has good reason to substitute legal aid for contingent fees but charge winning plaintiffs a modest amount for the services.

2.3.4. *Scope of cases*. The central questions here concern who and what should be considered in a case. These are interrelated questions revolving around two axes – the parties and the transaction or occurrence (their interaction). The topic can be divided into 'joinder of claims', 'joinder of parties', and 'class actions'.

In joinder of claims, one is concerned with what claims should be considered in one case. To reduce direct costs, it is best to handle as many claims as reasonably possible at one time. Thus, if Foster sues Gann for failure to pay on a contract, then in the same case Gann should litigate a claim of an offset for defective goods (Fed. R. Civ. P. 13(a)). These different claims all arise from the same transaction. Similarly, as long as Foster and Gann are in court, they might as well settle any other disputes between them. However, since these might involve entirely separate matters, for example, Gann's claim that Foster's delivery truck negligently backed into and demolished Gann's loading dock, it is not appropriate to require, only to permit, that this claim be litigated at the same time (Fed. R. Civ. P. 13(b)).

If a court is going to examine a transaction or occurrence, it is also efficient to join all parties affected by it in the case. For example, if Gann claims that some of the goods supplied by Foster were defective, and if they were Foster has a claim against the manufacturer, then the manufacturer should also be involved in the case (Fed. R. Civ. P. 14(a)). This procedure helps obviate the difficulty with the English warranty rule making sellers of products liable to consumers with a claim over against the manufacturer (see 5.2.7). However, it does not make the situation as efficient as the American products liability rule making the manufacturer directly liable to the consumer. Moreover, if some other person has an interest that might be significantly affected by a decision in the case, then that person should also be able to enter the case (Fed. R. Civ. P. 24(a) and (b)). For example, a decision might prevent a person adequately protecting an interest or some common issue might be involved. Finally, if two distinct matters are involved requiring separate evidence and law, as in Gann's claim for damages to the loading dock, a judge should be able to separate the issues and order separate trials (Fed. R. Civ. P. 42(b)).

A case illustrating joinder of both parties and claims is *Schwab v. Erie Lackawanna R.R.* (438 F.2d 62 (3d Cir. 1971)). A railroad worker sued his employer for injuries resulting from a train-truck collision. The railroad joined the truck driver and owner, claiming that the driver's negligence caused the accident, and thus the driver or owner was liable to the railroad for any liabilities to the worker. The railroad also filed a claim for damages to the engine. Although normally a cross-claim against such a third party is limited to payments for anything owed to the original plaintiff, the court found it both desirable and permissible to allow the additional claim for damage to the engine.

The primary justification for these procedures for joining claims and parties is reducing direct costs. If much the same evidence would have to be presented in separate trials, then both the parties and the public save money by having one trial. Considerations of fairness also pertain. Were there separate trials of the same matters, then inconsistent results might occur. For example, in *Schwab* the truck driver might be found negligent in the case for the worker's injuries but not negligent in a separate suit for damage to the engine. The problem can become particularly acute in criminal cases in which one person might be convicted of being an accessory yet the principal be found not guilty (see *State v. Spillman*, 105 Ariz. 523, 468 P.2d 376 (1970)). Joinder of claims and parties helps avoid these problems, although other legal doctrines are more important in preventing them (see 2.3.11). *(2-13) The principle of case scope: insofar as feasible, all claims and parties involving the same questions of fact or law should be considered in one case, and other claims involving the same parties should be permitted.* Several reasons might make it infeasible to consider all claims in one case, a crucial one being jurisdiction. However, even then, much of the preliminary fact gathering can be consolidated by having it handled by one court (28 U.S.C. § 1407 (1982)). The principle goes beyond issues arising from the same transaction or occurrence in two respects. First, as already noted, it permits other issues between parties to be considered in the same case, such as Gann's claim for negligent damage to his loading dock. Second, similar questions of fact or law can arise in a series of similar transactions although the parties are not the same.

This latter type of issue is often handled by class actions, the development of which has been a prominent aspect of legal procedure during the last half century. A class action is a suit by a few persons on behalf of themselves and many others similarly situated. If the plaintiffs prevail, then all members of the class obtain relief. Fundamentally, it is a method for aggregating many claims when joinder would not be practical. It is primarily used for discrimination, welfare, anti-trust, securities, and environmental cases.

The extant law contains many technical conditions for a class action that are not considered here. The primary reasons for allowing class actions stem from a combination of error and direct costs. Consider *Vasquez v. Superior Court* (4 Cal. 3d 800, 484 P.2d 964, 94 Cal. Rptr. 796 (1971)) in which 200 people had allegedly been subject to consumer fraud with most individual claims about $1,300 or less. Many of them might not find it profitable to sue individually, because the costs of the action would be large in comparison to the benefit should they win. However, the total amount involved is significant, approximately $260,000 plus other damages requested. If individual actions are not feasible, then the law is not enforced and the potential economic error cost is large. If all these individual claims are brought into one suit, then the direct costs can be reduced to make the case worthwhile and the error cost eliminated. So, by reducing direct costs, error costs can be decreased. One can prevent many small wrongs by one large case.

However, there is a risk in the process. Should the case fail because inadequately presented by the plaintiffs, then all the claimants lose. Consequently, before a few persons are allowed to sue on behalf of many, several requirements must be met (Fed. R. Civ. P. 23(a)). First, the group must be so numerous that individual actions and joinder are not feasible. Second, the claims must all have some matters of law or fact in common, otherwise there is no reason to combine them. In consumer fraud cases, the fact situations often vary so much that they should be considered separately. In *Vasquez*, the plaintiffs' alleged that the same information was given to each, because salespersons used a standardized sales pitch. Third, the claims of the actual or 'named' plaintiffs must be representative of those of the larger group; and fourth, the named parties must fairly and adequately represent the rest. These last two requirements ensure that the group's claims are adequately presented. For example, if the claims of the named parties are not the same as those for other members of the class, such as discrimination in promotion rather than hiring, then they might not adequately present the case for the latter (*General Telephone Co. v. Falcon*, 457 U.S. 147 (1982)).

Problems can arise with these conditions, many of which relate to fair representation. One set concerns settlement of the case. There are significant pressures for the case to be settled without a trial. A plaintiffs' lawyer might receive a sizeable contingent fee without the trouble of a trial. A defendant might face significant adverse publicity from the trial; and if he or she loses, a huge damage award with treble damages in antitrust cases. If the case has been certified as a class action, then a settlement cannot be made without the judge's approval (Fed. R. Civ. P. 23(e)). However, a judge might prefer a settlement to conducting a large trial. If the case has not been certified as a class action, then the judge's approval is not necessary. Nonetheless, the defendant faces a significant risk in such a settlement, because it will not bind the other members of the class. Hence, some of them could bring suit on the same grounds. Improper settlements, of course, involve error costs.

At least two steps can be taken to reduce the chances of inappropriate settlement. One is to prohibit contingent legal fees in class actions and compensate lawyers on the basis of reasonable fees (taking into account the chances of winning). A second is to require judges to at least note objections of members of the class and give a reasoned response to them (*Mandujano v. Basic Vegetable Products, Inc.*, 541 F.2d 832 (9th Cir. 1976)). Other steps might also be conceived.

A second problem concerns notice. Since almost any members of a class can bring a class action, without notice the other members of the class might lose their cause of action without ever knowing it was before a court. Thus, the principle of voluntariness supports all members of the class being notified. However, a requirement of notice can make it practically impossible for some class actions to be prosecuted. Consider *Eisen v. Carlisle & Jacquelin* (417 U.S. 156 (1974)). This was an antitrust suit on behalf of about six million odd-lot stock investors against two major dealers on the New York Stock Exchange. Providing individual notice to all identifiable members of the class was estimated to cost $225,000 for postage alone. The trial judge worked out another method of giving notice, with personal notice to the members most affected and to a small sample of the some 2,250,000 other identifiable persons as well as newspaper notices. However, the Supreme Court upheld the Court of Appeals in requiring individual notice. The result was that the plaintiffs could not afford to proceed with the suit. In short, the costs of personal notice mean that class actions in which many persons lose a very small amount cannot be brought. One can cheat many of the people a little, but not a few of the people a lot.

There are good reasons for individuals waiving and courts thus not requiring notice in such cases. As a plaintiff, one would not sue on one's own for the amounts in question. Consequently, if the class suit fails, one has not lost any claim one might reasonably expect to enforce. However, if the suit is successful, one might gain a small amount. The situation of plaintiff here differs from that of defendant which was assumed in considering notice (2.3.2). Were one to be sued as a defendant, then even though one's loss might be small, one would have reason to insist on notice. But as a plaintiff, the need for notice for small claims is significantly less.

As a defendant, one would certainly want the requirement, simply because it practically bars some large claims against one. The question, however, is whether the requirement of notice to plaintiffs is designed to benefit defendants, other than by practically barring some class actions. The primary benefit to a defendant is that if the action fails, no unnamed member of the class can bring a separate suit. Without notice, members of the class might claim they should not be bound by the decision in a prior case. But this argument is weak, because other legal doctrines might effectively bar successful suits by other members of the class, for example, stare decisis (2.3.9). More importantly, defendants should not be allowed to assert, as in *Eisen*, or effectively to waive notice to members of a plaintiff class, for example, because it might be disruptive to their customers (contra *Katz v. Carte Blanche Corp.*, 496 F.2d 747 (3rd Cir. 1974)). It would be acceptable not to require notice to all members of a class if the amount in question were below some fixed amount that would make individual litigation unfeasible. Otherwise, one risks the possibility of what, in *Eisen*, might amount to an eighty million dollar error.

Finally, problems can arise in providing remedies. If one allows suits by classes without individual notice, then one might not be able to locate all the plaintiffs entitled to receive damages. If they cannot all be located, then courts should be permitted to fashion other remedies that might benefit the members of the class. It is questionable whether courts should be permitted to distribute lump sum damages as they see fit (but see *West Virginia v. Chas. Pfizer & Co.*, 440 F.2d 1079 (2d Cir. 1971)). However, a form of injunctive remedy could be provided. For example, if a food producer has short weighted boxes of cereal for a time, it could be required to sell boxes with extra cereal at the regular price.

2.3.5. *Discovery*. Discovery is simply the ability to obtain information from other parties or persons. In the past, discovery was limited to information that was admissible at trial. In most U.S. jurisdictions, this close connection between discovery and admissibility of evidence no longer holds. Under Federal Rules, discovery extends to "any matter, not privileged, which is relevant to the subject matter" of the case (Fed. R. Civ. P. 26(b)(1)). The methods of discovery include statements under oath on oral or written questions ('depositions'), written answers to written questions ('interrogatories'), production of documents or things, examination of property, and physical or mental examinations of persons. In U.S. criminal cases, on request the prosecution must provide information that is material to guilt or punishment (*Brady v. Maryland*, 373 U.S. 83 (1963)).

Several aims are served by this broad use of discovery. First, error costs can be reduced. Testimony can be preserved if it is not likely that a person can be present for trial. Moreover, if each party has broad access to information, a better factual basis is likely to result in fewer errors. The elimination of surprise at trial can also result in a better presentation of the issues. Second, direct costs to the public are probably reduced, although it is less clear that overall direct costs are reduced. With information gathered and considered out of court, less time is necessary to ferret out information at trial. The issues are likely to be sharpened so that the trial is more focused and shorter. Admission of some matters can eliminate the need to prove them at trial, although their stipulation at trial would not occupy much time. Third, some process benefits might result, particularly fairness. Parties can also have more opportunity to participate by discussing the information with counsel.

Nonetheless, broad discovery has some drawbacks (see Wright 1983, 541-43). It can be an expensive process increasing the direct costs of the parties. It can be used to delay trial, for example, by asking for answers to many interrogatories or challenging requests for discovery. Thus, timeliness will be disserved. More wealthy parties or those that might benefit from delay can use lengthy and expensive discovery to deter people with legitimate claims from suing and to force lower settlements. Discovery can also involve invasion of privacy, for example, by filing a suit and then seeking discovery of business secrets, although courts have the power to protect business secrets by restricting or prohibiting discovery (Fed. R. Civ. P. 26(c)(7); Wright 1983, 564).

Some of these defects of broad discovery might be reduced by restricting its scope. As currently interpreted, being "relevant to the subject matter" of a case includes what can be called indirectly related matters. That is, one can discover A because it might lead to B which would help one's case (*Oppenheimer Fund, Inc. v. Sanders*, 437 U.S. 340, 350-51 (1978)). The result is that claims are sometimes filed without much or any evidence to support them on the hope that discovery will provide sufficient information to mount a plausible case. This is probably most common in negligence, products liability, discrimination, and antitrust cases. However, in these types of cases, it is also often difficult for plaintiffs to have adequate evidence before filing claims, because much of the crucial evidence is in the control of the other party. Consequently, severely restricting what can be discovered would result in more errors. Nonetheless, abuses could perhaps be curtailed without a great increase in errors by foreclosing discovery of indirectly related information. This might be accomplished by restricting discovery to information "relevant to a claim or defense," although such a verbal change could still be interpreted to include matters of indirect relation.

(2-14) The principle of discovery: discovery of all matters directly related to claims and defenses in the case, except for privileged and private matters not admissible at trial, should be allowed. This principle is meant to be more

restricted than the current one in U.S. federal practice, primarily by preventing discovery of indirectly related material. The indirect relation of material to the subject matter is not the central concern, but the low probability that one piece of information will produce something valuable. Speculation that information might lead to other useful information should not be permitted to ground discovery.

The difficult problems with discovery and this principle concern the exceptions. What material should be privileged presents several problems, but they are separate from discovery. For purposes of discovery, privileged material can be taken to include any material otherwise privileged. This includes, for example, self-incriminating statements (*Campbell v. Gerrans*, 592 F.2d 1054 (9th Cir. 1979)), government material under executive privilege (*Branch v. Phillips Petroleum Co.*, 638 F.2d 873 (5th Cir. 1981)), and perhaps journalists' sources (*Baker v. F & F Investment*, 470 F.2d 778 (2d Cir. 1972)).

The more difficult problems concern private matters. One's concern for privacy must be balanced against one's concern for truth and dispute resolution. Privacy interests vary from a weak concern about present salary to an intense concern about sexual activity. Thus, one would want courts to balance these concerns in individual cases. One's total wealth would be relevant to a property settlement in a divorce action, but not to a defamation case. One's mental and physical condition or opinions are among the more private matters and should only be discoverable if a good reason can be given for their relevance to claims and defenses. A defendant's eyesight would be relevant in a tort case involving a vehicle accident, although his or her bodily condition would not be absent a showing that the person seemed to be suffering some disease (cf. *Schlagenhauf v. Holder*, 379 U.S. 104 (1964)). Similarly, one's opinions would not normally be relevant, but they could be in cases of defamation where a crucial issue is whether one knowingly or recklessly disregarded the truth (*Herbert v. Lando*, 441 U.S. 153 (1979)). Finally, exclusion of the opinions or work product of one's counsel and other trial preparation material rests more on fairness than privacy (*Hickman v. Taylor*, 329 U.S. 495 (1947); Fed. R. Civ. P. 26(b)(3)).

2.3.6. *Evidence*. The admissibility of evidence at trial is probably the most troublesome aspect of procedure for the general public. Many of the perceived technicalities that allegedly defeat the achievement of justice occur here (see Frankel 1980, 106-09). An almost universal principle is to exclude irrelevant evidence (Fed. R. Evid. 402). If evidence is irrelevant to the dispute, then its admission will not lead to more accurrate decisions and will increase direct costs (Tullock 1980, 151). However, preventing the introduction of irrelevant evidence might not save much court time, since often extensive argument ensues about its relevance. Moreover, prohibiting such evidence indicates a lack of faith in the ability of judges and juries to determine the relevance of information. If a jury thinks evidence is relevant, then on what grounds can one argue that it is not? Presumably scientific grounds would suffice, but the law is notorious for its failure to recognize and admit scientific information. For example, computer printouts have been and are still often considered inadimissible evidence in some jurisdictions (but see Fed. R. Evid. 1001(3)) and blood tests showing nonpaternity have been considered inconclusive.

Perhaps the real concern is not relevance but the misleading character of evidence. Irrelevant evidence might mislead or confuse a jury about the issue in question. If it is likely to do so, then it should be excluded. This consideration does not apply as strongly to a judge, for a judge should be able to recognize and ignore misleading and irrelevant evidence. The underlying point is that unless it is misleading, a lawyer has little reason to introduce irrelevant evidence, for it will not further the lawyer's case with judge or jury.

Many unsupportable rules prohibit allegedly unreliable evidence such as the results of lie detector tests and hearsay testimony. The reliability of evidence can be brought out at trial, and a judge or jury can take its reliability into consideration (Tullock 1980, 150-51). A party has no reason to use less reliable evidence if more reliable evidence is available. Nonetheless, the exclusion of hearsay testimony might still be plausible. The likelihood of such information being distorted and therefore misleading is notorious. However, the concern is then the misleading character of the information, not its unreliability. Consequently, there is little reason to prohibit the introduction of evidence because of its unreliability, since that can always be brought out at trial.

Undoubtedly, the most objectionable rule of evidence so far as the general public is concerned is the exclusionary rule prohibiting the introduction of unconstitutionally obtained evidence in criminal trials (*Mapp v. Ohio*, 367 U.S. 643 (1961)). As technically applied in some instances, it must seem to be a gross misordering of priorities to allow patently guilty violent criminals to go free because niceties of search and seizure rules were not followed. Part of the difficulty has stemmed from a blanket rule prohibiting the introduction of such evidence in conjunction with difficult rules

as to the constitutionality of obtaining evidence. The Canadian requirement that such evidence be excluded if its admission "would bring the administration of justice into disrepute" allows some leeway for such
technicalities (Canadian Charter of Rights and Freedoms § 24(2)). The
modification of the U.S. exclusionary rule to permit use of evidence obtained by reasonable reliance on a search warrant subsequently invalidated
brings it closer to the Canadian test *(United States v. Leon,* 104 S. Ct. 3405
(1984)). The Court there recognized that use of the rule to impede truth
finding and to let the gulity go free might bring disrespect for law.

The exclusionary rule is an attempt to enforce substantive and other
procedural legal requirements by procedural sanctions. Many other extremely implausible evidentiary decisions, such as those concerning pater-
nity, are also often made to further nonprocedural policies, such as avoiding illegitimacy of children. Some uses of the exclusionary rule are procedural attempts to enforce procedures not practically directly enforceable.
The primary instance of this is the exclusion of evidence obtained from
suspects who have not been warned that they have a right to remain silent,
that any statements can be used against them, and that they have a right
to have retained or appointed counsel present (*Miranda v. Arizona*, 387 U.S.
436 (1966)). These procedures themselves are of questionable value, and
others might more adequately achieve their purpose (see Frankel 1980,
98-99). Instead of excluding evidence, it would be better to devise more
adequate primary remedies.

Even if procedures such as the *Miranda* requirements are not revised, it
is not clear that as a citizen one would not generally be better served by
an alternative to the exclusionary rule. There are two major alternatives to
the exclusionary rule – administrative action and private substantive remedies. Administrative action would involve sanctions against law enforcement officers violating constitutional (and nonconstitutional) rights. The
perceived problem with this approach is that law enforcement agencies –
police and prosecutors – are unlikely to take action against law enforcement officers, especially if their conduct assisted in obtaining a conviction.

The second alternative is a private cause of action, say, a tort remedy.
Such a remedy already exists (*Monroe v. Pape*, 365 U.S. 167 (1961); *Bivens
v. Six Unknown Named Agents of Fed. Bureau of Narcotics*, 403 U.S. 338
(1971)). This remedy may be adequate for innocent persons (Jones 1981,
250). The issue is whether it could be an adequate replacement for the
exclusionary rule. One objection is that it would not deter officers from
violating constitutional requirements, since their employer would probably

be liable, at least for negligent violations. If only the officers were liable, then they might not be able to pay the damages (Jones 1981, 248). Another objection is that if evidence could be used, then employers or officers would have to compensate offenders for their imprisonment (Jones 1981, 249-50). But there is no reason why damages could not exclude compensation for imprisonment, and there are good reasons of criminal law to do so. A carefully drafted tort rule with stipulated damages might be more effective than the exclusionary rule. The law enforcement agency need not be liable for knowing violations of rights. If officers were personally liable for them, they would be reluctant to commit them. Moreover, agencies would perhaps soon take effective action to reduce negligent violations, since otherwise the costs could become prohibitive.

Finally, instead of courts, an independent civil administrative agency could be established to hear cases of alleged violations of rights and to impose sanctions (see also *Bivens v. Six Unknown Named Agents of Fed. Bureau of Narcotics*, 403 U.S. 338 (1971) (Burger, C. J., dissenting)). It is certainly not clear that the exclusionary rule is preferable. However, this step goes beyond the framework of judicially used and enforced law that we are discussing. It thus illustrates the limitations of judicial legal procedure on the available principles and remedies.

(2-15) The principle of evidence: evidence should be excluded if, and only if, it would be misleading or waste time. This principle appeals to the aims of avoiding error and direct costs. One certainly has good reason to accept the exclusion of such evidence. The question is whether these should be the only grounds for excluding it. The principle does not directly exclude unreliable or irrlevant evidence, but some such evidence could be excluded as wasting time. For example, proposed evidence could be so unreliable that its introduction followed by testimony as to its reliability would be a waste of time. Similar considerations could apply to hearsay evidence. Moreover, the principle includes even relevant evidence that is misleading or wastes time (Fed. R. Evid. 403). While these two grounds for exclusion appear sufficient, further consideration might convince one that they are not.

2.3.7. *Burden of proof.* This topic does not require much comment. There are two types of burden, that of 'production' and that of 'persuasion'. The burden of production simply requires introducing evidence on a point first. In civil or criminal law, the obvious notion is that the party raising an issue should be required to produce some evidence to support his or her contention. Thus, plaintiffs and prosecutors must produce evidence to support all the elements of their claims. Most other requirements of production arise when a party introduces an issue that would not otherwise be raised, for example, a defendant in a tort action raises an issue of plaintiff negligence. The chief exception to these points arises when one party is thought to have special access to information. It would be uneconomical and unfair to make the party with less access to information produce it. However, with reasonably broad pretrial discovery, this consideration should rarely be applicable to presentation at trial.

The more significant question of burden of proof pertains to the burden of persuasion, that is, who has to carry the weight of the argument. Three levels of the burden of persuasion are often specified: the preponderance of the evidence, clear and convincing proof, and beyond a reasonable doubt. Theoretically, a preponderance means any amount over 50 percent likely to be correct, and the other standards require significantly more. However, some evidence indicates that judges and juries in fact translate preponderance of the evidence to mean 75 percent likely to be true, and beyond a reasonable doubt to mean 85 percent likely to be true (Tullock 1980, 79-80). This leaves little room for clear and convincing proof.

As we have already touched on grounds for the burden of persuasion in discussing moral costs (2.1.2), they need only be made explicit here. *(2-16) The principle of the burden of proof: (a) the burden of production should rest on the party that raises an issue unless it would be unfair because of another party's special access to and control of the evidence, and (b) the burden of persuasion should rest on the same party and be the preponderance of the evidence unless a higher standard is needed to avoid greater moral error costs by decisions adverse to the other party in such cases.* Due to the aim of avoiding punishment of the innocent, the moral costs of convicting the innocent are greater than those of not convicting the guilty, so criminal wrongdoing must be proved beyond a reasonable doubt. In most civil cases, moral costs are equal on both sides, so a burden of preponderance of the evidence is appropriate. In a few instances, moral costs might be greater with one type of error than another in a civil matter, so a burden of clear and convincing proof might be imposed.

It is important to distinguish between introducing a new issue and calling into doubt the other party's evidence on an issue. Consider *Texas Dep't of Community Affairs v. Burdine* (450 U.S. 248 (1981)). The plaintiff, Burdine, alleged that she had been discriminated against in not being promoted. Consequently, she had the burden of production of evidence that she was discriminated against. If the Department did not introduce any contrary evidence, Burdine would also have fulfilled the burden of persuasion by a preponderance of the evidence – some evidence in favor and none against. Thus, at this point the Department had the burden to present evidence that it did not intentionally discriminate, that it had a legitimate reason for not promoting Burdine. Nonetheless, the burden of persuasion on the issue remained with Burdine, for she raised the issue by filing the action. It is only when the other party introduces a new issue, rather than merely offering evidence in rebuttal, that the burden of production and persuasion shifts.

Finally, the burden of persuasion is sometimes made easier by various presumptions. Generally, a presumption merely shifts the burden of production, that is, it provides a party's prima facie case and makes it necessary for the other party to present evidence in rebuttal (Fed. R. Evid. 301). A doctrine that is sometimes taken to shift the burden of persuasion in tort law is that of *res ipsa loquitur* – the thing speaks for itself (Fleming 1968, 155-56). *Res ipsa* is involved, for example, if the plaintiff awakes from an appendectomy with a shoulder injury (*Ybarra v. Spangard*, 25 Cal 2d 486, 154 P.2d 687 (1944)). If the burden of persuasion is shifted, then the defendant must show by a preponderance of the evidence that he or she was not negligent. Practically, however, even if the burden of persuasion is not shifted to the other party, the presumption that negligence is involved is very difficult to overcome, although it can be done.

2.3.8. *Jury trials*. The jury trial is a source of many stories and dramas. Lawyers delight in talking about how jury sentiment can be played one way or another, and some psychological consulting firms exist to advise lawyers on jury selection. The United States probably uses the jury more than any other country in the world. The right to jury trial is enshrined, at least for federal courts and criminal cases, in the U.S. Constitution's sixth and seventh amendments. In contrast, the Canadian Constitution provides a jury trial by right only for criminal cases where the maximum punishment is five or more years of imprisonment (Canadian Charter of Rights and Freedoms § 11(f)).

Despite its prevalence in popular culture, not much solid knowledge exists about the functions juries actually perform, as opposed to the tendencies of classes of people to vote certain ways on juries. In theory, juries are confined to finding facts. A classic study of criminal juries found that when judges and juries disagreed, most of the time both facts and values were involved (Kalven and Zeisel 1966, 116). Room for factual disagreement provides leeway for juries to resolve issues in the direction of their value judgments. The chief reasons for judge-jury disagreement were issues of evidence, sentiments about the law, and sentiments about the defendant (Kalven and Zeisel 1966, 115). If juries think the criminal law too harsh, then they can find for the defendant (see Atiyah 1983, 21-22). Thus, a practical result of the use of the jury is to temper the law by contemporary standards of conduct as determined by ordinary citizens (L.R.C.C. 1980, 8-11).

There is little reason to think civil cases are much different. Juries can adjust the standard of negligence to changing social conceptions of appropriate care (Fleming 1968, 29). Whether a defendant behaved as a reasonably prudent person would have is not a purely factual matter. Value aspects are clearly relevant. Substituting judges for juries in tort cases is likely to have two effects (Fleming 1968, 149). First, findings of fact by a judge might be turned into conclusions of law. Even if findings of fact and legal conclusions are made separately (Fed. R. Civ. P. 52(a)), courts might take decisions as precedents for similar fact situations. Second, it is easier for appellate courts to overturn decisions; not only must the decision be supported by facts, but the reasoning must be correct. The first effect was one that Oliver Wendell Holmes gave for preferring judicial to jury decisions; conclusions of law amount to fixed rules and thus provide better guidance about permissible conduct (Holmes [1881] 1963, 89-91). The development of statutes and precedents make duties more precise. However, individuals are less likely to guide their conduct by precedents in civil than criminal law. Businesses do often use civil law as a guide, and the increased specificity of standards of negligence, except for traffic accidents, is most obvious in relation to commercial activities.

Room for juries to inject values into the application of the law stems from their immunity from sanction and the procedural difficulty in overturning jury determinations of fact. Except for bribery, jurors are immune from sanction for their decisions (*Bushnell's Case*, 124 Eng. Rep. 1006 (C.P. 1670)). One cannot punish jurors for making incorrect findings. Thus, in extreme situations, juries can nullify the law simply by refusing to convict. A major recent example of this has been the nullification of the abortion law in Quebec. Canadian law only permits abortions necessary for the health of the pregnant woman performed in hospitals after approval by a committe of three physicians. Twice juries refused to convict Dr. Henry Morgentaler, and the net effect is that abortion clinics are widespread in Quebec. In the first case, the Crown appealed as a matter of law, the

Quebec Court of Appeal reinstated the conviction, and the Supreme Court upheld the reinstatement (*Regina v. Morgentaler*, 42 D.L.R.3rd 448 (Que. Q.B. 1973), *rev'd*, 47 D.L.R.3rd 211 (Que. 1974), *aff'd sub nom. Morgentaler v. The Queen*, 53 D.L.R.3rd 161 (Can. 1975)). In the second case, the Quebec Court of Appeal upheld the verdict and the Supreme Court refused leave to appeal (*Regina v. Morgentaler*, 64 D.L.R.3d 718 (Que. 1976)).

About the only ways to overturn jury verdicts are by a decision that there was insufficient evidence to go to the jury ('judgment notwithstanding the verdict') or to show jury misconduct, for example, a compromised claim (decreasing an award to resolve differences about liability). In the first *Morgentaler* case, the Quebec Court of Appeal substituted a conviction for an acquital. Such a procedure is not permissible in U.S. law. With the widespread use of comparative rather than contributory negligence (see 5.3.3), a finding of a compromise verdict is now less likely. If a case has been given to a jury, it is puzzling how the jury's decision can be overturned because there was insufficient evidence for the jury to debate an issue. The contrary judgment is simply that of a judge, one person. How, on the traditional theory that juries only find facts, can the judgment of one person (or an appellate court that did not hear the testimony) show that jurors could not have reasonably decided as they did? Were the jury deciding a matter of law, then a judge's expert training would provide a basis for attaching more credibility to the judge's judgment. But since juries are supposed only to decide matters of fact and judges are not experts on such questions, the grounds for overturning a verdict are unclear. The traditional theory is a myth not actually followed in practice.

A central question is when, if ever, there should be a jury trial as a matter of right. The strongest case for such a right pertains to criminal trials. First, the world is and has been full of dictatorial governments. The jury's nullification power is a defense against unjust laws. One need not have a dictatorial government for the jury's power of nullification to be of value. It can be directed at particular laws, such as limitations on abortions as with Dr. Morgentaler, prohibiton of alcohol, or excessive mandatory punishment for minor offenses such as possession of marijuana. Moreover, jury trials need not be frequent for protection to be provided. Most criminal cases today do not involve jury trials but trials to lower court judges (Atiyah 1983, 21) or bargained pleas of guilty. Nevertheless, the possibility of a jury trial remains. Given that the jury is optional with the defendant, the only reason one might have to oppose such a right is the cost. In current practice, the marginal cost of jury trials to the public expense of law enforcement is small (L.R.C.C. 1980, 33). Should all criminal defendants receive a jury trial, that would change. The potential loss of liberty or life is significant to most defendants; a year in prison would be a major event to most people. It is callous and arbitrary to restrict, as Canada does, the right of a jury trial to cases in which the maximum incarceration is greater than five years. Thus, so long as jury trials are primarily a safety valve, the right of jury trial is acceptable for criminal cases.

The reasons supporting a right to jury trial do not carryover well from criminal to civil law. The costs of unjust laws are less, usually being payment of monetary damages or prohibition from certain activities. As indicated above, the functions of juries in some areas of civil law are much like those in criminal law. Questions of negligence are predominantly blends of fact and value that should be attuned to current society instead of based on outdated precedents. Certain other types of cases, such as defamation, might also importantly involve contemporary public attitudes. Moreover, if one party exercises a right to a jury trial, then the other party is forced into one. Although this is also true of criminal cases, the imposition is on the public as a whole rather than individuals. Consequently, it is hard to conclude that a right to a jury trial is necessary for civil cases. Reasonable people might decide either way, and stronger arguments can be made for the right in particular types of cases.

Two features of juries – size and unanimity – might also be considered central. The traditional jury consisted of twelve persons. However, smaller juries are or have been used in various places for both criminal and civil cases (L.R.C.C. 1980, 32; *Williams v. Florida*, 399 U.S. 78 (1970); *Colgrove v. Battin*, 413 U.S. 149 (1973)). Smaller juries are not likely to be as accurate in fact finding, simply because six people are more likely to be wrong than twelve. Other aspects of group dynamics could make a difference. Although jury size must be a difference of degree and no fixed number can be justified on normative grounds, at some point a jury becomes too small to fulfill its functions (*Ballew v. Georgia*, 435 U.S. 223 (1978)).

The requirement of unanimity is another matter. Here a difference exists between criminal and civil cases resulting from the standard of proof required. It is reasonable to allow for differences of opinion if the standard is preponderance of the evidence, so majority verdicts are acceptable. However, it is difficult to reconcile majority verdicts with the criminal standard of proof beyond a reasonable doubt. If, say, two jurors find the defendant innocent, how can one conclude that there was no reasonable doubt? One must, logically, conclude that the two jurors' doubts were unreasonable. Besides this concern with moral error costs, there is a concern for dispute resolution. Defendants might find unanimous decisions more acceptable. Consequently, unanimous verdicts should be required for criminal cases (*Burch v. Louisiana*, 441 U.S. 130 (1979) (disallowing nonunanimous criminal verdict by jury of six); L.R.C.C. 1980, 19, 28-32). *(2-17) The principle of jury trial: a right of jury trial with unanimous verdicts for conviction should exist in criminal cases.*

One final matter deserves note. It has recently been argued that some cases are too complex for juries to decide (*In re Japanese Electronic Products Antitrust Litig.*, 631 F.2d 1069 (3d Cir. 1980); Atiyah 1983, 22-23). As we have not accepted a principle requiring a right of jury trial in civil cases, we would have no trouble denying jury trials in complex civil cases. The matter is otherwise for criminal cases. If a case is too complex for a jury to understand and decide, then the matter appears to have been too complex for a defendant to have been able to know that the conduct was prohibited (see also Nocenti 1983, 26-27, 30-31). The principle of certainty ((6-9) in 6.2.3) would not be fulfilled. However, one should not immediately conclude that defendants in complex antitrust or conspiracy cases cannot be convicted, because juries might be capable of understanding very complex cases (L.R.C.C. 1980, 34; see *In re U.S. Financial Sec. Litig.*, 609 F.2d 411 (9th Cir. 1979)).

2.3.9. *Stare decisis.* In the previous section, we noted that the substitution of judge for jury decisions tends to turn factual matters into legal ones and provide more certainty. This certainty results from the common-law system of following precedent or 'stare decisis'. *(2-18) The principle of stare decisis: courts should follow precedents.* The precedents in question are those of that court or a higher one in the jurisdiction. The principle is not strict; that is, there can be sufficient reasons for not following precedent. However, stare decisis implies that a decision to depart from precedent cannot rest merely on slight substantive benefits of a rule or decision different from that dictated by precedent. In short, it amounts to a principle of stability of the law so that one is not justified in changing the law simply because one can think of a slightly better rule. Finally, the weight of the principle can vary between common-law fields. The principle of stability ((3-4) in 3.1.1) for property law provides extra emphasis to stare decisis in that field.

Many problems arise in determining what precedents require and which should be followed that are not discussed here. Two general interpretations are, however, worth noting (see Lyons 1985, 500-02). According to the historical model, if the same or similar factual features are found in the present case as in a previous one, then one should decide the same as before. In this model, the factual features are what control the present decision. According to the normative model, it is not the factual features themselves but acceptable principles justifying the previous decision that control the present case. The application of those principles in the present situation might justify a different decision for an apparently similar case. Although the factual elements present in the earlier case are also present in this one, there is a further feature that the principles pick out that justifies a different decision. However, the differences between the two approaches are not as stark as here indicated. A person using the historical model would sometimes distinguish a present case on the basis of an extra feature not mentioned in the previous decision.

The central difficulty in justifying stare decisis is that one must sometimes follow decisions that were not the best possible. One might think that this does not apply to the normative model of precedents, because one uses the most acceptable principles that will justify most previous decisions. Nevertheless, if a number of previous decisions were not the best, there may be no otherwise justifiable principle that will justify them. However, because we are considering a weak principle of stare decisis, one that sometimes allows not following precedent, one is not committed to following precedent though the heavens may fall.

The reasons supporting the principle of stare decisis are a blend of general purposes of law, error and direct costs, and process benefits. One reason is the certainty and predictability it provides the law. If people are to guide their conduct by the law, then they must be able to know what it requires. Often people do not guide their conduct by tort law; one does not consciously drive in one manner rather than another to avoid tort liability. Even so, one may still alter one's behavior in view of liability rules, for example, take out liability insurance. Frequent changes increase the economic costs of people adjusting their lives to the law.

As our discussion of the adversary system makes clear (2.2), stare decisis is not essential for legal certainty and predictability. Inquisitorial systems provide perhaps even greater certainty and predictability. However, if one is to have a common-law system in which judges make rules, then stare decisis is probably the only practical way to provide certainty and predictability. Otherwise one would likely face the wide variance that occurs in judicial criminal sentencing, only applied to findings of liability. The only alternative would be to have all cases heard by the same judge or judges, and even then one would face the uncertainty of a judicial change of mind about the relative merits of two substantive rules.

People also have reasons of reliance for the law to be stable. Reliance differs from certainty and predictability in that it pertains to effects on people who have arranged their affairs on the basis of predictions, not the mere ability to predict. Insurance companies rely on the rules of tort liability in considering their likely liability and setting rates. Changes can involve moral costs to those who have reasonably relied on the law; they have been led reasonably to expect one set of consequences and another set is substituted to their detriment.

Nevertheless, without stare decisis reliance on previous decisions would be unreasonable. Perhaps in deciding cases judges do commit themselves to following their decisions, but one must then ask whether they should make such commitments (Lyons 1985, 511). The crucial question is the reasonableness of the commitment and reliance. In some areas, judges do not in fact make such commitments; some lower court decisions and other discretionary ones (for example, whether to have separate trials for distinct claims) do not involve commitments. Nevertheless, such commitments are the norm, as evidenced by the principle of stare decisis, and the certainty and predictability of law provide reasons for making them. When a commitment has been made, if adequate advance warning has been given that a change might occur, then reliance is not reasonable. A proposed bill in a legislature provides such warning, but courts can also provide it by dicta or simple statements that it is time a precedent was reconsidered. The ability to rely on previous decisions also promotes repose in issues of continuing relationships. Otherwise, the decision of an issue in, say, an employer-employee relationship would be open to suit again should another similar matter occur.

A third reason for the principle of stare decisis is the efficiency of courts – a matter of direct costs. A heavy burden would be placed on courts if each case were treated as one of first impression. Many more appeals would be taken. Courts would have to hear and consider anew all the arguments for and against various rules. When cases clearly fall within the scope of precedents, time and money are saved and settlements encouraged.

A fourth reason is the coherence or consistency of the law. A change in one rule might require adjustments in many others. A change from contributory to comparative negligence might require abolition of other rules. A system of consistent or coherent rules can be worked out on a case by case basis only on the assumption that the previous rules are still binding. A coherent or consistent system contributes to intelligibility. This consistency is different from the logical consistency of any single judge, for a judge could hold a consistent but different set of rules and principles everyday.

The final reason is one of process benefits or perhaps moral costs, namely, the equal treatment of like cases. Stare decisis is not necessary to treating like cases alike; a system of statutory rules would also do so. Indeed, like cases can be treated alike without precedents or rules (see generally Lyons 1973, Winston 1974). Nevertheless, stare decisis is one way of helping to ensure that similar cases are treated alike, and the failure to do so is likely to make decisions less acceptable and thus decrease practical dispute resolution. Our assumption throughout has been that one is choosing principles for application to all similar cases. Dissimilar treatment of alike cases is thus contrary to our methodological assumptions. It would also destroy the intelligibility of the legal system. Consequently, equal treatment provides a reason for following precedent.

Sometimes the principle of stare decisis is treated as barring judicial change of common-law precedent. Often judges propound that any change in the law must be left to the legislature. However, nothing in the argument for stare decisis supports that conclusion. If a rule is completely out of step with current social conditions and works great substantive injustice, the principle of stare decisis is overridden. Whether that change should stem from the courts or legislatures is another issue.

Five factors are relevant to whether courts or legislatures should change nonstatutory rules. One is the interrelation of the extant rule with others; if it is embedded in a complex of rules, perhaps the required changes extend beyond the issues of the current case and failure to address them at the same time would create uncertainty and confusion. If so, then legislative change is preferable. Another factor is the complexity of the proposed rule. Even though the rule does not interrelate to many others, it might involve many complex elements which judges cannot settle within the confines of the current case whereas a statute could. The scope of a proposed new rule is also relevant. This consideration pertains to limits on a court's personal jurisdiction and authority over resources. For example, U.S. Supreme Court Chief Justice Burger suggested that perhaps the exclusionary rule should be abolished and a special court be established to hear tort claims for violations of constitutional rights (*Bivens v. Six Unknown Named Agents of Fed. Bureau of Narcotics*, 403 U.S. 388, 422-23 (1971)). However, as we have noted, establishing such a court is simply beyond the authority of a court. Similarly, abolition of tort claims for personal injury and property damage and the institution of comprehensive insurance, as we suggest in 5.5.2, is beyond the power of a court.

The lack of information available to a court is a fourth reason for leaving changes to legislatures. Especially within an adversary system that relies on private parties to gather and present information, courts might not be able to obtain and assess all the social information necessary to decide whether a rule should be changed. Courts cannot conduct the sort of social scientific inquiry that might be necessary to justify a change in a rule and work out the best alternative. However, given policy guidelines, courts do fairly well in devising and adjusting policies for complex local situations, as in school desegregation plans (Chayes 1979).

Finally, if a bright line needs to be established in a gray area, that provides a reason for changes to be left to legislatures. Setting a maximum amount of damages or temporal limitations on bringing suits are such matters. Essentially, the drawing of such bright lines, at least within some range, is discretionary. Settling on one line rather than another often involves compromise of various considerations with no one compromise clearly preferable. Courts are supposed to give principled reasons for their decisions, and that cannot be done for bright lines. Consequently, court changes of this sort are likely to bring courts into disrepute and cause litigants to feel unjustly treated, which decreases the chances of a practical resolution of their dispute.

These factors do not necessarily provide conclusive arguments against courts failing to follow precedent and for leaving changes to legislatures. They are all matters of degree, and various ones can be present to different degrees. Besides, the substantive injustice of the extant rule must be balanced with them. Finally, these same considerations apply to determining the types of issues that courts should refuse to handle even if they are cases of first impression. The factors determine the limits of adjudication as a method of dispute resolution and thus of substantive principles and rules courts can reasonably consider.

2.3.10. *Appeals.* If one wants to challenge a legal rule or its application in a particular case, then practically one must appeal the decision. A first question concerns the reasons, if any, for appeals as of right. Appeals obviously increase direct costs, so arguments for them must be based on avoiding error costs or gaining process benefits.

Of the process benefits identified earlier, only the principle of fairness might provide a reason for allowing appeals. But fairness concerns procedural equality between the parties, and procedural unfairness need not result in erroneous outcomes. Thus, one might query whether it is ever justifiable to reverse a decision on procedural grounds if there was no outcome error. A losing party in a case with procedural errors is likely to think it affected his or her chances of a favorable outcome. The opportunity to appeal such mistakes is likely to assist psychological and practical dispute resolution. But because of the major direct costs in a new trial, appellate courts should be permitted to let a judgment stand if they believe a procedural error did not affect the outcome – was a harmless error (Fed. R. Civ. P. 61). This consideration can apply even to mistakes of substantive law as in a charge to a jury. For example, in *Director of Public Prosecutions v. Morgan* (1976 A.C. 182), the Lords held that a trial judge had misdirected the jury in requiring them to find that the defendants' mistake must be reasonable. Nonetheless, the Lords let the conviction stand, because they did not think a reasonable jury could find that the defendants sincerely believed what they claimed – that the rape victim had consented.

Considerations of the consistency and development of law are a mixture of error costs and process benefits. Different trial courts often resolve similar issues differently. This is unfair in that different rules are applied to similar cases, although it is not a procedural unfairness between the plaintiff and defendant in a particular case. Also, there is an outcome error, because only one of the rules is correct. Appeals along with stare decisis can resolve this inconsistency by adopting one rule binding on all lower courts. The related factor is the development of the law. Common law developed from judicial opinions. As social conditions change, new situations arise sometimes rendering old rules inappropriate. Appeals permit higher courts to develop rules for changing circumstances. Nonetheless, these considerations do not require appeals as of right; indeed, they are better served by permitting appeals only at the discretion of appellate courts. The courts are in a better position than the parties to determine whether consistency or development of the law will be furthered by an appeal.

The major justification for appeals as of right must thus rest on avoidance of error costs. Such an argument must claim that appellate courts are more likely than trial courts to reach correct decisions. As appellate courts involve several judges – usually three or more – the claim must be either that appellate judges are better than trial judges or that groups of judges are more likely to be correct than single judges (Tullock 1980, 164). Although both of these contentions are plausible, there is little direct evidence to support them. Moreover, either factor could be instituted without appeals by having better judges or panels of them at the trial level (Tullock 1980, 165). However, one other factor supports the superiority of appellate decisions, namely, the time available for reflection before decision. A trial judge must often make rulings in the middle of trial without adequate time for researching precedent or reflecting on the situation. Appellate judges do have time and receive extensive briefs on the limited points being considered. Consequently, there is good reason to believe appeals will reduce errors.

The net result is that only avoidance of unfairness and error costs supports appeals as of right. Because the moral error costs are greater in criminal than civil cases, the argument for appeals as of right is stronger in them. Most common-law systems grant criminal defendants an appeal as of right (see Abraham 1975, 247; Jones 1981, 558). Moreover, acquitals cannot be overturned on appeal in most common-law systems (see Abraham 1975, 247; Jones 1981, 557), although we did note that Canadian courts reversed Dr. Morgentaler's first acquittal (2.3.8). Giving defendants appeals as of right reinforces the procedural safeguards to avoid punishment of the innocent. In effect, both the trial and appellate courts have a veto on punishment, so appeals as of right reduce the chances that an innocent person will be punished.

To decide whether appeals should be given as of right, one must balance the fairness and error cost considerations favoring them against the increased direct costs. Consequently, and ironically, the case for appeals as of right is greater the fewer appeals actually made, for the more appeals, the greater the direct costs. In the U.S. federal courts, out of every hundred civil cases filed, only five result in actual appellate submissions (Carrington and Babcock 1983, 355-56). Although even this rate puts considerable pressure on courts of appeal, disposition of easy cases without written or lengthy opinions probably makes it bearable. Nonetheless, one cannot conclude that formal and full appellate review should be available as a matter of right in civil cases. Discretionary review would still correct glaring errors.

A related question concerns the scope of appellate review. The common-law doctrine is that, with a few exceptions, appellate courts review matters of law but not of fact. In the past, courts of equity reviewed questions of fact, even permitting submission of further written evidence. As we have noted several times, the distinction between law and fact is not clear; many questions such as the reasonableness of conduct are a blend of value or law and fact. The U.S. federal compromise, at least for cases decided by a judge, is to allow findings of fact to stand unless "clearly erroneous" (Fed. R. Civ. P. 52(a)). Similarly, trial judges are to direct jury verdicts or give judgments notwithstanding the verdict only when there are no significant facts to support the party opposing the motion (see *Boeing Co. V. Shipman*, 411 F.2d 365 (5th Cir. 1969)). Appellate courts can give judgments notwithstanding the verdict rather than order new trials if they deem it appropriate, although that is rare (*Neely v. Eby Constr. Co.*, 386 U.S. 317 (1967)).

The standard argument for restricting appellate review to matters of law and its application to facts is that determination of facts often depends on matters which juries and trial judges have better evidence to evaluate. For example, findings often depend on the credibility of witnesses, which in turn depends on their demeanor, tone of voice, and so on. But if trials are video taped, trial judges do not have a significant advantage in these respects (Frankel 1980, 111-12). Moreover, in cases involving largely statistical evidence, for example, evidence of discrimination in hiring or promotion, there is little reason to believe a trial judge has access to significant information denied appellate judges.

A better argument for limiting the scope of appellate review rests on considerations of timeliness and repose. When appellate courts overturn verdicts and order new trials, decisions are delayed and the dispute remains open. Moreover, absent clear error, each party has had an opportunity to participate and present his or her case. Given the great costs of another trial, caution should be exercised in overturning findings of fact. However, instead of appellate courts assuming lower court judges or juries have better access to facts, a preferable approach is to consider whether the matter in question is one for which presence at the trial is apt to be beneficial. That is, instead of using a blanket law/fact distinction, appellate courts should consider whether the trial judge or jury did have access to evidence unavailable to it. *(2-19) The principle of appeals: appeals as of right should be available in criminal cases, and unless appellate courts have access to facts comparable to that of the trier, reversal on factual grounds should be limited to clearly erroneous findings.*

The principle of timeliness applies to the whole legal process, namely, that disputes be settled within an appropriate time. It therefore supports a limit to the time in which an appeal may be taken. The point is simply to get the appellate process started. No conclusive arguments can be provided for preferring one time period, say, ten days, to another, say, thirty days. Essentially, the point is to appeal as soon as reasonably possible after the judgment. However, for certainty a bright line of a definite time period is needed.

The rule of finality of appeals is that an appeal can be taken only from a final judgment (28 U.S.C. § 1291 (1982)). The chief purposes of the rule are to reduce direct costs and to prevent many appeals interrupting a trial and delaying it. The rule indirectly relates to repose by reducing the time before a dispute is conclusively settled. During the course of a trial, there might be several orders parties would like to appeal. But the appeal might not settle the case, and the trial would have to continue. Trial judges are usually correct, and mistakes will often turn out to be harmless – one wins the case anyway. However, sometimes failure to allow an appeal before final judgment can create errors or increase direct costs and delay. Courts have developed exceptions permitting appeals before final judgment if serious and irreparable harm is likely to occur should the trial court's decision be wrong (see *Cohen v. Beneficial Indus. Loan Corp.*, 337 U.S. 541 (1949); Wright 1983, 701-707). Moreover, courts of appeal have discretion to accept appeals from grants or denials of injunctions (28 U.S.C. § 1292(a) (1982)). Such exceptions are acceptable, for the possibility of irreparable serious harm is more important than the costs of delay.

2.3.11. *Repose.* A major application of the principle of repose is after all appeals have been exhausted. As the purpose is to put an end to a dispute once and for all, people should not be allowed to raise the same matter in another suit. In criminal law, this point is recognized in the rule against double jeopardy prohibiting a person being tried twice for the same crime. Both repose and avoidance of punishing the innocent support prohibiting retrial of a person who has been acquitted. As retrial with conviction is not possible, there is no point in permitting appeals of acquitals (see *United States v. Scott*, 437 U.S. 82, 90-91 (1978)). These reasons are not as strong when a mistrial occurs or a conviction is overturned on appeal. Unlike a factual finding of innocence, mistrials and overturned convictions cannot evidence innocence, only that guilt has not been properly proved. Consequently, retrials should be permitted if there is a strong reason for them (see Jones 1981, 560, 566-72).

In civil cases, repose underlies the doctrines of 'claim preclusion' or 'res judicata' and 'issue preclusion' or 'collateral estoppel'. Both of these doctrines prohibit relitigating the same subject matter, and they primarily differ in their scope. As the names suggest, claim preclusion prohibits relitigating the same claim, while issue preclusion prohibits relitigating the same issue. The problem is to determine what constitutes the same claim or issue.

Historically, claim preclusion was restricted to matters stemming from the same writ, but with the abolition of the writ system and adoption of modern liberal pleading, it has become much harder to apply. Whether two claims are the same could be based on their involving the same wrong or violation of a single right, the same transaction or occurrence, or the same evidence. These bases give different results. Suppose Hill and Iler have a traffic accident, Iler gets out of his car and calls Hill names, and Hill slaps Iler's face. On the same wrong or right basis, three court cases could stem from this incident. Iler could sue Hill for negligence. After that trial, Hill could sue Iler for defamation. In retaliation, Iler could sue Hill for battery. On the same evidence basis, although the negligence case could be tried separately, the defamation case would probably prevent Iler's suit for battery, since much of the evidence is likely to be the same, especially if Hill raises a defense of provocation. Finally, on the same transaction or occurrence basis, only one case might be permitted. The better basis is the same transaction or occurrence (Rest. 2d Judgments § 24(1)). In considering joinder of claims and parties (2.3.4), we concluded that considerable direct costs would be saved by trying all claims in one case. Applying claim preclusion on the same grounds promotes that policy. Although this amounts to compulsory joinder of claims, it still leaves much scope for permissive joinder of other issues (Rest. 2d Judgments § 22).

With this analysis of claim preclusion, the obvious basis for issue preclusion is same evidence. Consequently, in our hypothetical traffic accident, if Hill counterclaimed for defamation, both claim and issue preclusion would bar Iler's subsequent suit for battery. In other cases, however, only issue preclusion might apply. For example, suppose Johnson sues Klein on a franchise contract for provision of requirements, the existence of the contract is litigated, and a contract is found to exist. If two years later Johnson again sues Klein on the contract, Klein is precluded from arguing that no contract exists.

Historically, claim and issue preclusion were restricted to the parties in the case or those with whom they were in 'privity' (had a mutual or succesive relationship to property or by contract), for example, had sold a patent. But concerns for error and direct costs are not so limited. If an issue has once been litigated, why should courts litigate it again between different parties? (Claim preclusion is not in question here, since different parties would have separate claims.) Here one must distinguish 'defensive' and 'offensive' preclusion. Defensive preclusion occurs when a plaintiff seeks to litigate an issue that has already been decided against him or her. For example, if a plaintiff has sued one party for patent infringement and lost on the ground that the patent is invalid, he or she should not be permitted to sue another party for infringement of the same alleged patent (*Blonder-Tongue Laboratories, Inc. v. University of Ill. Found.*, 402 U.S. 313 (1971)). The defendant can use issue preclusion defensively to urge that the patent is invalid.

Offensive preclusion is another matter. It bars a defendant relitigating an issue he or she lost. Consider *Parklane Hosiery Co. v. Shore* (439 U.S. 322 (1979)). In a previous suit against it by the Securities and Exchange Commission, Parklane was found to have violated securities' laws. A stockholder then filed suit on the basis of the violations contending that Parklane was barred from contesting them. The Supreme Court upheld this contention. Again, it saves direct costs not to relitigate. However, there is an unfair possibility raised by this offensive use of issue preclusion. Suppose there is a mass disaster, for example, an airplane crash. Further suppose that Lawrence, an injured passenger, sues the airline for negligence and loses. Now suppose Manson sues the airline for negligence. As Manson has never litigated this matter, he is not precluded from doing so. Now if Manson wins, Neville can sue the airline and use offensive preclusion against it on the negligence issue. The net effect is that the airline is subject to continually relitigating its negligence until it loses. This will not, as the Supreme Court recognized in *Parklane*, save judicial time. Nor does it seem fair to the defendant. However, the Court was willing to rely on the powers and discretion of lower courts to try to prevent such situations. Absent a showing of how these situations can be avoided or that they are not unfair, such reliance is not acceptable.

Claim and issue preclusion significantly further repose and dispute resolution – putting an end to disputes so that parties can get on with their activities in peace. Another set of legal rules has the same effect by preventing lawsuits in the first place. Statutes of limitations prohibit bringing actions after a certain time has elapsed since plaintiffs became aware, or should have become aware, of their claims. Statutes of limitations avoid error costs due to difficulty in obtaining sufficient reliable evidence. They also prevent unfairness, for example, allowing a potential plaintiff to sit on a claim and run up damages. A major aim of the law is to prevent lawsuits, which are minus sum interactions, except as necessary for reasonable and timely resolution of disputes. Statutes of limitations further this aim (see also the principle of stale claims (3-16) in 3.4.1).

Nevertheless, statutes of limitation are one of the legal technicalities about which nonlawyers often rail. The objection is that if one can prove a valid claim, why should one be prevented from pursuing it, especially if the failure to file in time is one's lawyer's fault. Granted, sometimes evidence is lost, but this should not bar cases in which it is not true. It merely provides a technical shield for unscrupulous persons.

Two distinct issues are involved here. One is whether people should be allowed to bring cases after long periods of time, especially when evidence may have been lost or become less reliable (witnesses' recollections and testimony). One can reasonably agree, from both a plaintiff's or defendant's position, that some limit should be imposed. As a potential defendant, one wants to be able to get on with one's life without the cloud of a lawsuit. As a potential plaintiff, one can agree that one should proceed with reasonable speed in exchange for protection as a potential defendant.

The second issue is the use of a bright line or definite period without consideration for extenuating circumstances. It is probably this aspect that most upsets ordinary citizens and makes them view it as a "technical" defense. Courts have developed some rules to help mitigate this aspect, for example, the perpetuation of a debt if the debtor acknowledges it. However, there is no sharp point separating reliable from unreliable testimonial evidence. Consequently, either extensive investigation into the issue (and others) must be made in each case with high direct costs and considerable dissatisfaction by losing parties, or a bright line must be provided. Legislatures have recognized the need for bright lines and provided them.

Statutes of limitation provide a clear instance in which procedure affects substantive law. Indeed, it is sometimes a nice question whether statutes of limitation are to be considered procedural or substantive law. Nevertheless, it is clear that procedural considerations are importantly involved in restricting the substantive claims that can be brought in court. The entire procedural system set out in this chapter – courts deciding cases, the adversary system, and procedural elements from jurisdiction to repose – limit the substantive law that courts can develop and enforce. It is the common-law method of dispute resolution, and it is not necessarily the best method for resolving all forms of disputes, let alone the best method for achieving all aims one might have for a legal system (see also 5.5).

CHAPTER 3

PROPERTY LAW

INTRODUCTION

3.0.   Private property rights apparently exist in all societies (Becker 1980, 198-200; Hobhouse 1922, 11), but they vary greatly from society to society. Property law is fundamental to society and the other fields of common law, because it specifies the forms of, and control over, wealth in a society. It thus provides one set of rights with which the other legal fields are concerned (Epstein 1982, 49). Indeed, some social theories attempt to analyze all rights as forms of property rights. Contract law concerns the transfer of property and benefits of services. Freedom to transfer property, which did not widely exist in feudal society, may have been a precursor of freedom of contract (Atiyah 1979, 727). Much of tort law concerns damages to property, and part of the criminal law, such as theft and fraud, concerns security of property.

The judicial system settles disputes brought to it by disputing parties. Every parent is familiar with some problems judges face in property law.

"Alison won't let me play with the video game," Adam complains.

"It belongs to both of us," Alison protests. "He used it all morning. Now it is my turn."

Here is an issue of use and management of jointly owned property.

On the beach, Betty and Bruce are tugging in separate directions on a large conch shell.

"It's mine!" screams Betty.

"No, it's mine," yells Bruce. "I got it first."

"But I saw it first. I was going to get it when you grabbed it away," shouts Betty.

76

Here is a problem of original acquisition of property.

These disputes between children illustrate two of the three main topics in property law. The first topic is what is property. The forms of property involve two aspects – a concept of ownership and an account of the sorts of things that can be owned. A second topic concerns what one can do with property; much if not all of the value of property stems from what one can do with it. In turn, this depends partly on its form; one cannot do the same things with a copyright as with a farm. A third topic, as illustrated by Betty and Bruce, is how one can acquire property, and correlatively, since most property is acquired from others, how one can dispose of it. To address these topics satisfactorily, one first needs to specify the aims of property law.

AIMS

3.1.0. *Introduction.* Although it is an interesting problem that has exercised philosophers for centuries, the general justification of some form of private property is not our concern here (see Becker 1977; Lindsay 1922; Ryan 1984; Sartorius 1984). Instead, like the common law, we assume an institution of private property. The problem is to specify the main features of an acceptable institution of private property. Rarely do general justifications of private property directly answer the questions at issue in property law, but they do indicate acceptable aims for property law. These aims are tied to fundamental human purposes in society.

3.1.1. *Utility.* Some of the oldest and most common arguments for private property are based on utility – that it is useful to have private property (see Ryan 1984). The various arguments emphasize different benefits that accrue. Some emphasize economic considerations more than others, but a common thrust is that laws should promote well-being. We call these 'utilitarian' arguments.

One utilitarian argument for private property emphasizes the social instability that would result were people not secure in their possession and use of scarce resources. Suppose Carson has forty bushels of wheat but no law guarantees that she can continue to possess them. Others can take her wheat with impunity. Moreover, Carson is likely to consume the wheat as soon as feasible rather than save it. Although she might be hungry later, saving might not help, because others might take whatever she saves.

Disorder and an extravagant use of resources are likely if people are not assured the continued possession of things.

Another utilitarian argument emphasizes the efficient use of resources. Above we assumed that Carson had forty bushels of wheat, and we did not ask where or how she acquired them. But given the lawless situation described, why would anyone bother to plant and harvest wheat? One might as well let others do the work and then take the wheat. In that sort of situation, there is no incentive to use resources to produce goods that increase well-being. During the Vietnam war, North Vietnam annually invaded Laos and Cambodia at harvest time, collected the bulk of the harvest, and then returned to North Vietnam until the next harvest. The incentives for the Laotian and Cambodian farmers were radically decreased and production declined. In contrast, if people can count on the continued use and benefits of certain resources, then they have incentives to use them to create benefits. Resources will be used more efficiently. Although this argument indicates that private property is likely to be efficient, one cannot presume that a system of private property will be more efficient than a nonprivate property system in all circumstances (Michelman 1982).

Four aims of property law stem from these utilitarian arguments (see Posner 1977, 29-31). *(3-1) The principle of universality: all resources should be owned by determinate persons or it should be clear how determinate persons can acquire ownership of them.* This principle fosters efficiency and order. Although efficiency and order are not the only desirable conditions in society, they are desirable. If resources are owned, then someone has a good reason to use them to create more wealth or satisfaction. Resources need not be owned if they exist in such abundance that everyone can use all they wish. Few such resources exist now, but at one time, air and sunlight were such resources, and in many places so was water. Rules specifying ownership and how unowned resources are to be acquired decrease disputes over these issues. Of course, such disputes will never be entirely eliminated.

Suppose all resources were owned in common; that is, everyone owned everything. Then one would, in effect, be in a situation of no property. Anyone could use anything he or she wanted; it would be Alison and Adam arguing over the video game writ large. Inefficiency can also result, as in the well-known "tragedy of the commons" (Hardin 1976). If each farmer can graze cattle on the commons, then each will graze as many as possible. This will produce overgrazing destroying the land to the detriment of all.

If each farmer is restricted to grazing cattle on a particular and exclusive area, each will avoid overgrazing.

(3-2) The principle of exclusivity: ownership should be exclusive to the extent compatible with similar exclusivity of others' property. This principle has three aspects. First, ownership should enable one to exclude others from its use. Second, property should be owned by one or a limited number of persons rather than everyone in common, otherwise there is no one to exclude. (Corporations count as persons, at least for this purpose.) Third, this exclusivity should be limited to be compatible with the ownership of others. Many legal problems arise from incompatible uses of property, such as raising hogs in a residential area.

(3-3) The principle of transferability: (a) property should be voluntarily transferable from one person to another, and (b) involuntary transfers should not be allowed. Transferability permits more efficient uses of resources. If one person has grain but no water, and another has water but no grain, then both will be better off if they can exchange some of what they have. Moreover, such transfers should normally be voluntary. Involuntary transfer was a major problem in the above situation without property laws – disorder and disincentive. The importance of transferability varies with the type of property system; it is most important in a market economy, although some transfer occurs in others (Becker 1980, 208-9). By establishing and preserving the transferability of property, property law makes it possible to obtain the benefits of exchanges.

The fourth aim is more limited and qualified than the others, but nonetheless important. *(3-4) The principle of stability: legal ownership and possession should be stable.* A function of property law is to enable people to make plans on the basis of stable ownership and possession. This principle has two aspects. One pertains to the stability of laws of property (see Ryan 1984, 182-83). Such stability is a general principle for all law (Bayles 1978, 61, 65-66), but it is especially important for property law. Most contracts are at most for only a few years' duration, so changes in contract law will not usually disrupt long-term plans. Acquisition and use of real property, such as farms and factories, often involve long-range plans, perhaps over a lifetime or more. Frequent changes in the legal rules of ownership or possession can disrupt such plans. Suppose a section of land was zoned for residential use, and five years later, after a subdivision was constructed, rezoned for industrial use, and then in another ten years rezoned for agricultural use. Great disruption of plans and inefficiency would result, which is why no reasonable planning authority would make such changes (but see *HFH, Ltd. v. Superior Court*, 15 Cal. 3d 508, 542 P.2d 237, 125 Cal. Rptr. 365 (1975), *cert. denied*, 425 U.S. 904 (1976) (commercial to agricultural to residential but without development occurring)).

The other aspect of stability pertains to freedom from claims by others to ownership or possession of one's property, especially claims grounded in the distant past. Unexpected claims based on events of a half-century before can disrupt plans. Of course, the principle of stability carries more weight for some types of property than others; in general, stability is more important for 'real property' (land and things attached to it) than other or 'personal property', because often more is at stake and because most personal property has a comparatively short existence. This principle does not conflict with the principle of transferability, for it seeks to minimize involuntary loss of ownership or possession due to legal claims.

3.1.2. *Fairness.* Increasing social well-being, utility, is not the only rational purpose one might have; fairness is another which can provide aims for property law. Unfortunately, 'fairness' is an amorphous concept and needs to be specified.

One consideration of fairness is found in the dispute between Betty and Bruce (2.0). Both at least implicitly appealed to the principle that whoever obtained the conch shell first is entitled to it. *(3-5) The principle of first possession: ownership should be that of the first possessor of unpossessed property.* The principle of first possession resides in the distant past as the justification for ownership of all land in the United States. Ownership by the Europeans was based on the principle of first possession by explorers (*Johnson v. McIntosh*, 21 U.S. (8 Wheat.) 543 (1823)). Although first possession, like "first come, first served," seems to be a basic element of fairness, it has some utilitarian justification (see Epstein 1985, 217). To reduce disputes and forcible takings and to provide incentives for the use of resources, stability of possession is central. Consequently, one who has first possession of property should be able to retain it unless it is voluntarily transferred.

Fairness is an underlying concern of the labor theory of property. In a nutshell, the labor theory holds that, at least in the absence of reasons to the contrary, persons are entitled to the fruits of their labors. If a person under no obligation to others to do or not to do so cultivates a field and harvests the crop, then that person is entitled to the value of the labor – the crop. In the classical version, one owns one's body, so one should own that with which one mixes the labor of one's body. However, it is unclear why, on the classical version, one should gain ownership over that with which one mixes one's labor rather than lose ownership of the labor. A better view than mixing one's labor is that if one is not obligated to do the work, then absent a good reason to the contrary, one should be entitled to the benefits one produced. In the absence of good reasons, others do not have a claim to it, so one's claim based on labor should be sufficient (see also Sartorius 1984, 204).

There is a utilitarian reason to allow the person who grows a crop to have it; the crop is socially valuable and otherwise the person has no incentive to grow it. But fairness here seems to go further than utilitarian reasons would provide. Utilitarian considerations imply that property rights should be assigned to those to whom they are most valuable (Posner 1977, 36). But even if another person could make better use of some of a crop (perhaps that person has better access to buyers), without a further reason, as producer of the crop one could not accept assigning part of it to the other person. One would not accept another person receiving part of the benefits of one's labor simply because that person could make better use of it.

(3-6) The principle of labor: people should be entitled to a significant proportion of property that, without obligation to others, they produce, make, or create. This principle leaves open the possibility that someone else owns the material with which one works, and in such a case could be satisfied by compensation for the labor. At a minimum, a 'significant proportion' is that sufficient to provide an incentive for such production as justified by utilitarian concerns, but generally it is more than that. As principles only provide a good reason that can be outweighed by other good reasons, a principle of labor extending beyond that necessary for an incentive does not prohibit assigning a person less when there are good reasons for doing so. Finally, the principle of labor is an important addition to that of first possession. The principle of first possession partly underlies the classical labor theory, because that theory depends on one having first possession or ownership of oneself (Epstein 1979a, 1227). But our principle of labor extends beyond first possession, because it applies to products the materials of which were previously owned or possessed by others.

A final consideration of fairness is independent of utilitarian justification. Promotion of social utility or well-being sometimes requires collective activity, such as providing for national defense, building transportation systems, or running a court system. From a self-interested perspective, each person has good reason to avoid the burdens of producing such

82 CHAPTER 3

collective benefits while still receiving a share of the benefits. However, if each person so acted, these benefits would not exist, to the detriment of all. Rules requiring contribution from each for the production of collective benefits are needed.

Up to this point, the argument is straightforwardly utilitarian. However, a utilitarian would impose the necessary burdens so as to minimize the total burdens, even if some people received a significantly greater share. But by the method of argument being used, one must consider the situation from the perspective of all parties involved (here all persons in the society). The only acceptable solution from all perspectives is a roughly equal sharing of the burdens. *(3-7) The principle of social burdens: no grossly unequal burden should be imposed on a person for the production of collective benefits.*

3.1.3. *Freedom.* A final set of arguments for private property are concerned with freedom. One type of argument from freedom stems from Hegel (see Radin 1982, 971-77). One strain of this view is that private property is essential for liberty and the development of character (Rashdall 1922, 67). If one has an unlimited supply of some good, one will use it with abandon and fail to develop such traits as self-restraint. If one must provide for oneself from limited property, then one must learn to use deliberation and foresight to provide for the future (Lindsay 1922, 78). For example, if children who spend their allowance during the first part of a week are simply given more money by their parents, they usually fail to learn to restrain their impulses and to save for more expensive items they want.

Another strain of this view emphasizes how property can embody one's self and free expression. There is surely some truth in this notion. A person's clothes, household furnishings, house, and car indicate much about his or her preferences, and even if one did not choose them, after time they become part of one's identity. It is often argued that self-expression and identity do not apply to many forms of property, such as stock shares and trust funds. This objection surely applies to money and blind trusts where one does not know what is owned. However, stock shares and land holdings can express a person's self. Farmers and small businesspersons express themselves in their business property and view themselves as farmers, clothiers, grocers, and so on. Owners of stocks and bonds can do so; some people refuse to invest in certain companies on moral grounds, for example, South African companies. In effect, there is a continuum from what can be called 'self-expressive property' intimately connected with one's personality and identity at one end to property held only for wealth at the other (Radin 1982, 960).

Another type of argument from freedom focuses on the alleged value of private property as an element of political freedom (see also Epstein 1985, 138-39). One version is that in a supposed 'state of nature' (without government or laws) each person has full liberty, including the liberty to obtain, use, and modify things. Consequently, freedom of property – to possess, control, and use things – is one of the basic civil liberties or natural rights. On this view, regulation of property is permissible, just as is regulation of other civil liberties, but good reasons are required. And it would be no more justifiable to abolish private property than to abolish freedom of speech or security from unreasonable searches and seizures. Indeed, considerable criticism has been directed against the recent Canadian Charter of Rights and Freedoms for failure to include a right of property. A sociological version of this argument claims that only centers of power independent of political authority can restrain governments. Such centers of power are often based on wealth. In short, private property is not only a civil right but a defense against political oppression. We might at this point become involved in a long discussion of the relationship between private ownership and civil liberties in socialist and capitalist socities. Such an excursion would go too far afield and probably be fruitless.

Can these arguments from freedom for private property provide any useful guidance for property law? They do support one principle. The freedom to have and to do with property as one wishes is an aspect of freedom of conduct generally (see also Sartorius 1984, 204), and we have recognized freedom as a value rational persons would have (see 1.3). Wealth and the ability to dispose of it is often important for the realization of freedom. Suppose one wanted to place a political advertisement on television and had the wealth to do so, only one was not permitted to convert it to money to buy the television time. Then one's freedom of speech would be practically limited. Government thus should not interfere in the use of property without a good reason, which is merely part of the general burden of proof on government control of people's lives and activities. Moreover, freedom of conduct becomes more important as it is more expressive of one's self. Thus, a variant of the civil liberties and self-expression arguments support a principle of property. *(3-8) The principle of freedom: persons should be presumed to be free, compatible with a like freedom of others, to use, retain, and dispose of their property as they desire, the presumption being stronger the more property is self-expressive or identifying.*

It is now clear how property is tied to fundamental human purposes in society. Freedom to transfer and use property is an aspect of freedom of conduct in society, and some property is closely connected to one's personal identity and self-expression. Under the heading of fairness, we found property related to retaining the benefits of one's labors and not being subject to grossly unfair burdens. And the utilitarian considerations relate it directly to social order and increasing social well-being. It is because of these various connections to fundamental social values that property law plays a fundamental role in other fields of law.

FORMS OF PROPERTY

3.2.0. *Introduction.* The concept of property has changed over the centuries. Historically, it was closely tied to the notion of things – land, furniture, tools, and so forth. Property rights were said to be 'in rem' (claims to things and against all persons) rather than 'in personam' (claims against specific individuals). Today, that distinction breaks down in many cases. Property is still frequently said to consist of a bundle of rights. It is thus still important to distinguish property as rights or legal relations from the thing or 'res'; in many cases, there is no physical thing involved, for example, in ownership of a copyright or shares of stock.

Because 'rights' is ambiguous and people often confuse different meanings of 'a right', it is better to speak of the 'incidents' of property or ownership, since not all of them are rights in any sense. It is also necessary to clarify the concept of a right. The term 'a right' is often used to cover four distinct concepts – claim, liberty, power, and immunity (see Hohfeld 1946). In property law, these concepts are often kept distinct with 'right' being used only for 'claim' (Rest. Property § 1-4). 'Interest' is often used to mean a particular right in one of these senses or a group of them (Rest. Property § 5). Each concept has an opposite applicable to a person who lacks that sort of right. It also has a correlative concept applying to another person against whom the right is held.

First, a right can be a claim that another person act or forbear, the latter person then having a correlative duty to so act or forbear. The opposite is simply having no claim. For example, if Dent is owed $111 by Eaton, then Dent has a claim to be paid $111 and Eaton has a duty to pay $111. If Eaton does not owe any money, then Dent has no claim to be paid.

Second, a right can be a liberty or privilege to act or forbear, the correlative being that others have no claim that the person act or forbear. The opposite is a duty to act or forbear. If Faison has a liberty to slaughter his cow, then Gamble has no claim that he not do so. If Faison had sold the cow to Gamble but not yet delivered it, then he would have a duty not to slaughter it (no liberty to do so).

Third, a right can be a power and others have a liability to the exercise of the power. The opposite of a power is a disability. Hay has a power to exclude others from his land, and they are liable to be excluded. Hay might have a disability (no power) to exclude someone, for example, an employee of the electric utility repairing the power line.

Fourth, a right can be an immunity and others have a disability. The opposite of an immunity is a liability. If he were a minister, Hay might have an immunity from property taxes on his home, and the county have a disability (no power) to tax it. However, Hay would still be liable for income taxes.

These various relations can be illustrated in the following table.

RIGHT	CORRELATIVE	OPPOSITE
Claim	Duty	No-claim
Liberty	No-claim	Duty
Power	Liability	Disability
Immunity	Disability	Liability

3.2.1. *Ownership*. With this background, it is possible to analyze what has been called the liberal concept of full ownership, which is probably the common notion in Western society and that toward which the law has been tending over the centuries (Donahue 1980, 32). Traditionally, property was analyzed as involving the right to exclusive possession, the liberty of use, and the power of disposition (Donahue 1980, 32; Epstein 1985, 58-61; see Paton 1964, 467). We shall briefly list a more complex set of standard incidents of ownership or property (Honoré 1961; Becker 1980, 190-91). Although this longer list can be condensed to, and is more likely to have overlaps than, the traditional one, in some cases the specificity helps prevent confusion. Most but not all of these incidents are rights in one or the other senses discussed. We shall illustrate the incidents by the example of Ingram owning a piece of land (a mythical Riverview farm) and an automobile (Oldsmobile).

(1) The claim to possess. Ingram has a claim to exclusive possession of Riverview and the Oldsmobile. Others cannot simply move onto Riverview or take the Olds.

(2) The liberty to use. Ingram can come and go in her Oldsmobile as she wishes and hike and walk on Riverview as she desires. There are limits to the use Ingram can make of Riverview and the Oldsmobile, some of which are involved in other incidents, but within these limits she can do as she wishes.

(3) The power to manage. The power to manage is closely related to the liberty to use, but the latter is restricted to personal use. Ingram can let her sister live on Riverview or drive her Oldsmobile, lease Riverview or the Oldsmobile, or do a multitude of other things.

(4) The claim to income. Ingram has a claim against others to the crops produced on Riverview. If she leases Riverview or her Olds, she has a claim to the income it produces.

(5) The liberty to modify, consume, or destroy. Ingram has a liberty to modify Riverview, for example, clear trees for farm land. She can also make changes in the Olds and drive it until it wears out. It is not really possible to destroy Riverview considered as the land, although she can haul away top soil, cut timber, and mine minerals.

(6) The power to transfer. This crucial incident has two aspects. First, there is the power to transfer during one's lifetime – the power to 'alienate'. Ingram can sell or give the Olds or Riverview to someone. Second, there is the power to transmit property on one's death as by will or 'intestate succession' (inheiritance). Of course, if Ingram has not made a will, she has no control over to whom the property passes on her death.

(7) The immunity from 'expropriation' (taking away legal title). This provides security of legal title or ownership. Generally, if Ingram does not transfer ownership of Riverview or the Olds to someone else during her lifetime, she will continue to own it. Others cannot simply take ownership. A limit to this immunity is the government's power of 'eminent domain' to take the property for public purposes. But the government cannot take Riverview just because some administrator thinks it a good piece of land; a valid government purpose must be involved, and usually the owner (Ingram) must be compensated for the loss (3.3.5).

(8) The absence of term. Ingram's ownership is not for a specific period of time, a determinate period. Ingram can own Riverview as long as she

lives, but it will end when she dies. Of course, Ingram's ownership will also end if she sells or gives away Riverview or her Olds.

(9) The duty not to use harmfully. This incident and the next are not rights in any of the senses specified above but their opposites. This one is a general limitation on the liberty to use and the power to manage and is chiefly a matter of tort law. Although much dispute exists about what constitutes a harmful use, some cases are clear. Ingram may not use the Oldsmobile to run down pedestrians or knock down fences on other farms. Nor may she excavate her land so that her neighbor's house collapses or let her dam on the pond burst and flood the neighbors.

(10) The liability to execution. If Ingram has a loan on the car or a mortgage on Riverview and fails to make the proper payments, then it can be taken to pay the lenders. The Olds or Riverview can also be taken to pay other past due debts she might have. This liability limits her immunity from expropriation. It also limits her power to transfer voluntarily, in that the property might be transferred involuntarily.

(11) The residuary character. If Ingram transfers a right (interest) in her property to someone else, when that interest ends, it or a corresponding right returns to her. For example, if she lets her sister use the car for three days so that her sister has a claim to possess it, at the end of that period the claim to possess returns to Ingram. Similarly, if she leases Riverview, at the end of the lease the power to manage (determine what crops to plant and so on) returns to her. It is conceivable that such rights might simply cease to exist, but that does not seem to be the case anywhere. Allowing the rights to cease to exist would be contrary to the principle of universality, because there would then be unowned resources or aspects of them.

These incidents are related to the foregoing aims of property law. We just remarked that the residuary character is related to the principle of universality. That principle also supports the absence of term, for were ownership only for a determinate period of time, then at the end of it perhaps no one would own the resource. The principle of exclusivity supports the incidents of a claim to possess, the claim to income, and the power to manage (which includes the power to exclude others). The principle of transferability obviously supports the power to transfer. The principles of stability and social burdens support the immunity from expropriation. Finally, the principle of freedom supports the liberty to use; the liberty to modify, consume, or destroy; and the powers to manage and transfer insofar as these permit owners to do as they wish. It also indirectly supports the duty not to use harmfully, because an important class of harmful uses deprives others of

the freedom to use their property. This leaves only the liability to execution
not supported by one of the principles, but it involves a voluntary transfer
of a conditional claim to the property when debts are assumed. Consequently, directly or indirectly, all of the incidents of full ownership are
supported by the aims of property law.

We now examine how one might have less than full ownership, how the
various incidents can be divided. First, much physical property, such as
land, is capable of physical division. Ingram might sell part of Riverview
– an acre or lot. At various times promoters have sold parcels of one square
inch of land, for example, in Texas, so that purchasers could say they
owned land in Texas. Some objects are not easily divisible into valuable
physical parts. Ingram's Oldsmobile is not as readily divisible as Riverview,
although she could scrap it and sell off parts such as the radio and car-
buretor. Still other objects, such as a lamp or table, are virtually worthless
when physically divided.

Second, things that exist in time can be divided temporally, thereby
breaking the absence of term. Most simply, leases divide ownership by time
(as well as other aspects). In some resort areas, condominiums are sold on
a time-sharing basis (Cribbet and Johnson 1984, 431). One has possession
and use of them for a certain period each year, say, the month of August.
When property is divided by time, other incidents are also divided, for
example, the residuary character and liberty to destroy do not pertain to
lessees.

A more complicated division of property is among persons at the same
time. The common law has recognized three main forms of co-ownership
– 'tenancy in common', 'joint tenancy', and 'tenancy by the entirety'. The
differences between them primarily pertain to what one can do with the
property. Tenants in common each own the whole property, and if one dies
that person's share passes to his or her heirs or 'devisees' (recipients under
a will). Tenants in common can ask for a partition of the property so that
each gets half or whatever the proportional share is. If the property cannot
be physically divided, then it is sold and each gets a share of the money.
Joint tenants are like tenants in common except for the transfer of title on
death. If one of them dies, then the property does not pass to that person's
heirs or devisees; ownership is then that of the other tenant or tenants.
Tenants by the entirety are like joint tenants except that they are limited
to husband and wife and cannot demand a partition of the property (at least
while married). Also, if property is owned as a joint tenant and one goes
bankrupt, that person's creditors can force a sale of the property to pay the

debts. In many jurisdictions, this is not true of a creditor of only one spouse in a tenancy by the entirety (Cunningham, Stoebuck, and Whitman 1984, 214; *Donvito v. Criswell*, 1 Ohio App. 3d 53, 439 N.E.2d 467 (1982)).

The final aspect of divisibility of property concerns the other incidents. As full ownership consists of a bundle of incidents, most of them could be treated separately. Indeed, many of the incidents, such as the power to manage, are bundles of similar incidents that might be separated. Moreover, these incidents could be divided over time and perhaps space. Property is thus almost indefinitely divisible. People are apt to divide property into smaller units so long as they have value. For example, a recent development has been to 'strip bonds', that is, to sell the right to interest separate from the right to the principal on maturity. In one way this inclination to divide furthers transferability, since there are more things to be transferred. In another way it hinders transferability if someone wants to acquire full ownership, because incidents might have to be obtained from a number of persons. Thus, there are two tendencies at work – one to divide ownership and another to prohibit division. A possible solution is severely to limit divisibility of ownership of physical property, such as land and goods, but to allow divisibility full reign with respect to ownership of 'intangibles' (Lawson 1958, 80-81).

Several classifications of property are common. One such classification divides property into real and personal. Real property is limited to land and even excludes leaseholds of land. All other property is classified as personal property or 'chattels', but to increase confusion chattels are sometimes divided into real and personal, real chattels being leases. Another division, which cuts across the previous one, is between movable and immovable property, with leases and land being immovable and all else movable. Yet a third division is between tangible and intangible. Tangible property includes land, leaseholds, and goods such as furniture, computers, and so forth. We shall basically use the following division: real (land and buildings), leaseholds, and personal. Personal property will then be divided into several subgroups.

3.2.2. *Real property and leases.* The common law divides real property into various 'estates' which are in turn divided into those in possession and those in expectancy. Estates in possession are those of a person who currently has possession (except for leases), and those in expectancy or 'future interests' are those of a person who can expect to have possession in the future. All of this is further complicated by a distinction between legal and equitable estates. Historically, there were two types of courts – common-law courts and courts of equity. Essentially, law courts could only provide money damages for relief and applied a strict set of rules – the common law, whereas courts of equity could provide other types of relief and were originally designed to handle cases in which the operation of common-law rules worked inequity. Today, separate courts generally do not exist, at least in the United States, and the courts have both sorts of powers. Although courts do sometimes tailor their doctrines depending on whether the issue would previously have been classified as one of law or equity, whenever possible we shall ignore the law/equity distinction. Our purpose is to evaluate principles on their merits, not on the basis of historical classifications. Nevertheless, in some contexts the distinction is important.

There are three forms of 'freehold' estate (owning land in possession). The distinctions between them pertain to the transfer of the land. First, the 'fee simple' gives the rights of full ownership as described in 3.2.1; one can sell it, will it, or let it pass to one's heirs, and so on. Second, a person can own a 'fee tail'. This form requires that on one's death the property pass to one's children (traditionally eldest male heir). Consequently, the owner is effectively prevented from selling or devising it. Third, one can have a 'life estate', that is, own it so long as one lives. One can sell a life estate, although it is not easy. The purchaser has title (that which entitles a person to possession of land) so long as the seller lives – a life estate *pur autre vie*.

Future interests result from a temporal division of ownership and can involve any of the types of title. If Ingram transfers Riverview to her sister for her sister's life, then she might specify what is to happen to it after her sister's death. If the title is to return to Ingram (or her heirs), that is a 'reversion'; the title reverts to the previous owner. If it is to go to someone else, such as a charity, then it is a 'remainder'; the title remains away from the grantor. Remainders can be 'vested' or 'contingent'. A remainder is vested if the person to obtain it is identifiable, that is, one can definitely determine who will get it; if the person is not identifiable (perhaps not yet born), then it is contingent. There are also other types of reversion – 'possibility of reverter' and 'right of re-entry' or 'power of termination' – that can exist. For example, someone might deed land to a city so long as it is used as a park for whites only, and if the city does not or may not so use it, the land reverts to the grantor or the grantor's heirs (*Evans v. Abney*, 396

U.S. 435 (1970)). The differences between these reversions are not important for our purposes.

When these various estates and future interests in land are combined with the different forms of co-ownership, the complexity of ownership of land is overwhelming. Considerable legal effort is spent construing deeds and wills to determine what type of ownership has been given and who owns what. Title to land is sometimes so restricted or uncertain that it is difficult to transfer. The desirability and need for simplification has long been recognized. In the United States, various piecemeal approaches have been undertaken, such as abolishing or providing methods for eliminating the fee tail and abolishing or weakening tenancy by the entirety. Statutes of limitation have also limited the time during which various restrictions can apply. The simplification has been sporadic and varies from state to state. In England, much more radical reform occurred in the Law of Property Act 1925 (see Megarry and Wade 1975, 134-35, 408-9, 417-19; Lawson 1958, 83, 85). It abolished all but two legal estates – the fee simple absolute (no conditions) in possession and the 'lease for a term of years' – and limited concurrent or co-ownership to joint tenancy of no more than four persons without right of partition. However, many of the old forms of ownership, such as life estate and tenancy in common, were retained in equity.

A fundamental conflict of principles is involved in simplifying the law of ownership of real property, which might partly account for the greater reluctance of U.S. legislatures and courts to engage in radical reform in property law than other fields. That conflict is between the principle of transferability on the one hand, and the principles of stability and freedom on the other. The import of the principle of transferability is clear; complex forms of ownership make property less easily transferable. The complex of common-law forms of ownership can weigh heavily on the needs of a modern society. This is one aspect of the dead hand of the past, which is especially prominent in property law, in part due to the principle of stability.

The import of the principles of stability and freedom is less clear. First, a radical change in the forms of ownership, such as the Law of Property Act 1925, is a major shift in the rules applicable to property and thus contrary to the principle of stability. However, that shift was and can be eased considerably by the changes being made prospective. Moreover, such reform can introduce stability. The second aspect of stability (see 3.1.1) pertains to freedom from claims by others to ownership or possession of one's property. The complex forms of ownership increase the chances that some distant heir of a predecessor in title might lay claim to one's property and thus decrease stability of title. A striking example is *Brown v. Independent Baptist Church of Woburn* (325 Mass. 645, 91 N.E.2d 922 (1950)). In 1849 land was devised to the Church with a reversion (possibility of reverter) if it was not used for church purposes. By 1939, the area was commercial and the Church moved. However, the land reverted to the heirs. After the land was sold for $34,000, the lawyers received $9,000, the receiver $4,017, a genealogist $1,500, and the remainder was divided into more than 100 shares, the smallest being $6.25 (see Leach 1952, 743-44). The difficulties involved were not worth the benefit to the heirs, who undoubtedly found it a trivial windfall.

Second, the principle of freedom is not completely against radical reform. Limiting the forms of ownership does limit people's freedom to hold property as they want and to transfer it to people as they desire. However, the exercise of freedom by prior owners or generations can limit the freedom of subsequent owners or generations (see also 3.4.4). If prior owners can restrict ownership, say, to a life estate or to specific uses as in *Brown*, then subsequent owners have less freedom to use or transfer the property. Moreover, the conflict is not over freedom to dispose of wealth, but freedom to restrict that wealth to certain forms of property. The Law of Property Act 1925, by retaining a wide variety of ownership in equity, essentially preserved the freedom of prior owners to dispose of the benefits of property (wealth) as they desired. Thus, people retain the freedom to provide for the well-being of others as they desire, but not to specify what form that wealth must take.

(3-9) The principle of legal titles: the forms of legal title to land should be few in number and make transfer easy. Because our concern is with leading principles of law and not the details, this is not the place to specify all the precise changes that should be made. Moreover, alternative systems might well be rationally acceptable. Nonetheless, it is possible to note a few major changes that should definitely, and others that should probably, be made. In each case, the specific impact of the forms and alternatives to them on transferability, stability, and freedom should be considered. First, dower and curtesy (special rights of a husband and wife in the property of the other spouse) should be abolished if they have not been. Provision for spouses can be and usually is made by laws of inheritance (but see 3.4.4). Second, tenancy by the entirety should be abolished. In its worst form, it is a remnant of sexism denying women equal rights with men, for example,

by giving the male the exclusive right to possession and control (*D'Ercole v. D'Ercole*, 407 F. Supp. 1377 (D. Mass. 1976)). Part of its popularity is due to its ability to prevent creditors of one spouse reaching the property, but that does not make it acceptable. If the legislature wants to protect family property from creditors, it can do so by legislation. This would be more fair, because it would protect all couples, not just those who used tenancy by the entirety, and it need not protect assets not used for family purposes. Third, if it has not been, the fee tail should be abolished. There are other ways, such as creation of a trust, to provide for the following generation or generations, so the fee tail is an unnecessary and excessive restriction on the transferability of land.

Other forms of legal ownership should also probably be abolished. Life estates do not appear essential, and they are a primary cause of the complexity of ownership. Whenever a life estate is created, so is a future interest. In the contemporary world of high real estate taxes and rapid development, untransferable property can amount to an albatross rather than gold chain around the neck of descendants. The life estate is often used for tax planning purposes, but if the legislature wants to allow certain methods of avoiding taxes, it can explicitly and simply provide for them. Even from the point of view of the prior owner, trusts are often a better means than life estates of accomplishing goals. If life estates were abolished, most future interests would be too. Some forms of reversion would remain, and perhaps only the fee simple absolute should be permitted. Even if future interests are retained, they should be severely limited in duration (see 3.4.1).

Finally, it is less clear whether tenancy in common should be abolished, as it was in England. It is more likely than joint tenancy, due to succession, to make ownership complex. If one tenant in common dies with a half-dozen heirs, complexity is immediately introduced. However, tenancy in common has some beneficial uses, for example, in modern forms of home ownership. In condominiums, people own their homesites and are tenants in common of the common areas. Were tenancy in common abolished, this form of ownership of the common areas would not be permitted. However, a homeowners association or a cooperative could be used for the common areas. In homeowners associations, homeowners have a fee simple title to their land, and the association has such a title to the common areas. Members of the association are assessed fees for the expenses of the common areas. In a cooperative, a corporation owns all the land including individual apartments or homesites. A person then purchases shares in the corporation and the apartment is leased to the person.

Historically, the fee simple and leasehold were commercial forms of property, something that one might invest in; whereas the other forms of freehold were used to provide for the welfare of family members (Lawson 1958, 70-71). The above principle of legal titles recognizes changed economic circumstances. Wealth is no longer so significantly based on land; one can provide for the welfare of family members by other means, especially trusts. However, the various forms of leaseholds, unlike those of title, are still valuable and worth preserving.

In essence, a lease transfers most of the incidents of full ownership for a period of time. Subject to some general limitations and any limitations specifically provided for in the lease, the tenant has all the incidents of full ownership except the liberty to modify, consume, or destroy; absence of term; and the residuary character. The tenant has a limited power of transfer by subleasing to another, although often this can be done only with the permission of the landlord. A lease is for a definite period of time, not indefinite as the life estate. However, in some places a long-term lease is used as a practical equivalent of a fee simple. In parts of California, 99 year leases of land are common for homesites, and in England some leases are for as much as 999 years. Under the Law of Property Act 1925, leases for a term of years absolute are legal estates. A major reason for this is to provide for mortgagees' interests, but as we shall note (3.3.2), mortgagees need not have a legal estate to have their interests protected.

Types of leases largely depend on when and how they terminate. A 'term of years' is for a specific period, such as five years. 'Periodic tenancies' are for one period of time to another – year to year, month to month. A central element of such leases is the requirement of notice. In a lease for a term of years, the tenant has no right to stay after the end of the term. In a periodic tenancy, the lease continues to renew itself unless the landlord or tenant gives notice. When notice must be given depends on the length of the period; now it is usually specified in the lease or statutes. A 'tenancy at will' is for as long as one or the other party is willing. Rarely would a landlord or tenant be willing to lease solely at the pleasure of the other, and traditionally such leases were not permitted. Tenancies at will usually result from another lease being invalid. Finally, if a tenant holds over beyond the expiry of a lease without the landlord's consent, a 'tenancy by sufferance' is created. This is really a misnomer, because the person has no more right to possess than a trespasser. The major difference is that such a tenant, unlike a trespasser, is liable for an equivalent of rent.

3.2.3. *Personal property.* The forms of personal property are even more complex than of land but create fewer problems. Most of the common forms of ownership of real property are available for personal property. A useful division is between tangible and intangible property. Most intangible property is a claim to be paid money or to receive a fixed quantity of goods (Lawson 1958, 23). Tangible personal property consists of all those physical objects that are not fastened to land. Houses, for example, are attached to land, whereas cars, clothes, and most furniture are not. One can distinguish between 'fungible' and 'non-fungible' tangible personal property. Fungible goods are simply those for which others of the same type and quantity are substitutable. For example, bushels of wheat, pounds of nails, and shirts of the same material and size are fungible, whereas a diamond brooch is not for probably no others like it exist.

There are many forms of intangible property. First, there are 'debts', that is, claims to be paid a sum of money due. A second form is 'commercial paper', which is of two main types. One type consists of 'negotiable instruments' such as checks, bearer bonds, and so forth, which are also claims to be paid a sum of money. The second type consists of 'documents of title', which are claims to receive a quantity of goods. Another form is stocks and shares in corporations. Of course, some aspects of incidents other than the right to income pertain to some of the forms of property. Most shareholders in corporations have rights to vote at annual meetings, and one can claim and then use the goods in documents of title. There is little reason against the divisibility of such property, because it is unlikely to extend beyond the limits of commercial usefulness.

Two other forms of intangible property are closely related to the above. One is money, which in fact is a negotiable instrument. People think of money as a good, but most money is a promise by a government. Paper money is clearly a demand against a government's treasury, and now most coins are no more than that. In the past, coins were made of material – gold, silver, nickel – that was at least roughly worth the face value. Now most coins are made of cheaper materials, although it sometimes costs more to manufacture them than they are worth.

A more complex form of intangible property is a 'trust fund'. The trustees have the powers of management, and the beneficiaries have claims to the income. As with most intangible property, the claim to possess is somewhat fictional. The power to transfer the basis of the fund and thus modify it by selling and buying shares, bonds, real estate, and so forth, belongs to the trustees, but they lack the liberty to consume or destroy the capital of the trust – the underlying value. This is a very important form of property, and its existence provides one basis for limiting legal titles in land. One can provide for the future welfare of one's family by creating a trust and leaving titles to land more easily transferable. A trust's income can be directed to beneficiaries much as with a fee tail, life estate, and so forth without hindering the transferability of tangible property. Thus, although we shall not discuss trusts in detail, they are central to a rationally acceptable property law.

Another form of intangible property is reputation and image. A common type is goodwill – the reputation a business has which can command some value when it is sold. If a local clothing store has served customers well over the years and the owner wishes to sell it and retire, the goodwill of the customers and the name will be worth money to a purchaser. Similarly, the name and image of public persons can be valuable, as in posters and endorsements of products. Recently, several movie stars have sued businesses for use of their name or image (lookalikes) without consent. Even the use of an ordinary citizen's image can be valuable. This is usually considered a matter of privacy rather than property, but since one can charge for the use of one's image it comes to have value and might be considered a form of property.

One form of intangible property deserves special treatment, namely, intellectual (sometimes called industrial) property – patents, trademarks, and copyrights. This property consists of an exclusive claim for a limited time to methods, objects, forms, and words created by human beings. The name and image of public persons is also sometimes classified as industrial property. Intellectual property is a highly specialized field with many conceptual problems. Trademarks are much like goodwill and could as well be treated as property in reputation. Patents and copyrights are more difficult. Although it is said that one cannot acquire rights to ideas, one can come close to doing so. A patent is an exclusive right to use a new "process, machine, manufacture, or composition of matter" such as a newly discovered drug (35 U.S.C. § 101 (1982)). A perennial problem of patent law is to determine when a new entity is sufficiently different from previous ones to be entitled to patent protection.

A central problem of intellectual property is what can be patented or copyrighted. Laws of nature are not patentable, allegedly because not created but only discovered by persons. Similarly, copyrights in literature have been restricted to the forms of words used and not the ideas they express. Even this restriction seems weakened by *International News Service v. Associated Press* (248 U.S. 215 (1918)) which held that INS could not use news stories gathered by AP until they had lost commercial value (which meant there was no point in using them). INS was seemingly prevented from using not only the form of words but also the information in the stories. Music copyrights come even closer to rights to ideas, for it is not the printed score that matters but the sequence, length, and pitch of tones. A recent area of difficulty is copyrights to computer software. The form in which a program is presented (printout, floppy disk) is not important, but the sequence of logical relations that constitutes the program is. As computer programs are simply sequences of mathematical-logical operations, copyrights to them are much like copyrights to mathematical proofs (think what Euclid might have made!).

The point of intellectual property rights is brought to the fore by these examples, and it goes to the very foundation of private property. Computer software companies (like drug companies, publishers, and others) have little incentive to develop new products if others can immediately use them for free. It can cost a lot to develop a new computer program, money which might not be recovered if others can then manufacture, sell, and use the program without incurring the development costs. If a company will simply lose money, it has no reason to develop programs. The utilitarian justification for recognizing this form of property is apparent. The principle of labor also applies. If an individual works to develop a new computer program or bacterium (see *Diamond v. Chakrabarty*, 477 U.S. 303 (1979)), then that person should receive a significant proportion of the property (value) produced. Still, these considerations apply to the discovery of new physical laws: Newton labored long and hard to prove his laws; their discovery was of great social value; and incentives are needed for people to make such discoveries. Nor can one soundly argue from the intent of discoverors and inventors, for example, that people who discover new scientific laws do not do so to make a profit but those who develop computer programs do. The intent or purpose might depend on whether patents or copyrights are available.

Despite these arguments for the similarity of discovery of laws and creation of processes and so on, the distinction between what is and is not capable of being patented or copyrighted does depend on whether a person made or created it. It does not make sense to prohibit others from using a law of science or logic. People were using the law of gravity before Newton discovered it. The concept of a patent in it does not make sense – should each person be forbidden to stand on earth unless they pay a royalty for using the law of gravity? The same applies to laws of logic. People were using the law of noncontradiction before Aristotle formulated it. One cannot create or make laws of nature or logic, and they are used before they are discovered or formulated, but new applications of them to produce specific results is another matter. When Alexander Graham Bell invented the telephone, he did not create new scientific laws. Instead, he arranged matter so that the laws produced a new result. Similarly, computer programmers do not create new logical laws, but they use them in a way to create a new process and result. *International New Service* can be distinguished as a case of fair competition and not one of patent or copyright. AP did not have a right to the information itself, only to the benefit of its labor. INS could provide its readers the same information if it could obtain it other than from AP stories.

(10) The principle of intellectual property: one should have ownership for a limited time to new processes and results produced by the use of laws of science and logic but not to the laws themselves. This principle is primarily a specification of the principle of labor (see Sartorius 1984, 204-05). The time limitation is supported by utilitarian and fairness considerations. The utility of providing incentives for intellectual inventions must be balanced against the social utility of allowing others to use new and beneficial intellectual products. The principle of labor only specifies that one receive a significant proportion, not all, of the value of property created. It does not imply that one is entitled to take unfair advantage of others – to have the property when there are good reasons or obligations against it.

Usually, the time limitation of a patent or copyright is sufficient to prevent unfairness, but in some cases it might not be. Suppose Beta Pharmaceuticals develops a new drug that is safe and 95 percent effective against oat cell carcinoma (a form of cancer). Desperate cancer patients might pay all they could for the drug. Given that one might be either a cancer patient or an owner of Beta, one could not accept Beta demanding prices that during the life of the patent would reap many times Beta's total costs. One could accept Beta making a substantial profit, but not such an exhorbitant one. Should Beta try to do so, the government would no doubt change the law and license others to manufacture and produce the drug, perhaps requiring them to pay a fair royalty to Beta (cf. Patent Act, Can. Rev. Stat. ch. P-4, § 41 (1970).)

In asking whether something is or can be property or a form of property, it is often useful to ask for what purpose one wants to classify it. In the United States, many arguments about whether something is property stem from specific constitutional provisions, in particular the due process clauses which prohibit depriving persons of "life, liberty, or property, without due process of law," and the takings clause which prohibits taking property "for public use, without just compensation" (U.S. Const. amends. V, XIV). The point of classifying something as property is often to receive some due process protection or compensation. We shall consider takings later (3.3.5). Here we shall focus on statutory governmental benefits.

Consider the following types of government benefits – income tax refunds, social security and other pensions, television licenses, and prospects for continued government employment. Should they be considered property? It can be persuasively argued that they should be (see Reich 1984). From an economic point of view, they are aspects of wealth – income or streams of income. One can usually borrow money on the basis of them. Many Canadians assign their claim to an income tax refund to companies in return for a present discounted payment. The claim to an income tax refund is similar to any other claim on a debt and just as much property. One can also borrow against the other entitlements by personal loans, although such loans are less clearly against the particular payments as opposed to one's total income and wealth. Nonetheless, the benefits are often more certain than dividends from common stock. Consequently, for purposes of property law, they have a strong claim to being considered forms of property.

Why then the dispute about them? One reason is the failure to distinguish questions. In the constitutional contexts, the crucial issues are whether certain processes or compensation are required. These are questions of fair procedure and compensation and whether one has been deprived or had something taken, rather than whether something is property. A paycheck, for example, is property, whether or not one has a claim to continued employment. For a court to hold that an entitlement is not property is a conclusory statement that a requested process or compensation is not constitutionally required. Another reason concerns whether all the feasible incidents of ownership should be permitted. In particular, to view them as contractual rights creating property might prevent governments changing the conditions for them. Also, people might not be allowed to transfer directly some or all of their claim to income as Canadians do their income tax refunds. It is one thing for a social security recipient to borrow $5,000, and another for him or her to assign a year's payments. There are also reasons not to let just anyone have television broadcast licenses or jobs. Indeed, one cannot assign contractual rights to render personal services. However, these restrictions rest on policies and aims beyond the scope of property law. For present purposes, it suffices to include these sorts of benefits as a form of personal property, leaving open whether or not various actions deprive one of them and so on.

RIGHTS AND LIMITS

3.3.0. *Introduction*. Ownership, as we have seen, consists of a number of incidents most but not all of which are rights. The value of something largely depends on what one can do with it, that is, the rights one has (Lawson 1958, 8). Generally, the more one can do with something, the more one will personally value it. The economic value of something is what others are willing to pay for it, and that is likely to increase the more they can do with it. Thus, the value of a new invention is greatly increased by a patent claim to exclusive use. We shall now examine in more detail property rights and their limits. Although it is often difficult to separate rights from limits to them, the first two sections primarily emphasize rights and the following two limits. The fifth section concerns a particular problem in the clash between rights and limits, namely, when public limits are so great as to require compensation.

3.3.1. *To possess*. Common-law systems (and others) make a commonsense distinction between title and possession. Although title is what entitles one to possession, one might transfer that right for a time, retaining a residuary right. Also, legal possession is not the same as actual possession. If Jarman loans his property law text to Kuiper, he still owns it (has title) even though Kuiper has possession of it. Jarman's title gives him a right to possess the book after Kuiper is done with it or when he wants it depending on the terms on which he loaned it. Similar considerations apply if Jarman rents his house to Kuiper for a year. Kuiper has a right to possess it during the year, but Jarman has a residuary right to possess it after that time. Confusion is encouraged by saying Jarman's fee simple is in possession, which merely means he has current title, since Kuiper has actual and legal possession during the lease.

In placing property in the possession of others, a person exercises a power of management. So long as only a temporary right of possession is given to others, a person retains title. Thus, the right of another to possess depends on the intent or will of the owner in transferring possession, which is often expressed in an agreement between them. Consider *Fetting Mfg. Jewelry Co. v. Waltz* (160 Md. 50, 152 A. 434 (Ct. App. 1930)). Waltz and others leased a building to Fetting for five years. The lease contained a 'covenant' (clause or provision) by which Fetting agreed to become liable for any losses Waltz incurred should Fetting hold over beyond the term. The parties could not agree to a new lease, or even to an extention of the old one when Fetting found it might not be able to move into new quarters promptly. Fetting did not vacate the premises until almost a month after the term. Waltz then sued for a year's rent and the court upheld his claim. A landlord has an option either to evict a holdover tenant, who is a tenant at sufferance, or to convert the lease into a periodic tenancy.

Such a result is acceptable. As a landlord, one has a choice either to evict the tenant or to convert the tenancy into a periodic one. It might seem less acceptable from a tenant's point of view. A tenant would prefer tenancy at his or her will, but a landlord rarely has good reason to accept such a tenancy. The tenant has violated a duty to surrender the premises, a duty which the tenant voluntarily undertook. The holding over benefits the tenant, who still has possession of the premises. Moreverover, by the periodic tenancy, the tenant has a reasonable extension in which to find other premises. In *Fetting* the period might seem a bit long, but the original lease was for five years. Many apartment leases provide for converting a year's lease into a periodic tenancy by month with one or two month's notice.

Even so, a certain reasonableness should be exercised by landlords in converting holdover tenants to periodic tenants. In *Commonwealth Building Corp. v. Hirschfield* (307 Ill. App. 533, 30 N.E.2d 790 (Ill. App. Ct. 1940)), after being unable to remove all their belongings in three days of moving, the tenant Hirschfield and his family slept in the apartment overnight. When the landlord tried to convert to a periodic tenancy for a year and collect a year's rent, the court held for the tenant. In this case there was a covenant calling for double rent for any period of holdover.

'Bailments' of personal property correspond to leases of real property, only bailments cover almost all lawful possession of the personal property of another. The central element of bailment is the intention to transfer the right to possess. If Lipman stores his furniture in Marsh's warehouse, it is a bailment. Here, Marsh is not to use the furniture even though she has possession of it. There is also a bailment if Lipman lends his lawn mower to Marsh, even though neither pays money and Marsh can use it. If a store clerk hands a watch to a customer to examine, there is no intent to transfer the right to possess, so this constitutes mere 'custody' by the customer rather than a bailment. In parking lots, the crucial issue is whether the keys and thus control are turned over to the attendant. If they are not, the car owner merely has a 'license' to park. If they are, a bailment exists.

The importance of the distinction between bailment and other classifications such as custody and license stems from the duties of a bailee. The owner has a claim to possession of the property as determined by the agreement, and the bailee has a duty to deliver the goods and is liable for their value if he or she refuses to deliver them or delivers them to the wrong person. Moreover, while the goods are in the possession of the bailee, the bailee must provide the care of them an ordinary person would, that is, the bailee is liable for damage or loss of the object due to negligence. However, in recent years courts have been inclined to create bailments and hold parking lots responsible for damage even when keys were not surrendered or negligence was not proven (see *Parking Management, Inc. v. Gilder*, 343 A.2d 51 (D.C. 1975); *Heffron v. Imperial Parking Co.*, 46 D.L.R.3d 642 (Ont. 1974)). Because bailees have duties of care and delivery, one cannot become a bailee involuntarily; a bailee must accept possession or a bailment does not exist (*Cowen v. Pressprich*, 202 A.D. 796, 194 N.Y.S. 926 (App. Div. 1922)). (In some cases, a 'constructive trust' (one implied by law) might be found for someone who has involuntary possession, and the duties would then be similar.)

In general, a person with title to property can and should be able to recover it from the possession of others to whom possession has not been given, such as a trespasser, holdover tenant, or bailee who does not deliver. Problems arise, however, when the possessor is a bona fide purchaser for value without notice of the other's title. A number of distinct possibilities exist here, and the law treats them differently. (1) Suppose Nelson sells land to Orwell, and later sells it again to Parker who records his deed before Orwell does. Orwell cannot recover possession from Parker. In many jurisdictions, Orwell can recover if she records her deed after Parker purchases but before he records his. (2) If Orwell steals goods from Nelson and sells them to Parker, a bona fide purchaser, then Nelson can recover them. (3) If Orwell purchases goods from Nelson by deceiving him as to her identity, giving a bad check, or committing fraud, and then sells the goods to Parker, Nelson cannot recover (U.C.C. § 2-403(1)). The result varies in the purchase of land depending on the type of deception (Cunningham, Stoebuck, and Whitman 1984, 720-21). (4) If Nelson gives goods to Orwell, a merchant of such goods, say, for repair, and Orwell mistakenly sells them to Parker, Nelson cannot recover from Parker (U.C.C. § 2-403(2)). (5) Suppose Nelson has a 'security interest' in goods that Orwell bought on time; that is, Nelson has a claim to them as backing for money loaned. If Orwell sells them before the security interest is 'perfected' (it is established that payments have not been made on time), Nelson cannot recover them from Parker. Frequently this is true even if the security interest is perfected (U.C.C. § 9-307).

The traditional common-law rule is that one cannot pass a better title than one has. A thief or person who obtains goods by deceit as to identity has no title and so cannot pass title to a bona fide purchaser for value without notice. However, as the previous paragraph indicates, that principle is now riddled with exceptions, in fact, all the situations except for stolen goods and a few others. Moreover, the original logic based on title has disappeared, although attempts have been made to save it by changing the theory. For example, if Orwell acquires goods from Nelson by fraud (say, a bad check) and sells them to Parker, Nelson cannot recover, but he can if Orwell stole them (say, by shoplifting). The revised theory is that with a bad check, Orwell has a voidable title and a voidable title is converted into a full one by the bona fide purchase. But this is really no help, for in (4) the merchant does not even have a voidable title, nor does the seller of land in (1). Granted Nelson can sue Orwell for his loss or Orwell's gain from the sale, our question is whether Nelson should be able to recover the watch from Parker. Since Orwell did not have even a voidable title, she could not transfer title to Parker. Both Nelson and Parker are innocent. Parker is a 'good faith purchaser' of the watch, that is, he gave good value for it and did not know that Orwell had no right to transfer it. The Uniform Commercial Code has abandoned trying to analyze these situations on the basis of title passing (§ 2-101 comment), but it has limited application.

Regardless of the type of situation, either the original owner or the good faith purchaser will lose the same thing – the property in question. Sometimes the dollar value of the loss will differ, for example, if a security interest is less than the purchaser paid, or stolen goods were purchased for less than they were worth. All situations are the same from the point of view of a good faith purchaser – a fair purchase was made. The good faith purchaser is completely innocent. The original owner cannot have a stronger claim and often has a weaker one, for example, due to failure promptly to record a deed or to recover secured property. If both the original owner and good faith purchaser are wholly innocent, then the principle of first possession supports the original owner (except perhaps for land sales where actual possession might not have been acquired). However, the principle of transferability supports the good faith purchaser. The transfer of goods would be severely hampered if buyers had to assure themselves of sellers' titles, especially to goods.

The obvious resolution, acceptable as an original owner or good faith purchaser, is to split the loss (Coons 1979, 199). However, courts are generally unwilling to give compromise solutions, but they sometimes do split claims between an earlier owner and a good faith purchaser of land by contract when notice of the prior claim is received after some but not all payments have been made (Cunningham, Stoebuck, and Whitman 1984, 795-96). Another consideration can tip the balance. The good faith purchaser has done no wrong to the original seller, so the latter does not have a grievance against the good faith purchaser. The wrong to the original owner was by the seller to the good faith purchaser. There is no reason to shift this wrong to one against the good faith purchaser by allowing the original owner to recover the property. *(3-11) The principle of the good faith purchaser: a bona fide purchaser for value without notice should be entitled to property against all previous owners* (see also the principle of stale claims (3-16) in 3.4.1).

This principle also applies to negotiable instruments and documents of title. It would be awkward if all purchases had to be made with cash; consequently, negotiable instruments were developed. A negotiable instrument must contain only an unconditional promise to pay a certain amount of money on demand or at a particular time to a person named or the bearer and be signed by the maker (U.C.C. § 3-104(1)). Like the good faith purchaser, a 'holder in due course' has a clear title to it and usually gave value for it in good faith without notice of any defect (it has been cancelled, for instance). Negotiable instruments basically serve as replacements for money and to do so must be almost as good as money. In the United States, but not England, holders in due course of documents of title are protected like those of negotiable instruments (U.C.C. § 7-104; Lawson 1958, 25). The principle of the good faith purchaser supports the American rule.

For some especially valuable types of property, a record is kept of who has title and a purchaser is deemed to have notice of anything in the record or on a title ('constructive notice'). Transfers of land are recorded, and

automobiles, stock shares, and race horses are registered. In the case of
land and automobiles, the records are kept by public authorities, whereas
records of stock shares are kept by the companies. Recording of real
property is often indexed by years and parties to transactions, so that to
find all the transfers and conditions applicable to it, one must search by
names through volumes. A more sensible index is by the property so that
each transfer of the land is listed in one place. With computers, such a
system could be easily handled, saving much time and expense in searching
titles in land transactions. Unfortunately, the expense of entering all past
records and the dead hand of the past have often combined to prevent a
rationalized system. Title companies do keep such a record by tract. An
even better system is to register land and have all conditions listed on a
title. This system is being widely used in England, but seems to be declining
in the United States where it was never widespread.

Given the principle of the good faith purchaser, it is important for the
possessor of a security interest to be able to make that known to potential
purchasers or to be able to recover the property quickly in the event of
default. For registered property such as automobiles, mortgages on them
can be listed on the registration. A purchaser then has constructive notice
of the security interest. The more difficult situation pertains to goods
purchased on a conditional sales contract. Technically, a conditional sales
purchaser does not have even a voidable title. Nonetheless, so far as
subsequent good faith purchasers are concerned, there is no difference
between buying from people having a voidable title because obtained with
a bad check and from people having no title because they bought on time.
Thus, a good faith purchaser should be protected the same (cf. U.C.C.
§ 9-307). The advantage of assuming that not even a voidable title has
passed in conditional sales is to enable the original seller to recover by a
faster and simpler legal process before the goods are sold to a third party.
However, the issue of giving notice to the original purchaser is important
here (see 2.3.2).

Tenants under a lease have a right to possession or quiet enjoyment
against the landlord. However, this right is restricted to not being dispossessed by the landlord or persons with a superior title; it is not a guarantee
against trespassers or other wrongdoers (Cunningham, Stoebuck, and
Whitman 1984, 292-93). Severe interferences with the tenant's use of the
premises can constitute 'constructive eviction' if the tenant is driven to
abandon the premises. Constructive eviction can be a sword or a shield;
the tenant can either sue the landlord on it for damages or raise it as a

defense to a suit for rent. Consider the following situation in *Phyfe v. Dale* (72 Misc. 383, 130 N.Y.S. 231 (N.Y. App. Div. 1911)). A family rented an apartment. While living there, noise from other tenants in the building kept them awake until late at night. Acts of prostitution could be seen through the windows of the apartment below, and telephone coversations soliciting prostitutes could be heard from within the apartment. The wife was accosted and insulted in the elevator. The landlord knew of these matters and took no action to correct them. The family moved from the building, and when the landlord sued for the rent on the lease they successfully pleaded constructive eviction.

Owners of property also have an interest in not being bothered by such intrusions as noise, smells, and other things. For land, this generally falls under the law of nuisance, which is considered in 5.2.4 and 5.4.2. One should note that the law of nuisance provides both a right and a limit. One has a claim against others causing a nuisance, and one has a duty not to cause a nuisance to others.

3.3.2. *To use and capital.* In accordance with the principle of freedom, the law generally assumes that one may use (and thus manage and receive income from) one's property as one wants. An owner is normally interested in preserving or increasing the value of property and therefore will take care of it. Property law problems primarily arise when a person with an interest in property does not have possession, as when the property is in trust, under a life estate, or leased. Trustees, we have noted, are obligated to preserve the capital of a trust.

Under the law of waste a tenant for life has a duty not to decrease significantly the value of the property for the reversioner or remainderman. A life tenant can continue uses as a fee simple owner would, such as farm and operate existing mines – but not open new ones. A life tenant can generally improve the property, for example, tear down an old house next to a brewery on the same property (*Melms v. Pabst Brewing Co.*, 104 Wis. 7, 79 N.W. 738 (1899); see also Rest. Property § 138). If legal life estates were abolished as our discussion of the principle of legal titles recommends, the law of waste would no longer be needed. The equivalent of a life estate can be obtained by a trust. Trustees have control of a fee simple and are under a duty to preserve the capital for the beneficiaries. Any income, as from mining, would go into the trust fund. To the extent this depreciates the value of the land, it should not be treated as income owed to the present beneficiaries but used to preserve the principal, although the creator of the trust could impose other duties.

With rental property the situation is more complicated. The owner has an interest in preserving the property and the income from it, and the tenant is interested in the property being fit for use. We shall focus on the premises being fit for human habitation. In rental units, uninhabitability can arise in twelve ways due to the combinations of when the defect arises and its cause. The defect could exist prior to signing a lease, arise between the signing of a lease and the time for possession, or arise after possession. The cause of the defect could be the responsibility of the elements, the landlord, the tenant, or a third party.

Under the common law, the uninhabitability of leased dwellings was "tough beans" for the tenant. As waste also applied to leased property, the common law placed most of the burden of repair on the tenant. Absent a covenant or statute, the landlord had no duty to repair. The tenant had a duty to make minor repairs of damage due to the elements (*Suydam v. Jackson*, 54 N.Y. 450 (Comm. of App. 1873)). Moreover, tenants had difficulty covenanting out of a duty to repair. In *Polack v. Pioche* (35 Cal. 416 (1868)), the lease included a covenant that the tenant was not responsible for "damages by the elements or acts of Providence." As a result of heavy rains and the acts of third parties, a reservoir dam on noncontiguous property burst, and the resulting flood caused $6,000 worth of damage to the leased property for which the landlord sued. The court held that the covenant did not exempt the tenant from paying damages; because the tenant had helped reinforce the dam and some human intervention was involved (third parties), the damage did not result purely from the elements or Providence. Moveover, in the absence of a statute or covenant to the contrary, a tenant who leased land with buildings as opposed to part of a building had to pay rent even if the building was demolished by any cause (Smith and Boyer, 138; Chase and Taylor 1985, 619).

A central problem was that covenants were held to be independent, so even if the landlord failed to fulfill a covenant, the tenant was still liable for rent. The only exception was that a tenant did not have to pay rent if the covenant for possession or quiet enjoyment was broken and the tenant dispossessed. Constructive eviction broadens this exception, but it is not necessarily a sufficient revision since it requires one actually to abandon the premises (see also Chase and Taylor 1985, 598-610). Similar problems could arise for purchasers of newly constructed homes. If after the deed passed the house became uninhabitable due to hidden defects, the owner had no recourse against the builder. The deed was said to merge all the covenants in the contract for construction, and acceptance of title indicated fulfillment of all the covenants.

During the 1960s and 1970s, courts and legislatures in the United States began to require a warranty of habitability, overruling the doctrines of independence of covenants and merger in the deed, thus making leases and contracts for construction of houses closer to mainstream contract law. In rental units, court action primarily relied on housing code statutes. Although different courts took different approaches, the court's position in *Javins v. First Nat'l Realty Corp.* (428 F.2d 1071 (D.C. Cir. 1970)) is perhaps the most rationally acceptable and widely followed court case. The landlord, First National, sued for possession of apartments due to nonpayment of rent. The tenants admitted that they had not paid rent but offered to show 1500 violations of the housing code. The court held that a warranty of habitability as determined by the housing code was implied by law in leases of dwellings covered by the code. Usual contract remedies are to be granted for breach of the warranty. If code violations exist, a court must determine what portion of rent is suspended. If no rent is suspended, then the owner gets possession. If conditions are so bad that no rent is due, then the owner does not get possession. If some but not all rent is due, then the owner gets possession if the tenants do not pay that amount. Some courts have also extended the warranty to single unit dwellings (*Pole Realty Co. v. Sorrells*, 397 N.E.2d 539 (Ill. App. Ct. 1979)). (For the basis of much U.S. statutory development, see Uniform Residential Landlord and Tenant Act, 7A U.L.A. 503-59 (1972); for Canada, see Landlord and Tenant Act, Ont. Rev. Stat. ch. 232, § 96(1) (1980), and *Pajelle Investments Ltd. V. Harbold*, 62 D.L.R.3d 749 (Can. 1976).)

However, the implied warranty of habitability has been held not to apply to public housing (*Alexander v. United States Dep't of Housing and Urban Dev.*, 555 F.2d 166 (7th Cir. 1977), *aff'd on other grounds*, 441 U.S. 39 (1979); *Perry v. Housing Auth. of Charleston*, 664 F.2d 1210 (4th Cir. 1981)). It is alleged that a warranty of habitability would imply a warranty that the policy objectives of legislation providing public housing were met. This argument is invalid. Upholding a warranty of habitability in public housing would only imply that the policy objective was met as regards the particular tenant. It would not imply that all needy persons have habitable housing. Moreover, as a landlord, the government should be held to the same standards as others, standards imposed by government. From a tenants' viewpoint, there is no difference between the government offering defective housing on easier terms and private parties doing so.

A warranty of habitability has also been extended to the construction of new homes (*Petersen v. Hubschman Constr. Co.*, 76 Ill. 2d 31, 27 Ill. Dec. 746, 389 N.E.2d 1154 (1979)). In construction, the warranty is stronger than in rental units. It is not merely a warranty of habitability but one of quality, that it be constructed in a workmanlike manner – free from significant defects (Uniform Land Transactions Act § 2-309 (1975)). Other cases have held that the warranty applies even to subsequent owners and to used houses (*Redarowicz v. Ohlendorf*, 92 Ill. 2d 171, 65 Ill. Dec. 411, 441 N.E.2d 324 (1982)). Given the broader scope of the warranty of quality in construction, the law is approximating the contract law requirement of merchantability (see 4.3.2). A warranty of fitness for purpose should also extend to commercial property (see Uniform Land Transactions Act § 2-309 (1975) which is not restricted to residences).

(3-12) The principle of leases: leases and contracts for construction of buildings should be treated like other contemporary contracts. It can be argued that leases have always been treated as contracts, and therefore this principle merely states extant law, and in fact the whole discussion belongs to the chapter on contracts. However, it has been persuasively argued that property law concepts have influenced the interpretation of leases in many ways, even when courts have claimed to be using a straightforward contract approach (Chase and Taylor 1985).

Our principle of leases thus goes beyond using contract principles and requires full analysis in accord with contemporary contract analysis. The payor (tenant or purchaser) is paying in exchange for expected property. If the property does not meet the conditions in the agreement, then the payor should be able to get out of the agreement or receive damages or rent abatement so that he or she pays what the premises are actually worth, providing the defects are not the payor's fault. A warranty of habitability as broad as material breach should be implied (see Chase and Taylor 1985, 644). This approach implies that the parties should not be able to covenant out of the warranty of habitability to the minimum extent of meeting building and housing code regulations unless both parties benefit (see the principle of required conditions (4-12) in 4.3.2), otherwise it should amount to an unconscionable contract. One can find this sort of arrangement acceptable from the viewpoint of either party; each will be assured of receiving value for value given. Given that leases should be treated like other contracts, rent acceleration clauses making the whole due on default of a payment should not be permitted as they amount to penalties (*Ricker v. Rombough*, 261 P.2d 328 (Cal. Sup. Ct. Alameda Co. 1953)).

The landlord-tenant duties of repair are also resolved by treating leases as contracts with implied warranties of habitability and fitness for use. The landlord has a duty to keep dwellings in repair to meet the conditions in the lease and inducements to it and to keep commercial property fit for the intended use. In the absence of express covenants to the contrary, tenants should be liable to repair all damage beyond ordinary wear and tear caused by them or persons they permit on the premises (see The Landlord and Tenant Act, Ont. Rev. Stat. ch. 232, § 89 (1980)). The reasons for this liability are fairly simple. Tenants have control of their conduct and who is permitted on the premises, so they are best able to avoid such damage. Landlords are generally in a better position to insure against all other damage. Landlords could also insure against damage by tenants. In multiple unit property the costs would then be spread over all the tenants, and a tenant might reasonably be unwilling to assume a proportionate share of the risk of damage other tenants might cause. These considerations could be otherwise, and the landlord and tenant could make other arrangements for repair.

A property owner might want to use both the property and its capital value at the same time. This can be done by using the property as security for a loan. For real property, this involves a mortgage. The mortgagor (usually a purchaser) borrows money and provides the property as security for failure to repay the loan. The mortgagee has a claim to the property if the mortgagor defaults on payments. Although various technical questions arise, such as priority of mortgages (usually priority is in the order of time made or recorded), we consider only one aspect, namely, who holds the title. The English Law of Property Act 1925 introduced a legal estate of a definite term of years primarily so that mortgagees could have a legal estate to mortgaged property. The messy result is that two legal estates to the same land can exist simultaneously – the fee simple absolute of the mortgagor and the term of years of the mortgagee. In some U.S. jurisdictions, title passes to the mortgagee. If it does, the mortgagor has a right to the title when the loan is paid off. In most states, title remains with the mortgagor, but the mortgagee has a right to take it should the mortgagor default. Practically, there is little difference in overall results between these systems, but many details such as insurance and taxes have to be provided for differently. The point is to allow the mortgagee to have the property in case of default. So long as this element is provided and the mortgagor can transfer the property when and if he or she desires (subject to satisfaction of the mortgagee), either system is acceptable. However, the conceptual elements of the transfer of title and lease approaches are a nuisance (Lawson 1958, 184).

Security of personal property is more complex, because in some situations title passes and in others it does not (Casner and Leach 1969, 169-70). These differences are unimportant for our purposes. The crucial elements are that persons with a security interest be able to take the property if payment is not made. As we have noted, this requires a quick judicial procedure so that the property is not sold to a good faith purchaser. In some cases, such as pawnshops, this is not a danger because the person with a security interest already possesses the property.

3.3.3. *Private limits.* Because one may generally use one's property as one wants, the important questions concern limits to what one can do with it (Lawson 1958, 11). We have already mentioned that one cannot use one's property so as to create a nuisance to others. Most harmful uses of personal property, such as causing automobile accidents, are covered in tort law. This leaves two areas for consideration with respect to land – 'servitudes' and zoning. These limits can be for the benefit of specific private persons or for the public. Private limits result from servitudes, whereas public limits can stem from servitudes or zoning.

There are three types of servitudes as the term is used here – 'easements', 'profits', and covenants. Easements and profits can be considered together, and in the United States are often not distinguished. Both are the right of a person either to go onto the land of another for a limited purpose (profit or positive easement) or to prevent the landowner doing certain sorts of things on his or her land (negative easement which amounts to a restrictive covenant (Cunningham, Stoebuck, and Whitman 1984, 439)). An easement gives only the right to be on the land for some purpose, whereas a profit allows the person to take away things such as coal, gravel, game, or trees. The most common easements today are for utility pipes and lines and for public rights-of-way. Some easements, as for driveways, pertain to adjoining property, and others, as for utility lines, belong to persons.

Easements can be created by express agreement, implication, or 'prescription'. The principle of freedom supports rational and mature parties being able to create expressly any easements they want. It cannot support their creation by prescription, because then they are involuntarily imposed

on the owner. (Prescription is considered further in 3.4.1.) Implied easements usually arise when land is subdivided and courts must determine
whether an easement is implied to the benefit of a piece of property. Courts
often say that they are merely concerned with the intent of the parties, but
sometimes it is unlikely the parties had any intent. It is easy to imply
easements when the land is described in the deed by reference to a plat map
showing parks, easements, and so forth. Moreover, sometimes the necessity for the easement is so great that no reasonable person would have denied
it, for example, when the only access to one piece of land is across the other
(*Finn v. Williams*, 376 Ill. 95, 33 N.E.2d 226 (1941)).

In Appalachia, severe problems have resulted from easements or profits.
Most of the mineral rights were sold to corporations during the nineteenth
century. The deeds, so-called broad- or long-form deeds, gave the purchasers of the mineral rights an easement to come onto the land and do what
is necessary to extract the coal. In the nineteenth century, this largely
meant sink a shaft. Over time, courts interpreted the deeds to the detriment
of the owners of the surface rights. They permitted the coal companies to
cut timber for reinforcement of the mine shafts, to dig regardless of the
effects on the land above (such as sinking land), and, with the advent of
strip mining, to remove the top soil and pile rubble where they wished with
no duty to restore the land. Today, the results are apparent to the eye, and
the landowners have lost much more than the original owners expected.

Covenants running with the land (we ignore the distiction between real
and equitable) are like express easements and profits in that they must be
expressly stated, but unlike ordinary contractual promises that bind only
the promisor, they bind anyone who has possession of the land. Distinguishing those promises that are only between individuals from those
that attach to (run with) the land is sometimes difficult. The traditional
requirements are that the covenant be in writing, it be intended to run with
the land, its subject matter "touches and concerns" the land, and it involve
what is called 'privity of estate' – a relationship of the parties to the same
property rights (Smith and Boyer 1971, 348-49). The English rule of real
covenants requires horizontal privity (covenantor-covenantee) which in
effect limits it to landlord-tenant (*Austerberry v. Corporation of Oldham*, 29
Ch.D. 750 (Ct. App. 1885)). Most American jurisdictions were more generous, and now equitable covenants (restrictions, servitudes) which do not
require horizontal privity cover almost all cases.

An example of a covenant for private purposes is the case of *Dick v.
Sears-Roebuck & Co.* (115 Conn. 122, 160 A. 432 (1932); see also *Tulk v.*

Moxhay, 41 Eng. Rep. 1143 (Ch. 1848)). Dick ran a furniture store. He sold a lot across the street, with a covenant in the deed that it not be used for retail or wholesale furniture business for fifteen years. The original purchasers of the lot sold it to a corporation including the covenant in the deed. The corporation then leased it to Sears, without including the restriction in the lease. Sears opened a retail store in which it sold furniture. The court granted Dick an injunction prohibiting Sears from selling furniture. The purpose and intent of the covenant was to prevent the use of the lot across the street for a retail furniture business. Although the covenant was not contained in the lease, Sears could have discovered it by checking the deed.

(3-13) The principle of private limits: easements and covenants for private purposes should be construed to include only what is necessary for their purpose and should be implied or taken to run with the land only where necessary for the reasonable use of property. Mineral rights do not require a right to cut timber; that is a separate profit. Similarly, a right to a view, say, of the ocean, does not include the right to dictate the architecture of adjacent buildings that do not obstruct the view. One reason for this principle is to promote transferability by not encumbering real property any more than necessary. Although easements and covenants do not inhibit the transfer of property as much as fee tails and life estates, they do inhibit it. People are less likely to purchase land if a coal company has a right to cut the timber and disrupt the top soil. The principle also prevents imposing an unfair burden on individuals for the benefit of other private persons. Yet, freedom to transfer rights is preserved, because landowners can expressly grant servitudes if they wish.

3.3.4. *Public limits.* The public use of servitudes (and zoning) is often less problematic than the private use, because the limits will also benefit the owner of the property. For example, easements on homesites for public utilities clearly benefit the homeowner by providing electricity, gas, or telephone. Public purposes can be served by private covenants. An example is *Neponsit Property Owners' Ass'n, Inc. v. Emigrant Indus. Sav. Bank* (278 N.Y. 248, 15 N.E.2d 793 (1938)). Neponsit sued to foreclose a lien on land Emigrant had acquired by judicial sale. A covenant in the previous deed held that property owners pay a charge for the maintenance of roads, parks, and so forth. The covenant's purpose is clearly a public one and concerned with the land. Even though the Owners' Ass'n did not own land, the court found privity of estate since the association was formed to assert the common interests of property owners. Thus, judgment was given for Neponsit.

A central test of public purpose in private covenants is whether they bind several properties in a development. When they do, usually they are part of a private scheme of land development. As such, they should generally receive the respect courts give to legislative land planning. Thus, they should not be construed narrowly (see *Joslin v. Pine River Dev. Corp.*, 116 N.H. 814, 367 A.2d 599 (1976)).

Governmental zoning by type of use – residential, commercial, industrial, agricultural, and so forth – also often benefits the owners of property so zoned (see *Village of Euclid v. Ambler Realty Co.*, 272 U.S. 365 (1926); but see Epstein 1985, 131-33). Homeowners are benefited by not having factories built next door. As so beneficial, it is part of the police powers of state and local governments to promote the welfare. Whether the zoning is beneficial to the owners often depends on whether the entire area is largely of the same character – developed residential or undeveloped. When part is developed and another part not, the restrictions are often aimed to benefit one set of owners to the detriment of the others.

However, such regulations should be reasonably related to governmental purposes. The test need not be as stringent as the least restrictive alternative test (but see Epstein 1985, 131-33, 138), but it should be stronger than merely having some relation to some conceivable government purpose. The zones should be those a reasonable person might accept as furthering a stated governmental purpose, because otherwise individuals can suffer a significant burden. Property that can be used commercially is normally worth more than property that can only be used for residential purposes. So an owner can lose significantly if previously commercial property is rezoned as residential. If done unreasonably, it constitutes an unfair burden on the individual for the public benefit. In *Nectow v. City of Cambridge* (277 U.S. 183 (1928)), Nectow owned a large tract of land near industrial plants, with some residences across the street. A zoning ordinance restricted a 100 foot deep strip along the streets to dwellings, hotels, churches, schools, and so forth, while the rest of the property was left unrestricted. As a result, a prospective buyer backed out of a deal to purchase the entire tract. The Court upheld Nectow's claim for an injunction prohibiting the zoning, because the restriction would not significantly promote public purposes and the land had no practical use for residential purposes.

Zoning and servitudes can be used to preserve the character of the people living in an area. Historically, the most common use in the United States has been to promote racial discrimination. This is not the place to discuss the ethics of racial discrimination; we simply assume that it is morally and publicly unacceptable. Not only should the government not discriminate itself, but the law should not be used for racially discriminatory purposes. Consequently, racially discriminatory covenants, such as not to sell to blacks, should not be enforced as contrary to public policy (*Shelley v. Kraemer*, 334 U.S. 1 (1948)). If racial minorities are entitled to purchase land and live in any area, then they should have access to community facilities provided to people residing in the area, even if the facilities are nominally privately run by the residents (*Sullivan v. Little Hunting Park*, 396 U.S. 229 (1969); see also *Tillman v. Wheaton-Haven Recreation Ass'n, Inc.*, 410 U.S. 431 (1973)). Nor should a pattern of racial discrimination supported by zoning be permitted (*United States v. City of Parma*, 661 F.2d 562 (6th Cir. 1981)).

The difficult problems arise when zoning, covenants, and other devices can have valid public purposes but can also be used to discriminate. Residents of an area or apartment building have a legitimate concern with the character or ambience of their neighborhood or building. Crowded conditions, noise, odors, and other factors can detract from the desirability of living in an area. In urban areas, finding a residence allowing an amiable and quiet life is not easy. People have different desires for their residential conditions. Some desires are incompatible with others; activity fulfilling one interferes with that fulfilling another but not vice versa. For example, Quait's desire for reading in quiet does not interfere with her neighbor's desire to play the trumpet, but his trumpet playing interferes with her reading. Consequently, people with subordinate desires want protection from those with dominant ones. One can agree to techniques to provide such protection provided they are reasonably designed to do so and provide everyone an opportunity to fulfill his or her desires.

Thus, covenants in a housing cooperative contract permitting termination of membership after a finding that a person is an undesirable resident are acceptable and should be enforced if the resident creates noise, odors, and so forth (*Green v. Greenbelt Homes, Inc.*, 232 Md. 496, 194 A.2d 273 (1963)). However, a regulation limiting playing musical instruments to between 10:00 AM and 8:00 PM and no more than one and a half hours a day by any one person is arbitrary (*Justice Court Mutual Housing Coop., Inc. v. Sandow*, 50 Misc. 2d 541, 270 N.Y.S.2d 829 (Sup. Ct. 1966)). Several people playing consecutively would make as much disturbance as one playing for the same period of time.

It is more difficult to support public zoning to preserve or promote vague elements of the social ambience, both because the restrictions are imposed by government instead of voluntarily accepted and because vague concerns are more easily used for discriminatory purposes. In *Village of Belle' Terre v. Boraas* (416 U.S. 1 (1974)), the Village had a zoning ordinance restricting the whole Village to one-family dwellings defined as people related by blood, marriage, and adoption or two persons not so related living together as a housekeeping unit. The Village is a small one on Long Island near a large state university. A homeowner leased a house to six students, and the Village served the owner with an order to remedy the violations of the ordinance. The homeowner and some of the students sued to prevent enforcement of the zoning ordinance. The decision for the Village was based on constitutional and statutory considerations. However, given the small size of the village and the reasonable proximity of other places of residence, such limitations are reasonable. An ordinance defining a family more narrowly so as to exclude a grandmother living with two grandchildren, however, would surely go too far (*Moore v. City of East Cleveland*, 431 U.S. 494 (1977) (Stevens, J., concurring)).

One would consider such factors as opportunities for alternative types of housing in proximity to work, shopping, social services, and so forth in determining the acceptability of public limits (see *Berenson v. Town of New Castle*, 38 N.Y.2d 102, 378 N.Y.S.2d 672, 341 N.E.2d 236 (1975) (proximity to work)). If reasonable opportunities for others with different desires to reside in the area (as determined by the above factors) are available, regulations or zoning are acceptable. They are an attempt to provide for the many different desires in accommodations. *(3-14) The principle of public limits: reasonable restrictions to preserve or promote public purposes including ambience are acceptable provided alternatives are reasonably available.*

Reasonable availability of alternatives is a crucial element of this principle. The California Supreme Court has struck down apartment regulations prohibiting families with children (*Marina Point, Ltd. v. Wolfson*, 30 Cal. 3d 721, 180 Cal. Rptr. 496, 640 P.2d 115 (1982), *cert. denied*, 459 U.S. 858 (1982)) as well as condominium covenants limiting residency to persons over 18 years of age (*O'Connor v. Village Green Owners Ass'n*, 33 Cal. 3d 790, 191 Cal. Rptr. 320, 662 P.2d 427 (1983)). Although in both cases the court was construing a particular statute, it went beyond the statute's wording. Part of the court's concern was the limited availability of housing.

However, this concern is probably a short-sighted one. If restrictions limit available housing for families with children, market forces will likely develop to provide family housing. The same applies to apartment buildings prohibiting pets or students. By the court's ruling, those who wish to live free of the noise of children must take their chances. One might reply that reasonable regulations can be imposed for specific problems, such as noise. However, almost all children, students, and pets create excessive noise or other problems at some time even when regulations exist. It is reasonable to seek to avoid the problems altogether.

Other courts have permitted covenants to prohibit children (*Pomerantz v. Woodlands Section 8*, 479 So. 2d (Fla. Dist. Ct. App. 1985); *White Egret Condominium v. Franklin*, 379 So. 2d 340 (Fla 1979)). Such restrictions based on convenants seem more justifiable, because they are voluntarily agreed to. However, if most of an area has such covenants and market forces do not correct for it, then people are denied reasonably available alternatives. Should that occur or seem likely to occur, the government could set up a licensing scheme and, say, permit only so many housing units per thousand to exclude children.

The requirement of reasonable availability of alternatives can impose affirmative obligations on communities, for provision of alternatives can involve social burdens that should be shared equally. For example, communities should not be able to exclude all moderate and low income housing, although certain areas in a community may be zoned to exclude it (*Southern Burlington County NAACP v. Township of Mount Laurel*, 92 N.J. 158, 456 A.2d 390 (1983)). A related problem is posed by group homes for retarded persons, mental patients returning to the community, and so forth. If most citizens had their way, no locations would be available. Depending on the type of resident, the facilities often do not impose burdens on neighborhoods. Even if they do, the burdens should be shared equally. Thus, although prohibition of such homes is not acceptable, reasonable limitations on the number of them in an area is (see also *McMillan v. Iserman*, 120 Mich. App. 785, 327 N.W.2d 559 (1983) (prohibition contrary to public policy)).

3.3.5. *Takings*. We have just seen that the public benefit supports limits on the use of a person's property. It may also require that property be taken for public uses, for example, courthouses and highways. The principle of social burdens implies that persons whose property is taken for government purposes should be compensated the fair value of the property. To prevent persons holding out so that their property increases in value after a government project is announced, the compensation should be based on the fair market value of the property just prior to the announcement of the government project. A similar situation occurs in reverse when the government puts in improvements for property owners in a local area, such as sewers and sidewalks. Each property owner is required to receive the benefit and to pay a proportional amount of the cost of the improvement.

Both techniques can involve some unfairness, because the value of property to owners might be more than they receive in compensation, and the value of improvements might be less than they have to pay (Calabresi and Melamed 1983, 60). For example, an elderly couple that has lived in a house for half of a century might attach a sentimental value to it which the fair market value does not reflect; because of the self-expressive nature of the house, they would not have sold at the market price. Consequently, perhaps the payment should be somewhat more than the market value (see Epstein 1985, 183). Moreover, often there are relocation expenses and the cost of equivalent property has risen. These latter elements can be, should be, and sometimes are compensated for by additional payments (Uniform Relocation Assistance and Real Property Acquisition Policies Act of 1970, 84 Stat. 1894, 42 U.S.C. 4600 (1982); see also Gelin and Miller 1982, 184-95; cf. Epstein 1985, 51-56).

When the government acquires title or possession of property, whether permanently or for a limited time, it is clear that compensation is due. It is less clear whether compensation should be paid when the government does not acquire title or possession of property but regulates it in a way that decreases its value. Almost any restriction on the use of property might decrease its economic value. Two distinct but closely related questions are involved. One is whether the government can acquire or restrict the use of property, and the other is whether it must pay compensation.

In current U.S. law, the answer to the first question depends on whether a legitimate governmental purpose is involved (*Berman v. Parker*, 348 U.S. 26 (1954); Gelin and Miller 1982, 14). Given the broad purpose of preserving and promoting the public welfare, almost any program will pass that purpose. However, the current interpretation may be too generous. In *Berman*, a particular building in an urban renewal area was condemned and then sold with no changes to another private buyer. In this case, as it was part of the total plan for renewing an area, the action might be acceptable. One cannot object to all instances of government condemnation of proper-

PROPERTY LAW 119

ty for purposes of resale to private owners, for that would have prevented use of government condemnation power to acquire land for railroads and other such monopolies benefiting the public. However, one can seriously challenge condemning property and selling it to a large private corporation merely to promote economic development (see *Poletown Neighborhood Council v. City of Detroit*, 410 Mich. 894, 304 N.W.2d 455 (1981)). Although economic development is a legitimate aim of government, such preferences for a particular business are objectionable as compared to lower taxation or other advantages to attract a variety of firms. Moreover, if restrictions are involved, like the zoning restriction in *Nectow v. City of Cambridge* (277 U.S. 183 (1928)), the specific application must serve the public purpose.

The second question is more complex. It is also closely tied to the first, because if the government has to compensate property owners, it may not want to impose a restriction. Traditionally, U.S. courts have simply struck down legislation restricting property if compensation should have been provided but was not. However, in *San Diego Gas & Electric Co. v. City of San Diego* (450 U.S. 621 (1981)), a Supreme Court minority suggested that even if the restriction was rescinded, compensation might have to be paid for the period the restriction was in effect. Some state courts have adopted this approach (see *Suiss Builders Co. v. City of Beaverton*, 294 Or. 254, 656 P.2d 306 (1982); but see *Citadel Corp. v. Puerto Rico Highway Auth.*, 695 F.2d 31 (1st Cir. 1982)).

The primary principle supporting payment of compensation is that of social burdens. If possession or title of property were taken without compensation, say, for a school, a grossly unequal burden would be imposed on the owner for the benefit of all. A particular individual is singled out. To the extent the burden falls on a broad class of persons, as in zoning a district, the burden is more equally spread. The decrease in value also relates to the fairness of the burden imposed, because the greater the cost, the more likely it is an unfair burden. To the extent a restriction is not reasonably foreseeable or decreases the value of property, the utilitarian principle of stability also weighs against it (for an account of a strictly utilitarian approach to takings, see Michelman 1967, 1214-18).

These considerations do not point to a rule that clearly demarcates cases in which compensation should be paid from those in which it need not. Instead, they indicate three factors to be taken into account and balanced against one another. *(3-15) The principle of takings: whether compensation is due depends on the extent to which individual property is singled out, owners had no reason to expect limitations when the property was acquired, and property rights are curtailed.* The first factor is relevant to whether an unfair burden is imposed. The larger the class over whom the burdens are imposed, the less the affected owners have an unfair burden. The second factor pertains to stability. If owners had reasonable grounds for expecting limits, then there is no harmful instability (see Michelman 1967, 1238-41). Presumably, as in any other contract, they took the risk of foreseeable events and acquired the property at a lower price.

The third factor rests on both social burdens and stability. The greater the restriction on property, the more likely it is that a grossly unequal burden is being imposed and that expectations are affected. Stability of property is less affected the less property rights are curtailed. One aspect of the third factor is the centrality of the incident affected to the property. Courts have generally construed the right to exclude others as central, so that any physical invasion is sufficient for compensation, for example, requiring landlords to permit the installation of cable television wiring (*Loretto v. Teleprompter Manhattan CATV Corp.*, 458 U.S. 419 (1982)). But this doctrine goes too far; even though the liberty to use and exclude is a central incident, a physical invasion need not seriously curtail that liberty. Such invasion might be temporary, for example, minor use of the edge of a homeowner's lot during construction of sidewalks. Even permanent invasion, as in the installation of wires for cable television, need not be serious. Thus, a second aspect of the curtailment of property rights is the effect on the value of the total property. Installation of a television cable does not significantly decrease the value of the property; indeed, it probably makes apartments easier to rent. A different situation is posed by *Kaiser Aetna v. United States* (444 U.S. 164 (1979)) in which owners of a marina had been denied the right to exclude the general public from its use. A right was largely abolished, and the property lost much of its value.

Two arguments based on methods similar to ours lead to quite different results. Thus, it is important to distinguish our methodology and principle. Joseph Sax (1971) has argued that many restrictions, even if they deprive an owner of almost the total value of property, do not require compensation, because they are not for public use but to settle conflicting uses of private property. The use of property can have spillover effects on neighboring property, for example, strip mining can cause mud slides onto lower lying property or pollute rivers. In such cases, there is a conflict between uses of different parcels of private property. The use of land for strip mining conflicts with the use of lower lying land for residential purposes. As each owner has a claim to be free of the burdens of the other, settling such a dispute simply determines the extent of the rights of each (Sax 1971, 162). In settling such conflicts, the government should seek to maximize the output of all the resources involved (Sax 1971, 172). In effect, the decision should be that which an individual who owned all the affected property would make, that is, utilitarian maximization.

Although very similar to our approach of determining whether a principle would be acceptable from each position, Sax's method differs importantly. By conflating the question to what a single owner would do, it ignores differences due to different positions of persons. Consequently, the principle of social burdens is denied; one person can be sacrificed for the public well-being. If one were developing principles for unsettled land, his procedure might be acceptable. But when people have developed reasonable expectations and paid money on the basis of assumptions the law fosters, it is not an acceptable approach. One could not accept it from each position considered separately; indeed, the point of compensation is precisely to avoid sacrificing one person for the social good.

Suppose a private airport is built some distance from a city. Over the years the city expands, and people purchase land and build houses near the airport. Now suppose the government enacts legislation to restrict the use of the airport to preserve quiet in the residential neighborhoods (compare with facts in *Hadacheck v. Sebastian*, 239 U.S. 394 (1915)). On Sax's approach, if the residential use is more valuable than the airport's use, no compensation should be paid to the airport even if it has to shut down. However, from the position of the airport owners, steps were taken to construct it where it would be compatible with existing uses of neighboring land. Those who purchased residences knew of the existence of the airport, and the proximity to the airport undoubtedly decreased the price they had to pay. Moreover, if the residential use is more valuable, then it should be possible to tax the residents enough to compensate the airport (cf. *Spur Indus., Inc. v. Del E. Webb Dev. Co.*, 108 Ariz. 178, 494 P.2d 700 (1982)).

Richard Epstein's recent analysis of takings does take seriously whether a principle would be acceptable from both positions (1985). He starts with full property rights, in particular, to exclusive possession, use, and disposition. In a taking, each individual must be made better off – this is what just compensation and public use imply. By just compensation, the person is indifferent to the loss of the property, and the person gains by the benefits of public use. Finally, Epstein does not accept our factor of fair warning but requires the person explicitly or actually to assume the risk as in tort law (Epstein 1985, ch. 11; see 5.3.1 (assumption of risk)). Interestingly, in the airport example above, he would agree with Sax that no compensation is due because the airport constitutes a public nuisance that can be regulated under the police power; airport noise causally interferes with the enjoyment of adjoining property and to think otherwise exhibits confusion about the concept of causation (Epstein 1985, 118-20).

Our method differs from Epstein's in three important respects. First, we do not take the limits of property rights as fixed absolutely by natural law. Instead, we take the limits of property rights to be fixed by those principles rational persons would accept. Thus, like Sax, we do not assume that the right to use property adjacent to an airport anyway one wants cannot be limited without compensation. Second, Epstein requires that each person be better off after a taking (Epstein 1985, 199-202). In contrast, our principle of social burdens does not prohibit regulations making some people worse off, only imposing a grossly unfair burden on one or a few individuals. Thus, our method is more utilitarian than Epstein's, though still less so than Sax's. Finally, on the warning issue, our argument is from the stability of property and resulting expectations. It thus involves setting the limits of property rights, not a confusion about causation in creating a nuisance (cf. Epstein 1985, 115-21). We in part settle the respective property rights by a consideration similar to foreseeability and acceptance of risk in contract law, not assumption of risk in tort law.

In sum, our method is less utilitarian than Sax's, for we do take into account the differences of position of individuals affected. However, it is more utilitarian than Epstein's, for we do permit individuals to bear a burden, but not a greatly disproportionate one, for the public good. Moreover, we do not start from fixed absolute property rights. Consequently, our approach cuts a middle path between Sax and Epstein and is more congruent with court decisions.

It is instructive to consider how our principle of takings would apply to the leading case of *Pennsylvania Coal Co. v. Mahon* (260 U.S. 393 (1922)). This involved the long-form deeds discussed with respect to easements (3.3.3). Reserving the mineral rights, Pennsylvania Coal had sold the surface rights to land for a residence. By covenant the purchasers assumed the risk of, and waived all rights to, damages resulting from the mining of coal. The Pennsylvania legislature passed an act that, among other things, prohibited the mining of coal if it would cause the subsidence of dwellings. The homeowners sued to enjoin Pennsylvania Coal from mining in such a way as to cause their land and house to sink. Mr. Justice Holmes rendered an opinion holding the law to be an unconstitutional taking without compensation. He argued that the law was not for the public benefit as the subsidence of a house was not a threat to others, and that the damage to the coal company's interests was so great as to amount to a taking. In dissent, Mr. Justice Brandeis claimed that the law merely prohibited a noxious use and did benefit the public even if some individuals received much more benefit.

None of these arguments are persuasive. First, the noxious use argument faces the problem that the respective rights – to residential use without mining, or mining despite disruption to residential use – need to be settled. There are incompatible uses just as in the airport example above. In fact, here the matter was settled by private agreement in the deed; the homeowners had accepted the possible disruption due to mining. Second, the magnitude of harm argument, on the facts, is not persuasive. For all that is said, the cost to Pennsylvania Coal of leaving whatever coal was necessary to support such buildings was negligible. The effect on the value of the total property (mineral rights) should be considered, because that indicates how great the proportional burden is. Sometimes restrictions on part of a parcel of land significantly decrease the total value, because the remainder cannot be used for intended purposes. Third, the public versus private benefit arguments are irrelevant to the compensation question. Surely, regulation of mining and preventing the collapse of residences is within the power of the government. The question is whether compensation is required. Of course if it is, the state might want to repeal the law.

On the view proposed here, the crux of the case depends on the principle of private limits requiring a narrow construction of servitudes for private purposes. If the covenants are interpreted narrowly, then Pennsylvania Coal should not be permitted to cause subsidence of property unless it is necessary. Such a showing was not made. Moreover, by the principle of takings, the magnitude of the loss of coal to the total to be mined in a particular area should be a factor. As noted above, no evidence of the magnitude of the loss was given. Pennsylvania Coal was not singled out as opposed to other coal companies, so in this respect there is no claim for compensation. However, Pennsylvania Coal had no warning of the possible restriction on its use, but the homeowners did have warning of the possibility of collapse due to mining. This factor alone is probably insufficient to require compensation. In any case, if a statute held that coal companies could not cause subsidence unless necessary to mine a significant quantity of coal in proportion to the total, then surely compensation should not be required.

In conclusion, the principle of takings can be illustrated by applying it to *Penn Cent. Transp. Co. v. New York City* (438 U.S. 104 (1978)) which involved the designation of Grand Central Station as a landmark. Under the New York City law, owners of landmarks are to keep the exterior in good repair and to obtain a commission's approval before making changes to it. Penn Central's application to build an office skyscraper atop Grand Central was denied, and it sued claiming that this amounted to a taking. The Supreme Court upheld the application of the law as not requiring compensation.

Application of the factors for takings makes this a close case. First, since the law applies to others (some 400 landmarks had been designated), the Court denied that Penn Central was singled out. This argument is not acceptable, for in each case a property owner is singled out on the basis of the unique property owned. It is not like destroying all red cedar trees within two miles of apple orchards (*Miller v. Schoene*, 276 U.S. 272 (1928)). Second, Penn Central had no fair warning when it acquired the property that such a restriction was likely. However, it did have warning before it developed plans for the office tower. That is, the specific use was not contemplated before warning. Third, the liberty to use airspace above ground is a central incident of property. The inability to construct an office tower could amount to a significant financial loss of rental income. However, in its existing state a reasonable return on investment could be had from the site, and the air space rights were still valuable, because in New York City they could be sold to owners of other locations. (The law, like many others, allowed for variances if a sufficient return could not be obtained.) Unlike the usual zoning, it is unclear how Penn Central received any advantage from the law, although the Court claimed that the preservation of landmarks benefits all citizens economically and by improving the quality of life. Tax breaks or subsidies to help maintain landmarks would modify this point (Grand Central was already tax exempt). The two elements that make the Court's decision acceptable are the size of the financial loss to the total value and the warning Penn Central had before developing specific plans. Absent these two factors, compensation would have been appropriate.

ACQUISITION AND DISPOSAL

3.4.0. *Introduction.* The acquisition and disposal of property usually go together, because one person acquires property from another. However, there are three ways in which one can acquire property other than by transfer from another: by creating property, by obtaining possession of unowned or lost property, and by possessing or using property adversely to the owner. Here we do not consider acquiring property by creating it. This leaves two methods of acquiring property by possession. Property is usually acquired from others by gift, succession, or exchange. We emphasize the elements involved in disposing of property rather than acquiring it, although in these interactions the two go together. The exchange of property is basically a matter of contract law and considered in the next chapter. However, we consider conveying real property by deed, which, although often involved in exchange, can have elements of gift or succession.

3.4.1. *Possession.* Common-law systems operate on a basis of relative rather than absolute title. One need not prove that one has a claim to property better than anyone else, only that one's claim is better than that of the other party in a case. This use of relative rather than absolute title is essentially an outcome of adversarial procedure, since courts are limited to issues between the parties to a case and cannot adjudge their claims versus nonparties. Present possession of property is a strong claim that can be defeated only by a title or, in some cases, prior possession. The principle of first possession is thus enshrined in the law, because if no one had a prior possession, then one has a claim against any conceivable challenger. Acquisition by first possession is limited to tangible property, because intangible property depends on someone creating it, often by separating the intangible rights from tangible property.

The difficult question concerns what constitutes possession of unowned property. The law requires that one have and intend effective control over the object. One can accept such a principle. First, if no control at all were required, then someone could merely state that he or she possessed all unowned property. As everyone could do that, nothing would be accomplished in determining who owned the property. Moreover, one has no reason to accept a mere making of a claim as a basis for excluding one. Second, if one has effective control, one reasonably wants to retain it unless one voluntarily transfers it. Third, the requirement of intent indicates that the person wants or claims the object.

What constitutes effective control depends on the character of the property and the type of control normal for such property (*Brumagim v. Bradshaw* (39 Cal. 24 (1870); *Eads v. Brazelton*, 22 Ark. 499 (1861)). Early discoverers and explorers would land from a ship, plant a flag, and claim the whole land mass for their sovereign. No one today would contend that this constitutes effective control of land.

The requirements for actual possession of personal property are especially difficult due to its many varieties. Perhaps the best one can do is obtain a "feel" for what is required by looking at some fact situations. For example, a person in hot pursuit of a wild animal, such as a fox, even though capable of catching and killing it, does not have possession although it might be unsporting for another to come along and kill the fox (*Pierson v. Post*, 3 Cai. R. 175 (N.Y. Sup. Ct. 1805)). Similarly, fishermen who have trapped mackerel in a net but not yet closed a small portion of the net do not have possession (*Young v. Hichens*, 115 Eng. Rep. 228 (Q.B. 1844)). However, if one has killed a whale that sinks to the bottom and is later found on the beach and the practice is for the killer to obtain the whale, then killing it is sufficient for possession (*Ghen v. Rich*, 8 F. 159 (D. Mass. 1881)). If one is recovering abandoned manure on the road and has raked it into piles to be picked up the next day, then one has possession (*Haslem v. Lockwood*, 37 Conn. 500 (1871)). A person might normally let the piles remain for a reasonable period before removing it. And finally, a meteor that strikes the earth and imbeds three feet in the ground becomes part of the land and belongs to the possessor of the land (*Goddard v. Winchell*, 86 Iowa 71, 52 N.W. 1124 (1892)).

In the foregoing personal property cases, the property was previously unowned or held to have been abandoned so that no one had title to it. The situation is different when a person finds property that is not abandoned but lost, for then someone has title to it. Due to the relativity of title, the first person to obtain possession of it has a right against everyone except the true owner. If the true owner is known or can be found, the finder has a bailment. This might appear to be an exception to the rule against involuntary bailment, but at least the person voluntarily obtained possession of the object. If the true owner is unknown and cannot be found, the finder can exercise all the rights of ownership, although should the finder sell the item and the owner subsequently show up and claim it, the finder might be liable to the owner for the value. In *Armory v. Delamirie* (93

Eng. Rep. 664 (K.B. 1722)), a chimney sweep found a jewel and took it to a goldsmith's shop to find out what it was. The goldsmith's apprentice removed the stone from the setting. The sweep refused to sell it to the goldsmith, who returned the setting but not the stone. The sweep sued for the jewel and the court held for him.

When one person finds a lost article on the premises of another, a question arises as to who has possession – the finder or the owner of the premises. The original English rule appeared to favor the finder. In *Bridges v. Hawkesworth* (21 L.J.Q.B. 75 (1851)), a traveling salesman found a parcel of banknotes on the floor of a shop and asked the shopkeeper to hold them for the owner. The shopkeeper advertised in the paper for the owner, but no one came forward. After three years, the salesman asked for the notes back, but the shopkeeper refused. The salesman sued and won on appeal. Similarly, a passenger who found a gold bracelet on the floor of an executive lounge at an airport was granted it over the airline operating the lounge (*Parker v. British Airways Bd.*, 1982 Q.B. 1004 (C.A. 1981); see *Hannah v. Peel*, [1945] 1 K.B. 509). In other cases, especially involving employees and bailments, the owner of the property on or in which something is found has been held to have possession (*South Staffordshire Water Co. v. Sharman*, [1896] 2 Q.B. 44; *Grafstein v. Holme and Freedman*, 12 D.L.R.2d 727 (Ont. 1958); and *Cartwright v. Green*, 32 Eng. Rep. 412 (Ch. 1802).) One English commentator has claimed that the tendency is to say that a thing lost on premises is in the possession of the person possessing the premises (Lawson 1958, 57), but a more accurate view is that the English rule is unclear and deficient (Harris 1961, 98).

Most American jurisdictions distinguish between lost and misplaced property. Property is misplaced when a person intentionally puts it down and then forgets where it was left. The possessor of premises where misplaced property is found is held to have possession instead of the actual finder. Thus, if a person finds a wallet on a table in a barber shop, the owner of the barbershop is entitled to it over the finder (*McAvoy v. Medina*, 11 Allen (Mass.) 548 (1886)). However, one must still be able to distinguish between lost and misplaced property. Would the bundle of notes on the floor in *Bridges v. Hawkesworth* be considered lost or misplaced? It is unlikely that the owner deliberately or intentionally placed the bundle on the floor.

A reason often given for according possession of misplaced property to the owner of premises is to provide the true owner a better chance of recovering it. Owners of valuable misplaced property might return to places they have been to look for it. This point does not really distinguish between misplaced and lost property, because owners of lost property might do the same. Moreover, it does not settle the issue between the finder and the owner of the premises. In *Bridges*, the traveling salesman left the notes with the shopkeeper for three years so that they might be found. Similarly, I once found over a hundred dollars in bills in a drawer of a motel room chest. I turned the money over to the motel which returned it to the previous occupant of the room. But suppose the owner had never been found. Although the property was clearly misplaced rather than lost, why should that have given the motel a better claim to it than I? Matters would be different had the money been discovered by a maid, for it is reasonably part of a maid's job to turn found property over to the employer (*Jackson v. Steinberg*, 186 Or. 129, 200 P.2d 376 (1948), *reh. den.*, 205 P.2d 562 (Or. 1949)). Moreover, instead of turning property over to the owner of premises, it would be better to turn it over to the police. A uniform practice of this sort, which is legally required in some jurisdictions, provides people who have lost property a central location to seek to recover it and saves them retracing their activities in many places.

Acquiring property by adverse possession or prescription differs from finding it, because the person with title is known or could be found. Adverse possession involves actual and exclusive occupancy which is open, continuous, and held against all others (hostile) for a specified period of time (Cunningham, Stoebuck, and Whitman 1984, 758; Smith and Boyer 1971, 157-58). After so possessing property for a period of time varying from five to twenty years or more depending on the jurisdiction, the possessor has title to the land even against the previous title holder. The title is not acquired from the previous owner but is original, so liens against the property for debts of the previous owner do not apply. Prescription is similar but gives a claim to use, an easement rather than title (Cunningham, Stoebuck, and Whitman 1984, 451-52; Smith and Boyer 1971, 387). The primary differences between adverse possession and prescription stem from the nature of the right acquired. Prescription does not involve occupancy but use and need only be adverse to the owner, not all persons. An owner can break the uninterrupted use by verbal denials of acquiescence (*Dartnell v. Bidwell*, 115 Me. 227, 98 A. 743 (1916)), but that is insufficient to break uninterrupted possession.

The point of adverse possession and prescription is to settle claims after a period of time (see also the principle of repose (2-9) in 2.1.3). Indeed, they are simply an instance of the use of statutes of limitation (2.3.8) to achieve

repose (Cunningham, Stoebuck, and Whitman 1984, 764). They also decrease disputes and settle some without expensive adjudication. Transferability of property is promoted by clear titles, and adverse possession provides a way of giving a clear title. Moreover, stability of possession
(although not stability of title) is promoted. Thus, the principles of repose,
transferability, and stability support the following more specific principle.
*(3-16) The principle of stale claims: after a reasonable time, claims of title
against a possessor or user of property should be void, unless proper notice is
given of the continuance of the claim.* What constitutes a reasonable time for
purposes of the principle varies depending on the nature of the property,
the mode of acquisition of possession, and the nature of the claim. However, twenty-five years appears to be a reasonable maximum even for land.
Although from the viewpoint of the possessor stability of possession is
provided, it might seem that from the viewpoint of a claimant the principle
is not acceptable. After a certain time, the owner has probably adjusted to
not having the property, and the possessor should be able to rest assured
in ownership. Moreover, the principle does permit claims to continue
provided one makes an effort to keep them open by providing notice. A
diligent claimant need not lose anything, and one who is not diligent loses
by his or her fault.

This principle also covers finders of property. Turning the property over
to a public authority provides a uniform method for owners to recover it.
Finders should be held to have possession while the property is in police
custody. After a reasonable time, a finder should have title even against the
previous owner. A reasonable time for found personal property should be
comparatively short, at most a couple of years. The actual finder rather
than the possessor of premises on which it is found should be considered
the possessor. The two exceptions are finders who are criminally on the
premises or who are employees with a duty to deliver found property to the
employer.

This approach largely coincides with a proposed statute modelled on the
New York law (Cribbet and Johnson 1984, 124-5). It differs from the
proposed statute in one important respect. The proposed statute would
return property found in safe deposit premises to the company and eventu-
ally have it escheat to the state. Perhaps the reason is to conform with the
state's right to acquire abandoned or unused safe deposit boxes and bank
accounts, but there is no reason to prefer conformity with that policy rather
than one of finders. Moreover, the prospect of possibly receiving the
property would encourage honesty by depositors.

The principle of stale claims applies to other areas besides finders, prescription, and adverse possession. For example, it applies to possession of stolen property such as paintings. In *O'Keefe v. Snyder* (83 N.J. 478, 416 A.2d 862 (1980)), O'Keefe sued to recover a painting in Snyder's possession and allegedly stolen in 1946. The court held that provided the owner has diligently sought to find and recover the property, title rests in the possessor six years after the owner has discovered who the possessor is. Here the reasonable time can be significantly extended because of the difficulties of discovering who possesses stolen personal property. It is doubtful that this significant extension should be permitted. On the one hand, if claimants do not know who possesses the property, notice cannot be provided and they could lose rights through no fault of their own. On the other hand, often victims will have received compensation through insurance, the property probably belongs to a good faith purchaser, and no such allowance is given to persons who lose property. The principle also applies to reversionary interests if they are not abolished by simplification of titles to land (see also *Presbytery of Southeast Iowa v. Harris*, 226 N.W.2d 232 (Iowa 1975)). A person with a reversionary interest need not lose it, provided the claim is recorded. The principle also supports allowing other sorts of claims, such as to mineral rights, to lapse after a sufficiently long period of time (*Texaco v. Short*, 454 U.S. 516 (1982)).

3.4.2. *Abandonment and gift.* One may want to dispose of property during one's life without receiving anything in return. Such voluntary disposition of property involves abandonment or gift of it. In abandoning property one does not direct to whom, if anyone, it is to go, whereas in giving a gift one does. When one abandons property, one voluntarily parts with possession intending to give up all rights to it (Smith and Boyer 1971, 458). Gifts are present transfers of property to another that are not in return for something. If something (including a promise) is received in return, then it is normally considered in contract law.

(3-17) *The principle of present gratuitous disposition: people should be able, without a return benefit, presently to dispose of property voluntarily to anyone or no one as the owner and recipient (if any) desire, subject only to conditions necessary to establish that it was such.* The principles of transferability and freedom support this principle. That of universality of ownership is against abandonment, but at least for personal property, is outweighed by the others. As an owner one has no reason to object to this principle and every reason to support it since, presumably, such disposition is what one wants to do. Assuming the property is of some value, presumably the recipient will be benefited, and normally one has no reason to object to being benefited. Sometimes a recipient might not consider the property a benefit suppose someone gave you a dead whale (see Casner and Leach 1969, 25, on "unwilling" possession of dead whales). Consequently, voluntary acceptance by the recipient is also necessary.

Normally, the abandonment and subsequent acquiring of personal property does not pose a problem, but there are two possible problems. One concerns restrictions on how, when, or where one abandons property. In New York City during the late 1960s, many automobiles were abandoned along freeways. One could watch them practically disappear over a a few days as people stripped them. As the costs of disposing of the wrecks became great, steps were taken to make owners of automobiles pay for their disposition. Public welfare considerations can limit the power to abandon property – such as requiring people to pay for garbage collection and not permitting them to create a public nuisance by abandoned property.

The second possible problem concerns a presumption that property is abandoned. Should one presume that all interests in bodily tissue excised in surgery are abandoned? Rarely does one want one's excised gall bladder, appendix, tumor, and so forth. However, one might want to retain some control. One might not be willing for a hospital to use one's tissue for research. Most people probably do not care about research studies done on such material, but for a few types of tissue – fetal and genetic – they might. A woman might not want to allow researchers to remove eggs from an excised ovary and use them to produce children by in vitro fertilization. In these sorts of cases, it is reasonable to assume people retain an interest in such tissue and to require their consent to its use.

The aim of universality might be more important for abandoned real property than for personal property. In the common law of England, abandoned real property 'escheated' to (reverted to) the state. In the United States, this doctrine was not generally followed. In the settlement of the country, new settlers might move in and acquire it. American law does not recognize abandonment of estates in land (Cunningham, Stoebuck, and Whitman 1984, 465). In urban areas slumlords sometimes actually do abandon property rather than continue its unprofitable operation. Public health and safety can be endangered. Today, the government will either have or soon acquire a lien against such property for taxes.

Consequently, if the government wants the property, it can acquire it or sell it, if a buyer can be found. Whether or not it does so, in the contemporary world, governments should be responsible for seeing that actually abandoned real property is not a threat to public health and safety.

The legal doctrine of gifts requires a donative intent by the donor (a voluntary intention to transfer the property to another), delivery of the property, and acceptance of it. The elements of donative intent and acceptance are clearly required by the principle above, for they ensure that each party acts voluntarily. The requirement of delivery is both an element of evidence that the donor intended to make a gift and part of what it means to make a gift. If Rahner says to Strong, "I will give you this book tomorrow," Rahner has not given the book to Strong; at most, he has promised to give it to her even though his statement is evidence of donative intent (see *Cochrane v. Moore*, L.R. 25 Q.B.D. 57 (1890) (Esher, L. J.)). To put the point another way, for a gift to have occurred, it must be correct to use the past tense – "Rahner gave the book to Strong." Such a past tense statement would not be true until Rahner had surrendered possession of the book. However, for this point, Rahner could surrender possession by saying on the phone, "It's yours; come and get it when you can."

Most of the problems with gifts concern delivery. Above it was stated that Rahner had to have surrendered possession, not that Strong had to have possession. The donee might have possession in an attenuated sense. In *In re Stevenson's Estate* (79 Ohio App. 315, 69 N.E.2d 426 (Ct. App. 1946)), Stevenson gave Newman the key to a safety deposit box and told him to get what was his from it. The box was not opened until after Stevenson's death. It contained an envelope marked as having items belonging to Newman, these being some bearer bonds and stocks endorsed by Stevenson. The court held that delivery was made when Newman received the key. Moreover, the property itself need not be delivered; delivery of a written instrument symbolically representing the property will suffice (*In re Cohn*, 187 A.D. 392, 176 N.Y.S. 225 (N.Y. App. Div. 1919)). A gift need not even be delivered to the donee; it can be delivered to a third person for the donee. In *Matter of Mills* (172 App. Div. 530, 158 N.Y.S. 1100 (Sup. Ct. 1916), *aff'd* 219 N.Y. 642, 114 N.E. 1072 (1916)), a father wanted to give a million dollars each to his son and daughter. It was agreed to do so by transferring some stock and $8,000 to each. He wired his bookkeeper to make an entry in the books to transfer the stock, and the entry was made before the father's death. However, no entry was made transferring the money. The court held that the entry was sufficient for delivery of the stock but that the money was not delivered.

Thus far the discussion has concerned 'gifts inter vivos', that is, while alive. The law treats specially gifts given in view of possible death – 'gifts causa mortis'. They must meet the general conditions for gifts as well as be made because of likely death from a specific cause, such as an operation. These gifts do not transfer all rights; donors reserve the right to revoke them and have the property back if they do not die from the cause in view.

A major problem with such gifts is the legal distinction between 'conditions precedent' and 'conditions subsequent' (see Smith and Boyer 1971, 472). A condition precedent is one that must occur before a legal status is changed, and a condition subsequent is one that will revoke a legal change. If the requirement of death is a condition precedent, then the transfer is not made until the person dies. Unfortunately, dead people cannot make gifts; any transfer of property must be by devise or intestate succession. The problem arises in interpreting the words a donor uses. Most people would probably say, "I want you to have this if (or when) I die," which technically amounts to a condition precedent. A statement of a condition subsequent would be "I want you to have this unless I live," but that is unusual and pessimistic. Most persons using the former expression would intend a condition subsequent if delivery were made, so unless a contrary intention is clearly evident courts should presume a condition subsequent is intended.

Grymes v. Hone (49 N.Y. 17 (1872)) illustrates most aspects of a gift causa mortis. A grandfather made an absolute assignment in writing, under seal and witnessed, of twenty shares of stock to his granddaughter. He kept the paper with him for a while, and later, in failing health, he gave it to his wife saying that he meant it for the granddaughter and not to give it to the executors of his estate if he died. When his wife asked why he did not give it to the granddaughter then, he said that they might need it. After his death five months later, the granddaughter successfully sued the estate for the shares. First, it is clear the grandfather intended to give the shares to the granddaughter. Second, he made delivery by giving the instrument to his wife. Third, the granddaughter accepted the shares, at least by suing for the gift. Fourth, the grandfather reserved the right to revoke the gift by saying not to give it to the granddaughter now because they might need it. Finally, the court (referee) found that the grandfather died of a specific illness he had in view at the time. Here one should note the broad concept of illness – failing health.

Bank accounts that are joint or in trust are also covered by the principle of present gratuitous disposition (see Uniform Probate Code § 6-104 (1969)). There are two legal theories of joint bank accounts. According to the contract theory, the signing of papers at the bank constitutes a contract giving each the right of surviorship (like jointly owned real property). Even if one person keeps the passbook and is the sole user of the account, on his or her death, it all belongs to the other. The other theory is that such accounts constitute gifts. Hence, on the death of one person, all the elements of a gift must be shown. Usually, making the account joint evidences donative intent and delivery, but questions can arise concerning the amount given. The gift theory is unacceptable. Most persons intend such accounts to provide for survivorship and expect the law to carry out their intentions. There is no reason for it not to do so.

Courts have looked to people's use and expectations in establishing so-called Totten trust accounts. The name comes from *Matter of Totten* (179 N.Y. 112, 71 N.E. 748 (1904)). In that case, the New York Court of Appeals held that an account in trust for another person establishes a revocable trust. The person establishing the account can use it as he or she desires, including withdrawing all money. It passes to the beneficiary on the death of the trustee or when that person clearly confers the account as a gift, for example, by handing over the passbook. In effect, a Totten trust provides a half-way between keeping the money oneself and a gift causa mortis. Unlike simply keeping the money, the trust provides for its transfer on death. Unlike a gift causa mortis, no specific cause of death need be considered when it is created and the owner has the present use. A Totten trust would have served the purposes of the grandfather in *Grymes v. Hone*.

3.4.3. *Deeds*. The discussion of gifts was restricted to personal property. The principle of present gratuitous disposition also applies to land. The law requires all transfers of interests in land (except intestate) to be evidenced by a signed writing. This requirement stems from the Statute of Frauds (1677) and is retained in modern statutes. As the name indicates, its point is to prevent fraud by allegations of oral transfers. This purpose is discussed in more detail in section 4.3.5 as the statute applies to certain types of contracts. For land, in addition to its evidentiary function, the writing requirement also serves, in conjunction with recording or registration requirements, to provide a public record of ownership. These two considerations together suffice to justify the requirement as a condition necessary to establish a voluntary gift of land.

Interests in land other than leaseholds are transferred by 'deeds' which should be treated similarly to gifts, because a transfer of land by a deed can simply be a gift. The requirements for the forms of deeds vary between jurisdictions, usually being established by statute. In some areas, the dead hand of the law still operates to make the matter quite complex. Rationally, only a few elements are needed. First, who is deeding and who receiving the property should be noted. Second, a description of the property sufficient to demarcate it clearly from other property should be provided. Third, the precise interest being transferred (mineral rights, life estate, and so on) should be noted. Fourth, it should be dated and signed by the grantor. No other requirements appear necessary, although one would usually expect a deed to contain a statement of any guarantees given by the grantor.

Deeds are distinguished by the warranty or guarantee of title the grantor provides the grantee. A warranty can be against all defects prior to the date of the deed ('general warranty' deed), only against defects arising during the grantor's ownership ('special warranty' deed), or against nothing ('quitclaim' deed). It might seem useful to abolish all forms of deeds except the general warranty deed, but there is no special reason to do so since the warranties do not provide significant protection. Purchasers of real property are normally better protected by warranties of marketable title in contracts of sale, recipients of land by gift should not look the horse in the mouth, and 'fiduciaries' (persons having an obligation of trust to another) cannot personally warrant the title of property under their control. Moreover, quitclaim deeds can be useful in clearing up any doubts about title.

Delivery is also required for deeds to be effective, but the legal theory of what constitutes delivery differs from that for gifts. Making a deed with the intent that it operate is sufficient for delivery of even a gratuitous deed and even if the grantor retains possession, although the mere making of a deed without intent is not sufficient for delivery (see also *Ferrell v. Stinson*, 233 Iowa 1331, 11 N.W.2d 701 (1953)). Physical delivery of a deed is simply strong evidence of intent but independent evidence can establish the intent, whereas in gifts of personal property, physical delivery (at least surrendering possession) constitutes part of what it means to give a gift. One reason for this difference is simply that making a deed serves much the same purpose as physical delivery of personal property. Even for personal property involving a written instrument, such as stock, signing it over to another person and separating it from one's property can be effective to transfer it, not as a gift but as a trust with the original owner as trustee (Smith and

Boyer 1971, 476-77; see *Smith's Estate*, 144 Pa. 428, 22 A. 916 (1891)).
When a written instrument is involved, physical delivery should not be
required. A written instrument effective when signed justifies one's use of
the past tense – saying that the property has been given. Only when there
is no written instrument do evidentiary and conceptual problems justify
requiring physical delivery.

It is sometimes said that acceptance is not necessary for a deed of land,
but there is no reason to treat transfers of land which might be gratuitous
differently from gifts of personal property. Thus, the operation of deeds
should depend on their acceptance by grantees when they learn of it. One
should also require acceptance of grants taking effect on the grantor's
death; should the property not be accepted, it should then pass by devise
or intestate inheritance. Although some courts state that acceptance is
required for gratuitous inter vivos transfers by deeds, the cases rarely so
hold (Smith and Boyer 1971, 282). Instead, it is generally assumed that a
person accepts valuable property. Such a presumption might reasonably
apply to both deeds and gifts, the burden of proof being on the recipient
to show that it was not accepted. Nonetheless, if intended recipients clearly
do not want property, it should not be forced on them.

The question remains whether a person she ald be able to make a deed
to become effective at some future date. This might be desired in the case
of sales or gifts of land. In sales, the point is normally to make the deed
effective on fulfillment of a condition such as full payment of the price. In
donative deeds, the point is normally to make it effective on the grantor's
death. In both situations, the traditional view is that delivery must be made
'in escrow' – to a third party to hold until the condition is met; the deed
cannot remain with the grantor or be given to the grantee. If the grantor
retains control over the deed, for example, the ability to revoke it, then the
deed is not operative, for there was no present intention to pass title. If it
is given to the grantee, then title might not be secure because a grantor
might later allege that an oral condition was imposed. This view does not
withstand the logic of the traditional concept of delivery as the intention
of the grantor. If the intention without any physical delivery suffices for
nonconditional delivery, then it should suffice for those operative on a
condition whether the physical document is in the hands of the grantor,
grantee, or a third party. Moreover, while a grantor can perpetrate fraud
on a grantee by subsequently alleging conditions not made at the time of
delivery, a grantee can also perpetrate fraud on a grantor by denying that
conditions were made. Some courts have held that a conditional delivery

can be made to the grantee (*Lerner Shops of North Carolina, Inc. v. Rosenthal*, 225 N.C. 316, 34 S.E.2d 206 (1945); *Chillemi v. Chillemi*, 197 Md. 257, 78 A.2d 750 (1951)). Similarly, it should be possible for the grantor to retain the deed. Admittedly, proof of intent and conditions might be harder in such situations.

The intent that a deed take effect at a later date creates another problem. The principle of legal titles holds that legal estates should be few and easily transferable. Delivery in escrow or conditional delivery creates many of the same problems as the other forms of legal estates. In the sales situation, it is not so bad. But the practical effect of delivery conditional on the grantor's death is to create something equivalent (except for waste and so on) to a life estate in the grantor, remainder to the grantee (technically a 'springing executory interest' (Cunningham, Stoebuck, and Whitman 1984, 743)).

It would better comport with the reasonable desires of most people were the law turned on its head and such deeds treated like Totten trusts, leaving the fee simple and the right to revoke in the grantor with a right of survivorship in the grantee. This approach would leave the land freely alienable at all times, and people would be more free to dispose of property as they desire. Of course, the same effect could be achieved by creating a trust, but so can the present effect. Although conditional delivery of a deed would be essentially the same as a will, there is no reason why the law cannot allow more than one way of accomplishing the same practical result.

3.4.4. *Succession.* On the death of the owner, unless otherwise provided for, property transfers by devise or intestate succession. Our previous discussion assumed that owners should have a right to determine who has their property after death. A principle of succession that underlies most of the common law is that persons should be able by clear written evidence to direct the disposition of their property on their death, and failing such direction, it should pass to those persons to whom the average person would want it to go (Lawson 1958, 168; Paton 1964, 493).

One might challenge the succession of property in general; it has been suggested that all property or all property over a certain amount should escheat to the state on the death of the owner (Haslett 1986). Large gifts would also have to be prohibited to prevent people using them to avoid the restrictions on succession. This proposal would not be acceptable to most people. After originally abolishing all succession of property, the Soviet

Union reintroduced it (Paton 1964, 497). Unless most people agree, such a policy would be undemocratic and probably unenforceable (see Haslett 1986, 142-43 (recommending against present imposition of such a law for these reasons). However, even widely shared beliefs are not necessarily justified, although the presumption is that they are rational and the burden of persuasion is on those who contend the contrary.

Succession and the common-law principle appear to be strongly supported by the principle of freedom. They extend that freedom from use and disposition while alive to disposition after death. However, it has been claimed that prohibition of succession is at least consistent with freedom (Haslett 1986, 131-37). The argument is that prohibition of succession will more equally distribute wealth; given the declining marginal utility of wealth, more people will be able to do more of what they want, that is, they will be more free. This argument, however, equates freedom with the ability to satisfy desires. We defined freedom as being free from some limit to do something (1.4). We did not require that one want to do something in order to be free to do it. That would imply that a person locked in a room who wants to stay there is free (see Feinberg 1973, 5-6; Bayles 1978, 75-76). What needs to be shown is that one could accept the principle from any position, that of donor, recipient, or general citizen. It is obvious that donors will lose the freedom to dispose of property and recipients the freedom to accept it.

A utilitarian argument can also be advanced for succession and the common-law principle. Many people work to accumulate property to pass on to others. To prevent their doing so would remove an incentive for work and diminish the public well-being. This argument has a couple of weaknesses. First, some empirical evidence indicates that passing property upon death is not a significant incentive to productivity (Haslett 1986, 144 n. 23). Second, most people pass their property to their family, and that does not require freedom to direct its disposition. In the Middle Ages, the common law did not provide for wills, and primogeniture passed property automatically to the eldest male heir.

Whether or not succession is ultimately justifiable, given that it exists, the question is whether the common-law principle for it is acceptable. Undoubtedly, the primary argument for restricting the principle pertains to dependents – spouses, children, and others (Haslett 1986, 138-39; Sartorius 1984, 208). If a person supports others while alive, should that person be required to provide for them after death? Suppose Taney's minor niece lives with and is dependent on him, and Taney dies without making a will.

Should Taney's son, who is a well-off lawyer, be permitted to receive his entire estate with no provision for the niece? Suppose the dependent were a stepchild by a second marriage? One argument to require provision for dependents is that if people voluntarily undertook to care for others while alive, then they should be presumed to have also accepted making provision in the event of death. But that argument is weak. Many people fail to provide for the care of dependents after their own death, for example, by purchasing life insurance. Moreover, people might be able and willing to provide for such dependents out of current income but assume that on death their property will pass to their immediate family. A second argument is that such a requirement relieves the state of the burden of caring for indigent persons. But in a welfare state, why should specific individuals have to take on burdens in addition to paying taxes (including estate taxes on death)? While alive these people relieved the state of a burden it would otherwise have, and this burden is simply returning to the state.

These arguments are inconclusive, but an argument can be made for one specific restriction on the general principle, namely, to provide for one's own children. People can and should make fully voluntary decisions whether to have children (see Bayles 1984a, 16). Deciding to repoduce makes one responsibile for the children's existence. They should have an equal opportunity for a reasonable life, and this requires adequate material provision for them during their minority. This argument does not extend to stepchildren or spouses, although it does extend to children voluntarily accepted as one's own by adoption or by consent to conception with donor genetic material, as in artificial insemination or in vitro fertilization. The voluntary act of reproduction or adoption imposes an obligation that cannot be avoided by later voluntary acts (except for relinquishment prior to death). Note that a reverse argument will not work for provision for parents, because one does not voluntarily choose or take responsibility for them prior to birth. *(3-18) The principle of succession: except for adequate provision for dependent children, people should be able by clear writing to dispose of their property to others after death as they desire; and if no such disposition is made, it should pass as the average person would desire.*

One might object that this principle does not provide adequately for spouses. In the current world, this failure could be quite disadvantageous to women who have worked as housewives and thereby contributed significantly to their husbands' life and accumulation of property. There are several replies to such an objection. First, it is assumed that household personal property is held jointly, although couples can make other provisions. Second, most homes are also held jointly, and if they hold it in another form, couples should be aware of the possibilities on death of one of them. Third, in community property jurisdictions, only half of the property is held by a spouse, so only half could be given to someone else (see also Uniform Marital Property Act (1983)). Fourth, each spouse should have a duty to support him or herself on the death of the other as on separation or divorce (see also Family Law Reform Act, Ont. Rev. Stat. ch. 152, § 15 (1980)).

Recipients of property by succession should have the power to refuse it; that is, as in all other transfers, acceptance should be a condition. The law usually permits beneficiaries to repudiate under a will but not in intestate succession. This power is primarily used by spouses who would benefit more by intestate succession than under a will. If the above principle were followed for intestate succession, that would not be true. Other reasons can be imagined why someone would want to decline receipt of property by succession. For example, the beneficiary might not approve of the way the property was acquired (illegally) or of the property itself (shares in South African companies). As with deeds and gifts, courts might plausibly presume acceptance and place the burden of proof on those who claim nonacceptance, but this does not eliminate the point.

The principle of succession concerns to whom property should pass; it does not specify that owners should be allowed to direct that their property be destroyed. In a recent case, a woman of substantial wealth directed that her fashionable old house and its furnishings, some of which were antiques, be burned after her death. Under court supervision, this wish was carried out by the fire department ("Home Razing" 1984). Clearly, the utilitarian argument for permitting persons to direct the disposition of property on their death does not support this result. Its point is to benefit the public by providing an incentive for persons to create wealth. Such wanton destruction does not benefit the public. The property could have been given to charity or sold at public auction and the proceeds given to the government for public uses. Sometimes the destruction of property on death, such as letters and manuscripts, has a reasonable purpose. Consequently, judges should perhaps have discretion to declare directions to destroy valuable property contrary to public policy and either transfer it by succession or have it escheat to the state.

It is unnecessary to provide details about the form of wills or the specific order of succession intestate. Historically, wills for land were included in the Statute of Frauds and required to be in writing. Given the evidentiary problems of the intent of deceased persons, that requirement is quite acceptable. Most modern statutes require that they be signed at the end by the person, be witnessed by two or more other persons, and be dated (see, for example, Succession Law Reform Act, Ont. Rev. Stat. ch. 488 (1980)). Some also permit valid wills without witnesses, if made completely in the person's handwriting and signed. Most statutes for intestate succesion provide for spouse or descent (children and grandchildren), ascent (parents and grandparents), and then siblings and so on (see Ill. Rev. Stat. ch. 3, § 2-1 (1983)). This accords fairly closely with what the average person in North America would do. The principle of succession permits other orders, say, parents first, if that is what the average person in that society would desire.

The 'rule against perpetuities' is the last topic to be considered in this chapter. It is also one of the most difficult topics in property law. Fortunately, as our purpose is only to consider the underlying principle, we need not get into the complicated details of the rule. The rule essentially states that no interest is good or valid unless it must vest, if at all, within twenty-one years after lives in being at the creation of the interest (Casner and Leach 1969, 255; Smith and Boyer 1971, 111; Lawson 1958, 138-39). If Umstead wills or deeds Mountainview to her son for life and then to his youngest child to reach the age of forty years, it will be invalid with respect to the youngest child, because the interest might not vest within twenty-one years of the death of Umstead's son. The rule is not restricted to disposition of property by will but also applies to disposition by deed and trust.

Although the rule pertains to the vesting of contingent interests, its original point was to promote the alienability of property. However, that purpose is no longer primary, as property can almost always be alienated (Morris and Leach 1962, 2; Lawson 1958, 143). Simplifying legal titles would remove many of the occasions for application of the rule, at least as far as alienability is concerned. Part of the argument for limiting legal titles depended on the ability to use trusts to achieve the same result without rendering property inalienable. Nonetheless, even property held in trust is not as freely transferable as other property (Smith and Boyer 1971, 124; Lawson 1958, 144). Thus, a problem, though a lesser one, still remains with transferability. But that is not the rule's primary aim.

The purpose of the rule is to prevent persons lining up successors to property in perpetuity. It does practically permit them to be lined up for about a century by specifying the living members of a long-lived family, which gives the duration of their lives plus twenty-one years. In England it has been common to use the Royal family as a basis. Thus, the primary question at stake is how far into the future current property owners should be permitted to control the use and benefit of property in any form (including capital value and income). Thus, the question goes beyond that discussed in relation to the principle of legal titles in 3.2.2, which was restricted to control over the form of property.

The central issue is a balance between the interests of present and future generations (Morris and Leach 1962, 17; Lawson 1958, 144). Freedom of one generation to determine the use and benefit of property in the next limits the similar freedom of subsequent generations. The freedom one might gain to dispose of property is balanced by a possible loss of freedom to control property received. Persons' concerns can easily extend to provide for people currently in existence, for example, children or grandchildren. Of course, any provision for them would usually be vested interests. Concerns for the well-being of currently nonexistent persons are another matter. It is plausible that concerns for nonexistent persons are not strong beyond the offspring of persons presently in existence. After that, concern would be for the nonexistent offspring of nonexistent persons, and that is surely weaker than the desires of such persons to control their own lives and property. Allowing for the first generation of nonexistent offspring to reach majority gives one the limitations of the rule against perpetuities, lives in being plus twenty-one years.

The catch is that often the lives in being used are not those about whose welfare the transferor is concerned. Consequently, one reasonable tightening up of the rule is to restrict the lives in being that can be used to those who benefit under the instrument. Of course, this would involve considerable variation in the length of time people could prescribe property, but that is also present under the current rule. An alternative would be to wait and see if interests vest and allow courts to reform limitations to approximate the transferor's intention (Morris and Leach 1962, 34-5). This change is not incompatible with the restriction of lives in being to beneficiaries, and would provide some flexibility should a beneficiary die sooner than expected. The resulting rule is that no interest should be valid unless it vests within twenty-one years of the lives of beneficiaries in being at the creation of the interest, with courts having the power to modify instruments to approximate the transferor's intention. This rule incorporates the wait and see doctrine by using 'vests' rather than 'must vest'.

CHAPTER 4

CONTRACT LAW

INTRODUCTION

4.0. Contract law can be defined narrowly or very broadly. Contracts are
often defined as promises or agreements enforceable at law (Corbin 1952,
5; Treitel 1979, 1). Contract law might then be taken to be the law pertaining to the enforcement of promises or agreements. However, this narrow
conception of contract law is inadequate for material normally included in
contract law, let alone for evaluating the law. Many court cases normally
included in contract law do not, for one reason or another, involve enforceable agreements or promises. Indeed, often it is found that no contract has
been made. In short, contract law concerns more than enforceable contracts and agreements; it also concerns failed attempts to make them. The
narrow conception of contract has made possible talk of the death of
contract (Gilmore 1974), because principles similar to those in tort law
have come to play such an important role in failed attempts to contract.

An extremely broad conception of contract law is as the law pertaining
to private transfer of property or services. So conceived, contract law
includes many subjects not usually thought to belong to it, such as wills and
inheritance, gifts, restitution, fraud, and conversion of property. Contract
law in this sense includes all the law developing the principle of transferability of property (3-3). Thus, providing for the possibility of contractual
transfer is one reason why in the previous chapter we emphasized keeping
property alienable. Because of this close relationship between contract and
property, conceptions from the two can often be mixed together. In the
previous chapter we found that property and contract conceptions have
often been mixed together in leases (3.2.2).

This extremely broad conception of contract law can be subdivided by
the use of two distinctions. The first is simply whether an intended transfer
is a present or future one. The second distinction is between 'plus sum',
'zero sum', and 'minus sum' interactions. In plus sum interactions, more
value exists after the interaction than before; that is, value is increased. The
general concept of a plus sum interaction has three subcases. One party
might lose but the other gain more than the first loses; one party might

143

CHAPTER 4

remain the same and the other gain; and both parties might gain. If Arnold purchases a watch from a store, then presumably both he and the store benefit and the interaction is a plus sum one of the last type. Each party obtained something it wanted more than than what it gave. In zero sum interactions, the same amount of value exists after the interaction as before. If two people each mistakenly take the other's similar umbrella from a stand, the interaction is a zero sum one. An interaction would also be a zero sum one if one party gained precisely what the other lost. In minus sum interactions, less value exists after the interaction than before. If two people have an automobile accident, value is decreased. Either one party is the same and the other worse off or both are worse off.

How one classifies some interactions depends on how value is conceived. For example, gifts are usually treated as zero sum interactions, probably because there is only a one way transfer. But the parties to a gift transfer might think of it as a plus sum interaction. The recipient of a book might value it more than a donor who has already read it. The donor might value the recipient having the book and indicate this by paying to mail the book to the donee. Voluntary gifts can then increase economic value and be plus sum interactions. Gift interactions can also be minus sum ones, for example, when a recipient places less value on a gift than the donor or the market. One often receives gifts that one did not want and puts away in a drawer or closet. Perhaps on average gifts are zero or modest plus sum interactions, the plus sum ones barely offsetting the minus sum ones.

With these two distinctions, we can classify transfers of property or services as follows.

	ZERO SUM	PLUS SUM
PRESENT	gift inter vivos gift causa mortis	barter cash sales
FUTURE	conditional deeds succession	executory contracts

All of the transfers in the zero sum column were considered in the previous chapter. (Note that only gratuitous conditional deeds are intended, the qualification being omitted for lack of space in the table.) Gifts causa mortis and conditional deeds are placed near the border of present and future, because gifts causa mortis are present transfers with a right to revoke, whereas conditional deeds involve future transfers when the condition is met. Note that all the examples of zero sum interactions are traditionally considered in property law.

One might thus expect contract law to concern all and only transfers in the plus sum column. However, before one can accept that view, three points must be clarified. First, the concept of a plus sum interaction needed is a special one. Contract law is not limited to interactions which are in fact plus sum ones; it includes cases when something goes wrong and the interaction is not a plus sum one. One must view the interaction from a prospective perspective; it is expected to be a plus sum interaction. As noted above, one party can lose and the interaction still be a plus sum one so long as the other party gains more than the first loses. Nonetheless, if the interaction is voluntary, rational parties expect it to be beneficial to them, although they need not expect or even consider whether it will be beneficial to the others. The concept then is of mutually expected beneficial plus sum interactions. Each party expects to get something that is of more value to it than what is given. Because each party expects to benefit, based on the parties' expectations, *ex ante* the interaction is a plus sum one of the third type – in which both parties gain. Court cases arise when something goes wrong and the transfer does not occur or is for some other reason not mutually beneficial as expected.

Second, our classification is broader than that implied by some conceptions of contracts. Many commentators claim that contracts necessarily involve a promise (Calamari and Perillo 1977, 1; Corbin 1952, 7). If promises always relate to the future, then contract law excludes all present transfers such as barter (Corbin 1952, 6). This creates a problem for cash sales of goods as in purchasing groceries. Of course many sales of goods are partially 'executory', for example, one party is to perform at a future date. Moreover, even most present sales involve commitments to the future, for example, warranties. Nonetheless, a cash payment for goods "as is" (no warranties) is included in the Uniform Commercial Code (§ 2-316(3)(d)) and thus part of what is usually considered contract law. We have placed cash sales of goods in the present category, but near the border because of the future effect of warranties. If one party in a sale is to perform in the future, then sales of goods belong to executory contracts as that term is meant in the table, namely, as all those in which at least one party makes a commitment to something in the future.

Third, we have used 'interaction' rather than the more usual 'transaction' because of its durational openness. 'Transaction' suggests a discrete event, whereas 'interaction' can apply to a long-term relationship. Much tradition-al contract law focuses on brief interactions between strangers. Yet, in the contemporary world, many contracts, such as employment, franchise, and installment contracts, pertain to a course of dealing between parties (see generally Macneil 1980). Although many of these long-term or relational contracts are treated in special fields, such as labor law, it is desirable to develop contract principles that can cover both them and discrete tran-sactions. Discrete transactions within a relational contract need not be plus sum ones, provided the whole relational contract or course of dealing is expected to be such.

Thus, with these qualifications and clarifications, contract law can be taken to concern mutually expected plus sum interactions. The main function of contract law is then to regulate such interactions transferring property or services between private persons (see Kronman 1980, 472) and to provide civil remedies when they go wrong. Failed mutually expected plus sum interactions usually become zero sum or minus sum ones. Most minus sum interactions are treated in tort law, but because many failed mutually expected plus sum interactions become actual minus sum ones, there is an overlap of tort and contract principles, especially for remedies. This does not mean that tort and contract law are the same; they take different perspectives (see 5.0). Criminal law also regulates plus sum and minus sum interactions, but it can be distinguished by its remedy – punish-ment (6.1.0 and 6.4.1). The distinctions between contract, tort, and criminal law thus depend on the type of interaction or the remedy.

AIMS

4.1.0. *Introduction.* Most theories of contract law adopt a single aim – the enforcement of agreements or promises, maximizing economic value, or fulfilling reasonable expectations. As in other fields, no single aim provides an adequate basis for evaluating the law. Nevertheless, it is useful briefly to examine their claims, and then to bring together the insights they provide.

4.1.1. *Agreement and promise.* The classical view is that contract law is to enforce the agreement or promises of the parties. On the agreement version, the purpose of contract law is to carry out the wills of parties who intended to be legally bound by an agreement (Fridman 1983, 631). On the promise version, the purpose of contract law is to enforce the moral obligation to keep promises when the institution of promising is intentionally invoked (Fried 1981, 16; see also Atiyah 1981a, 3). Three claims are central to both versions. (1) The parties intend to bind themselves. (2) The parties freely choose to bind themselves. (3) Legal enforcement increases freedom or autonomy by enabling people to make definite arrangements for the future (Fridman 1983, 636; Fried 1981, 20-21).

There are problems with this view as the sole purpose of contract law. First, as we have remarked, much of contract law concerns situations when, for one reason or another, agreements or valid promises were not made. The purpose of enforcing agreements or promises thus does not reach them. The heroic approach is to call such situations contractual accidents or gaps falling outside of contract law proper (Fried 1981, 69). But this is like saying principles of building construction pertain only when they are followed and have no relevance to situations when they are not.

Second, the first two claims are sometimes denied in the law. Parties can be legally bound although they did not intend to bind themselves legally. Indeed, it is not unusual for parties to find they have legally binding contracts or promises when one or both of them did not so intend. Contrarily, some contracts are not legally enforced even if the parties want and intend them to be, for example, gambling contracts. Whether one is legally bound depends on the rules of law, although often one can avoid legal obligations by explicitly stating that one is not making legal commitments. It follows that parties do not always freely choose to bind themselves. One should distinguish two aspects of freely binding oneself – entering a contract and choosing the terms of a contract. Terms of a contract are often set by law (for example, a marital contract), but one is free to enter it or not. In a few cases, a contract is not even entered freely. Different conceptions of freedom can pertain here, but on almost any of them some contracts are not entered freely, for example, an agreement with a judge not to do some act (Atiyah 1981a, 23).

One's overall freedom is increased by being able to make legally binding agreements. One has options to bind oneself in the future. But it is the ability to bind others to one, not the ability to bind oneself, that is the most valuable aspect of contract, although being able to bind oneself and doing so might be necessary to get others to bind themselves. One is freed from worry and actions to ensure the promised performance. Thus, enforcement of agreements or promises cannot be the sole aim of contract law, because it simply fails to cover a multitude of situations arising in it. Nonetheless, it, and especially the freedom it provides, can still be purposes of contract law.

4.1.2. *Maximizing economic value.* Economic analysts view law, at least private law, as designed to maximize economic value or wealth (Posner 1983, 88-115). The point or test of legal enforcement (imposition of liability) is to create incentives for value maximizing conduct in the future (Posner 1977, 68). A more contract specific and sophisticated aim is to "maximize the net beneficial reliance derived from promise-making activity" (Goetz and Scott 1980, 1321). 'Beneficial reliance' is reliance on commitments that are kept so that one benefits. 'Detrimental reliance' is reliance when a commitment is not kept and one loses. A balance must be struck between the benefits from fulfilled commitments and the losses from unfulfilled ones. In reciprocal or bargained for contracts, these two considerations can be balanced by the parties in their negotiations. For example, if Bradford is entering a contract to loan Caswell a sum of money, the interest to be charged will reflect Bradford's estimate of the likelihood of Caswell being able to repay. The greater the risk of nonrepayment (loss), the higher the interest (benefit) will be. In nonreciprocal contracts, the law must be more active, because these considerations are not balanced by the parties adjusting the terms.

On this economic view, freedom is subordinated to increasing wealth. Freedom of parties is not important for its own sake but because value is determined by the free preferences of persons. Free choice in entering contracts and fixing their terms is essential, because it ensures that both parties expect to benefit from them and value is thus increased. If a person did not (freely) intend to make a commitment, then its enforcement is not justified, because there is no reason to believe the person thought it would be beneficial (Kronman and Posner 1979, 5). The economic view supports a freedom the promise theory does not, namely, the freedom to breach contracts. If a party finds that another deal can provide more benefit even if damages are paid, then that party is free to break the contract. Indeed, to maximize value, the person should do so. Similarly, if the original judgment about expected benefit from the contract was incorrect and one will lose from completing the deal, one is free to and should breach if the damages would be less than the costs of performance.

The economic view focuses on the fact that contracts are mutually expected to be beneficial, that is, value increasing interactions. One has good reasons to accept the economic purpose. Laws facilitating mutually expected beneficial plus sum interactions are desirable, since one can expect to benefit whichever party one is. Moreover, one has no reason to object to rules that enable others to break contracts provided one receives benefits equivalent to what one would have received had the contract been performed. However, economic theorists tend to discount the costs of breach by the other party, in particular, the costs of suing for compensation. Possible legal expenses and judicial error are costs of another's breach that must be subtracted from the benefits of the contract. Consequently, one would not accept allowing others to breach whenever, after subtracting one's expected benefits, they gain.

Maximizing beneficial reliance comes close to maximizing the trust which promise theorists see as central. On a promise view, the principles of mutual trust and respect are the basis for enforcing promises (Fried 1981, 17). Beneficial reliance amounts to action in trust that promises will be fulfilled. Thus, both views fasten on essentially the same element but describe it in different terminology – mutual trust and beneficial reliance. They have different views as to the ultimate purpose or benefit of enforcement. Promise theorists view the benefit as freedom, while economic theorists view it as material gain. The difference is subtle, because an important point of contractual freedom is to be able to improve one's situation materially by arranging the future. The close relation between material gain and freedom is shown by the principle of transferability of property (3-3) being justified by considerations of utility in the previous chapter (3.1.1). However, freedom to contract includes the freedom to make expected detrimental commitments as well as beneficial ones, although a rational person would not do so.

4.1.3. *Reasonable expectations.* Another view contends that "the fundamental purpose of contract law is the protection and promotion of expectations reasonably created" (Reiter and Swan 1980, 6). In a contractual setting, only those reasonable expectations of which the other party was or should have been aware are to be protected (Reiter and Swan 1980, 7). This view emphasizes one being responsible for another reasonably relying on, or having expectations due to, one's words or actions (Reiter 1980, 242). If one is or should have been aware that one's actions would create reasonable expectations in another, then one is responsible for fulfilling (not frustrating) those expectations.

The central problem for this view is to specify when expectations and reliance are reasonable (Atiyah 1981b, 68). One might determine reasonableness of contractual expectations and reliance by social practices. Courts often use commercial customs and practices as a basis for interpreting contracts (Rest. 2d Contracts §§ 219-22). However, for many contracts no such commercial basis exists. Instead, one has to turn to what the average person would have expected or to a normative theory about reasonable expectations. Using the expectations of the average person will not provide a sound normative basis for contract law. Even if one thinks it valuable to satisfy people's expectations, this will not help. The average person's expectations are often determined, directly or indirectly, by what the law is. Thus, the argument might be circular: the law should be such and such because that complies with what people expect, but they expect that because the law is such and such. A normative basis should thus enable one to evaluate the expectations of people. The concept of a rational person as we are using it can fulfill that role. But then the view simply amounts to claiming that contracts should be enforced when rational persons have good reasons for doing so. This does not provide an aim for contract law.

The aim of protecting reasonable expectations and reliance is closely related to the aims of the promise and economic views. Reasonable expectations arise from promises, and their protection and promotion largely involves enforcing the promises. Promoting and protecting reasonable reliance is similar to the economic view's concern to maximize beneficial reliance. The economic theory, however, provides a criterion for determining when and how reliance should be protected, thereby specifying what reliance is reasonable. The reasonable expectations view does not provide guidance here.

4.1.4. *Specific aims.* With different language and emphasis, each of the views is concerned to promote and protect mutually expected beneficial plus sum interactions involving the transfer of property or services and the interests arising therein. It is possible to pick out specific aims common to these views and to add one that they ignore. Both the promise and economic views emphasize freedom to enter contracts and fix their terms. Although the reasonable expectations view does not emphasize freedom, it does emphasize responsibility for the exercise of freedom, for expectations and reliance voluntarily created. Consequently, the freedom to transfer property and services in mutually expected beneficial interactions is common to each. This aspect is already incorporated in the principles of transferability (3-3) and freedom (3-8). The principle of transferability is a very general one, covering gifts and testamentary dispositions as well as contracts (Fried 1981, 39). Property is not voluntarily transferable unless people are free to transfer it, and the principle of freedom reinforces this. The stronger presumption of freedom as property is more closely related to self-expression and identity primarily applies to the use and retention of property, not its disposition. Indeed, one might argue that there should be greater freedom to dispose of property the less closely it is related to one's expression or identity, but that claim need not be pursued here.

The expected benefit of entering interactions involving commitments about the future rests on the assurance that they will be fulfilled. The views' emphasis on trust, beneficial reliance, and fulfillment of reasonable expectations all support legal assurance. Promises are more trustworthy if supported by law; beneficial reliance is more likely when the law enforces most commitments; and expectations and reliance are reasonable if the law will protect them. Not all commitments about the future need be or should be legally enforced. Much depends on whether the interaction is expected to be a plus sum, zero sum, or minus sum one. One has good reasons for the promotion and enforcement of commitments in mutually expected beneficial plus sum interactions, because one can expect to benefit from them.

This rationale does not apply to other forms of plus sum, zero sum and minus sum interactions. In an expected minus sum interaction, at least one party and often both will lose, so one has no reason to support commitments to them. Similarly, in plus sum interactions in which one party gains more than the other loses, the losing party has no reason to support commitments. In zero sum interactions, either both parties will be left as they were or one will gain what the other loses. With an equal chance of being either party, one would be indifferent to them. Again, however, whether an interaction is zero sum depends on what counts as value. If one counts the psychological satisfaction of a donor or the greater value to the donee, then the giving of gifts can be a plus sum interaction. One might thus rationally desire to bind oneself legally to giving a gift in the future. These situations are basically the same as plus sum interactions in which one party benefits and the other remains the same. Finally, as a potential donee in a zero sum interaction, one does not want it turned into a minus sum interaction with oneself the loser.

(4-1) The principle of enforceable commitments: commitments to future transfers of property or services should be supported and enforced (a) in mutually expected beneficial plus sum interactions, and (b) in zero sum interactions if (i) it is necessary to prevent loss due to reasonable reliance by intended beneficiaries or (ii) donors indicate they are enforceable. This principle encapsulates the reasoning of the previous two paragraphs. It extends to wills and gratuitous conditional deeds, for by making such instruments a donor indicates that they are enforceable. It also protects reasonable reliance on gratuitous promises. This principle assumes that, in accordance with the principles of transferability and freedom, the commitments are voluntary.

Of course, as with all principles, there can be sufficient reasons against complying with it. In law, because of the direct costs of legal procedure, a crucial concern is not bothering with de minimis or trivial matters. This consideration is largely met by the costs imposed on parties in lawsuits for enforcement of commitments. Although none of the views considered makes note of the point, one also has another good reason to limit enforcement of commitments. *(4-2) The principle of collective good: enforcement of commitments should be limited by social policies for the collective good.* Courts have always so limited commitments, refusing to enforce contracts contrary to public policy.

This principle is merely a specification of more general political principles supporting limits on freedom for the common good (Bayles 1978, 141-63), which also justify public limits on property and some criminal laws. One stands to benefit from justifiable policies of this sort. Although one might want to enter into an arrangement involving a commitment contrary to such a policy, for most people the chances of this being so are small. Even if one would want to make or receive such a commitment in a particular case, it does not follow that a legal principle of enforcing such commitments would benefit one. One would have to consider the detrimental effects on one as a member of society from their enforcement. Consequently, for almost everyone, the expectable benefits from the principle outweigh the expectable benefits of not having it. However, few policies are likely to restrict enforcement, because mutually beneficial interactions do not usually impose harm on others. The primary instances of this occur when collective restraint from conduct is necessary for some good, for example, refraining from anticompetitive business practices.

CONTRACT FORMATION

4.2.0. *Introduction.* The principle of enforceable commitments is too general to be applied directly in contract cases. In specifying it, one should keep distinct several issues related to contract formation. What commitments should be legally enforceable? What should be required to make a contract? When should contracts be considered to come into existence? The enforceability of contracts is related to their being made, because people tend to use 'contract' to mean 'enforceable contract'. However, there can be contracts that are not enforceable. The hoary doctrine of consideration primarily pertains to the first question, although it is often said that consideration is necessary to make a contract. Offer and acceptance primarily pertain to the last two questions, for no contract is made without an offer and acceptance and contracts come into existence when an offer is accepted.

4.2.1. *Consideration.* The doctrine of consideration has created despair for hundreds of students as well as several scholars. A primary, though not the only, purpose of the doctrine of consideration is to distinguish those promises or commitments that are legally enforceable from those that are not. According to classical legal theory, only those commitments for which consideration is received are legally enforceable. Consideration for a promise is an act, a forbearance, a change in a legal relation, or a promise, bargained for and given in exchange (Rest. Contracts § 75). It is either a detriment to the promisee or a benefit to the promisor (Chitty 1983, § 146). One difficulty is that, given a court's view of the justice of the case, almost anything can count or not count as consideration. In *Hamer v. Sidway* (124 N.Y. 538, 27 N.E. 256 (1891)), a nephew's refraining from smoking, drinking, swearing, and playing cards or billiards for money constituted consideration for an uncle's promise to pay $5,000; but in *Kirksey v. Kirksey* (8 Ala. 131 (1845)), a widow and her children moving sixty miles across rural Alabama in the nineteenth century was not condsideration for a brother-in-law's promise of a place to live .

One scholar claims that the doctrine "is too internally inconsistent" to serve as a basis for contractual obligation (Fried 1981, 35). He is referring to a deeper inconsistency than the seeming one between the cases just mentioned. Although consideration is required for a binding contract, the adequacy of consideration is supposedly not examined by courts (Rest. 2d Contracts §§ 17, 79). In practice, under other names courts do sometimes evaluate the adequacy of consideration (Atiyah 1981a, 105), but they do so much less than were it official policy to do so. In any case, the theoretical problem remains. The failure to inquire into the adequacy of consideration implies that people's free arrangements should be respected and enforced, but the doctrine of consideration limits the free arrangements that are respected and enforced (see also Atiyah 1981a, 94).

The conflict involved here goes to two purposes underlying the enforcement of plus sum interactions – freedom and maximizing value. The failure to inquire into the adequacy of consideration recognizes the freedom of persons to make their own arrangements. The requirement of consideration helps ensure that the interactions are mutually expected to be beneficial and thus increase value. Consider the following hypothetical contract. Didway transfers goods "as is" to Evans in exchange for Evans's paying Didway $100. Didway prefers $100 to the goods, and Evans prefers the goods to $100. The transaction is mutually expected to be beneficial, each party receiving something valued more than he or she gives, and thus a plus sum interaction. Moreover, Didway receives a benefit of $100, which constitutes a detriment to Evans. Similarly, Didway's detriment (giving up the goods) is a benefit to Evans. The doctrine of consideration rests on these elements of mutual benefit and detriment. Yet, courts will not inquire into whether the goods are worth $100. The economic rationale is that only Evans can determine what the goods are worth to him. Even if no one else would pay more than $75 for them, it does not follow that Evans has not benefited, only that he probably could have obtained a better bargain. For a court to refuse to enforce the deal because the goods are not worth $100 is to interfere with Evans's freedom to make his own value judgments and lead his own life.

This exchange does not involve commitments, but one can easily modify it into an executory contract with mutual commitments by simply having Didway and Evans exchange promises to act as above. Here one has mutually exchanged promises, and the promises are taken to be consideration for each other. Around the beginning of the twentieth century, there was much academic debate as to how a promise could be consideration for another promise (Bronaugh 1983), and some contemporary scholars still query how promises can provide consideration (Atiyah 1981a, 94). Promises cannot be beneficial to promisees or detrimental to promisors unless they are binding, but they are not binding unless consideration is given and a contract is formed.

The answer to this alleged problem lies in two factors. First, as we discuss more fully below (4.2.2), a central element of consideration is that it is bargained for the promise, which occurs in this case. Second, not just any promise will do. The promise must be to something that itself would be consideration. For example, if a person is already under an obligation to the other to do the promised act, the promise will not constitute consideration (Rest. 2d Contracts § 73; *Lingenfelder v. Wainwright Brewery Co.*, 103 Mo. 578, 15 S.W. 844 (1891)). There is no benefit to the promisee or detriment to the promisor, so the interaction would be a zero sum rather than plus sum one; neither gives or receives anything. If one is still inclined to contend that a promise is not sufficient to constitute consideration, one should note that it is just as valuable as what is given, namely, a promise. Reciprocal bargained for promises constitute consideration for each other if the promised acts would constitute consideration, because each gets as much as he or she gives. One simply discounts the promised acts of each by the probability of their occurrence.

In the standard case, the benefit is received by the promisor and the detriment is that of the promisee. These relations are not essential (Rest. 2d Contracts § 79). If Frick hires Graham to drive her son's car from Ontario to Florida, then Graham clearly performs a detrimental act, but Frick's son receives most of the benefit. Nonetheless, the interaction is still reasonably foreseen as a plus sum one. Frick thinks that she is better off having her son's car driven to Florida than retaining the money paid to Graham. Nor does it make any difference if Graham's brother drives the car, that is, the detriment for Frick's promise is to someone other than the promisee.

The mistake of classical contract theory is to turn good evidence of an interaction being a plus sum one into a necessary condition for enforcing a commitment. *(4-3) The principle of consideration: consideration should be treated as evidence that an interaction is mutually expected to be beneficial and thus as providing a reason to enforce a commitment.* Consideration indicates that the promisor expects to obtain something valued, although it need not pass to that party. In *Hamer v. Sidway*, the uncle wanted his nephew to refrain from smoking and so on. When a person is to receive something asked for in exchange for a promise, there is reason to believe that the person expects to gain from the interaction. In *Kirksey v. Kirksey*, there was little reason to believe the brother-in-law wanted the widow to live on his land, that he received anything he valued. However, there may have been other reasons for enforcing the brother-in-law's promise. Consideration is not a necessary condition for enforcing commitments (see also Eisenberg 1982, 640), but it is a good reason for doing so. It shows that the interaction is likely to be a plus sum one, and there are good reasons for enforcing commitments to promote such interactions.

4.2.2. *Past benefits.* The general English rule is that past consideration or benefit is not sufficient to make a promise legally binding (Atiyah 1981a, 97-98; Chitty 1983, § 162; Davies 1977, 27). The argument is that the benefit was not bargained for and the promise was not given for it. Thus, the bargain requirement of consideration is used as a necessary condition for a commitment to be enforceable. However, there are certain situations in which even English law allows past consideration to make a promise enforceable – where an act was done or promise made at the promisor's request or a debt unenforceable by a statute of limitations is acknowledged (Chitty 1983, §§ 165-6, 171). American courts are more generous with respect to past benefits.

A case illustrates past benefits. In *Sheldon v. Blackman* (188 Wis. 4, 205 N.W. 486 (1925)), a niece gave up her job and took care of her aunt and uncle for thirty-four years. After thirty years, his wife having died, the uncle made a note for $30,000 payable to the niece on his death. The court upheld the note and provided reasonable compensation for services rendered thereafter. A reasonable person could certainly value thirty years service as worth $30,000 even with the dollar's much greater value then. In this case, there was no past legal obligation rendered unenforceable by law nor a bargaining for the service and note.

This sort of case is recognized by *Restatement (Second) of Contracts* § 86 which allows enforcement of promises made in recognition of previously received benefits to the extent necessary to prevent injustice, provided the amount is not disproportionate to the benefit. However, it does not permit recovery if the benefit was conferred as a gift or otherwise the promisor was not unjustly enriched (Rest. 2d Contracts § 86(2)(a)). The underlying principle of this section is 'unjust enrichment' – benefits given for which compensation is expected. However, it allows for variation from the market value of the benefits, since they can be worth more to one person than another.

This principle is not compatible with the case law or logical. In *In re Hatten's Estate* (233 Wis. 199, 288 N.W. 278 (1940)), a man whose estate was valued at $3,000,000 had given a $25,000 note for meals and other services (such as being driven to various places) rendered over a number of years. Although the value of the services was $6,000, the plaintiff was allowed to recover on the note. The meals appear to have been provided originally as gifts – having a friend to dinner. After Hatten had told the plaintiff that she would be compensated, she might have expected compensation and failure to compensate then constitute unjust enrichment. However, if there is unjust enrichment, the promise is unnecessary since the plaintiff can sue under the law of restitution (Eisenberg 1982, 664). In *Webb v. McGowan* (27 Ala. App. 82, 168 So. 196 (1936)), a promise to pay a weekly sum to a worker injured in saving the employer's life was upheld. It is highly unlikely that at the time he acted the worker expected to be compensated for any injuries. Moreover, failing to compensate a good Samaritan is not obviously unjust; indeed, if compensation were expected for good Samaritanism, it would no longer be such. Physicians can expect payment for emergency services, so one does not view their services as good Samaritanism. The *Restatement*'s theory tries to force these situations into a mold they do not fit.

There are good reasons to accept § 86 without the limitations for gifts and lack of unjust enrichment. Two mistaken assumptions underlie the failure to recognize past benefits as a broad basis for enforcing commitments. Perhaps the major one is treating bargaining as a necessary condition for enforcement (see also Levin and McDowell 1983, 40). A bargain is evidence of a mutually expected plus sum interaction. However, there can be actual plus sum interactions without a bargain and consideration, including some gifts. The second mistaken assumption is treating contracts as discrete transactions. On a relational view, one can consider the receipt of the original benefit and the later return as one interaction. As a benefit was received, the entire interaction is a plus sum one. Granted, it might not have been mutually expected to be beneficial, for the promisee might have rendered the benefit without expecation of recompense, although many people today do expect reciprocation of gifts. Contract law might have originated in reciprocal gift giving in primitive societies. Reciprocity, or reciprocity along with benevolence, is the primary motivation in the past benefit cases (Henderson 1971, 1158).

As a promisee, one will benefit from enforcement of a promise in return for a past benefit. As a promisor, one can view it as a mutually beneficial interaction. If one does not, one need not make the promise. However, the amount involved should be such that the promisor could reasonably consider it reciprocation for the benefit received. *(4-4) The principle of past benefits: a commitment made in recognition of a previously received benefit should be enforceable unless a reasonable person in the promisor's position could not view it as reciprocity for the benefit.* To avoid fraud, especially when the promisor is dead, one might reasonably require clear and convincing proof of the promise. If the amount promised is in excess of reasonable reciprocity, a court could either not enforce it or reduce the amount to a reasonable sum. The practical results are likely to be the same in either case, because if the court refuses to enforce the promise, a valid claim for compensation for unjust enrichment is likely to remain. Both the principle of past benefits and that of consideration indicate that situations come under part (a) of the principle of enforceable commitments – that the interaction is a mutually expected beneficial one.

4.2.3. *Reliance.* Suppose a promisor has not benefited, but the promisee detrimentally relied on the promise. Except for the psychological benefits a promisor might have received from the promise, the interaction was not mutually expected to be beneficial. In *Ricketts v. Scothorn* (57 Neb. 51, 77 N.W. 365 (1898)), a grandfather gave his granddaughter a note payable on demand for $2,000 plus interest so that she would not have to work, and she quit her job for about a year. The court held she could recover from his estate. Here, one might argue, there was as much consideration as in *Hamer v. Sidway* (124 N.Y. 538, 27 N.D. 256 (1891) (uncle requests nephew to cease smoking)).

A clear instance of no benefit being received by the promisor is *Feinberg v. Pfeiffer Co.* (322 S.W. 2d 163 (Mo. Ct. App. 1959)). In 1947, Pfeiffer's board adopted a resolution providing Mrs. Feinberg, an employee since 1910, $200 a month for life on retirement. She retired two years later, and payments were made until 1956, when they were reduced to $100. The court did not find consideration in the extra two years Mrs. Feinberg worked, because she was paid for that. Although the board made the resolution in recognition of Mrs. Feinberg's long employment, that could not constitute past benefit, for she had also been paid for it. Instead, the court specifically relied on *Restatement of Contracts* § 90 which provides that "a promise which the promisor should reasonably expect to induce action or forbearance of a definite and substantial character on the part of the promisee and which does induce such action or forbearance is binding if injustice can be avoided only by enforcement of the promise." In *Restatement (Second) of Contracts*, the corresponding section (90(1)) has been modified to drop the requirement of definite and substantial character, to cover third parties as well, and to provide that the remedy can be limited.

The *Restatements'* requirement that reliance be reasonably expectable by the promisor has been criticized as redundant, for the very purpose of a promise is to induce behavior. The crucial element, it is claimed, is whether the reliance is reasonable (Eisenberg 1979, 20-21; Eisenberg 1982, 659). At one level, whether reliance is reasonable, like reasonable expectations (4.1.3), depends on whether a promise is enforceable. Consequently, reliance is reasonable to the extent the promise will be enforced. At a more specific level, what is reasonably expectable by the promisor and what is reasonable reliance by the promisee are interdependent. Conduct in reliance that is not of a sort foreseeable by the promisor is not reasonable, and unreasonable conduct in reliance is not usually foreseeable. It is preferable to use a promisor's foreseeability as the test, because that indicates the extent of commitment undertaken. It designates the scope of the promisee's conduct for which the promisor is responsible. Also, it more clearly covers third parties.

Except for the psychological benefit to the promisor, these situations involve zero sum interactions. However, if such commitments are not enforced, then zero sum interactions become minus sum ones. A relying promisee will have incurred costs. For example, Mrs. Feinberg is likely to have spent savings on the assumption that she would have a continued $200 a month income. Thus, these cases fall under the principle of enforceable commitments (b)(1) of preventing loss due to reasonable reliance by intended beneficiaries. *(4-5) The principle of reliance: a commitment should be enforceable to the extent necessary to prevent loss due to foreseeable reliance.* This principle is acceptable whether one is promisor or promisee. It enables one to make enforceable promises in zero sum interactions and still withdraw from them at an anticipated cost. As a promisee, one can place more trust and reliance in such promises, because one need not fear loss.

It is worth noting that *Kirksey v. Kirksey* (8 Ala. 131 (1845) (widowed sister-in-law invited to come live on land)) could have been decided on this basis had it been available. A similar case decided on this ground was *Greiner v. Greiner* (131 Kan. 760, 293 P. 759 (1930)) in which a mother promised to give her son land if he came and lived on it. Indeed, *Kirksey* is better supported, because the widow asked only $200 damages, not a continued place to live, whereas in *Greiner* the son requested and received the land, which was more than necessary to prevent loss.

For the principle of reliance to operate, a promise need not be definite enough to constitute an offer and form a contract were there consideration (see 4.2.5). In *Hoffman v. Red Owl Stores* (26 Wis. 2d 683, 133 N.W.2d 267 (1965)), Red Owl had been engaged in extended negotiations with Hoffman concerning his purchase of a franchise grocery store. At first Red Owl told Hoffman that the $18,000 he had would be sufficient. Hoffman sold his bakery and bought a small grocery for experience, then Red Owl told him to sell it and purchase a larger one, which he did. On Red Owl's recommendation, Hoffman also bought a lot and moved to another city. Finally, Red Owl escalated its demands to $24,000, then $26,000 and finally broke off negotiations. The court used § 90 of *Restatement of Contracts* to require Red Owl to compensate Hoffman.

It has been objected that this case is not the enforcement of a promise at all but a tort action, because there was no promise sufficient to establish a contract and the plaintiff received only the costs of reliance (Fried 1981, 24). But these contentions rest on the narrow concept of contract law as enforcing promises and are contrary to the jury and appellate court findings. The jury found that representations (commitments) were made by Red Owl and relied on by Hoffman, and the appellate court explicitly used *Restatement of Contracts* § 90. Commitments were made even if they were not sufficient to constitute a franchise contract.

The principle of reliance does not require that the action itself be detrimental. Instead, the loss could result from the failure to enforce the commitment. The point is illustrated by *Central London Property Trust Ltd. v. High Trees House Ltd.* (1947 K.B. 130 (1946)). High Trees leased a block of flats from Central London just prior to World War II and subleased flats, but the building was not full. Consequently, Central London agreed to accept payment of half of the rent. In 1945, the receiver of Central London sued for the full back rent. The court held that the promise was intended to create legal relations and the promisor knew that the promisee was going to act on it. Consequently, it held that back rent could not be collected, but as the promise was made because of the low tenancy rate in the flats, it did not extend beyond the time income from them became reasonably sufficient to pay the full rent on the lease.

This case does not directly involve detrimental reliance, because High Trees' reliance was beneficial to it. However, not enforcing the promise and permitting Central London to recover all back rent could have involved a loss for High Trees. If it did have the money, it might have made other uses of it (new investments, dividends, and so on) just as Mrs. Feinberg might have spent some of her savings. As there is no way accurately to determine this matter, it is reasonable to use the amount promised. However, in *High Trees* it is reasonable to take the promisor as foreseeing reliance only while rents were low, whereas in *Feinberg* the promisor should have foreseen reliance during retirement, that is, for the rest of Mrs. Feinberg's life.

4.2.4. *Gratuitous commitments*. Finally, none of the subordinate principles discussed this far covers zero sum interactions in which donors indicate that promises should be legally enforceable – part (b)(2) of the principle of enforceable commitments. Historically, such promises could be made enforceable by making them under seal, but in many American (but not English and Canadian) jurisdictions the use of the seal has been severely restricted or abandoned (Fuller and Eisenberg 1981, 16; U.C.C. § 2-203 comment 1; Chitty 1983, § 25; Fridman 1976, 188-90). As a result, in *Dougherty v. Salt* (227 N.Y. 200, 125 N.E. 94 (1919)), an aunt's promissory note payable to her eight year old nephew was held not enforceable. Rational persons might want to commit themselves legally to a future gratuitous transfer of property or services, and from an economic viewpoint even a completely gratuitous promise can increase value (Kronman and Posner 1979, 8) and thus be a plus sum interaction.

There are a number of arguments against enforcement of gratuitous promises (Eisenberg 1979, 3-5), but none of them are completely decisive. First, it is claimed that the injury from breach is slight, for if a promise were relied on it would be covered by the principle of reliance. Although the injury might be slight, a child promisee in a situation like *Dougherty* might be counting on the gift to attend college. The frustrated expectations can be as great as with any promise. Second, the promisor is not enriched at the promisee's expense. Again this is true. These first two points only show that, ignoring the psychological benefits to the promisor, the situation is not covered by the principles of past benefits and reliance. Third, it is claimed that no social interests are implicated in such promises. However, they can increase economic value, and there can be social interests in trust irrespective of reliance. Fourth, there are serious problems of proof, for people might simply fabricate claims. But this only requires limitations on the promises that will be enforced, not denying legal enforcement to all of them.

Two more serious objections arise even for formalized or written promises where the evidentiary problems are not great, namely, the difficulties created by improvidence and ingratitude (Eisenberg 1979, 13-16; Eisenberg 1982, 661). For example, suppose an aunt promises to pay her nephew $5,000 in two years, but when the time comes, due to unforeseeable losses, she will be unable to provide for herself or her family if she does. Alternatively, suppose the nephew has, without her consent, taken her automobile for a cross country trip and wrecked it. While European countries recognize improvidence and ingratitude as defenses, the contention is that common-law courts are not equipped to analyze difficult family situations. But this surely exaggerates the point. These concerns are quite similar to impossibility of performance and frustration of purpose (see 4.4.1), which courts do consider. Proof of financial hardship is addressed by courts all the time in child support and bankruptcy cases. Ingratitude is perhaps a more difficult point, but it should not cover such factors as a nephew's political or social views. It might be restricted to damage to property (an offset) or personal injury. At the weakest, one could even allow the promise to be revoked in writing for any reason prior to the time for performance; this would still permit enforcement of unrevoked promises.

(4-6) The principle of gratuitous commitments: a written and notarized commitment, stating that it is to be legally binding, should be enforceable, without consideration, past benefit, or reliance, to the extent appropriate in view of any changed circumstances. This principle is clearly acceptable from a promisee's viewpoint, and since one need not make a promise but can legally bind oneself if one wants, it is acceptable from a promisor's viewpoint. The restriction on enforcement 'in view of changed circumstances' permits courts to consider improvidence and ingratitude on the basis of individual cases. This principle basically corresponds to the Model Written Obligations Act (9C U.L.A. 378 (1943)). American law accords with this principle when the promise is of a charitable donation, although a mighty effort has been made to find consideration (*Allegheny College v. National Chautauqua Co. Bk.*, 246 N.Y. 369, 159 N.E. 173 (1927)). Moreover, Totten trusts and gifts by written instruments delivered to third parties (3.4.2) are similar to such enforceable commitments.

A distinct form of gratuitous commitment often arises when parties seek to modify a contract by agreement. The traditional common law implicitly if not explicitly viewed modification as equivalent to making a new or additional contract. The rule was that consideration is necessary for a promise made in modification – a gratuitous commitment is not enforceable (see *Stylk v. Myrick*, 170 Eng. Rep. 851 and 170 Eng. Rep. 1168 (1809) (seamen in Russia demand higher pay when two desert the ship); a consideration interpretation has been strongly criticized, Gilmore 1974, 22-28). In *Alaska Packers' Ass'n v. Domenico* (117 Fed. 99 (9th Cir. 1902)), Alaska Packers hired workers as sailors and fishermen to go to Alaska for the salmon season. Once in Alaska, the workers quit and refused to work until the superintendent promised them higher pay. On their return, the workers were paid the original wages and signed a release. They then sued for the extra pay promised in Alaska. The court held for Alaska Packers on the ground, among others, that there was no consideration for the extra pay. The workers only promised to do what they were already legally obligated to do, so they incurred no detriment and the packers no benefit.

Consideration is not appropriate for settling *Alaska Packers'*. Our principle of consideration would not resolve the issue, for it only holds that consideration provides a good, not a necessary, reason for enforcing a contract. Failure of consideration thus does not provide a sufficient ground for not enforcing a contract. The stronger traditional doctrine of consideration is not needed to settle the case. The sailors had Alaska Packers' superintendent over a barrel. If no promise was made, the fishing season was likely to be a total failure. In effect, the agreement was economically coerced (see Rest. 2d Contracts § 175).

There are cases where the request for modification by one party seems more reasonable. In *Gilbert Steel Ltd. v. University Constr. Ltd.* (67 D.L.R.3d 606 (Ont. 1976)), Gilbert Steel requested a price increase in steel being furnished for two apartment buildings under construction by University. An oral agreement was reached to modify the written contract, but a written agreement was never made. While University Construction accepted deliveries with invoices indicating the new prices, it did not pay in full. Gilbert Steel then sued for the remainder due. The court found for the defendants, holding that there was no consideration for the variation, and rejecting detrimental reliance as a legal basis for claims and on factual grounds.

Should modifications be enforceable? Contractors supplying goods assume risks of price increases unless they specifically contract otherwise. An alternative available to University Construction was to refuse to agree to the price increase and, if Gilbert defaulted, to purchase the steel elsewhere and sue for the difference in price. As the apartment buildings were only partially constructed at the time, this alternative might have involved a delay in construction. However, it is doubtful that the delay would have been significant; there is no showing that the needed steel was not available from other sources. By agreeing to the change, University seems to fall under the principle of reliance so its promise should be enforced. The court, of course, did not accept the principle of reliance. Moreover, it claimed that Gilbert could not show detrimental reliance. The reason is that had University refused to pay the higher price, Gilbert would have been liable for the increased costs of steel University purchased elsewhere. Thus, such modifications do involve gratuitous commitments.

(4-7) The principle of modifications: good faith modifications of contracts regardless of consideration, past benefit, or reliance should be enforceable. One has a good reason to accept this principle. Many modifications are routinely made by businesspersons without significant cost to either party, for example, modifying time and place of delivery. Also, on a relational view of contracts (see 4.0), modifications occur in the context of ongoing business dealings between parties. If one agrees to a modification in favor of the other party in this contract, a modification might be made in one's favor in a subsequent one. In short, neither party need be worse off, and both might benefit in the long run. One can at least partially protect oneself from unacceptable modifications by refusing to agree. If there is excessive economic pressure, the modification would not be in good faith. The requirement of good faith is discussed below (4.3.7); here we need only note that it rules out more than extortion and coercion.

It has been suggested that the chief goal of the law should be to enforce voluntary modifications and not to enforce involuntary ones (Hillman 1982, 681). But that is too narrow a basis for refusing to enforce modifications, unless one takes an exceptionally broad view of coercion and includes any exploitation of unfair advantage within it. Although the Uniform Commercial Code does not require consideration for modifications in contracts for the sale of goods, it does impose a duty of good faith requiring a "legitimate commercial reason" for the modification (U.C.C. § 2-209(1) and comment 2). The *Restatement (Second) of Contracts* (§ 89) enforces modifications if fair and equitable in view of unanticipated circumstances or required by justice in view of reliance on the promise, but this is too restricted a principle (Hillman 1982, 692-702). There is no reason to require that reasons for modification stem from unanticipated circumstances. Detrimental reliance need not arise in contract modifications, and in any case, it is covered by the principle of reliance.

4.2.5. Offer and acceptance. The concepts of offer and acceptance are most at home in reciprocal or bargained for contracts. One party makes an offer, and its acceptance by the other party creates a contract. They are less at home in unbargained for 'unilateral contracts' in which only one person makes a commitment and the other performs an act, for example, where a reward is offered for the return of an article. The negotiations that precede a contract often make it unclear when a proposal constitutes an offer.

An offer should be definite enough so that both parties know generally what the deal is. One would not rationally accept being bound by contracts when one did not know what one was committed to or was to receive in return. Without such general knowledge, one cannot determine whether it is likely to be beneficial. Problems can arise when the commitments are not definite. A simple and frequent instance arises in having a car serviced. Suppose Jason takes her car to a garage and says that she wants an oil change and lubrication, and that the motor has been stalling and she wants it checked. Has Jason agreed to a $39 inspection that includes brakes, radiator, and other items in addition to the motor? Work costing twice the expected price does not appear to be part of the deal. Not all the terms need to be specified, provided the other terms are reasonably expectable so that one is not unduly surprised. Courts often have a sufficient basis for filling in unspecified terms (U.C.C. § 2-204(c)). Often they can fill in even the price on the basis of the reasonable value in the market. Consequently, no particular term must necessarily be specified in all contracts.

(4-8) The principle of offers: offers should involve the communication of a reasonably definite commitment in return for a reasonably definite act or commitment. The paragraph above explains what a reasonably definite commitment is and why it should be required. Obviously, a commitment must also be communicated, or else one cannot evaluate the deal. A commitment can be communicated by words or conduct. For example, even if she does not sign a service order, by leaving her car at the service station, Jason indicates commitment to having it serviced. If the offeree does not receive the communication, for example, a letter never arrives, there is no offer. Thus, an offer should take effect on its receipt (*Caldwell v. Cline*, 109 W.Va. 553, 156 S.E. 55 (1930)).

The aspect of commitment by the offeror is crucial. One could not accept being bound to a contract when one did not commit oneself to a deal. A statement that indicates further discussions are necessary does not constitute a commitment. A seller of property who writes to a prospective purchaser giving a description and saying "If you are really interested, you will have to decide fast, as I expect to have a buyer in the next week or so" has not made a commitment even if the terms are definite (*Lonergan v.*

Scolnick, 129 Cal. App. 2d 179, 276 P.2d 8 (Dist. Ct. App. 1954)). The sentence indicates that the seller is not committing him or herself to the sale, and the usual practice in real estate is for the purchaser to make a written offer. Most newspaper ads or form letters sent to a number of people are not offers but merely quotations of prices inviting offers.

More troublesome situations arise when a contract is sent but not signed, and the covering letter indicates that the recipient should sign and return it whereupon the sender will sign it. The question is whether the sender has made a commitment to sign the agreement. If there is such a commitment, then an offer has been made. If a commitment to sign is not made, then the sender reserves the right to change his or her mind. This problem arises in many situations, for example, contracts of employment and for publishing books (such as this one). One of the major difficulties is the risk to which one can be exposed. For example, suppose State U. sends a contract to Professor Kemper signed by the Dean of the College. The contract states that it is not valid unless signed by the President; and the covering letter says for Professor Kemper to sign all three copies and return them, a completed copy will then be returned to him. Does he have a contract? It may be three months or more before he receives a completed copy, and meanwhile he must resign his current position.

A central question is who should bear the risk of the nonexistence of a contract. If the exchange of signed copies is expected to be reasonably quick, then it is reasonable to leave it with the recipient (*Schenck v. Francis*, 33 App. Div. 2d 91, 305 N.Y.S.2d 217 (1969); *aff'd*, 26 N.Y.2d 466, 260 N.E.2d 493 (1970)). However, if the risk is significant and the recipient must begin performance before receiving the countersigned contract, then the risk should be with the sender. The principle of reliance will not help here if the original letter was not an offer or commitment. However, the same reasoning as supported that principle supports construing the letter as an offer. In the position of Professor Kemper, one would not agree to surrendering employment and waiting months for the other party to accept. Courts tend to analyze such cases by whether the writing merely confirms a previous agreement; if it does, then a contract exists; if not, then there is no contract. The risk analysis is a better approach when assignment of the risk is not clearly indicated.

Two major questions concern acceptance. One is when an acceptance takes effect, and the other is whether an acceptance can modify any terms of the offer. The former question is more easily handled. The choice is between when the acceptance is sent and when it is received. With rapid telecommunications, there is little difference between the two. The issue primarily arises when slower methods of communication are used, such as the mail. In Canada, it usually takes a week or more for a letter to travel across the country (or often even a province). In either case, one party will be bound for a while without knowing it. The better rule is that an acceptance takes effect on its sending (*Morrison v. Thoelke*, 155 So. 2d 889 (Fla. Ct. App. 1963)). This rule involves only one communication for both parties to know that a contract exists, from the acceptor to the offeror. The other rule requires two communications before both parties know that a contract exists, because the offeror has to notify the offeree that the acceptance has been received. There is no reason for the added delay and trouble involved.

Whether an acceptance can modify terms is more difficult. The traditional common-law rule required acceptance of the exact terms of the offer (*Poel v. Brunswick-Balke-Collender Co.*, 216 N.Y. 310, 110 N.E. 619 (1915)). Any changes constituted rejection and the making of a counteroffer. The problem became acute with the development of printed forms for sale and acceptance. Often an acceptance form contains conditions that significantly modify the offer, for example, disclaiming all warranties. If the offer is accepted and different or additional terms are merely proposed for altering the contract, then a contract should exist. The acceptor has indicated willingness to accept the original terms, and the offeror can either agree to the changes or not. In effect, one has the elements of a contract modification.

The difficult situations are when the offeree makes acceptance expressly conditional on the offeror's assent to changes (including additions). A test should be whether the changes are such that a reasonable offeror would probably not agree to them. If a reasonable person in the offeror's position would not accept them (they materially alter it or the offeror has expressly limited acceptance to the terms offered), then the acceptance should not be binding. Otherwise, as an offeror one would be stuck with unreasonable commitments foisted on one by another party, which is contrary to the principle of transferability's (3-3) requirement that transfers be voluntary.

This leaves those cases in which a reasonable offeror might or might not accept the changes. The choice is between presuming a contract to exist unless the offeror indicates the unacceptability of the conditions, or presuming it has not been accepted and does not exist. The latter position, like that of making the time of acceptance depend on receipt by the offeror, requires another communication for conclusion of the contract. As the offeror is the one who stands to lose if the changes are not acceptable, it is appropriate to place the burden of objecting on the offeror. Thus, these changes can be presumed to be binding unless the offeror promptly communicates an objection to them. As an offeror, one can always reject the changes, and one can avoid any possibility of them by stating in an offer that no changes are acceptable.

These conclusions basically correspond to those in the Uniform Commercial Code (§ 2-207) and the *Restatement (Second) Contracts* (§ 59). It differs, however, by not distinguishing between different and merely additional terms. Since the offeror can object, this distinction is not relevant. It thus avoids the complex problem of what happens when the terms differ but the parties act as though a contract exists (see *C. Itoh (America) Inc. v. Jordan Int'l Co.*, 552 F.2d 1228 (7th Cir. 1977)). *(4-9) The principle of acceptances: acceptances should take effect when sent to offerors provided that if they are expressly conditional on changes, (a) the changes are reasonable and (b) offerors have a reasonable time to object to them.* By the test above, changes are unreasonable if no reasonable person in the position of the offeror would agree to them.

The usual offer can be legally revoked at any time before acceptance, although a revocation, like an offer, takes effect only when received (*Henthorn v. Fraser*, [1892] 2 Ch. 27 (C.A.)). This rule can lead to absurd or unseemly situations, such as the offeree standing at the door willing to pay off a debt and the offeror inside shouting that the offer of discounted payment is withdrawn (*Petterson v. Pattberg*, 248 N.Y. 86, 161 N.E. 428 (1928)). A way out of such situations is for offers to be made 'firm' or open for a definite period of time. Traditional common law did not permit firm offers unless something was paid or given for them – an option contract was made. The classic case is *Dickinson v. Dodds* ([1876] 2 Ch. D. 463 (C.A.)). On Wednesday, Dodds gave Dickinson a note agreeing to sell property for a stated price and wrote that the offer would be held open until 9:00 AM on Friday. On Thursday, learning that Dodds was offering or agreeing to sell the property to another person, Dickinson delivered a note of acceptance to Dodds' place of residence, which Dodds did not receive. At 7:00 AM Friday morning, Dickinson had a duplicate note given to Dodds, who replied that it was too late for he had already sold the property on Thursday. Dickinson sued to enforce the contract, but the Court of Appeal held that Dodds was free to sell the property before Friday. Lord Justice Mellish thought it absurd to hold that the offer was binding, for there was no simultaneious agreement or meeting of minds to form a contract.

There is no good reason to accept such a rule, for it limits one's possibilities of interaction. As one commentator has noted, the rule implies that 'You may have until Friday to accept and I also promise that I will not revoke the offer before Friday' means the same as 'You may have until Friday to accept but I may revoke the offer at any time before acceptance' (Gilmore 1974, 30). Now it may be puzzling why a person would want to make an irrevocable offer, but if a person does, surely the law should enable the person to do so. One has no reason to accept such a limitation on one's powers to make irrevocable offers, since it is always in one's control not to make them. The Uniform Commercial Code (§ 2-205) recognizes this possibility for the sale of goods, and there is no reason to limit it to the sale of goods. Firm offers should be allowed, provided they are made in writing (see N.Y. General Obligations Law § 5-1109 (McKinney 1978)). The proviso is to prevent disputes and fraud.

In the construction business, a problem arises as to whether revocable offers, firm offers, or actual contracts are made. Often primary contractors submit bids on the basis of offers from subcontractors. Suppose the subcontractor makes a mistake and submits a bid that is too low by half, but the primary contractor has no reason to believe there is a mistake and relies on the offer in making its bid. Should the subcontractor be allowed to revoke its offer after the primary contractor's bid has been accepted or should the subcontractor be deemed to have made a firm offer? To allow revocation makes the primary contractor responsible for the accuracy of the subcontractor's bids. As a primary contractor, one has no reason to to assume the risk of other's errors, and as a subcontractor one should be willing to assume the risk of one's own errors to avoid assuming those of others. Thus, a subcontractor should be held to the bid (*Drennan v. Star Paving Co.*, 51 Cal. 2d 409, 333 P.2d 757 (1958)). Here, reliance should turn an offer into a firm offer, just as it should turn an invitation to deal into an offer in the hypothetical case of Professor Kemper.

Should the reliance of the primary contractor on a subcontractor's bid be considered acceptance making a contract? This is justifiable when the primary contractor knows or should know that the subcontractor knows its bid was used (in effect, acceptance is communicated). Both parties then receive a benefit – the subcontractor assurance of the work, and the primary contractor assurance of a price. Otherwise, the subcontractor is bound but the primary contractor is not. The contract is conditional on the primary contractor receiving the prime contract. Some courts have arrived at the same results on other grounds (*Industrial Elec.-Seattle, Inc. v. Bosko*,

67 Wash. 2d 783, 410 P.2d 10 (1966)). As silence cannot be construed as acceptance, when the primary contractor does not inform the subcontractor of use of its bid, a contract would not normally exist. Still, if the primary contractor knows or should know that the subcontractor is aware of the use of its bid, perhaps because of a public filing requirement, a contract should exist. At least one court has found a statutory basis for holding the primary contractor liable in such a case (*Southern California Acoustics Co. v. C. V. Holder, Inc.*, 71 Cal. 2d 719, 79 Cal. Rptr. 319, 456 P.2d 975 (1969)).

DUTIES, DEFECTS, AND DEFENSES

4.3.0. *Introduction.* Because of the reciprocal character of most contracts, it is not possible to separate clearly duties and defenses; the failure of the other party to fulfill a duty can often be the basis for a contract action or a defense to one. Mistake or incapacity can be a basis for a lawsuit or a defense to one. We begin with duties arising under a contract, that is, what is enforceable as part of the contract. Then we consider defects in the formation of contracts – mistake, incapacity, or lack of a written memorandum. If there is a defect, either no enforceable contract exists (it is void) or one party can cancel it (it is voidable). Lastly, we consider duties that are independent of the contract, most of which concern the bargaining process. Failures to fulfill these duties have effects similar to defects.

4.3.1. *Types of terms.* The duties under a contract depend on its 'terms' or provisions, so an understanding of contractual duties requires an understanding of the types of terms. Contractual terms are classified in different ways for different purposes, and there is no general agreement on the terminology of these classifications. There are three main bases for classifying terms: indicating (1) how they came to be, (2) the effects of their not being fulfilled, and (3) whether a party made a commitment to their being fulfilled.

Terms can be classified by their origin as 'express', 'implied in fact', or 'implied in law' ('constructive'). Express terms are those stated by the parties, while implied terms are read in by the courts. Terms implied in fact are supposed to follow from or be presupposed by the express ones, while those implied in law are simply legally required. The principles of transferability (3-3) and freedom of property (3-8) support contractors being free to set the terms of their contract. Although express terms constitute the primary source of duties under a contract, through the courts society has always imposed or prohibited some terms, and during the twentieth century this practice has increased. Often, but not always, the parties can explicitly reject these legal requirements and thus still set their own terms.

Terms can also be distinguished by the consequences of their nonfulfillment. If some terms are not fulfilled, then the other party does not have to fulfill duties; the contract is at an end. If other terms are not fulfilled, the other party must still fulfill duties but has a claim for damages. In English and Canadian law, it is well established usage to call the former 'conditions' and the latter 'warranties' (Chitty 1983, § 746; Davies 1977, 54; Fridman 1976, 268-69). American legal use of 'condition' generally conforms to this, except for a dispute over whether it refers to a contractual term or a fact. Some authors reserve 'condition' for the state of affairs that fulfills a term rather than the term itself (Corbin 1951, 583; Rest. 2d Contracts § 224 Comment a and Ill. 1). One could speak of terms of condition, but there need be no confusion if an expression is classified according to the effect of its referent. In fact, 'condition' is probably better applied to the term than its referent, since 'condition' is used to indicate a logical relation. There is no standard American word for terms that are not conditions; 'warranty' is used variously in American law for terms that in English terminology are conditions or warranties. The English terminology is used here.

Suppose Lefler contracts to buy Mayer's boat for $2,500, and Mayer assures her that the boat does not leak. If Mayer fails to deliver the boat to her, Lefler need not pay. Delivery of the boat is a condition of Lefler's duty to pay. The logical structure of Lefler's duty is 'if X, then duty Y'. If after receiving the boat Lefler discovers that it has a small leak, she can sue for damages. Mayer's commitment that it does not leak is a warranty. It is not a requirement that must be fulfilled before Lefler has an unconditional duty to pay, but it might be used to offset the amount to be paid.

Unfortunately, even express terms rarely come neatly labeled as conditions or warranties. Obviously, conditions are the more important terms and warranties the less important ones (Davies 1977, 54), or conditions are vital to the contract while warranties are subsidiary (Atiyah 1981a, 148). In determining whether terms are conditions or warranties, courts often consider either the effect of their nonfulfillment on a party or the intention of the parties at the time of contracting. Often, the parties have no clear intentions, and, of course, the seriousness of the nonfulfillment would affect their intentions. The best that can be done is to clearly frame the issue.

(4-10) The principle of conditions and warranties: if a reasonable person in the promisee's position at the time of contracting would not have agreed to fulfill duties rather than adjust them if a given term was not fulfilled, then it should be a condition; otherwise it should be a warranty. Although this principle is definitional, use of the classification affects underlying duties. It prescribes when some duties of the other party should be dependent or independent of the term. The notion of adjusting duties is meant to cover paying a lower price or some other change such as time of performance. The failure of a condition makes it unreasonable for a party to complete the contract, because that party cannot expect it to be beneficial even if some other terms are modified.

The third classification of terms is by whether a party made a commitment to their fulfillment. The fulfillment of some terms is beyond the powers of the parties. For example, a contract for crop insurance might make the insurer's duty to pay conditional on the crop being destroyed by hail. Destruction of the crop by hail is a condition, but no one made a commitment to its fulfillment. In contrast, parties make commitments to the fulfillment of some terms. In this chapter, we have generally used 'commitment' instead of 'promise' because the law enforces more than what are ordinarily considered promises; it enforces commitments. In some contracts, people commit themselves to the existence of certain contemporary states of affairs or facts. If Mayer tells Lefler that the boat he is offering to sell is fourteen feet long, Mayer commits himself to the truth of the statement, to the boat being that long. Other commitments are to future states of affairs, usually that the person will do something or bring something about. These can be called promises proper. For example, Mayer might promise to deliver the boat within one week. One is generally liable for all one's commitments in a contract.

Commitments of fact and promises can be either conditions or warranties. The various possibilities are shown in the following table with examples of terms from the hypothetical contract between Lefler and Mayer.

COMMITMENTS

	Fact	Promise
Conditions	boat exists	to deliver
Warranties	boat's length	delivery date

The problems of classifying terms leads to an important point about the so-called objective interpretation of contracts. It is often said that courts enforce the intent of the parties, what they agreed to. But Justice Holmes said, "The law has nothing to do with the actual state of the parties' minds. In contract, as elsewhere, it must go by externals, and judge parties by their conduct" (Holmes [1881] 1963, 242). Much confusion results from failing to note that 'objective' and 'subjective' are relative terms with different meanings in different contexts.

First, courts must interpret what the contract is, so the interpretation is objective in the sense that the meaning is what others take it to be, not what the parties take it to be. In this sense, the very nature of a court case (decision by a third party) requires objectivity in the sense of judgment by other persons. Second, there is a difference between trying to determine what the parties meant and determining what someone else would have meant. Courts are concerned with the former, and in this sense their interpretation is subjective. Third, courts must primarily base their interpretation on what the parties said and did (objective), not what they thought but did not express (subjective). Contrary to Holmes's comment, they are concerned with the parties' states of minds (cf. also Hall 1960, 152-55, 163). If Mayer sincerely said the boat did not leak, then Mayer thought or believed it did not. Whether Mayer was sincere or honest is also based on what Mayer said and did. If Neal testifies that she rode in the boat with Mayer the day before and she showed Mayer that a small amount of water leaked in, then one has reason to believe that Mayer's statement to Lefler was not sincere.

Fourth, courts must often address issues or points that the parties did not consider; they must fill in missing terms implied in fact. Then the question is what reasonable persons in the parties' positions would have agreed to. Even here, the question is not what term some abstract reasonable person would have agreed to (objective), but what reasonable persons in the parties' positions and with their particular interests might reasonably have agreed to (subjective). This subjective interpretation amounts to interpreting the contract so that the parties could mutually expect it to be beneficial. For example, a person who takes a car to a garage for minor repairs and has a second car for use in the meantime might agree to wait three days for the repairs to be completed. A traveling salesperson who has no other means of transportation would not agree, because the time delay would be too costly. If the time for repairs is not specified and the garage is aware of the person's situation, different interpretations of a reasonable time for repair would be appropriate depending on the situation. All this is mere common sense used by courts; only commentators become confused by asking whether interpretation is objective or subjective, concerned with the parties' states of mind or objective facts, without clearly specifying the senses involved.

An extreme expression of an objective approach to contracts is the 'parol evidence rule'. This rule prohibits extrinsic evidence to add to, vary, or contradict a written contract which 'integrates' the agreement (says it contains all the terms). The point is that the written agreement provides the best evidence of the meaning of the parties. Although sometimes called a rule of evidence, it is actually a substantive rule, for even if the excluded evidence is introduced at trial, it is to be ignored (Calamari and Perillo 1977, 113). However, the rule has become so riddled with exceptions that prominent English commentators consider it practically obsolete (Atiyah 1981a, 163; Treitel 1979, 143). It still has importance in American law (Rest. 2d Contracts § 213).

There is little reason to keep the rule. In most interactions, even a written contract is not considered by the parties to be more than a statement of their agreement. Rarely are all the elements of an agreement reduced to writing, as is evidenced by the many cases in which courts must find terms implied in fact. Although a written agreement is better evidence than oral testimony or other evidence, that is surely a matter which a trier of fact can weigh. However, complete abolition of the rule would mean that parties could never bind themselves to a written contract that definitely settles the terms negotiated between them. In complex negotiations between businesspersons, that is sometimes desirable. Nevertheless, many printed forms contain a statement that they integrate all the terms and are signed by people without realizing the legal implications. Consequently, the rule should be limited to contracts where a written statement of integration is made, explained, and separately signed. Even then, it is apt to be abused.

4.3.2. *Implied terms.* Implied terms serve two main functions. First, as we have seen, the express terms can imply or presuppose certain other terms. Parties cannot be expected to state expressly all the implications of the terms of their contracts. Terms implied in fact fulfill this function. Second, if some terms are set by law, then the parties need not negotiate over them or bother to incorporate them explicitly into the contract. This is especially useful where there is a standard practice in a commercial setting. In both instances, parties are saved the time and expense of settling terms. Usually, if they wish to do so, the parties can expressly vary from legally implied terms.

(4-11) The principle of implied terms: in the absence of clear evidence parties intended otherwise, if necessary to settle a case, terms to which reasonable people in the parties' positions would agree should be implied.. By 'the parties' positions' is meant 'with their interests in the particular social-economic circumstances'. The first part of the principle allows parties freely to set terms. It promotes contractual freedom by not authorizing judges to override the agreement of the parties and not licensing them to insert terms not necessary for resolving the dispute. It thus promotes maximal freedom of transfer compatible with the judicial function of dispute resolution. The main part of the principle imposes reasonable conditions for persons in the circumstances. It promotes maximization of wealth, because reasonable parties would agree to terms only if they could still expect to benefit from the contract. By courts reading in such terms when necessary to settle a case, parties are saved the time and expense of negotiating and specifying them, unless they want terms contrary to the usual implication.

Examples of terms commonly implied in law are the 'merchantability' and fitness for particular purpose of goods for sale. Merchantability applies to sales by persons in business and generally means that the goods are of standard quality (U.C.C. § 2-314). People would not want to bother putting such a condition on a sales slip everytime they bought clothes or other items. But of course, they might want to waive such a requirement, for example, in purchasing floor samples "as is" (U.C.C. § 2-316(3)(a)). Fitness for a particular purpose applies to any seller, whether or not in the business, who knows that the buyer wants the goods for a particular purpose. Thus, if Lefler told Mayer that she wanted the boat for a particular purpose which required speed of at least twenty-five miles per hour, then Mayer would impliedly warrant that the boat would go that fast. As we saw in 3.3.2, similar warranties of habitability and quality construction should apply to leased premises and new buildings.

A further question is whether there are any terms that the law should not permit parties to include or exclude even expressly. The principles of freedom and implied terms support parties being able to include or exclude any terms they desire. A background assumption of contractual freedom is that people have alternatives; that they are free to make the best deal they can among a number of alternatives. To the extent one lacks alternatives, one lacks freedom. In modern economic conditions, that background assumption is not always true. If Odell wants to take a train from Toronto to Montreal, there is only one passenger railroad, Via Rail. Suppose Via includes a term ('exemption clause') on the back of the ticket exempting it from any liability for damage to baggage or personal injury. Is it reasonable for Odell to agree to this term? "Nobody in his senses would agree to a contract which permitted the other party to commit negligence with impunity, unless, perhaps, by doing so he were to get the goods or services offered at a cheaper price" (Atiyah 1981a, 168). Is Odell to stand at the wicket and negotiate with the clerk over the term?

These considerations suggest another principle limiting that of implied terms. *(4-12) The principle of required conditions: if one party has no reasonable opportunity to choose, the minimal contractual conditions to which rational persons would agree were there reasonable alternatives should be required by law and the parties prohibited from changing them unless they can show that it is to the advantage of both to do so.* This principle does not require that all rational persons would agree to the terms whatever their situation, only that most would do so in most situations. It sets minimal conditions that almost everyone can be expected to want. For example, airlines are required to provide basic liability in case of accidental death. People who want greater protection can purchase additional flight insurance. Obviously, a number of people want more than the required amount, since companies make a profit selling flight insurance.

The principle uses rational persons (1.2) rather than reasonable persons in the parties' positions as the principle of implied terms does. This means that idiosyncratic interests, whether rational or not, and special circumstances are ignored. However, the principle permits parties to avoid the requirements in such cases, although it does require a showing that both parties benefit, for example, a passenger receives a lower fare (see Rest. 2d Contracts § 195(2)(b) and Comment a). In England, the Unfair Contract Terms Act 1977 simply bans exemption clauses for negligent personal injury or death (§ (2)(1)) and for merchantability of goods sold to consumers (§ (6)(2)(a)). Other exemption clauses must meet a condition of reasonableness, and one of the tests of reasonableness in sales is whether the other party received a benefit or had an opportunity to contract with someone else without that term.

Perhaps the most difficult aspect of using the principle of required conditions arises in interpreting 'no reasonable opportunity to choose' and 'reasonable alternatives'. So far we have discussed the principle in the context of 'contracts of adhesion' – standard form contracts made between consumers and virtual monopolies. In these situations, there are no market alternatives to the supplier. One might object that Odell had alternatives to Via Rail; he could have flown or gone by bus. But these are not directly competing services in the way alternative beauty shops are, although they are closer alternatives than there is for local telephone service. The range of alternatives can vary, and judgment is needed in determining whether reasonable alternatives exist.

The mere existence of reasonable alternatives does not necessarily imply that a person has a reasonable opportunity to choose. A person's characteristics or circumstances might also prevent a reasonable opportunity to choose. Indeed, one feature of high pressure sales tactics is to prevent a person making reasonable choices among alternatives, for example, by claiming that there are other buyers and the item might be sold if one waits to look elsewhere. Thus, there are two elements to determining whether a person has or had a reasonable opportunity to choose – the availability of competitive sources of similar goods or services and the person's particular situation. If competitive alternatives existed and a contractor did not obtain the minimal conditions a rational person would accept, then there is good reason to suspect that the contractor's particular situation prevented an opportunity for reasonable choice. However, the contractor might have had a reasonable opportunity and simply made an unreasonable decision. Freedom involves the freedom to make mistaken choices; protective intervention would go beyond the bounds of a justifiable paternalism (Bayles 1978, ch. 6; but see Kennedy 1982, 638-49).

For the sale of goods, the Uniform Commercial Code in effect implements the principle of required conditions by permitting courts to refuse to enforce terms or whole contracts which were unconscionable at the time the contract was made (§ 2-302). Because 'unconscionable' is not defined, courts are empowered to exercise a broad discretion to reject or modify contracts. Even the commentary to the section does little to help elucidate its meaning, saying that such clauses are those "that are so one-sided as to be unconscionable" (which defines the term by itself) and that the point is to prevent "oppression and unfair surprise" (U.C.C. § 2-302 comment 1). By another section (U.C.C. § 2-719(3)), exemptions from liability are also often found to be unconscionable, and exemption from liability for personal injury is deemed prima facie unconscionable.

In a number of cases, courts have required that unconscionability involve no meaningful choice and quite unfavorable terms (*Patterson v. Walker-Thomas Furniture Co.* 277 A.2d 111 (D.C. Ct. App. 1971); *Jones v. Star*

Credit Corp., 59 Misc. 2d 189, 298 N.Y.S.2d 264 (Sup. Ct. 1969); *Williams v. Walker-Thomas Furniture Co.*, 350 F.2d 445 (D.C. Cir. 1965)). These amount to requiring minimal conditions when a party has no reasonable opportunity to choose among alternatives. Perhaps one of the clearest cases of unconscionability is *Frostifresh Corp. v. Reynoso* (52 Misc. 2d 26, 274 N.Y.S.2d 757 (Dist. Ct. 1966)). A door to door salesman for Frostifresh sold the Reynosos a refrigerator freezer for $900 plus $245.88 credit charges, although the unit cost Frostifresh only $348. While the negotiations were in Spanish, the contract was in English. Moreover, when Reynoso said that he could not afford it because he had only one week left on his job, the salesman suggested that it would not cost them anything because of commissions they would make on sales to friends and neighbors. Thus, because the Reynosos could not understand the language of the contract and were orally misled by the salesman, although alternatives were available, they had no reasonable opportunity for choice.

Some commentators distinguish between procedural and substantive unconscionability (Leff 1967; Epstein 1979b, 94). The lack of a reasonable opportunity to choose is a procedural aspect of contract formation, while the onerousness of the terms is substantive. They deny that substantive unconscionability alone should be sufficient to negate a clause or contract. We have suggested that lack of minimal terms suggests but does not always imply a lack of reasonable opportunity to choose. Some courts have been inclined to deduce a lack of meaningful choice from grossly unfavorable terms (*Jones v. Star Credit Corp.*, 59 Misc. 2d 189, 298 N.Y.S.2d 264 (Sup. Ct. 1969)). Other courts have simply said that a grossly unfair purchase price alone is sufficient for finding unconscionability (*Toker v. Westerman*, 113 N.J. Super. 452, 274 A.2d 78 (Dist. Ct. 1970)). The principle of required terms would not support that result; further evidence of lack of opportunity for reasonable choice is required. However, grossly unequal bargaining power can be sufficient for finding a lack of reasonable opportunity. In particular, a franchisee dealing with a franchisor might have little opportunity for reasonable choice, as where a franchisor simply presents a contract waiving liability for its negligence to a poorly educated person without counsel (*Weaver v. American Oil Co.*, 257 Ind. 458, 276 N.E.2d 144 (1971)). This would be particularly true if other franchisors of that type had similar conditions.

Despite the unease with which it was originally greeted, some possible excesses by courts, and the criticism of some commentators, the doctrine of unconscionability has become embedded in American law (Rest. 2d

Contracts § 208; U.C.C.C. § 5.108; Rest. 2d Property § 5.). The principle
of required terms supports this incorporation.

4.3.3. *Mistake.* The first defect in contract formation we shall consider is
mistake. Earlier we noted that an offer need not specify all the terms, but
it must provide enough so that the promisee has a general idea to what he
or she is agreeing (4.2.5). For a contract reasonably to be mutually expected
to be beneficial, both parties need to know what they are getting into.
Expectations of benefit are not well-founded when due to mistake the
parties do not understand the conditions.

Mistakes can be divided into mutual (both parties) and unilateral (one
party) mistakes. Some authors divide mutual mistakes into two categories.
Unfortunately, American and English terminology does not coincide, and
'mutual' is used by each for a subclass of two party mistakes. 'Misunderstandings' (American) or 'mutual' (English) mistakes occur when the parties
do not mean the same thing. 'Mutual' (American) or 'common' (English)
mistakes occur when both parties mean the same thing, but their assumption is false. For clarity, we use 'misunderstanding' and 'common' for
these subclasses and 'mutual' for the general term including both.

It is not clear that the distinction between misunderstandings and common mistakes makes much difference (Fridman 1976, 84). *Raffles v. Wi-
chelhaus* (159 Eng. Rep. 375 (Ex. Ch. 1864)) would be classified as a
misunderstanding. The plaintiff contracted to sell the defendant 125 bales
of cotton "to arrive ex 'Peerless' from Bombay." The plaintiff meant a ship
named "Peerless" to sail in December, but the defendant meant another
ship named "Peerless" due to sail in October. When the cotton arrived, the
defendant refused to accept it and the plaintiff sued. The court held that
because there was no agreement on the term, no contract existed.

Another famous case, *Sherwood v. Walker* (66 Mich. 568, 33 N.W. 919
(1887)) would be classified as a common mistake. Sherwood sued Walker
to deliver a cow sold to him. The defendant had told the plaintiff that the
cow was probably barren. An arrangement was made to purchase the cow
for $0.055 a pound, which was the going price for a barren cow; a fertile
cow would sell for about ten times that. Before the plaintiff came to get the
cow, the defendant discovered that it was with calf and refused to deliver
it. The court held that there was no contract, because of the mistake about
the fertility of the cow. Had it been known that the cow was not barren,
there would not have been a contract. The result is the same as in *Raffles.*

This case has been strongly criticized. The main line of argument is that one should consider the allocation of risk in the contract or how the parties would have allocated the risk had they foreseen the contingency (Posner 1977, 73; Swan 1980, 232). The point is to decrease the costs of mistakes, and this generally occurs by placing the burden on the best avoider of mistakes (Kronman 1978a, 4). Walker owned the cow and so had the best opportunity to determine whether it was fertile; moreover, Walker told Sherwood that the cow was probably barren. Thus, it seems that Walker assumed the risk of the cow being barren.

Risk analysis does not provide as clear an answer to *Sherwood* as might be thought. At the time, it was not possible to determine with certainty whether a cow was barren. Had Walker thought that there was a significant chance the cow was fertile, he would probably have demanded a higher price – somewhere between those for barren and fertile cows. A price term can be continuously varied to reflect differences in the probability of a contingency. Thus, a court can use the price to help determine the assignment of risk in a contract (cf. Rest. 2d Contracts § 351 Comment f). If the price is low, then the parties assume that some desirable feature is lacking, but if the price is high, then they assume that the feature is present. If the price is in a middle range, then one can assume that the risk was allocated between the parties. In *Frigaliment Importing Co. v. B.N.S. Int'l Sales Corp.* (190 F. Supp. 116 (S.D.N.Y. 1960)), it was found that due to the low price, the buyer should have known the seller did not mean a high grade of chicken. Alternatively, one might say that the buyer assumed the risk of the chicken being low grade, even though the seller was clearly in a better position to determine risk. This case is probably best considered to be like *Raffles* where the parties did not agree on the same terms.

Mutual mistakes usually result in no contract, unless one party knew or should have known what the other meant or one party has assumed the risk as perhaps in *Frigaliment*. In *McRae v. Commonwealth Disposals Comm'n* (84 C.L.R. 377 (Aust. 1951)), the defendants sold the plaintiff salvage rights to a tanker wrecked on a reef. In fact, no such tanker existed. The court held that the defendants had committed themselves to the existence of the tanker, and as the plaintiff would not have made the deal without the tanker existing, it was a condition of the contract. Consequently, the plaintiff was allowed damages for breach of contract. (Due to the difficulty of calculating expected profits, the court only awarded compensation for expenses incurred.)

Unilateral mistakes are normally the responsibility of the mistaken party. We have already mentioned this matter in connection with subcontractors' bids to primary contractors (4.2.5). However, in some situations the matter is otherwise. First, contractors are sometimes relieved of the burden of mistaken bids if the consequences of enforcement would be unconscionable and 'rescission' (voiding the contract, see 4.4.2) would not impose a significant burden on the other party (Calamari and Perillo 1977, 306; *Kenneth E. Curran, Inc. v. State*, 106 N.H. 558, 215 A.2d 702 (1965); *Crenshaw County Hosp. Bd. v. St. Paul Fire and Marine Ins. Co.*, 411 F.2d 213 (5th Cir. 1969)). These cases usually involve clerical errors in computing bids that are discovered shortly after bids are opened. Second, if a party knew or should have known of the other's mistake, then liability falls on the party that knew of the mistake (Rest. 2d Contracts § 20(2); *White v. Berenda Mesa Water Dist.*, 7 Cal. App. 3d 894, 87 Cal. Rptr. 338 (1970)). The mistaken party can either rescind or enforce the contract. This latter frequently occurs when people purchase goods under false names. The seller wants its meaning enforced so that title to the goods did not pass to the fraudulent purchaser and it can recover from a third party purchaser. However, our principle of the good faith purchaser ((3-11) in 3.3.1) already supports the third party purchaser retaining the goods.

(4-13) The principle of mistake: a contract should not be enforceable against a party who has made an innocent and substantial mistake of fact if either (a) that party has not assumed the risk of the mistake or (b) the other party knew or should have known of the mistake. A substantial mistake of fact is one but for which a reasonable person in the party's position would not have assented to the contract. In contracting, each party expects to benefit. If that expectation is based on an innocent mistake of fact the risk of which has not been assumed, then one cannot rationally expect the contract to be beneficial. If both parties make an innocent mistake, as in *Raffles*, then the contract cannot be enforced against either party. Neither party could expect the contract to be beneficial on the other's terms. Similarly, in *Sherwood*, Walker could not expect the contract to be beneficial.

The second condition of the principle applies to unilateral mistakes. For example, contractors who innocently make computational errors in bids ('innocent' here means 'without negligence') are entitled to rescind if the other party knew or should have known of the mistake. Because parties assume the risk of their own unilateral mistakes, this principle will not by itself justify rescission in cases of innocent unilateral mistakes when the other party did not and need not have known of the mistake. But if enforcement of the contract would impose a significant burden on the mistaken party and its rescission would not impose such a burden on the other party, the principle of good faith (4.3.7) supports rescission. Without rescission, the interaction will be at best an expected zero sum rather than plus sum one, and it would not fall under principles for gratuitous commitments.

The difficult question concerns those situations in which the other party has acted on the contract or will otherwise lose. In cases of unilateral mistake, the burden falls on the mistaken party because rescission is not permitted. In cases of mutual mistake, however, there may be no enforceable contract but part performance by one party. In *Raffles*, one of the parties had shipped cotton, and in *McCrae* the buyer had fitted out a ship for salvaging. In some cases restitution is required, in others costs are split (see *National Presto Indus. Inc. v. United States*, 338 F.2d 99 (Ct. Cl. 1964), *cert. denied*, 380 U.S. 962 (1965)), and in others the loss lies where it falls. Here it does seem appropriate to make the best mistake avoider pay, as in *McCrae*. When there is no difference in the parties' abilities to avoid mistakes, as in *Raffles*, then costs should be split. Parties then assume the risk of the mistakes they can best avoid when these have not been explicitly or implicitly assumed (as by price).

4.3.4. *Incapacity*. Another defect that can prevent an enforceable contract being formed is the incapacity of one party. A prime aim of contract law is to enable private persons to improve their situations by making arrangements for transfers of property or services that are mutually expected to be beneficial. The focus is on interactions in which persons make free and reasonable choices. If people are not capable of making such choices, then the aim will not usually be furthered by enforcing their commitments. *(4-14) The principle of contractual incapacity: a contract should not be enforceable against a person who, at the time of contracting, lacked capacity to make a reasonable choice to contract.* In general, incapacity can be used only by the incapacitated person; that is, the incapacitated party can enforce the contract should he or she want. A capable party is able to make a reasonable choice and determine that the contract is probably beneficial, so there is no reason to let that person out of it when the other person wants to continue.

Legal minors lack the capacity to make many contracts. Two types of contracts by minors are enforceable, namely, those for the purchase of 'necessaries' and those for employment beneficial to them. What constitutes necessaries is a highly variable matter involving what goods are proper or suitable for maintaining a person's position. In the nineteenth century, rather extravagant items were found necessary for upper class minors. Given the current restrictions on child labor, there are few forms of legal employment that would not be beneficial to a minor.

Instead of making exceptions on the basis of the subject matter of contracts, it would be better to inquire directly into the capacity of minors to make reasonable decisions about the given contract. A person can lack the capacity for some decisions but not others. In other areas, such as capacity to consent to medical treatment, the law recognizes variable capacity of minors. One might object that this approach would be unacceptable from the position of the other party, because one could not know for sure whether a minor had the appropriate capacity. However, the same uncertainty arises concerning whether an item is a necessary. Moreover, rules of thumb could still be used, for example, that twelve year olds have the capacity to purchase baseball gloves.

A persistent problem arises from minors lying about their age when making contracts, especially purchases of automobiles. Should minors be permitted to lie about their ages to purchase goods such as cars, use them for a while, and then rescind or disaffirm the contract demanding their full money back? The extant rules on this matter are complex and riddled with exceptions (see Calamari and Perillo 1977, 239-42). So long as minors are permitted to disaffirm contracts, a good faith seller who took reasonable precautions to determine that the buyer was of age should be compensated. This policy represents a reasonable balance between protection of minors and protection of sellers against fraud. It would be of considerable help in this area if the age of majority for contracts and ownership of property was the same as the driving age. By one means or another, courts have usually held that the seller must be compensated for loss in depreciation of the goods (*Petit v. Liston*, 97 Ore. 464, 191 Pac. 660 (1920); *Doenges-Long Motors, Inc. v. Gillen*, 138 Colo. 31, 328 P.2d 1077 (1958)).

The other type of incapacity is mental illness. Traditional common law voided contracts only if the mental illness affected a person's cognitive capacities. However, contemporary psychology recognizes that people's capacities to make reasonable choices can be affected even if they know what they are doing and vice versa. Moreover, people should be able to presume that persons on their own in society are competent. Disallowing that assumption would place too great a burden to determine the sanity of those with whom one interacts. Of course, the presumption is rebutted if a person's conduct indicates mental incompetence. Thus, disaffirmance of contracts because of mental illness should be permitted only if the other party believed, or had good reason to believe, that the person was mentally incapacitated. In *Ortelere v. Teachers' Retirement Bd.* (25 N.Y.2d 196, 250 N.E.2d 460 (1969)), a sixty year old teacher with cerebral arteriosclerosis was on leave for mental illness. Two months before her death, she selected a retirement benefits option payable only during her lifetime. The retirement board was or should have been aware of her illness, since she was on leave for medical reasons. On suit by the estate to overturn the selection of a retirement option, the Court of Appeal reversed a lower court finding that as a matter of law there was insufficient evidence of mental incompetence and ordered a new trial.

4.3.5. *Written memorandum.* A third possible defect of contract formation is the failure to evidence a contract by a writing signed by the party against whom enforcement is sought. This stems from the Statute of Frauds 1677 which required written evidence for six types of contracts – of an administrator or executor to pay charges from his or her own estate, to guarantee another's debt, to provide a consideration for marriage, to sell land or interests therein (real property), that cannot be performed within a year of their making, and to sell goods worth more than ten pounds. In England, the Law Reform (Enforcement of Contracts) Act 1954 abolished the requirement except for guarantees and contracts relating to land. In the United States, the primary applications are to contracts for the sale of land, incapable of performance within a year, and for the sale of goods with a price of $500 or more (U.C.C. § 2-201(1)).

Rational reasons for the requirement of a writing are not obvious. As its name states, the statute was originally adopted to prevent fraud. But it also creates the possibility of unfair dealing. A person can avoid a commitment by arguing that it is not in writing. For example, in *Morsinkhoff v. De Luxe Laundry & Dry Cleaning Co.* (344 S.W.2d 639 (Mo. Ct. App. 1961)), Morsinkhoff had a job for $7,200 a year. He received an oral $10,000 a year contract to work for De Luxe; employment was to commence in six weeks so that he could give a month's notice to his present employer. After he gave notice, he was told he did not have the job. The court held that either his contract was for more than one year, in which case it had to be in writing, or it was for less than a year, in which case it could be terminated for no reason. Similarly, I once had an oral agreement to purchase a townhouse, and the lawyers were told to prepare a contract. The sellers kept the for sale sign in the window, and before the contract was prepared, they sold it at a higher price to another buyer.

Besides preventing fraud, the requirement of a writing can fulfill other purposes (see Fuller 1941, 800-01). It can make a person think before entering a contract. If one is to sign a written memorandum, one is apt to be more judicious. It can also channel actions into particular frameworks – legal and nonlegal commitments. These are also valuable functions. Channeling can save courts time in considering cases. However, the extent to which the requirement of a writing serves these purposes is questionable. Many people become so accustomed to signing forms that they sign without reading them or thinking. Court time might not be saved, because many cases involve arguments about whether the requirement applies and whether a memorandum is sufficient. Under the Uniform Commercial Code, a trial is never avoided, because it permits enforcement if a party admits to the contract at trial (§ 2-201(3)(b)).

(4-15) The principle of a written memorandum: a written memorandum of a contract authenticated by the party against whom it is enforced may be required for contracts of significant value. This principle does not state that there should be such a requirement, only that there may be. A requirement of a writing protects the person against whom a claim is made by treating it as void. Although fraud or unfairness can be perpetrated against promisees, they can protect themselves against detrimental reliance by not acting on the commitment until it is reduced to writing. Thus, when I attempted to purchase the townhouse, I did not detrimentally rely on the oral agreement, and Morsinkhoff could have waited for a writing before giving notice. In situations like our hypothetical Professor Kemper who waited over three months for a signed contract (4.2.5), the principle of reliance should protect those who rely. Our principle does not refer to the time in which a contract is to be performed (within a year). Instead, it is the value or significance of the contract that should count. Some long-term contracts might not be of significant value, although all employment contracts should be. Finally, it is up to courts or legislatures to specify what constitutes significant value, but the appropriate amount in 1986 dollars is probably more like $2,000 than $500 (cf. U.C.C. § 1-206 ($5000 for sale of personal property)).

4.3.6. *Contrary to law.* The last defect considered here concerns contracts contrary to law or public policy. The principle of collective good supports not using the law to enforce contracts contrary to laws and policies promoting or protecting collective goods. There are two approaches to this restriction. One is to prevent courts being used to support agreements contrary to law; the other is to use nonenforcement of contracts to help deter undesirable conduct. It is the first approach that is acceptable. Contract law is not a useful deterrent, because it is random and therefore possibly not effective, and the sanction is often excessive (Treitel 1981, 104 and 108; see also Atiyah 1981a, 255). Suppose, due to economic restrictions, the law makes it illegal to sell goods of type *X*. If such contracts are void and Patton sells $8,000 worth of *Xs* to Quinn but after delivery Quinn refuses to pay, then Patton is out $8,000. If Quinn pays before delivery and Patton refuses to deliver, then Quinn is out $8,000. Which party loses is completely independent of any subjective guilt, for the losing party might not know of the regulation while the defaulting party does. Moreover, $8,000 is probably a larger fine than the legislature would impose. Finally, even if both parties know of the regulation, they will not be deterred from direct exchanges of money for goods.

(4-16) The principle of illegal contracts: if a purported contract or its performance is contrary to a law, regulation, or judicially recognized public policy necessary for a collective good, then (a) it should be modified so as not to be contrary to the policy; (b) if that is not possible, the parties should be restored to their positions prior to the contract; and (c) if (b) is not possible, any losses from nonenforcement of the contract should be divided between them in proportion to their respective culpability. 'Culpability' here includes negligence, and various culpable mental states should be ranked as in criminal law (see 6.4.2). This principle is acceptable, because it permits a mutually beneficial interaction if that is possible without detriment to the collective good; and if it is not, restores a zero sum situation or shares losses on the basis of guilt. A completely innocent party need not fear loss, except to the extent equally shared by another completely innocent party.

An essential part of the principle of illegal contracts is the requirement that the law or policy be necessary or important for the promotion or protection of a collective good. Two common grounds for not enforcing contracts probably do not meet this requirement – wagering contracts and those pertaining to sexual immorality. Although the judgment that gambling contracts are immoral is legislatively imposed, those against some forms of sexual immorality are not. For example, in England and Canada prostitution is not illegal, but courts sometimes hold contracts related to prostitution, such as leases of premises, to be contrary to public policy. It is doubtful that refusal to enforce wagering and prostitution related contracts promotes a collective good; indeed, they probably create collective harm. Much criminal activity related to illegal gambling stems from the coercive collection of gambling debts. Criminal activity in this area might be significantly reduced were gambling debts enforceable at law. Similar considerations apply to prostitution.

It has been suggested that nonenforcement of these contracts serves two other purposes, namely, preventing indignity to the courts of even trying such cases and enabling undesirable situations to be brought to an end, for example, by allowing a landlord to evict a prostitute (Atiyah 1981a, 256). However, the dignity of the court surely takes second place to prevention of strong-arm collection of gambling debts; and if courts recognized the contracts, hearing the cases would not appear so undignified. Moreover, landlords could be given grounds for evicting prostitutes, for example, zoning laws, without failing to enforce all such contracts, especially where prostitution is legal. Besides, they can and often do put a clause in the lease for this purpose.

A common type of contract which can be reformed is one that involves restraint of trade. Suppose Rankin sells her cab company to Slayton and agrees not to operate a cab company anywhere in the state or province for twenty-five years. This noncompetition clause is in restraint of competition and contrary to law or public policy in most if not all common-law countries. If ten years later Rankin starts a cab company in a city fifty miles away and Slayton sues, the courts can and would hold the clause to be void but maintain the rest of the contract of sale. In such cases, courts usually modify clauses as need be in light of the type of business and the economic conditions (but not always, see *H & R Block, Inc. v. Lovelace*, 208 Kan. 538, 493 P.2d 205 (1972)). Finally, it should be noted that sellers have good reason for reasonable limitations on their competitive activity, namely, it can increase the price they receive for the sale of their business.

In *Sears, Roebuck & Co. v. Kelly* (1 Misc. 2d 624, 149 N.Y.S.2d 133 (1956)), the parties could be and were returned to a position as though the illegal conduct had not occurred. As a buyer for Sears, Kelly had accepted $12,500 worth of gratuities from various suppliers. The court upheld Sears' claims to be repaid the amount of the gratuities and to refuse to pay a bonus for the period of employment (thus penalizing the culpable party).

McConnell v. Commonwealth Pictures Corp. (7 N.Y.2d 465, 166 N.E.2d
494 (1960)) illustrates both how wrongdoers can be made to suffer losses
and how illegality can be in the performance of a contract and not the
contract itself. McConnell sued for an accounting of the gross receipts from
the distribution of certain movies. In exchange for his securing the distribution rights, Commonwealth had contracted to pay him $10,000 and a
percentage of the gross receipts. Commonwealth claimed that it had paid
the $10,000, but that to obtain the rights McConnell had paid it as a bribe
to a representative of movie producers. The parties could not be restored
to a position as though the contract had never occurred. Although neither
party would lose more than it expected if the defendant paid the contractual
percentage, that would amount to enforcing an illegally performed contract.
Consequently, if the contract is not to be enforced and one party is to suffer
a loss, that is the culpable party, and McConnell lost.

4.3.7. Duties independent of the contract. Most of the duties considered in this
section do not arise from express or implied terms of the contract. Thus,
their violation usually renders a contract voidable; that is, the wronged
party can rescind and the parties are to be put in a position as though it
never took place. The chief exception to the foregoing statements is the
duty of good faith, which is more a catchall for a number of duties than a
specific one. Some violations of it permit rescission of the contract, while
others provide a basis for damages.

The duty of good faith can be approached by considering the definition
of 'good faith'. It is commonly defined as "honesty in fact" or that plus
"observance of reasonable commercial standards of fair dealing" (U.C.C.
§§ 1-201(19) and 2-103(1)(b)). However, this is probably too narrow a
definition (Summers 1968, 207-16). Robert Summers suggests that 'good
faith' is best considered an "excluder" that excludes certain types of conduct – bad faith (Summers 1968, 200-01). Although it is often easier to
identify bad rather than good things or conduct, there is some value in
having at least a vague positive concept. This can perhaps be achieved by
considering its normative basis in the foundations of contract law. A
primary reason for enforcing contracts is to promote mutually expected
beneficial plus sum interactions. This purpose requires a minimal trust in
the whole course of dealing between the parties. One needs to trust that
the other party is sincerely involved in an interaction that will probably be
mutually beneficial, even if the other party seeks to reap as many benefits

for him or herself as possible. *(4-17) The principle of good faith: contract law should require conduct necessary for the minimal trust rational people need to interact with a reasonable prospect of it being mutually beneficial.* Honesty in fact or sincerity is a crucial condition for such minimal trust, but not the whole of it.

The Uniform Commercial Code imposes a duty of good faith on the performance or enforcement of a contract (§ 1-203), but obviously the duty of good faith must extend to the process of contract negotiation and formation, in short, throughout the contract process (Summers 1968; Reiter 1983, 710-12). Good faith is a common requirement of North American labor-management negotiations. Bad faith has been found in contractual negotiation and formation, as in negotiating without serious intent to contract and taking advantage of others in driving a hard bargain. It has been found in contract performance, as in wilfully rendering only substantial performance and abusing powers to determine contractual compliance. It can occur in raising or resolving disputes, as in making up disputes and taking advantage of another to obtain a favorable settlement. Finally, it can pertain to remedial actions such as refusing performance for no reason or abusing the power to terminate a contract. Seen this way, the duty of good faith (or not to act in bad faith) is the most general expression of duties independent of the contract.

Although they might be seen as an aspect of good faith, it is useful to emphasize specially duties necessary to ensure that interactions are voluntary. The principle of transferability of property (3-3) is against involuntary transfers of property which should include transfers of services. In considering unconscionability and the principle of required conditions (4.3.2), we saw that parties should have a reasonable opportunity to choose to contract. Without that, the contract is not voluntary. The traditional common law was more concerned to ensure contracts were voluntary than it was to ensure other aspects of good faith. Thus, there were specific duties concerned with voluntariness.

The duty not to misrepresent requires that one's commitments during negotiation and contract formation be sincere. The basic concern is with factual claims, and the duty is often said not to extend to promises and statements of opinion and intention. However, in making promises and statements of opinion or intention, one at least commits oneself to one's state of mind, to the sincerity of the statements. Thus, if one has no intention of fulfilling a promise or acting as one says one intends, or does not really hold opinions expressed, one has made a false commitment.

Legally, the exclusion of opinions has almost been swallowed up by its exceptions (Calamari and Perillo 1977, 285).

Some jurisdictions have developed a complex classification of misrepresentation (see *Maxey v. Quintana*, 84 N.M. 38, 499 P.2d 356 (N.M. Ct. App. 1972); cf. Davies 1977, 87-91). If it is knowing or reckless, then it constitutes fraud and damages are possible (*Derry v. Peek*, 1889 App. Cas. 337). If it is innocent, then the other party may rescind the contract but damages are not available. If it is negligent, then it falls in tort instead of contract law and damages are available. This tortuous set of distinctions is not acceptable. Although there are historical reasons for it, this distinction between contract and tort law, with negligent misrepresentation in tort law and intentional and innocent in contract, is artificial. It simply reflects the dead hand of the past. The only relevant normative issue concerns possible remedies. If there is doubt about the appropriate remedies for negligent or innocent misrepresentation, then courts should have discretion as to remedy, as they have in England under the Misrepresentation Act 1967.

In practice, courts can often avoid questions of fraud or innocent misrepresentation by construing a factual commitment as an implied term in the contract. For example, if a truck is sold as a 1958 model when it is a 1956 model with a 1958 cab, the seller can be taken to have warranted the truck as a 1958 model (*F. and B. Transp. Ltd. v. White Truck Sales Manitoba Ltd.*, 51 W.W.R. 124 (Man. 1965)). This technique is not readily available for contracts other than for the sale of goods. If the seller of an automobile dealership states that other dealers in the area make a certain sum, when in fact some are losing and others are making signicantly less, one cannot take the seller as having warranted an income from the dealership. This sort of case must be treated as fraud (*Hanson v. Ford Motor Co.*, 278 F.2d 586 (8th Cir. 1960); see also *Esso Petroleum v. Mardon*, 1976 Q.B. 801 (C.A.)).

The *Restatement (Second) of Contracts* (§ 161) treats certain failures to disclose information as equivalent to assertions and thus constituting misrepresentation. It might be better simply to recognize a duty of disclosure. The problem is formulating it. One approach is to specify that there is no duty to disclose information except under certain circumstances, such as where it is required by law, it amounts to concealment, partial disclosure would be misleading, one discovers that one's prior statements are mistaken, or there is a fiduciary duty to do so (Calamari and Perillo 1977, 288-91). However, this approach is not very satisfactory. It does not give guidelines as to when the law should require disclosure or failure to disclose amounts to concealment.

An alternative approach suggests a positive duty to disclose material information that is not the result of a deliberate search (Kronman 1978a, 9). In effect, information acquired by a costly search is treated as a property right – a form of intellectual property (Kronman 1978a, 14). Material information is that which a reasonable person would take to be relevant to a decision to contract. One has good reasons to agree that one should not be required to disclose information acquired by a deliberate effort, for such information is analogous to property produced by one's labor. It is less clear that one has good reasons to agree to disclosure of all information obtained without a search. Why should one disclose if the other party's ignorance is due to negligence or sheer stupidity. However, if one has not made an effort to obtain information and the other party is unlikely to be able to obtain it, then a duty of disclosure makes sense. Thus, there is at least a duty to disclose material facts of which one has knowledge without a deliberate search and which the other party is unlikely to be able to discover.

This duty appears to underlie many specific duties of disclosure imposed by statute, for example, on applicants for insurance, companies in stock prospectuses, and lenders of interest rates charged. In each case, the information is primarily under the control of one party. It also applies in other situations in which the law imposes a duty to disclose, such as those that amount to concealment. In *Obde v. Schlemeyer* (56 Wash. 2d 449, 353 P.2d 672 (1960)), the Obde's were successfull in obtaining damages for termite infestation of an apartment building they purchased. Schlemeyer knew of the termites, and he had had the building treated, although perhaps inadequately. He had made repairs so that the termites and damage were not noticeable by the usual inspection of buyers. Without the knowledge, the Obde's could not make a reasonable decision to purchase.

The final duties concerning an opportunity for a reasonable choice are not to use duress or undue influence. Both of them prevent a party having a reasonable and so free or voluntary choice. Duress is often characterized as making an improper threat or carrying it out (see Rest. 2d Contracts § 175; Atiyah 1981a, 231). Problems arise in determining what threats are improper. Obviously, threats of illegal conduct are improper, while threats not to conclude a contract are perfectly proper. Today, the most common forms of duress are probably economic pressure or threats not to fulfill contractual obligations. In the latter cases, lack of consideration is often

used as an alternative basis for not enforcing the contract (*Alaska Packers'*
Ass'n v. Domenico (117 Fed. 99 (9th Cir. 1902)). The central element,
however, is whether a party removed reasonable alternative choices from
the other or took advantage of the other's lack of such alternatives (Trebil-
cock 1980, 395).

Legally, undue influence involves unfairly taking advantage of a dominant psychological position or a position of confidence and trust, such as
parent/child, lawyer/client, or even rest home-operator/elderly patient
(*Public Trustee v. Skoretz*, 32 D.L.R.3d 749 (B.C. Sup. Ct. 1972)). In the
latter situations, one party is presumed to have special power or influence
over the decisions of the other. In the former, due to circumstances, one
party is specially vulnerable. For example, in *Odorizzi v. Bloomfield School
Dist.* (246 Cal. App. 2d 123, 54 Cal. Rptr. 533 (1966)), undue influence was
attributed to the superintendent and principal of a school who visited a
teacher at home and secured a resignation. The teacher had just been
released on bail for a charge of homosexuality (subsequently dismissed)
and had not slept for forty hours.

DISCHARGE AND REMEDIES

4.4.0. *Introduction.* Contracts can terminate in a variety of ways. Usually,
both parties fulfill their duties and courts are not involved. However,
problems can arise requiring court action. In the next section, we consider
several ways contractual obligations end. The three following sections
consider principles to govern remedies for failed contracts – instances in
which the expected plus sum interaction for one reason or another did not
occur as expected. Remedies are needed for two basic types of cases – those
in which an enforceable contract did not exist or was rescinded, and those
in which a commitment is enforced. The former cases are usually said not
to involve contract remedies or be part of contract law but belong to the
law of 'quasi-contract' or 'restitution'. However, as we saw (4.0), failed
attempts to make contracts should be included in contract law. The section
on 'rescission' includes all these cases in which a contract is void or voided.
The other cases – those enforcing a commitment – can be divided into
enforcement by payment of money damages and by 'specific performance'
– making a party actually keep contractual commitments.

4.4.1. *Discharge.* When the obligations or duties of a contract are ended,
they are discharged. One form of discharge, 'frustration', is much the same

as mutual mistake and has similar effects. When an unforeseen happening deprives one party of the expected value of the contract and it was the basis on which they both entered the contract, then that party is discharged from having to perform. The classic case is *Krell v. Henry* ([1903] 2 K.B. 740 (C.A.)). The defendant had rented a room from the plaintiff to use to view the coronation procession of King Edward VII. The procession was cancelled due to the unexpected illness of the King. The exceptionally high rent for a short time showed that viewing the coronation procession was contemplated by the parties. The court found the defendant not liable for the rent.

The similarity to common or mutual mistake can be seen by supposing that the King had become ill and cancelled the coronation the day the contract was concluded (*Griffith v. Brymer*, 19 T.L.R. 434 (K.B. 1903)). Mutual mistake pertains to existing facts, while frustration and 'impossibility' pertain to future ones (Calamari and Perillo 1977, 498-99). The difference between frustration and impossibility is that in the former performance is possible – the defendant in *Krell* could have paid for the room. If, however, the building had burned down, it would have been impossible to use the room (*Taylor v. Caldwell*, 122 Eng. Rep. 309 (K.B. 1863)). Slightly different situations arise when, although it is physically possible to perform, it is commercially impracticable.

Discharge for frustration or impossibility is acceptable. Frustration and impossibility prevent an interaction being mutually beneficial and thus defeat the point of contracting. From a promisor's viewpoint, discharge prevents a significant loss. If the promisee has done nothing to perform the contract, he or she does not lose. As one might equally be either party, one has no reason to prefer enforcement of the contract, which would necessarily amount to enforcing a transaction that, through no fault of either party, is at best a zero sum one.

An economic analyst might object to this conclusion, claiming that impossibility is not relevant and that the question is which party is the better risk bearer because better able to prevent the risk or to insure against it (Posner 1977, 77-78; Posner and Rosenfield 1977, 90-91). But this approach does not suffice, since the event cannot be prevented by either party and being unforeseen is not something either would insure against. One might reply that the possibility of the King's illness was foreseeable and impossibility cases usually involve events of a type one insures against – fires and so on. However, one must also consider the costs of determining who is the better insurer. If the analysis were applied on a case by case analysis, the costs of a legal determination of the better insurer might exceed the benefits. A similar consideration might apply to the acquisition of insurance. Should homeowners take out insurance for the full contract price whenever they have their houses painted to protect against loss should the house burn before the painting is done? The costs of administering the additional insurance, even if it is made a standard clause of house insurance, is probably greatly in excess of the benefit.

It hardly needs mentioning that a contract can be discharged by mutual agreement or 'performance' (keeping the commitments). If neither party wishes to complete the contract, then whatever the law might say, there is no legal case, for neither will commence one. (In a very few cases, a third party might do so.) Performance, one must realize, need not be the performance of actions. The commitments in a contract for the sale of goods are rarely all fulfilled by the transfer of goods and payment of the price. Warranties of merchantability and other terms can bind the seller or even buyer for a time after that.

'Breach' of a contract by one party, that is, failure to keep one of its conditions, usually permits the other party to consider his or her commitments discharged. This is true if the breaching party does not perform at all, 'repudiates' the contract (states that he or she will not continue), or fails to keep or defectively keeps a condition. If an unfulfilled term is only a warranty, the innocent party must perform and settle for damages. As we have seen (4.3.1), determining whether a term is a condition or warranty is not easy. If the innocent party treats the contract as ended, neither party has a duty to perform any more. But the commitments of the breaching party are turned into duties to pay damages. Of course, the innocent party might want to insist on performance. We examine that in 4.4.4.

The traditional theory of common law, although probably not the practice, was that parties must perform conditions exactly as specified in the contract. That could work significant injustice, and the doctrine of 'substantial performance' has modified it. In *Jacob & Youngs, Inc. v. Kent* (230 N.Y. 239, 129 N.E. 889 (1921)), a contractor built a house according to specifications calling for use of about 2,000 feet of wrought iron pipe by a specific manufacturer. When only 1,000 feet was delivered, the contractor substituted pipe of equivalent quality from another manufacturer for the rest. The owner refused to pay $3,483 of a total cost of about $77,000, and the builder sued for the remainder. Given the trivial nature of the failure to follow specifications, the court determined that the plaintiff had substantially performed, and that the defendant was entitled only to payment for any demonstrable damage from failure to follow specifications, which in this case was none. One can contrast *Jacob & Youngs* with *Kreyer v. Driscoll* (39 Wis. 2d 540, 159 N.W.2d 680 (1968)). Kreyer did poor work and left unfinished half the plumbing, electrical, heating, and tile work as well as all of the linoleum and a fourth of the decorating. The court did not consider this substantial performance.

Some authors think that the doctrine of substantial performance requires distinguishing conditions from promises (Calamari and Perillo 1977, 396-7). Conditions must be fully performed, but not promises. But this analysis only creates confusion. This would change the requirement of building according to specifications from a condition to a promise. In many cases, the terms can be divided into conditions and warranties, for example, some house specifications are conditions and others are warranties. The manufacturer of plumbing pipe is a warranty (*Jacob & Youngs*), while that there be plumbing is a condition (*Kreyer*). In other cases only one item is involved, for example, time. Substantial performance occurs when the promisee received most of what he or she wanted and would have contracted for that, although probably for a lower price. For example, suppose a courier service makes a commitment to deliver by noon the next day, but does not deliver until 1:00 PM. Depending on the situation, one might agree to a later delivery for a reduced rate or one might choose another firm or method of delivery. The issue is a factual question as to the importance a reasonable person in the party's position would attach to exact compliance with the term (cf. Levin and McDowell 1983, 70).

Breach can arise before the time for performance. This is called anticipatory repudiation. In the classic case of *Hochster v. De La Tour* (118 Eng. Rep 922 (Q.B. 1853)), the defendant hired the plaintiff in April to accompany him on a tour to start on June 1st. On May 11th, the defendant wrote to the plaintiff saying he had changed his mind and would not hire him, and the plaintiff commenced an action on May 22nd. Prior to June 1st he found other employment but not starting until July 4th. The court held that the plaintiff had sufficient grounds for treating the contract as discharged, not keeping himself available until June 1st, and starting the action. One could certainly accept such a result. By seeking other employment as soon as possible, the plaintiff not only made the best of a bad situation for himself but also for the defendant (who would not have to compensate him the amount he earned).

4.4.2. *Rescission.* We here consider remedies for all the failed attempts to make a contract – when it is void or voided. The primary purpose of enforcing contracts is to enable people to enter mutually expected beneficial plus sum interactions. In default of that, people would rationally prefer a zero sum interaction in which neither gained or lost. Purely risk neutral people, those concerned only with average expectable outcomes, would be indifferent to the allocation of benefits and losses in a zero sum situation, for the average is always no gain or loss; but few people are purely risk neutral. By having remedies restore them to zero sum situations with neither party gaining or losing, people have nothing to lose and a reasonable prospect of gain by trying to contract. If, however, the failure necessarily turns the interaction into a minus sum one, then in the absence of any fair basis for allocating the loss, beforehand people would rationally agree to splitting the loss. A fair basis for allocating the loss would stem from a justifiable principle. *(4-18) The principle of rescission: when contracts are void, voided, or rescinded, (a) parties should be restored to the position they were in prior to the interaction; and (b) if there is a net loss not allocable on the basis of other principles, it should be split between them.*

If neither party has acted, there is no problem applying the principle and restoring people to the previous position. For example, in *Sherwood v. Walker* (66 Mich. 568, 33 N.W. 919 (1887) (contract for sale of cow void due to mutual mistake), see 4.3.3), Sherwood had not paid Walker and Walker had not given Sherwood the cow. But these types of cases are not frequent. If one party has received some benefit from the other, then obviously that benefit should be returned. For example, if a contract for the purchase of goods is void or voided, then the goods should be returned. However, this does not necessarily restore the parties to their previous position. There might have been some use and depreciation of the goods. If so, then usually the person who used them has received a benefit equal to the loss or depreciation and should also compensate for that.

An exception might be made here for minors. Suppose a minor does not misrepresent his or her age in purchasing a home computer and then wants to rescind the contract. The seller will have a used rather than new computer which will be worth significantly less. In cases of this sort, one might rationally permit losses to remain with sellers, because they have various means to protect themselves. They can include the losses as part of the cost of doing business or institute procedures to avoid selling to minors. Thus, although the seller loses in the particular interaction, this need not be an unanticipated or uncovered loss. In effect, the seller is the best insurer against this type of risk and there are special reasons to protect minors. The matter is different if the youth lied about his or her age; the seller should receive an offset for depreciation (see 4.3.4). Sellers cannot reasonably protect themselves against selling to minors who lie about their age and use false identification.

In many cases of a net loss, other principles will provide for its allocation. For example, the principle of illegal contracts provides for allocating losses on the basis of culpability. However, in at least one type of situation, there is a net loss and other principles do not suffice. Suppose one party orders special machinery built, but after considerable work has been done but no deliveries made, the contract is frustrated (Posner and Rosenfield 1977, 92-94; Atiyah 1981a, 306). One party has a net loss and the other party has no benefit. Here a mutually expected beneficial plus sum interaction has turned into a minus sum interaction. One might try to apply the principle of reliance and contend that the buyer could foresee that the manufacturer would rely on the promise to begin work, but that simply makes the second performer liable for unforeseen frustrating events. The same is true if one maintains that it is part of the manufacturer's cost of doing business. Nor is it clear who is the better risk insurer. At this point, a principle of sharing the loss is appropriate (see Fried 1981, 70-73). The parties intended a mutually beneficial plus sum interaction. Since they cannot be returned to a zero sum situation, the next best choice for a rational risk averse person is a minus sum situation in which neither bears the full loss. In Britain, the Law Reform (Frustrated Contracts) Act 1943 permits this result. We have already suggested the same result for mutual mistakes, which as we saw in the previous section are similar to frustration.

4.4.3. *Damages.* We are here primarily concerned with money damages for breach, although our principle also covers damages for warranties. The rescission remedy can involve the transfer of money, and an action for rescission might properly be for money, for example, to recover monies paid.

A party's receipt of the expected benefits of a contract depends on the other party fulfilling his or her commitments. In making commitments, one realizes or should realize that the other person is counting on their fulfillment to receive a net benefit, and one assumes the risk of their not being fulfilled. One function of contracts is to shift risks (Atiyah 1981a, 186). This does not settle the extent or scope of the risk assumed. One might only

assume risks that are within one's power to control; so if a commitment
is not fulfilled through no fault of one's own, one is not liable. Such a
restriction would severely limit the types of contracts people could make;
some contracts, insurance contracts for example, are simply to shift risks
over which neither party has significant control. The restriction would be
contrary to the aim of enabling people freely to enter mutually expected
beneficial interactions. Consequently, it is not rational to restrict the assumption of risk to failures to fulfill commitments that are within the
parties' control, although parties might so contract if they wished.

We have not specified what is meant in the principle of enforceable
commitments by 'supported and enforced'. This could involve penalizing
people who break commitments to deter people from breaking them, or it
could involve simply compensating promisees so that they do not lose
(Barton 1979, 155). A promise theory is more likely to support a deterrence
approach than an economic theory. As we have seen (4.1.2), an economic
approach implies that people should break commitments whenever they
can make more than required to compensate injured parties for their losses.
However, we also noted that due to expenses involved in obtaining compensation, merely obtaining the contract benefits would not always provide
complete compensation. The deterrence and compensation approaches
usually coincide, but they do diverge in some situations (Barton 1979, 157).

*(4-19) The principle of contract damages: if the contractual commitments of
a party are not fulfilled, that party should place the other party in the position
he or she would have been in had the contract been fully performed insofar as
the other party's failure to be in that position is the foreseeable result of the
commitments' nonfulfillment.* This principle is the one rational parties would
normally probably agree to at the time of contracting (see Cooter and
Eisenberg 1985, 1462-68). It provides each party with an efficient incentive
to perform, for unless a breaching party can gain more than the other one
expected from a contract, it will not benefit from breaching and paying
damages. Thus, it provides incentives to take proper precautions against
possibly breaching. For if precautions are not taken, one might lose more
than the cost of precautions. It also protects each party's reasonable
reliance on the other's performance, but not unreasonable reliance.

The restriction to foreseeable loss is also acceptable from the prospective
position of either party. As a potentially injured party, one can warn the
other of possible losses. If one fails to do so, then although one might not
be in as good a position as if the contract had been performed, it is one's
own fault; in effect, one assumed the risk. As a breaching party, one is liable

only for losses for which one could reasonably have accepted the risk. One is not liable for losses independent of commitments made to the other party, nor for losses one could not reasonably foresee at the time of contracting. To determine whether it is likely to be beneficial to enter a contract, one must consider the risk of paying damages should one default. This calculation cannot be made for unforeseeable losses the other party might suffer (see also Levin and McDowell 1983, 60). To reasonably accept such a risk, one would have to receive more in return, but one has no way of knowing how much more. By our principle, one is not liable for unforeseeable losses unless one explicitly assumed the risk.

The principle of contract damages and its rationale imply that a breaching party need not make the other better off than he or she would have been had the contract been fulfilled (*Freund v. Washington Square Press, Inc.*, 34 N.Y.2d, 357 N.Y.S.2d, 314 N.E.2d 419 (1974)). This could arise in several types of situations. First, the cost of performance might be considerably greater than the value to the injured party. For example, in *Peevyhouse v. Garland Coal & Mining Co.* (382 P.2d 109 (Okla. 1962), *cert. denied*, 375 U.S. 906 (1963)), the cost of regrading strip mined land in conformity with the contract was estimated at $29,000. The total value of the land was estimated at less than $5,000, and the increased value from regrading at $300. The court restricted damages to the loss in value of the property.

Second, in breaches of contracts to employ a person, other benefits received by the plaintiff, such as unemployment insurance, might result in injured employees receiving more than they would have from employment. Unemployment benefits are in lieu of salary, and at least in part are paid for by employers. In the United States, employers pay higher rates for unemployment insurance if there are claims from previous employees. Consequently, these benefits should be deducted. However, some courts fail to do so (*Billetter v. Posell*, 94 Cal. App. 2d 858, 211 P. 2d 621 (1949)). Other benefits, such as social security and annuity benefits, should not be deducted, or at least not in full. Were the person working and not receiving them, further contributions would be made and due to later retirement greater benefits then received. Due to wrongful dismissal or whatever, the person receives lesser social security and annuity benefits than were the person employed. If the full benefits are deducted from damages, the person receives less than he or she would have if employed. Again, however, some courts wrongly deduct them (*United Protective Workers of Am., Local No. 2 v. Ford Motor Co.*, 223 F.2d 49 (7th Cir. 1955)).

Damages are commonly analyzed as involving three separate interests – the 'expectation', 'restitution', and 'reliance' interests (Fuller and Perdue 1936-37, 53-57; Rest. 2d Contracts § 344). The expectation interest consists of the benefits a party expects from the contract. The restitution interest is that in having back any benefits conferred on the other party. And the reliance interest is that in being compensated for any losses. The principle of rescission primarily concerns the restitution interest, although the reliance interest is involved when the interaction is a minus sum one. Under the Uniform Commercial Code, one can sometimes rescind and obtain damages for expectation as well (§ 2-711(1)).

All three interests can be involved in an action for damages (Calamari and Perillo 1977, 579). Suppose Gamma Computer Store agrees to purchase ten microcomputers from Delta Computer Corp. for $1500 each for resale at $2300 each and makes a partial advance payment of $2000. Further suppose that due to production problems, Delta fails to deliver the micros and Gamma sues for $5750. First, Gamma asks for the return or restitution of its $2000. Second, Gamma asks for $250 reimbursement for newspaper advertising of the new Delta computers it expected to have in stock to sell. This is its reliance interest. Third, Gamma also asks for $3500 which is the profit it would have made in selling the computers – $350 each for ten, assuming that $450 of the difference between the purchase and resale price goes for overhead and that Gamma is not entitled to recover that. This is its expectation interest. If all of the requested damages are paid, Gamma will be in the position it would have been in had Delta delivered the computers. If effect, it has its profit or expected benefit.

A court might not include the full $3500 lost profit; it might find that Gamma sold or could have obtained and sold other micros instead. This involves the duty to 'mitigate' damages. A party is required to keep its losses as small as reasonably possible. Parties should be able to expect others to take reasonable steps to avoid losses rather than simply let them mount. In *Rockingham County v. Luten Bridge Co.* (35 F.2d 301 (4th Cir. 1929)), when Luten had done little work on building a bridge, the County repudiated the contract. Luten completed construction and sued for the full contract price. The court denied payment of the contract price and gave Luten only the cost expended to the time it was notified of repudiation and its expected profit. Luten could have limited the damages by ceasing construction when it learned that the County would not go through with the contract.

The assumption above that Gamma might have obtained or sold other micros instead is close to a problem that presents the one exception to the principle of contract damages. Suppose Temple orders an automobile from Epsilon Motors, makes a deposit of $400, but repudiates the contract before delivery. Even if Epsilon sells the car to another buyer, should it be permitted to claim that it would have sold a car to that buyer in any case, so it is entitled to the full profit it would have made on the sale to Temple, say, $1500? This largely depends on how Epsilon does business or the business conditions (Davies 1977, 218). If Epsilon can sell as many cars as it can get, then it did not lose profit and should not receive any damages (*Charter v. Sullivan*, [1957] 2 Q.B. 117 (C.A.)). If it could not have sold all the cars it obtained, then it seems Temple should pay the lost profit (*W. L. Thompson Ltd. v. Robinson (Gunmakers) Ltd.*, 1955 Ch. 177; U.C.C. § 2-708(2); *Neri v. Retail Marine Corp.*, 30 N.Y.2d 393, 334 N.Y.S.2d 165, 285 N.E.2d 311 (1972)).

However, one might better use what has been called "statistical expectation" (Cooter and Eisenberg 1985, 1477). Epsilon, and especially other enterprises such as airlines, can calculate the likely number of cancellations or repudiations. Thus, they are entitled to the normal profit they statistically expect making allowance for cancellations. In practice, this amounts to a cancellation fee or loss of deposit. This variation on the principle of damages would be acceptable from either position, whereas full profit would not be (Cooter and Eisenberg 1985, 1471-75). Buyers are unlikely to be willing to assume the risk of the full profit plus reliance and restitution, for that often amounts to paying the full contract price without obtaining any benefit. Moreover, sellers can make business allowances for an expected rate of cancellations or repudiations. Thus, airlines overbook seats on the expectation that there will be a certain percentage of cancellations.

In contracts for the purchase of many goods, on default by the seller one may 'cover' by purchasing similar goods elsewhere without unreasonable delay and receive the difference between the contract price and the price actually paid (U.C.C. § 2-712), or one may simply sue for the difference between the contract price and the market price at the time one learned of the breach (U.C.C. § 2-713). In *Oloffson v. Coomer* (11 Ill. App. 3d 918, 296 N.E.2d 871 (1973)), Oloffson unreasonably delayed in covering. In April, Coomer contracted to sell 20,000 bushels of corn to Oloffson for October delivery at $1.1275 a bushel, and 20,000 more bushels for December delivery at $1.1225. On June 3rd, Coomer told Oloffson that he would be unable to fulfill the contract. Oloffson continued to insist that Coomer deliver, and after the delivery dates passed purchased corn for $1.35 and $1.49 a bushel. He then sued for the difference between the price he paid and the contract price. The court limited damages to the difference between the contract price and $1.16, the price on the day Coomer notifed Oloffson that he could not deliver. In such markets, if one covers immediately, there is no difference in the remedies. The effect of the market price remedy is to mitigate damages. One may cover part and use the market price for the rest (*Interior Elevator Co. v. Limmeroth*, 278 Or. 589, 565 P.2d 1074 (1977)).

The part of our principle that parties are only liable for foreseeable losses is encapsulated in the common-law rule of *Hadley v. Baxendale* (156 Eng. Rep. 145 (Ex. Ch. 1854); see also Rest. 2d Contracts § 351(1); *Security Stove & Mfg. Co. v. American Rys. Express Co.*, 227 Mo. App. 175, 51 S.W.2d 572 (1932)). The plaintiffs, mill owners, arranged to ship by the defendant carriers a shaft for use as a model in making a new one. Meanwhile, the mill could not operate. Due to the carrier's neglect, the plaintiffs did not receive the new shaft until several days later than need be and sued for lost profits during those days. The court held that a party in breach is liable for damages that (1) arise naturally or (2) as may reasonably have been contemplated by the parties at the time of contracting, which requires sufficiently notifying a party of special circumstances so that it can foresee abnormal losses. In effect, this rule reduces to losses foreseeable at the time of the contract, because normal or natural losses are reasonably foreseeable. The foreseeability of damages is also implicit in the principle of reliance. The foreseeability of the reliance should carryover to the foreseeability of the losses. Note that the principle of reliance also limits damages to the reliance interest.

A number of factors influence courts in determining whether damages are foreseeable or, as it is often put, too remote. The concerns differ in personal injury and economic loss, courts being more likely to find personal injury foreseeable (Swinton 1980, 89). Even in considering the foreseeability of economic loss, a variety of factors affect court decisions, such as the identity of the parties, type of goods or services involved, and the price or other consideration in relation to the loss (Swinton 1980, 70). These different factors do affect the reasonableness of parties foreseeing loss or having assumed the risk in a commitment. Different types of goods are likely to cause different types of loss.

As we noted in discussing mistakes (4.3.3), different risks assumed would be reflected in the price. The latter point is exemplified in *H. Parsons (Livestock) v. Uttley, Ingham & Co. Ltd.* (1978 Q.B. 791). The plaintiff received compensation for lost and diseased pigs. The defendants had left closed a ventilator on a feed hopper they installed, and stored feed became mouldy making the pigs that ate it ill. As the court in *Hadley v. Baxendale* recognized, the test of foreseeability is in the context of what the parties might reasonably contemplate as the assignment of risks. Consequently, one can ask whether the parties in such a case would reasonably assign the risks of diseased animals to the farmer or to the supplier of feed hoppers. The price of a hopper is not likely to be sufficient to include such risk. Moreover, the risk of diseased animals is a risk of farming and more easily insured against by farmers (see also Atiyah 1981a, 322; *Photo Production Ltd. v. Securicor Transp. Ltd.*, 1980 A.C. 827 (Diplock, L. J.). Here analysis by actual price charged and by who is the better risk bearer coincide and point to a result different from the court's.

Two points pertain to funds due a party that does not fulfill commitments. First, when the commitment is a warranty, the injured party is not discharged from performance but is entitled to an offset for damages. Suppose Gamma had received the ten microcomputers, but one of them was defective. Then it should pay the contract price less the loss due to the defective computer. Gamma would thus owe only $11,500 – the contract price of $15,000, less $1,500 for the defective computer and the $2,000 already paid (U.C.C. § 2-714).

Second, if one has partly performed but breached a condition, one should be entitled to payment or an offset so long as the injured party is in as good a position as had the contract been performed. This means that the injured party should be liable for the value of any benefit received or a lesser amount that will leave the breaching party in as good a position as though the contract had been performed (Waddams 1980, 174). This was not the recognized common-law rule, which theoretically denied the part performer anything (see *Sumpter v. Hedges*, [1898] 1 Q.B. 673 (C.A.) (builder who failed to complete a house denied any compensation)). Nonetheless, there are good reasons for the rule suggested. The injured party does not have to pay for any more than received and in no case more than he or she contractually agreed to pay. The breaching party is entitled to receive some compensation for losses. If an injured party's benefits are greater than his or her losses, then the breaching party can recover. This principle was followed in *Kreyer v. Driscoll* (39 Wis. 2d 540, 159 N.W.2d 680 (1968)), where a builder failed to substantially perform in constructing a house.

For various reasons the parties to a contract might stipulate an amount
for damages – 'liquidated damages'. Courts have not looked with favor on
such terms. Three criteria are used in determining whether liquidated
damages are to be allowed – the difficulty in estimating damages, the
intention to provide damages rather than a penalty, and the reasonableness
of the amount as an estimate of damages – yet the later is usually the more
important one (Calamari and Perillo 1977, 565). Recently, the courts'
hostility to liquidated damages and penalty clauses has been challenged by
commentators, especially economic analysts. Among the advantages
claimed for such clauses are providing compensation for persons who think
ordinary damages will be inadequate, perhaps because of 'special personal
value' of performance; saving court time in reviewing cases of legitimate
liquidated damages; and allowing sellers without a reputation for reliability
to provide assurance (see Kronman and Posner 1979, 260; Goetz and Scott
1979, 207). The doctrine of unconscionability can provide protection
against unduly onerous terms (Goetz and Scott 1979, 207). Indeed, one
might contend that the courts' emphasis on the reasonableness of the
amount is an implicit concern with unconscionability.

One of the main arguments against penalties is that they discourage
persons from breaching contracts when the benefits from breach are more
than enough to compensate the injured party. They thus prevent the efficient allocation of resources. However, as we have noted several times,
the extant legal system does not provide full compensation for legal expenses, time, and so on in recovering.

The element of special personal value is important for evaluating liquidated damages, penalties, and cases where the cost of performance is greater
than the increased market value from performance. Special personal value
is basically value that a person attaches to something that is not reflected
in the market. This personal value will often rest on the self-expressive or
identifying nature of property recognized in the principle of freedom ((3-8)
in 3.1.3). Damages are primarily assessed on market value, but a party's
expected benefit from a contract is the value to that person, not the market
value. Besides liquidated damages, personal value can also be involved in
situations where the cost of performance exceeds the increased market
value from performance (Harris, Ogus and Phillips 1979). For example, in
Peevyhouse, the value to the owners of restored strip mined land might have
been greater than the added market value of restoration. Moreover, penalties may not be such but only include personal value. Personal value
should be treated like other abnormal damages and allowed when a

defaulting party knew or should have known of it. Thus, when a clear case for personal value is made, courts should permit liquidated damages in excess of a reasonable estimate of market value rather than consider them penalties, and they should give cost of performance rather than additional market value.

4.4.4. *Specific performance.* An injured party might not be satisfied with damages but want the contract actually performed, for example, a contract to purchase a house. A primary reason for wanting actual performance is the personal value to be obtained. Sometimes courts order specific performance – actually fulfilling the commitments. Note that this might involve ordering a person not to do something, for example, not go into competitive business.

Courts have been very reluctant to order specific performance (Atiyah 1981a, 324-5). First, it is ordered only when damages would be inadequate. Second, even if damages would be inadequate, for a variety of reasons courts might not grant specific performance. One reason often given is the difficulty of supervising performance. Here is a procedurally based reason for limiting substantive rules. However, given the recent experience of courts supervising desegregation of schools and other decrees in public law cases, this reason is not very persuasive. It has some plausibility as a reason for not ordering specific performance in contracts for personal service, such as an actor performing. It is difficult to ensure that performance is not merely made, but made reasonably well. It is also said that ordering personal services would constitute a considerable restraint on freedom of the person. However, in North American labor law, companies are frequently required to reinstate wrongfully dismissed workers not involving personal service, which seems to be a significant restraint on the freedom of employers.

Granting specific performance when damages would be inadequate is surely acceptable. The issue arises only for cases of breach. It does not arise for rescission cases, because the parties are to be put in the position they were in prior to the interaction, which cannot involve specific performance. Nor does it arise for failure to fulfill warranties, for one has had performance, albeit defective. As the purpose of a remedy for breach is to place the injured party in the position he or she would have been in had the contract been performed, specific performance will often do this.

The real issue is the acceptability of the general presumption against specific performance, which amounts to the requirement that damages be found inadequate. The presumption stems from the historical distinction between law and equity. Courts of equity provided specific performance, and they acted only when the legal remedy of damages was inadequate. The question is whether the presumption is simply the dead hand of the past or has a legitimate basis.

First, the presumption makes no difference when an object is unique, for the presumption is met. Land and real property, art objects, and at least some goods supplied by franchisors to franchisees are considered unique. When objects are unique, there is no reliable market for determining price or an adequate substitute. Moreover, an individual is more likely to attach personal value to a unique item than a common one. The costs of court time in calculating damages and the risks of not adequately calculating personal value make specific performance preferable (see Kronman 1978b).

Second, in many cases, by the time a case gets to court, specific performance might not do any good. For example, Gamma Computer Store in our hypothetical example in the previous section would probably not need ten microcomputers by the time its claim against Delta got to court. The requirement to mitigate damages also often makes specific performance unwanted or irrelevant to the injured party. In *Oloffson v. Coomer* (11 Ill. App. 3d 918, 296 N.E.2d 871 (1973), also discussed above), had Oloffson covered by purchasing corn when Coomer breached, he would not have been interested in specific performance. Thus, in many or most cases, the injured party will find specific performance useless.

Third, that the injured party will often, even usually, not desire specific performance does not justify a presumption against it. It is one thing to leave the injured party discretion to ask for damages or specific performance; it is another to allow specific performance only when, in the court's judgment, damages would be inadequate. It has been forcefully argued that specific performance should be as routinely available as damages, because damages often fail to compensate adequately, promisees are unlikely to request specific performance unless damages are inadequate, and promisees are in a better position than courts to determine whether damages would be adequate (Schwartz 1979, 276-9). These are clearly reasons why, as an injured party, one would want specific performance at one's option.

Fourth, from a defaulting party's point of view, the routine availability of specific performance could be costly. By requesting specific performance, plaintiffs would avoid the duty to mitigate damages. Breaching parties might find that the costs of specific performance have significantly increased due to delay. For example, if a builder breaches after partial performance, a requirement of specific performance a couple of years later might cost significantly more due to increased costs of labor and materials. Even in a falling market, damages might not be mitigated if injured parties were permitted reliance costs in addition to specific performance. The costs of reliance could exceed any fall in market price. This possibility could be prevented by not allowing damages in addition to specific performance, but then home purchasers, for example, would be denied compensation for rent until performance. In the end, courts might be required to make judgments of the balance between mitigation of damages and the personal value of performance.

Given the unlikeliness of wanting specific performance as an injured party and the possible increased costs as a breaching party, one would not accept routine specific performance. *(4-20) The principle of specific performance: specific performance should not be ordered unless damages would be inadequate and courts can easily supervise performance.* Besides the problems for either party mentioned above, were courts to try to sort through the concerns to see that breaching parties are not improperly harmed, a significant burden would be placed on court time and resources. In short, court cases would become more complicated, and the economic direct costs of the court system increased (see 2.1.1). Concerns for economic costs and certainty of relief for plaintiffs underlie the restriction to easily supervised performance. The purpose of remedy for breach is to place the injured party in the position he or she would have been in had the contract not been breached. If damages will do so, injured parties have no complaint. Thus, the procedural nature of a court system justifies the restrictive substance of the principle of specific performance.

CHAPTER 5

TORT LAW

INTRODUCTION

5.0. Tort law is concerned with "interactions" in which one person has caused another harm (Seavy 1942, 73). Special quote marks are used, because unlike contract interactions, usually the parties do not knowingly deal with one another. For example, a car might run off the road and smash the plaintiff's fence. As the interactions involve harm, tort law is concerned with interactions that from an after the fact perspective are minus sum ones. Because contract law is based on whether before the fact an interaction is mutually expected to be beneficial, it concerns some interactions that after the fact are minus sum ones. Most of these contractual interactions that turn out to be minus sum ones can also be addressed in tort law.

It might be claimed that not all tort cases involve minus sum interactions, that some involve zero sum interactions. For example, in wrongfully taking another's property with the intent to keep it ('conversion'), one person has acquired another's property, which appears to be a zero sum interaction. One contemporary view of tort law contends that it is concerned with both wrongful gains and losses (Coleman 1983, 66). However, tort law is concened only with losses. First, the tort remedy is based on the loss suffered by the plaintiff, not, as in restitution or quasi-contract, the gain of the defendant (Williams 1951, 170-71). For example, if due to frustration a contract is void, one party must return to the other what he or she has benefited. If, however, one person has converted and consumed perishable goods of another, that person must pay for the loss – what the goods were worth to the person who owned them – not for the gain – what they were worth to the person who converted them. If the conversion was deliberate, then the plaintiff usually has a choice between the tort remedy of the amount of his or her loss or the restitutionary remedy of the benefit gained by the defendant (Epstein 1985, 36-37).

This does not mean, however, that the difference between tort and contract is simply a matter of remedy. In most, if not all, cases of wrongful gains, the one who parts with property does not do so voluntarily but by force or fraud (including misrepresentation). Thus, from an economic perspective one has no basis for claiming that the property was worth as much to the gainer as to the loser, because the loser did not make a reasonable judgment that the interaction was beneficial. Thus, one has no basis for an economic claim that the interaction is a zero sum rather than minus sum one. Indeed, inasmuch as the interaction involves the violation of a right of the plaintiff, from a broader perspective there is a moral harm. The tort remedy focus on recitfying a loss results from the focus on the interaction as a minus sum one. Consequently, it is misleading to say that tort law is concerned with wrongful gains or unjust enrichment. It is concerned with losses by one party.

If tort law is concerned with harms or losses, it is important to be clear what a harm or loss is. A person is harmed or suffers a loss if something occurs that is contrary to or sets back that person's interest, that is, makes the person less capable than before of fulfilling his or her self-regarding wants (see Bayles 1978, 96-104; Feinberg 1984, ch. 1). The person is worse off than before the interaction. One must distinguish harm or loss from non-benefit. In non-benefit, something fails to be in a person's interest. The person is no better off after the action than before, which is especially significant when the person thought he or she would be. For example, the failure of a promisor to perform under a contract is frequently a non-benefit. The promisee's position is not improved, as it should have been. Indeed, expectation damages are for non-benefit, while reliance damages are for harms or losses. However, not all interests are or should be protected by tort law. We shall consider what kinds of harms or interests should be protected by various torts.

The tort law question is "Who should be liable to whom for what losses?" or more specifically, "Which defendants should be liable to which plaintiffs for what harms?" Courts confront cases in which a plaintiff claims to have suffered or be about to suffer a loss. The question is whether to shift some or all of this loss to the defendant either by making the defendant pay the plaintiff or by prohibiting the defendant acting in ways that will harm the plaintiff. Recall that we are concerned with principles to support judicial decisions applied to the parties to a case or controversy (1.4). If the government is not a party to the case, judges cannot order it to pay the plaintiff simply because they think it would be best if the government paid for the plaintiff's loss. At the end of this chapter (5.5), we drop this assumption and briefly consider whether litigation is the best way to achieve the aims of tort law.

In considering tort actions, it is useful to make causation an explicit element of a legal case in addition to the three elements indicated in 1.5. The traditional elements of a tort action are: (1) the defendant had (has) a duty to the plaintiff; (2) the defendant acted (is going to act) contrary to that duty; (3) the defendant's act causally affected (will causally affect) the plaintiff; and (4) as a result, the plaintiff suffered (will suffer) harm. The emphasis on these elements varies among particular torts. Element (4) is basically the claim that a response is appropriate, either payment of damages or issuance of an 'injunction' – order that the defendant do or not do something. Elements (3) and (2) together constitute the claim that the defendant violated the duty. If all tort duties are viewed as duties not to cause harm, they are violated only if acts contrary to duty cause harm. Thus, these two elements are prominent in tort law defenses.

AIMS

5.1.0. *Introduction.* In the mists of medieval law, tort and criminal law arose together. To drastically oversimplify the law and history, if one person claimed to have been harmed by another, he or she could bring an action against the other. Money damages were often paid to both the plaintiff and the state. Over time, criminal actions by the state became separate from private ones, although some of them, such as assault and battery, still overlap. Moreover, although originally both crime and tort were concerned primarily with physical harm, both have broadened their scope to include other forms of harm.

Given the historical connection between tort and criminal law, it is not surprising that similar aims are claimed for them. One aim is often said to be appeasement or prevention of self-help by victims against those who cause injury (Christie 1983, 5; Williams 1951, 138-40). This aim is not specific to tort law or even tort and criminal law. Instead, it is one of the aims of a legal system – to provide for the peaceful resolution of disputes (see 2.0 and the principle of peacefulness (2-3) in 2.1.3). Although it might explain a few features of tort law, it provides little normative guidance for most problems.

5.1.1. *Retribution.* The central idea of 'retribution' is that a person should "pay" for wrongdoing. In criminal law, this payment involves punishment;

in civil or private law, it primarily involves payment of money damages to victims. This aim can be developed by considering the fact situation in *Fisher v. Carrousel Motor Hotel, Inc.* (424 S.W.2d 627 (Tex. 1967)). Fisher, a black mathematician, was an invited guest of corporations having a conference at Carrousel. Plate in hand, he was about to be served at a buffet luncheon, when an employee of the hotel snatched the plate from his hand and shouted that a black could not be served. The retributivist view is that such conduct should not be tolerated, that the wrongdoer should pay for his wrongdoing, and that he should make it up to Fisher. In short, a culpable wrongdoer should pay for his or her wrongdoing by making reparations to the victim. In *Fisher*, the court awarded damages for mental suffering resulting from an assault even though there was no physical harm.

Several objections can be raised against retribution as an aim. A common objection to retribution as an aim of criminal law is that it seems pointless to inflict suffering on a wrongdoer if no good will come from it (see 6.1.2). However, that objection is inapplicable to tort law, because the typical relief is for the wrongdoer to pay damages to the victim. Good always results, because the victim receives a benefit. Another objection is that other culpable wrongdoers who perhaps fortuitously do not cause harm will not be penalized at all by the tort law, so the retributive aim of penalizing wrongdoers is undermined (Coleman 1975, 171-72; Chapman 1983, 16). This objection ignores another difference between retribution in tort and criminal law. Because criminal law has a societal perspective, it is concerned with all wrongdoing. The tort law perspective is that of the individual plaintiff, not society as a whole. The individual plaintiff seeks retribution for wrongful injury to him or her, not for all wrongdoing. Culpable conduct that does not cause the plaintiff injury is not usually more of a wrong to the plaintiff than to any other member of society, and so it does not give rise to a particular complaint of harm. Moreover, even if tort law does not and cannot fully achieve the retributive aim, it does not follow that it is not an aim to be pursued in tort law (see also Calabresi 1970b, 208). Most other criticisms of the retributive aim (Chapman 1983; Coleman 1983, 46-50) are based on it not providing an explanation of much of tort law. As our purpose is justification, not explanation, and an acceptable aim need not justify the whole of a legal field to be one of its legitimate aims, these arguments are irrelevant.

(5-1) The principle of civil retribution: ethically culpable wrongdoers should make reparations to their victims. The concept of 'ethically culpable' wrongdoers is a difficult one to spell out, although almost everyone has a

good idea of what it involves. For present purposes, we construe it narrowly to require that the act was voluntary (not due to duress, coercion, and so on), that the actor was aware that the act was contrary to the victim's interest, and that the actor did not reasonably believe he or she was justified. These restrictions certainly prevent the retributive aim applying to much tortious wrongdoing; the concept of fault in tort law is not this ethical one (see Coleman 1975, 170-71). Thus, the principle has, quite limited scope. However, instead of disqualifying it as an acceptable aim, this limited scope makes it more acceptable. As a defendant, one could not rationally accept a retributivist aim if one was not aware that one was inflicting harm, or if aware, was not acting voluntarily. But given the restrictions, one can always avoid inflicting such harm, so the principle is acceptable. As a plaintiff, one can easily accept ethically culpable wrongdoers making reparations.

Some theories of civil or tort law try to develop a more general aim in the retributivist tradition, although it is often not clear whether they are primarily designed to explain or to justify it. For example, an Hegelian view contends that there is a moral fault of moral mistake or ignorance and that reparations are due for acts exhibiting such fault (see Prichard and Brudner 1983, 154-59). A wrong involves the violation of rules that reciprocally guarantee freedom. However, the further one gets from the narrow conception of ethical culpability, the less likely it is that one can accept the principle from the defendant's perspective. This approach suffers from the common problem we have noted before, the belief that only one aim accounts for a field of law. Consequently, we do not consider it further.

5.1.2. *Deterrence*. Another traditional view is that the aim of tort law is to deter people from harming others. This aim also overlaps with an aim of criminal law, but in criminal law deterrence is to be achieved by punishment and in tort law by liability for damages. If they have to pay damages for harming others, people will avoid injurious conduct. This aim has some limitations. First, like the retributivist aim, this one also assumes that people can avoid the injurious conduct, but unlike the retributivist aim, it does not require that a person be ethically culpable. For example, inadvertent negligence is not ethically culpable, because the person is not aware that the conduct will probably inflict harm. Nonetheless, the prospect of having to pay damages can make people more careful and thus prevent negligently caused harm. Still, for specific individuals to be deterred, it must be possible for them to avoid the injurious conduct. Consequently, a 'subjective' standard of negligence should be used – could this individual have avoided the conduct (Williams 1951, 159). Another limitation is that achievement of the deterrence aim also requires that the individual who commits a tort – 'tortfeasor' – pay. The aim is at least significantly weakened if the tortfeasor can shift the burden, say, by insurance (see Williams 1951, 165-68).

Another alleged limitation of the deterrence aim is that the tort sanction will be too great or too little for deterrence (Williams 1951, 147). The typical tort sanction is to pay for the harm caused. The amount is adventitious. The damages might be more or less than required to deter the conduct. This difficulty is partly, but only partly, met by the money being paid to the victim. Deterrence in criminal law arises from imposing a loss (imprisonment), and there is no point in imposing more than necessary. The payment of damages, however, is not a net loss in that sense, because the plaintiff gains whatever the defendant loses. Thus, if the sanction is more than needed to deter, it is not a net loss. However, this point does not help when damages are too little.

In recent years, inspired by the economic analysis of law, economic deterrence has become a popular aim. It is suggested that the aim of tort law is the efficient avoidance of accidents (Calabresi 1970a, 26; Posner 1977, 143). Although there are several versions of this view, the general idea is to assign liability so that accidents are avoided in the most efficient manner whenever it is economical to avoid them. This approach is sometimes called general deterrence (Calabresi 1970a, 27; Calabresi 1970b, 208-09). The approach is one of 'general' rather than 'specific' deterrence, that is, of deterring others rather than just the individual held liable. However, one could have general deterrence approaches that are not solely concerned to minimize the economic costs of accidents, so it is preferable to call it economic deterrence.

One of the inspirations for this approach, at least in negligence cases, is the so-called Learned Hand formula. Judge Hand suggested that the test for negligence is whether the cost of a defendant preventing an accident is less than the cost of injury times its probability (*United States v. Carroll Towing Co.,* 159 F.2d 169 (2d Cir. 1947)). In short, would defendants taking precautions in such situations pay off by avoiding accidents the total costs of which would be greater than the costs of the precautions? If so, they should be liable. But the Learned Hand formula is not quite the prescription of economic deterrence. Even if it would pay off for defendants to take precautions, on economic grounds it might be better if the losses remained with plaintiffs, because they could avoid them more cheaply. Losses should be assigned to the cheapest risk avoider. (Note that this is similar to the economic analysis of mistake in contract law (4.3.3).) If neither party can reduce the risks for less than the costs of the accidents, then neither should take precautions. In such situations, losses should remain with plaintiffs to save the 'transaction costs' of shifting them to defendants. Transaction costs are any costs of an interaction transferring property or services, in this case, primarily legal costs.

It is useful to compare and contrast the traditional and economic deterrence aims. First, the traditional aim does not distinguish among defendants who could be deterred from injurious conduct – they should all be held liable. The economic version does not hold all deterrable defendants liable. They should not be held liable if the costs of precautions are greater than the costs of harms or if plaintiffs could more cheaply avoid the harms.

Second, economic deterrence takes a rule-oriented or statistical approach (general deterrence), while traditional deterrence takes an individual case approach (specific deterrence). Damages in individual cases are adventitious. By the rule approach, in determining whether precautions are worthwhile and liability should be imposed, one considers the costs in similar situations, including those in which fortuitously no harm results from lack of precautions. This partially avoids the objection or limitation that damages are more or less than needed to deter. The sum of damages paid will not be either more or less than needed to deter inefficient failures to avoid accidents, although in individual cases it will. Moreover, the statistical approach will not deter poor persons from committing wrongs from which they will benefit, such as converting others' property. Either they cannot pay damages or they have to return what they have gained; they cannot lose by the interaction and so will not be deterred. However, deterrence (like retribution) can still properly be an aim even if it will not always be achieved. The rule-oriented approach seems to be the more appropriate one, because principles are to be applied to many situations.

Third, the rule orientation of economic deterrence helps make it compatible with defendants shifting losses by insurance. Economic deterrence is primarily concerned with determining liability, although if those persons held liable did not incur any costs people would have no incentive to modify their behavior and there would be no deterrence effect. The average insurance premium must be greater than the average cost of harm, for it must include administration costs and profits. Thus, each insured person has an incentive to take precautions slightly greater than the average cost of harm. If insurance premiums are adjusted for frequency of accidents, then the greater one's risk of accident, the greater one's insurance costs. However, because of the delay in raising premiums and the fact that they are spread over time, the cost of insurance is probably not as effective a deterrent as having to pay damages. Of course, insurance companies are competitive and to keep their premiums low sometimes quit insuring high risk persons or organizations. The uninsured person will then bear the full costs of future accidents, but it might be too late to deter or save money, for the accidents might be relatively rare but expensive ones.

Fourth, the economic as well as the traditional deterrence view might require a subjective standard of negligence. One might think that it too would be avoided by the rule orientation, that the most efficient rule would be based on an 'objective' standard or interpretation of the average or reasonable person. This is not necessarily so. A rule with an objective standard might not deter any more accidents than one with a subjective standard. After all, persons subjectively incapable of complying with the law will not be deterred. Although applying a subjective standard at trial is more time consuming and expensive than applying an objective one, a subjective standard might save transaction costs (especially direct costs of the legal system) by removing cases from courts. Thus, a subjective standard excluding some classes of persons from liability might be as effective a deterrent as an objective one and save transaction costs.

After all this, deterrence surely remains one plausible aim of tort law. One rationally wants to decrease the risks of being harmed. As a potential plaintiff, then, the aim of deterrence is acceptable. The question is whether it is acceptable as a potential defendant. From that viewpoint, one would want to minimize the chances of being liable. On the whole, economic deterrence does so more than traditional deterrence. Although economic deterrence might support an objective standard so that one might be liable when one is incapable of avoiding accidents, it reduces liability when plaintiffs could more cheaply avoid harms or one's benefits are greater than the harms. Moreover, it permits loss spreading by insurance. These gains are almost certainly greater than the costs of an objective standard. Given equal probability of being a plaintiff or defendant, one would rationally prefer the economic to the traditional version, for it reduces the average cost. Whatever one might lose from it as a plaintiff, one would more than gain as a defendant. In short, with an equal probability of being a plaintiff or defendant and other things being equal, one would prefer liability rules providing the most economic avoidance of losses. *(5-2) The principle of economic deterrence: uneconomical harm should be deterred by imposing liability on the cheapest risk avoiders.* Because we do not contend that this is the only aim of tort law, our overall view of tort law differs from that implied by a strict economic analysis.

5.1.3. Compensation. Many authors take compensation to be the primary aim of tort law (Fridman 1978, 9; Prosser and Keeton 1984, 5-6; Seavy 1942, 72; Williams and Hepple 1976, 3). Moreover, the aim of compensating plaintiffs for their losses is implicit in those of retribution and economic deterrence. One version of retribution has been called ethical compensation – justice requires that the victim of a wrong receive compensation (Williams 1951, 141). We have indicated this compensatory aspect by speaking of reparations. To appreciate it, one need only ask whether a plaintiff's retributive aim would be satisfied if the defendant suffered a penalty but the plaintiff did not receive any damages. One has no reason to support a tort law system of this sort; the chance of the satisfaction of seeing the defendant penalized without any possible recovery for harm would not be worth the cost in time and money of bringing a lawsuit. Even if plaintiffs received legal costs, in most situations one would not bother to sue simply for the satisfaction of retribution. Although some plaintiffs, for example, in defamation cases (see 5.2.1), might be satisfied with 'nominal' or minimal damages, few would sue without a chance of receiving larger damages.

Compensation is perhaps only contingently involved in economic deterrence. The correct amount of deterrence is provided by making injurers compensate their victims for the harms (Posner 1977, 143). The same penalty could be provided but not given to plaintiffs, that is, not given as compensation; but then plaintiffs would have no reason to sue and deterrence would not result from tort law.

The aim of compensation is broader in scope than those of retribution and deterrence; that is, it supports more tort actions. Compensation differs from reparation by not requiring the loss to result from a wrong. It makes no difference whether the defendant is ethically culpable or could have avoided the injurious conduct, for the concern is to make good the injured party's loss. Nor is it a defect that injurers might be insured; indeed, insofar as this helps guarantee that victims are compensated, it is a benefit. Thus, compensation turns what for other aims are limitations into virtues.

This broader scope of the compensatory aim might, however, make it unacceptable. From a plaintiff's perspective, one would have no objection to it. Of course one would rationally want to be compensated for a harm. It is another matter altogether from a defendant's perspective. Suppose Archer's fence is damaged by Baldwin's car running off the road. Further suppose Archer sues her next door neighbor Cox for compensation for the damage to the fence. If the sole aim of tort law is compensation for losses, this would fulfill it (see Weinrib 1983, 125). But if one were in Cox's position, one would find such liability completely unacceptable. Nor would the argument that Cox is rich and can easily afford to pay for the fence while Baldwin is poor and unable to compensate Archer render it any more acceptable were one Cox. Even if this "deep pocket" theory explains part of tort law, such as 'vicarious liability' (5.2.5), it is surely normatively unacceptable (cf. Calabresi 1970a, 40-42). Cox's chief complaint would be that she had nothing to do with the damage to Archer's fence, so she should not be the one to compensate Archer. Thus, a minimal condition for the acceptability of compensation as an aim is that the defendant be someone related to the production of the harm.

This restriction alone might not be sufficient to make compensation an acceptable aim. One must still consider how the defendant is related to the production of the harm. It makes no difference to a pure compensatory aim whether the injurer was ethically culpable or could even avoid the harm. As a defendant, how could one rationally accept a principle holding one liable for harms one could not avoid causing? Suppose Baldwin's car went out of control, because a defective tire made by Zeta Rubber blew out. Further suppose that Zeta Rubber has excellent quality control procedures, and that the cost of procedures to exclude more defective tires would be greater than the cost of harm prevented. (Thus, economic deterrence would not directly justify Zeta's liability, because the costs of avoidance exceed the costs of accidents.)

Could one, in the position of Zeta, rationally accept a principle of compensation imposing liability on one for the damage to Archer's fence? One might. The reason is the ability to spread the cost. Zeta need not suffer any major loss by having to pay in such cases, because it could spread the costs of such liability over all its customer's by charging slightly more for tires. By avoiding severe economic losses for any one person and consequent economic social dislocations, such loss spreading could even lower the total costs of harm (Calabresi 1970a, 40, 44).

Even if total costs are not reduced, the ability to spread costs or risks can render a principle of compensation acceptable even if defendants cannot avoid the harm resulting from their activities. Cost spreading effectively turns compensatioon into a form of insurance. The basis for insurance is risk aversion – one wants to avoid risks of significant harm. One is willing to pay a small amount (have a certain small loss) to avoid the possibility of a very large one. It cannot be shown that risk aversion is irrational, although it seems more plausible when the harms are major (see Rawls 1971, 154). Indeed, we have already used it in justifying the principle of rescission ((4-18) in 4.4.2). Given an equal chance of being plaintiff or defendant, with risk spreading and aversion to the risk of major losses, the potential benefits as plaintiff outweigh the losses as defendant. *(5-3) The principle of compensation*: : *people should be compensated for their losses by those whose activities produced the harms and who either could have conducted the activities without producing them or are able to spread the costs.*

We have thus arrived at three acceptable aims of tort law. In the classical view, retribution, deterrence, and compensation were all achieved together (cf. Fleming 1968, 8). If defendants' liability was based on ethical fault, then making them pay damages would exact retribution on wrongdoers, deter them from similar conduct in the future, and compensate victims. However, these aims need not all be satisfied together, and they rarely are in the extant tort law. It is perfectly rational to pursue one aim primarily in one type of tort and another aim primarily in another type. It is not irrational to pursue retribution in defamation actions and compensation in personal injury cases. As we have seen, some aims have a broader scope than others.

Nor need one rank the aims in order of importance. One aim might be more important in one context, and another in a different context. For example, plaintiffs in defamation actions might primarily be interested in elements of retribution – showing that what was said about them is false and that the defendant was at fault in making the statements – than in compensation. Nor is it sound to object that an aim is not or cannot be fully fulfilled in tort law. It is perfectly rational to pursue an activity that only partly fulfills an aim. After examining the structure of tort law, we briefly consider whether the aims might not be better fulfilled by a social arrangement other than tort law. That they might does not constitute an objection to their being aims in tort law, but to using tort law as a method of achieving the aims. That one might make more money investing in stocks than in gold does not imply that making money is not a justifiable aim in investing in gold.

DUTIES

5.2.0. *Introduction.* Torts can be classified in various ways (Fridman 1978, 31-40). Classification can be by the interests of the plaintiff, such as physical safety, possession of property, and so on. A closely related approach is to classify torts by the harm suffered – physical injury to the person, mental suffering, and so on. Crimes are generally classified in this manner – homicide and rape for examples. Of course, as harm is something contrary to an interest, an invasion of an interest, this classification does not differ significantly from that by interests.

For present purposes, it is preferable to classify torts according to the mental state with which the defendant acted – intentionally, negligently, and so on. This approach indicates more clearly the type of conduct and duties involved than an approach based on interests. A duty not intentionally to act contrary to an interest specifies the wrongful conduct more than a duty not to invade an interest. One can then distinguish different torts involving the same type of conduct by the interests protected.

Torts basically require one of three mental conditions. The actor must have acted (1) intentionally, (2) negligently, or (3) with 'strict liability' – any mental state will suffice, or better, no specific mental state is required. Sometimes another mental condition – wilful, wanton, or reckless – is specified; this condition is often considered an aggravated form of negligence (Prosser and Keeton 1984, 212-14). In a few situations, such as libel of public persons in the United States, recklessness is classified with intent in that either suffices for liability. In tort, to act intentionally is to desire an outcome or to believe that it is substantially certain (Rest. 2d Torts § 8A; Williams and Hepple 1976, 85). To act negligently is to fail to act as a reasonable, prudent person would have. For strict liability, it is enough that a voluntary act caused the harm.

5.2.1. *Intentional torts.* As just explained, intentional torts involve the actor either desiring a consequence or believing that it is substantially certain to occur. We will often use 'know' or 'knowingly' for the latter condition. Moreover, it suffices if a reasonable person would know that a consequence is substantially certain. 'Recklessness' differs from knowledge with respect to the likelihood of the consequence occurring. In recklessness, a consequence is not substantially certain to occur, only strongly probable.

A more difficult question about intentional torts pertains to what consequences must be intended. The problem can be illustrated by the intentional tort of 'battery'. Battery requires unconsented to contact or touching of another. An ambiguity is whether a defendant must (1) intend both contact and that it be harmful or offensive, or (2) intend contact which happens to be harmful or offensive. By (1) the defendant must intend harm or offense, whereas by (2) the defendant need not know that the contact will be harmful or offensive. Interpretation (1) seems to require a desire for or knowledge of harm, whereas (2) does not, only that contact occur.' Some cases require only sense (2) (*Masters v. Becker*, 22 A.D.2d 118, 254 N.Y.S.2d 633 (App. Div. 1964); *Garratt v. Dailey*, 46 Wash. 2d 197, 279 P.2d 1091 (1955)). A similar point concerns trespass to land – invasion of the interest in exclusive possession. Historically and even today to some extent, one need only have intended the act that constituted trespass, not trespass itself (Christie 1983, 62; Prosser and Keeton 1984, 68). Essentially, only a voluntary act is required, not knowledge of consequences, so though called an intentional tort, it is more one of strict liability (Cane 1982, 35).

In both battery and trespass, a necessary condition is that the other person not consent to the touching or going on the land. As lack of consent is essential, it is appropriate to require that the defendant be aware that the victim does not consent. The chief historical reason for not requiring this in trespass was that trespass was often used to settle titles to land. One person would go onto disputed land and the other would sue for trespass. The latter could win only if he or she and not the other had title to the land. The effect was to vindicate rights regardless of damages, of the interaction being a zero sum one (see Cane 1982, 36; Prosser and Keeton 1984, 67-68). But today, there are other ways of settling disputes about ownership and the vindication of rights is not appropriate here (Cane 1982, 39).

If the defendant in battery or trespass is required to know that the contact with person or land is without the victim's consent, then intent and not strict liability is involved and the retributive aim is relevant to all intentional torts. In 5.1.1, we specified ethical culpability as involving a voluntary act with awareness that it is contrary to the victim's interest and without a reasonable belief that it is justified. In intentional torts the behavior is voluntary, and for now we can ignore the belief in justification such as self-defense. If the actor knows the contact is without the victim's consent, then the actor knows that it is contrary to an interest of the victim, namely, the interest in not having such contact without one's consent.

Here one must distinguish between an act being contrary to an interest of the victim and it being contrary to the net interests of the victim – all interests considered together. An actor might think that contact is in the victim's net interests, for example, a surgeon who removes diseased tissue. The normative question is who should make this judgment of the victim's net interests. The law of tort leaves it to the victim, and there are good reasons for doing so. At best, the actor is causing one harm to avoid greater harm or to provide a benefit. As a potential victim, one would not leave judgments of the balance of interests to all others, although one might give specific persons (such as a surgeon) permission to make such decisions for one in specific contexts. By requiring that one consent either to specific acts or to others making such judgments in particular contexts, tort law prevents intermeddling by others.

The class of intentional torts is both the narrowest and the broadest category of torts. It is the narrowest in that it encompasses the smallest range of defendant conduct, because the other categories also include intentional conduct. It is the broadest category in that it includes interests and harms not included in other torts (see also Smith 1984, 111). There is good reason to be more inclusive of interests protected from intentional invasion than from nonintentional invasion. Given that the invasion is desired or knowing, from a victim's perspective it expresses less respect than an unintended invasion. To have one's reputation damaged by a person knowingly stating falsehoods is a personal attack and affront, whereas to have it damaged by careless misstatements does not indicate personal disrespect and affront (although the law also protects the latter). From a defendant's perspective, as one is aware of the invasion, one can more easily avoid it and the consequent liability than with other torts.

One fundamental interest protected by intentional torts is that in the person. Broad interests such as this can be divided into more specific ones. The interest in one's person includes freedom from unconsented to contact (battery) as well as from the fear of such contact ('assault'). It can also be taken to include freedom from limits to one's movement ('false imprisonment' and 'malicious prosecution') as well as from disturbance of one's mental or emotional tranquility ('emotional distress').

Courts have been slow to include not causing emotional distress alone (without other injury) within the ambit of tort duties, in part because of the difficulty in setting limits. Emotional distress is an unavoidable element of daily life. However, one has no reason to suffer more of it than necessary, especially when it is inflicted for no ulterior purpose. One way of narrowing the scope of such a tort is to require that the conduct causing the distress to be "extreme and outrageous" (Rest. 2d Torts § 46(1)). Another way is to require that the distress be severe. The problem is to affix a meaning to 'severe'. One might require that some form of psychiatric disorder result, but that might be a difficult hurdle to meet. Perhaps it is best to leave it to the trier of fact, who will have a reasonable sense of what is beyond the limits of social tolerance. Most people would find it outrageous and likely to cause severe emotional distress to tell a six-year-old girl that her mother took a man away from another woman, was sleeping with a man, and would be punished by God (*Korbin v. Berlin*, 177 So.2d 551 (Fla. Dist. Ct. App. 1965)).

Another broad interest to be protected by duties in tort law is that in property. This clearly includes the interest in not having it intentionally damaged or destroyed as well as those in exclusive and continued possession (trespass and conversion). It can also include the interest in not transferring property due to falsehoods (fraud). Although sometimes classifed as special torts, interference with certain economic relationships, such as contracts and customers, can also be viewed as contrary to an interest in property (wealth). However, the mere intent to create economic loss for another, as by attracting away another's customers, is not sufficient to violate a duty. Instead, special considerations of means (threats) and motive are required.

A special group of torts can involve either interference with the person or property. These are torts involving the misuse of legal process. We have already indicated that intentionally procuring the imprisonment of another without a sincere belief that there is probable cause for it is contrary to an interest in freedom. But some forms of malicious prosecution involve civil actions that primarily affect property. For example, in *Bank of Lyons v. Schultz* (78 Ill. 2d 235, 399 N.E.2d 1286 (1980)), the bank tied up payment of $30,000 of a husband's life insurance for over nine years on groundless claims, and as a result the plaintiff, unable to make mortgage payments, forfeited her house. Even in these cases, some consideration is given the personal interest in being free of frivolous and vexatious court cases independent of the property value involved, although courts still require a showing of actual property loss.

An interest in privacy has become the basis of an independently recognized tort law duty only in this century. Privacy can involve seclusion, intimacy, or private affairs (Bayles 1978, 89-90), but legally a broader conception is used and some "privacy" torts protect other interests. The first type of case to make a major impact on the law involves the use of a person's picture or name in advertising a product (Prosser and Keeton 1984, 851). In these cases, people are recognized to have a proprietary right to the use of their names or pictures for commercial purposes. In recent years, courts have become conscious that such 'right of publicity' cases are really protecting interests in property similar to goodwill or trademarks (see 3.2.3; *Grant v. Esquire, Inc.*, 367 F. Supp. 876 (S.D.N.Y. 1973); *Zacchini v. Scripps-Howard Broadcasting Co.*, 433 U.S. 562 (1977)).

The core privacy cases involve intrusions on seclusion, intimacy, or private affairs such as physical invasions of one's home, eavesdropping on conversations by the use of wiretaps, and unauthorized examination of bank accounts (Prosser and Keeton 1984, 854-55). In all of these situations, the central interest is control over who has information about one. People have good reasons to protect such an interest (Bayles 1978, 90-91). In these cases, the primary aims must be deterrence or retribution instead of compensation, because these invasions rarely involve significant financial losses to be compensated.

Another group of cases usually classified as involving privacy, so-called false light cases, also often protect an interest in reputation (but see Prosser and Keeton 1984, 864). A person is falsely portrayed in a detrimental way. The common law's traditional method of protecting an interest in reputation was by an action for defamation. However, a false light privacy case can protect a person even when the statements are not defamatory. Nonetheless, if statements are defamatory, one is more likely to recover by a defamation action (Prosser and Keeton 1984, 866).

Conduct injurious to reputation is almost always linguistic – verbal or written. Given the importance of freedom of speech, presently courts are understandably reluctant to allow a broad action for defamation. However, the traditional restrictions on defamation actions go far beyond any reasonable concern for freedom of speech. One of the recognizably unjustifiable restrictions is the difference between speech ('slander') and writing ('libel'). In slander actions, unless the language falls within a narrow class of specific comments, such as accusation of a crime or infection with a loathsome disease, special damages must be proven. The result is that some verbal statements are not actionable although they would be were they written. As courts have recognized, these differences are almost entirely due to the historical origins of the two actions, but courts have refused to modify them (see, for example, *Jones v. Jones*, [1916] 2 A.C. 481 (Haldane, L. J.)). Here is the dead hand of the past with a vengeance. One has no reason to accept a distinction that as early as 1812 was recognized to have no basis on the merits (*Thorley v. Lord Kerry*, 128 Eng. Rep. 367 (Ex. Ch. 1812) (Mansfield, L. C. J.)).

The conflict between freedom of speech and interests in privacy and reputation can be examined by considering the weight to be attached to the truth of statements and to the intentional character of the invasions. If what is said about one is true, then while it might damage one's reputation, one has little ground for complaint. If truth will damage one's reputation, then either the reputation was undeserved or the damage is undeserved, that is, people improperly take certain facts to reflect negatively on one. In the latter case, the fault lies with those people who improperly adopt a negative view, not the person who made the information available. The same consideration applies to false light privacy cases. However, one would not accept truth as a bar to invasion of actual privacy interests. It is precisely making known the true state of one's private affairs that constitutes the invasion.

The distinction between privacy and reputation interests can also help resolve whether, out of a concern for freedom of speech, only intentional invasions of them should be torts. The common-law action for defamation was not restricted to intentional conduct. From a concern for freedom of speech, the U.S. Supreme Court has in effect restricted mass media defamation of public officials and public figures to statements known to be false or involving reckless disregard for the truth (*New York Times Co. v. Sullivan*, 376 U.S. 254 (1964)). Technically, the Court recognized a mass media privilege for negligent defamation of public officials and figures. However, it has allowed private persons to sue in negligence and taken a broad view of who is a private person (*Gertz v. Robert Welch, Inc.*, 418 U.S. 323 (1974); *Time, Inc. v. Firestone*, 424 U.S. 448 (1976)).

Although the Court has not always articulated its reasons well, perhaps the central element is that defamation of private persons involves invasion of privacy. 'Public persons' are those who have thrust themselves into the public eye or been so thrust by reasons beyond their control. One may infer that the former have implicitly consented to be the subject of discussion, and the latter are unfortunate victims of the vicissitudes of life, such as being disaster victims. Private persons have neither voluntarily consented to be the subject of discussion nor been forced to be so by unfortunate circumstances. Consequently, defamation of private persons often involves an unwanted publication of private affairs as well as injury to reputation, in effect, two torts in one. Given this probable invasion of two interests, one would desire that due care be taken to publish only what is at least true. Moreover, the publication of true information that does not involve forcing people into the public eye, for example, information contained in public records, does not invade either interest and so should not be prohibited

(*Cox Broadcasting Corp. v. Cohn*, 420 U.S. 469 (1975); but see *Briscoe v. Reader's Digest Ass'n*, 4 Cal. 3d 529, 483 P.2d 34, 93 Cal. Rptr. 866 (1971) (publication of name of rehabilitated criminal years later may invade privacy)).

(5-4) The principle of intentional torts: persons should be liable for intentional invasions of others' interests in (a) their person, including bodily integrity, freedom, and emotional tranquility; (b) property, including economic loss by deceit and legal actions not in good faith; (c) privacy; and (d) reputation. This principle is stated in terms of 'intentional invasions' of interests rather than 'acts contrary to people's interests' to imply or at least suggest the causal element of actually harming. We have briefly mentioned a few problems of balancing this principle with others to work out the details of specific torts, particularly the balance between freedom of speech and interests in privacy and reputation.

5.2.2. *Negligence standard.* The tort of negligence requires only that one negligently or carelessly cause injury. Unlike recklessness, which involves an awareness of a strong probability of a consequence, negligence does not require actual awareness of the possibility of harm, only that a person should have been aware of an unreasonable risk of harm. The test is how a reasonable, prudent person would have acted (*Vaughan v. Menlove*, 130 Eng. Rep. 490 (C.P. 1837)). In practice, this often means what a jury, with hindsight, thinks should have been done. The standard is probably higher than what jurors would actually have done in the situation. Serving on a jury, they know what in fact resulted, which is likely to make them more conscious of possible injury than they would have been in the situation. Moreover, they are in a calm condtion, not distracted by other things, and are able to reflect more fully and adequately. Nevertheless, the standard does allow juries to vary judgments in accordance with changing social conditions and standards of conduct (Fleming 1968, 28).

This standard is said to be objective, because it does not allow for the particular capabilities of the defendant. A person of limited mental capacity might not be able to recognize the dangers that a reasonable person would. However, one must be precise about the characteristics of the defendant that are ignored. These might be divided into physical and mental characteristics (cf. Seavey 1927, 1-3). In each case, some allowance is made for limited capabilities. First, allowance is made for physical defects of a person. A blind person is held to the standard of care of a reasonably prudent blind person, not that of a sighted person. Second, children are not held to the standard of adults but to the standard of children of their age and experience. Neither of these modifications makes the test depend on the particular defendant's capabilities.

Two other factors reinforce the objectivity of the standard, that is, its independence of the characteristics of the actual defendant. First, many more tort cases are being decided by judges than formerly. In England, hardly any cases are decided by jury. Judges, unlike juries, often render written decisions stating the reasons for their judgments. (This is less true of Canada and England than the United States.) Consequently, the fact situation they describe might be treated as a legal rule for future cases. If a defendant is found negligent in one case, so will future defendants in similar fact situations (Fleming 1968, 28-29). Second, failure to comply with statutory standards of conduct, such as speed limits, is often held to be strong or even conclusive evidence of negligence. Courts have considerable trouble deciding which statutory and regulatory standards should also be standards of conduct for tort law (see Prichard and Brudner 1983, 150-54; Williams and Hepple 1976, 97-104). Here we only note that to the extent courts accept such standards, negligence is made more objective. Indeed, sometimes statutory standards go beyond negligence and constitute strict liability, because their violation is considered conclusive evidence of negligence even if a person could not reasonably comply with them.

A central question is whether one has good reasons to accept the reasonable prudent person standard of care for negligence tort actions. To ask the question is almost to answer it. As a reasonable person, one would be able to meet the standard, recognizing that one might occasionally lapse from it. One would also want others to exercise the same degree of care towards oneself. Consequently, a reasonable person standard is acceptable.

It is less certain that one would accept it being applied objectively rather than subjectively, that is, as not excusing persons incapable of meeting it. Were one mentally deficient and unable to meet the objective standard, would one still want it applied? As a potential defendant, one would prefer a subjective interpretation. But for every defendant, there is a plaintiff with an interest in compensation. As a plaintiff, one could not have a legitimate retributive aim towards a defendant who was subjectively incapable of being more careful, for such a defendant would not be ethically culpable. Indeed, the retributive aim is completely irrelevant to negligence torts, because no merely negligent defendant is ethically culpable (aware of acting

contrary to another's interest). Nonetheless, to adopt a subjective application would place one at risk of bearing the costs of harm unintentionally
caused by persons of lesser capacity. In effect, persons of lesser capacity
would be permitted to cause uncompensated harm others are not permitted
to cause, which seems unfair (Weinrib 1983, 137-38). However, it is not
obvious that a reasonable person would consider this to be unfair. Each
person would be held to a standard of a reasonable use of his or her
capacities, and it is not necessarily fair to make persons of lesser capacities
pay for harm they could not avoid causing.

Two further considerations come into play at this point. One is that
society needs common standards that most people can meet. Thus, one can
rely on, say, other drivers meeting a common standard rather than having
to guess whether some less capable drivers might not be required to be as
careful as others. Another point is that the aims of economic deterrence
and compensation generally support an objective interpretation. As we saw
in 5.1.2, economic deterrence involves a complicated balancing of increased deterrence and transaction (direct court) costs. Rules recognizing physical and age disabilities are relatively clear and unlikely to decrease deterrence or increase transaction costs. More complicated analyses concerned
with the abilities of particular defendants are less likely to be economical.
Although the compensation aim is limited to recovery from people who
could have conducted activities without producing harm, many incapable
persons could and should recognize the limits of their capabilities and
avoid activities they cannot conduct safely. *(5-5) The principle of care:
persons should exercise the care that reasonable, prudent persons of their age,
experience, and physical characteristics would exercise in the circumstances.*

The reasonable person standard implies that some injuries result from
reasonable risks. The Learned Hand formula discussed in 5.1.2 comes into
play. If the likely benefits to the actor outweigh the likely harm to others,
then the risk is reasonable. Or, put negatively, if the likely benefits do not
outweigh the risk, the conduct is unreasonable (Rest. 2d Torts § 291).
Determining the benefits to the actor includes considering the importance
of the interest; the advance to it that is expected; the likelihood of the
advance; and the availability of alternative, less risky, actions that will
advance it. The *Restatement (Second) of Torts* mentions "the extent of the
chance that this interest will be advanced" (§ 292(b)), but this is confusing.
The extent of the advance of an interest – how much one might benefit –
is distinct from the chance of an advance or benefit. To speak of the "extent
of the chance" is nonsensical. Factors in determining the risk to others

include the importance of the interests, the likelihood of their invasion, the extent of such invasion (the degree of harm), and the number of persons whose interests are at risk (cf. Rest. 2d Torts § 293).

Such a calculation need not be, indeed, is unlikely to be, in monetary terms. Juries might well decide that risks are not worth taking even though in strictly monetary terms they pay off. For example, Ford Motor Company apparently decided that the costs of moving the gas tanks on Pinto automobiles were greater than the costs of harm likely to result from not moving them. Assuming that Ford included all deaths that would result and was correct in its calculations, a jury might still decide that the risk was unreasonable. A sophisticated economic analysis could perhaps account for this difference, because the costs would simply be determined by people's preferences between the two alternatives, thereby increasing the costs of harm. If one uses an economic benefit/cost analysis, one must use such a sophisticated one and not a simple one based only on direct financial costs.

5.2.3. *Scope of negligence.* We must now consider the scope of the duty of care. This has two aspects: towards whom must one be careful and with respect to what injuries. Good reasons exist to adopt a foreseeability standard for both. One could not reasonably accept a duty to take care to avoid injuries which a reasonable person could not foresee, because that would impose a duty that one could not meet. Nor does one have any reason to accept a lesser scope, for that would in effect deprive one of compensation for injuries that a reasonable actor could have avoided. With some twists and turns, the foreseeability standard is the one generally used in the law.

A classic legal statement of the foreseeability standard with respect to persons was given by Lord Atkin.

You must take reasonable care to avoid acts or omissions which you can reasonably foresee would be likely to injure your neighbour. Who, then, in law, is my neighbour? The answer seems to be – persons who are so closely and directly affected by my act that I ought reasonably to have them in contemplation as being so affected when I am directing my mind to the acts or omissions which are called in question. (*Donoghue v. Stevenson*, 1932 A.C. 562, 580.)

Of course, the second part of this quote is somewhat redundant; in effect, it defines "your neighbour" as anyone to whom one can foresee injury. This

statement is usually taken to be limited to physical injury to person or
property and to exclude omissions (Smith 1984, 99, 125). We consider the
interests to be protected in 5.2.4. In short, a duty of care is owed to those
persons whom one can reasonably foresee might be injured by one's conduct.

A famous American case also established that one's duty is limited to
persons to whom injury can be foreseen. In *Palsgraf v. Long Island R.R.* (248
N.Y. 339, 162 N.E. 99 (1928)), a man running to catch a departing train was
assisted on board by two guards. He dropped a wrapped package contain-
ing fireworks that then exploded. The shock knocked over some scales
many feet away injuring Ms. Palsgraf. On one interpretation, the court held
that risk of injury to Ms. Palsgraf, as opposed to the boarding passenger,
was not foreseeable by the guards. (However, one reason injury to her was
not foreseeable is that an explosion causing such damage was not foreseeable.)

Once one adopts the foreseeability standard for persons, it is only
reasonable to adopt it for injuries. However, for a while English courts, or
at least some of them, did not use the foreseeability standard. Instead, it
was held that one is liable for the direct consequences of a negligent act,
whether or not they are foreseeable. The source of this doctrine was *In re
an Arbitration betweeen Polemis and Furness, Withy & Co., Ltd.* ([1921] 3
K.B. 560 (C.A.)). In that case, the defendant's workers negligently knocked
a board into the hold of a ship, which caused a spark that ignited petrol
vapors and burned the ship. It was foreseeable that knocking a board into
a hold might cause injury to workers, cargo, or slight damage to the ship.
However, no reasonable person would expect it to cause the destruction
of a freighter by fire. Nonetheless, the fire was held to be a direct consequence of the act of knocking the board into the hold, so the defendant was
liable for the full damage to the ship.

The unacceptability of the direct consequence doctrine can be easily
shown. Suppose injury to Debnam is foreseeable, but injury to Eddy is not
foreseeable. Further suppose that due to Ferrell's negligent act both Debnam and Eddy suffer injuries of a kind that were not foreseeable. If one
allowed damages for all direct injuries but only to persons to whom injury
is foreseeable, then Debnam would recover and Eddy would not, although
in fact the defendant could not foresee the injuries to either. Ferrell has no
reason to accept liability to Debnam, since he could not foresee the injury
and so avoid it. Moreover, Eddy would find it unacceptable. "Why," she
might ask, "should Debnam be compensated and I not, when Ferrell could

no more foresee the injury to Debnam than to me?" This result is avoided if not only the plaintiff but the kind of injury must be foreseeable.

In a pair of famous cases, the *Wagon Mound* and *Wagon Mound No. 2*, the British Privy Council rejected the direct consequence standard of *In re Polemis* and recognized the foreseeability standard. The Wagon Mound was a ship docked in Sydney harbor, and oil it was loading was negligently spilled. The next day the oil was ignited by hot metal from a nearby repair wharf causing a conflagration. In the first Wagon Mound case, it was held that the owners of the Wagon Mound were not liable for the damage the fire caused the wharf, because it was not reasonably foreseeable that furnace oil in such circumstances would catch fire (*Overseas Tankship (U.K.), Ltd. v. Morts Dock and Eng'g Co.*, 1961 A.C. 388 (P.C.) (Austl.)).

In the second case, the owners of the Wagon Mound were found liable for fire damage to two ships docked nearby (*Overseas Tankship (U.K.), Ltd. v. Miller S.s.Co.*, [1967] 1 A.C. 617 (P.C. 1966) (Austl.)). Again, forseeability of damage was held to be the standard. The difference between the holding in this case and the previous one was attributed to the trial court having found that while remote, the possibility of fire was foreseeable, and that the defendants had no reason not to try to disperse the oil (the cost of precautions was less than that of the possible harm); whereas in the first case, the trial court had found that the risk of fire was not reasonably foreseeable. These cases clearly exhibit the difficulty in applying the foreseeability standard to particular facts. For however one cuts it, in the same situation the risk of fire was found reasonably foreseeable by one court and not by another. Of course, the evidence presented in court undoubtedly differed, although the extent of the difference is questionable (see Christie 1983, 323-27).

A problem still exists about what injury must be foreseeable. It could reasonably be foreseen that the Wagon Mound's spilt oil would pollute the water and make the docks slippery. The question was whether fire was foreseeable. Courts often claim that one is liable if the kind of injury was foreseeable even though the extent of injury was not. Thus, if a child knocks a lamp into a hole with a resulting large fire severely burning the child, the workers are liable for the burns. It could be foreseen that a child might be burnt by a lamp, although it could not be foreseen that an explosion might occur (*Hughes v. Lord Advocate*, 1963 A.C. 837). But, the *Restatement (Second) of Torts* (§ 281) claims that if an actor is negligent towards another with respect to one interest, he or she is liable for the invasion of any other interest protected from negligent invasion. This seems to imply that if

Ferrell's conduct is negligent because it risks injury to Debnam's property, then Ferrell is liable if Debnam receives personal injury. This result faces the same objections as the direct consequence doctrine and is just as unacceptable.

Nonetheless, there is an acceptable interpretation of the distinction between kind and extent of injury. Instead of distinguishing kinds of injury by the interests affected, one should distinguish them by the kinds of causal factors involved. In the Wagon Mound cases, the question was whether fire could be foreseen, not whether loss of life or damage to property could be foreseen. The *Hughes* decision might be confusing because their Lordships spoke of burns rather than fire. Another case indicates that it is the type of cause, not interest, that distinguishes kinds of injury. In *Doughty v. Turner Mfg. Co., Ltd.* ([1964] 1 Q.B. 518 (C.A. 1963)), an asbestos cement cover was negligently knocked into a vat of 800 degree Celsius liquid. After a couple of minutes, the lid exploded and the spewing liquid injured nearby workers. The court held that there was no liability, because the workers could not reasonably foresee an eruption of the liquid. However, there would have been liability had the liquid splashed on people when the lid slipped in, and the injury in that case would have been the same – hot liquid on the person. Similarly, in an American case, a can of rat poison negligently left near a stove in a coffee shop exploded injuring a worker. Liability was denied because the kind of injury was not foreseeable (*Larrimore v. American Nat'l Ins. Co.*, 184 Okl. 614, 89 P.2d 340 (1939)). Leaving rat poison near a stove is dangerous because food might be contaminated, not (at least beforehand) because of the likelihood of an explosion (see Keeton 1986; Feinberg 1986). Again, it is the kind of cause, not the interest invaded, that makes the difference.

(5-6) The principle of foreseeability: the duty of care should extend to, and only to, harms from foreseeable kinds of causes to foreseeable persons. One must be able to foresee harm resulting from a type of cause. The acceptability of this principle should be evident from the foregoing discussion.

This principle justifies the so-called thin skull rule, that one takes victims as one finds them. Thus, if one negligently injures a person, one must pay for damages suffered by a person with a thin skull that a person with a normally thick skull would not have suffered (see Prosser and Keeton 1984, 291-92). In such a case, although the extent of the injury is not foreseeable, the person and injury from that type of cause are. Thus, the principle of foreseeability applies and justifies liability, but a principle that required the extent of injury to be foreseeable would not justify liability. Moreover, the conduct must be likely to cause harm to an ordinary person, for otherwise harm of some sort is not foreseeable. That is, there must first be negligent harm, however slight, to an ordinary person. Being hit in the head would be a harm to a normal person, although perhaps the damage might be minimal. Consequently, plaintiffs who are especially sensitive to noise are not protected if the noise would not bother an ordinary person in ordinary activities. For example, mink farmers are especially sensitive to noise, because it makes mother minks eat their young. But courts have held that they are not protected in negligence from low flying airplanes (*Nova Mink, Ltd. v. Trans-Canada Airlines*, [1951] 2 D.L.R. 241 (N.S. Sup. Ct.)) or in strict liability from the noise of blasting (*Foster v. Preston Mill Co.*, 44 Wash. 2d 440, 268 P.2d 645 (1954); Rest. 2d Torts § 524A). Nor are specially sensitive persons protected from even intentional noise from carillons (*Impellizerri v. Jamesville Federated Church*, 104 Misc. 2d 620, 428 N.Y.S.2d 550 (Sup. Ct. Onondaga Co. 1979)).

5.2.4. *Interests protected from negligence*. The interests protected alone from negligent invasion are not as extensive as those protected from intentional invasion, because the retributive aim is inapplicable to negligently caused injury. However, once harm occurs to a protected interest, harm to other interests caused by the same act can usually be included in damages. Clearly, because of the centrality of physical well-being and property, these interests should be protected, and the law has always done so. Thus, one has a duty to take care not to cause foreseeable harm to persons or property. But not all the interests in the person protected from intentional invasion should be included. First, the negligent invasion of an interest in freedom is not a tort. The torts of false imprisonment and malicious prosecution must be intentional, at least as to the acts of imprisonment and prosecution. However, an element of these torts could be based on negligence, for example, negligence in determining whether there is probable cause for an arrest. Indeed, the existence of probable cause is based on what a reasonable person would believe or do, and although "actual malice" is also required, some courts take the absence of probable cause or recklessness with respect to it to imply actual malice (*Boose v. City of Rochester*, 71 A.D.2d 59, 421 N.Y.S.2d 740 (N.Y. App. Div. 1979)). Given the importance of freedom, it is surely reasonable to accept recklessness and probably negligence as to probable cause for this action.

The other controversial personal interest is that in emotional tranquility or mental stability, disruption of which is usually called nervous shock. The standard case involves someone (usually a relative) who sees an accident or the victims. Two issues are involved – who should be allowed to recover and what harm is necessary to justify recovery. Traditionally, both of these have been answered in relation to physical injury. As to the harm, American cases first usually held that one must suffer direct physical harm, and then broadened the rule to include cases in which physical harm resulted from emotional shock, for example, nervous disorders or fainting and hitting one's head. The English cases never clearly required that emotional shock be manifested in physical illness (Clerk and Lindsell 1982, § 10-15; Christie 1983, 512). Some American courts have adopted the English view (*Molien v. Kaiser Found. Hospitals*, 27 Cal. 3d 916, 167 Cal. Rptr. 831, 616 P.2d 813 (1980)).

How serious must the nervous shock be? Although one does not desire unpleasant surprises, one's primary interest is in retaining the capacity to be reasonable. Thus, the primary forms of mental injury are those that make one less intelligent or mentally abnormal (Bayles 1978, 109). In effect, this means that the injury should be a recognizable psychiatric disorder, not mere mental suffering (*Hinz v. Berry*, [1970] 2 Q.B. 40 (C.A.)). One should also remember that grief from the loss of a loved one is always an emotionally disturbing event, and it is one of the expectable tragedies of life to be avoided only by dying first. Moreover, the shock should be such as to cause disturbance to the ordinary person, otherwise harm is not foreseeable.

The other issue concerns who should be able to recover for nervous shock. The issue should be treated as who is foreseeably at risk of nervous shock. For some time, one had to be physically injured or likely to be physically injured. Then some courts included persons who witnessed an accident (*Dillon v. Legg*, 68 Cal.2d 728, 69 Cal. Rptr. 72, 441 P.2d 912 (1968)). More recently, other courts have included persons who subsequently saw victims (*McLoughlin v. O'Brian*, [1983] 1 A.C. 410 (1982)). The best approach is to consider various factors that might make the injury foreseeable. Among these are the relation to the primary victim, witnessing an accident, and seeing victims shortly after an accident (see Linden 1977a, 360-67).

We have already implicitly considered the negligent invasion of interests in reputation and privacy in discussing intentional torts (5.2.1). In effect, we suggested that reputation should be protected from negligent invasion only when privacy is also often involved – private persons. The mass media privilege in defamation for public persons and figures should extend to everyone. Most negligent invasions of mere privacy do not merit compensation; instead, there should also be a requirement of the invasion of another interest, usually property or economic advantage. The careless intrusion on seclusion or intimacy, such as opening a door without knocking, is one of the risks of modern life that one would reasonably endure to avoid the vexation of being a defendant in such cases. But when other interests are involved, as in private affairs, one would find the benefits of compensation to outweigh the burden of defending. For example, a lawyer who negligently discloses information about a pending contract should be liable for any resulting financial losses should the deal not go through. The lawyer has a special duty of confidentiality.

One might contend that in this situation privacy is irrelevant if economic loss is a protected interest, so we need to consider whether economic advantage by itself should be protected. Of course, only foreseeable economic losses should be protected. Moreover, there are reasons for not usually recognizing economic loss beyond that stemming directly from a physical injury, such as loss of work from personal injury, loss of income to dependents from wrongful death, or loss of production from damage to equipment (see Rabin 1985). Even these restrictions are sometimes insufficient. During construction, water and gas pipes, as well as electric and telephone lines, are frequently damaged and supplies to others interrupted. The disruption of power will foreseeably cause economic loss to factories and other businesses dependent on it. Most people do not suffer physical damage and so cannot recover for economic loss. Sometimes, however, there is also physical damage. For example, in a leading Canadian case, a motel was allowed to recover for loss of business when electric cables a mile away were cut, because some food in the electric refrigerator spoiled (*Seaway Hotels Ltd. v. Gragg (Canada) Ltd. and Consumers' Gas Co.*, 17 D.L.R.2d 292 (Ont. 1959); see *George A. Hormell & Co. v. Maez*, 92 Cal. App. 3d 963, 155 Cal. Rptr. 337 (1979)).

Such a result is unacceptable. First, recovery is purely fortuitous. Suppose another motel across the street had equally lost business due to lack of lights and so on, but had had a gas refrigerator and so suffered no property damage. Then it would not have been able to recover. One cannot reasonably accept such arbitrary results. Second, the potential liability as a defendant would be extreme. Suppose one negligently drives into a power line pole and the resulting power failure blows a fuse in a factory. As there is physical damage, one would be liable for all loss of production during the power outage. As a potential defendant, one could not accept such great liability, even though this kind of loss is foreseeable and physical injury occurs. In *Gilbert v. New Mexico Constr. Co.* (39 N.M. 216, 44 P.2d 489 (1935)), the defendant negligently broke a water main and was held liable for a fire that destroyed the plaintiff's house while water pressure was reduced, despite the fact that the city failed to increase the water pressure after repairs were completed. Third, one should instead consider the assumption of risk. Businesses and individuals in their home expect some interruptions in utility service. It is one of the hazards of living in society. The considerations underlying economic deterrence do not support liability in these cases; businesses and home owners are the better insurers against such risk and assume them as part of the cost of doing business.

It hardly needs stating that liability for negligently caused economic loss alone would be unacceptable. The number of potential plaintiffs if one negligently drove into a power pole in a business area would be overwhelming (see Rabin 1985, 1534-38). Nonetheless, in some situations, like the above hypothetical of a lawyer's negligent disclosure of a client confidence, liability for economic loss alone appears appropriate. These are situations in which the defendant has undertaken to perform a task or has special skills or knowledge on which the plaintiff would foreseeably rely (see also Smith 1984, 122-25; cf. Solomon and Feldthusen 1977, 187; Rabin 1985, 1518-26). This is merely an extension to tort of the contract principle of reliance (4-7), which explains the overlap of contract and tort law in this area. Such cases would include negligent misstatements of banks, financial advisors, accountants, and others. Professionals and others with special skills should be worthy of trust which includes being competent and careful (Bayles 1981, 68-71; *Hedley Byrne & Co. v. Heller & Partners*, 1964 A.C. 465). It would also include negligent failures of government building inspectors to find defects in new contructions, and other negligent conduct of professionals on which third parties are known to rely.

It is appropriate here to mention nuisance, because its is similar to negligence. A private nuisance is an unreasonable invasion (whether intentional, negligent, or strict liability) of the interest in quiet enjoyment or use of property. Traditionally, the unreasonableness of the invasion was determined much as one determines whether a defendant in negligence should have taken precautions – does the benefit to the defendant outweigh the risk of loss to the plaintiff. If it was reasonable, then there was no liability. However, in recent years, some courts have held defendants liable to compensate plaintiffs even when the benefit of the conduct exceeds the harm (*Boomer v. Atlantic Cement Co.*, 26 N.Y.2d 219, 309 N.Y.S.2d 312, 257

N.E.2d 870 (1970); *Jost v. Dairyland Power Coop.*, 45 Wis. 2d 164, 172 N.W.2d 647 (1969)). The *Restatement (Second) of Torts* (§ 826) has endorsed this when the harm is serious and the defendant can feasibly bear the financial burden of compensating for the harm and continue its activities. Such a result is supported by the principle of compensation when the costs can be spread, for example, to the purchasers of cement (*Boomer*) òr users of electric power (*Jost*).

(5-7) The principle of interests protected from negligence: the duty of care should primarily extend to interests in (a) physical and mental integrity; and (b) property, including economic loss resulting from reasonable reliance on a person's undertaking, special skill, or special knowledge. As explained above, the interests in freedom and reputation are only partially to be protected from negligent conduct. The interest in privacy is not a separately protectable interest. We thus have three distinct principles of negligence. They could be combined into one: people have a duty to exercise the care of a reasonable person to avoid foreseeable harm to persons' interests in their person and property. However, such a simple statement omits many of the important qualifications, and a statement including them all would probably be too complex to be readily intelligible. Moreover, the qualifications concern important normative issues in negligence law.

5.2.5. *Vicarious liability.* In strict liability, one need not prove that the defendant acted intentionally or failed to exercise care. A person violates a duty even if all possible care was exercised. Thus, the second and third elements of the standard tort action, proof of violation of a duty and proof that one was causally affected, are basically collapsed. There are three situations in tort that essentially use this criterion.

In 'vicarious liability', one person, such as an employer, is held liable for the conduct of another, the employee. This amounts to strict liability, because the employer need not have intentionally or negligently caused harm, although the actor might have done so. It is also possible to be vicariously liable for strict liability torts of another. In early cases, courts often argued as though the employer was personally negligent. For example, it might be said that an employee's supervisor should have control and direction of the work. In some situations, that is not plausible. Consider an employer riding in a car with an employee driving. If the employee drives negligently, this negligence is imputed to the employer. However, if the employer were to try to take control of the car, this would also constitute negligence (see *Weber v. Stokely-Van Camp, Inc.*, 274 Minn. 482, 144 N.W.2d 540 (1966)). Also, as many professionals and other experts are now employees, it is no longer required or expected that supervisors know how to direct the work of an employee (Fleming 1968, 174). One can imagine a hospital administrator trying to tell the chief of surgery how to perform an operation! As a consequence, employers need not be negligent in any respect.

Several reasons based on deterrence and compensation can be advanced for accepting vicarious liability of employers (Williams and Hepple 1976, 113-14). Perhaps the chief reason for its introduction is the deep pocket theory – to assign liability to one who is likely to be able to pay – but we have rejected that aim (5.1.3). A related reason for vicarious liability is to promote compensation, and the elements of the principle of compensation are met. First, the harms result from the employers' activities. Second, often they could conduct their activities without producing harm. Third, employers can spread the costs over a large number of persons by including them in the price of their products or services. Moreover, since employers benefit from the activities of their employees and can spread the costs, they will not be significantly harmed by paying damages. Vicarious liability can also have some deterrence effect in that it might encourage employers to be careful in selecting their employees. Consequently, vicarious liability of employers is acceptable. The same considerations apply to one's unpaid agents.

There is no justification for extending vicarious liability of employers beyond employee conduct on the job – furthering the employer's interests. If an employee commits an intentional wrong without the employer's knowledge or authorization and not in the furtherance of the employer's business, the employer should not be liable. For example, if a bus driver hits a motorist with a change box after the motorist's vehicle has struck the bus, the employer should not be liable (*Houston Transit Co. v. Felder*, 146 Tex. 428, 208 S.W.2d 880 (1948)). Although the employer could spread the costs, the conduct was not part of the employer's activities from which benefit would be received. However, in some cases, one might argue that an intentional wrong by an employee violates a duty of care that an employer owes to a patron, for example, a taxi cab driver who rapes a passenger (*Co-op Cab Co. v. Singleton*, 66 Ga. App 874, 19 S.E.2d 541 (1942)). This might be viewed as violating an implied required condition of the contract rather than a strict liability tort. If no one would reasonably waive negligent personal injury in such situations, no one would reasonably waive intentional personal injury.

This same rationale extends beyond employers. It includes people engaged in a 'joint enterprise'. Usually, but not always, a joint enterprise is a business arrangement with a sharing of economic costs and benefits. Although the other members of the enterprise are not strictly employees, as long as one has some part in the decision-making, the relationship is similar – the activities are one's as much as the others'. The chief difficulty in applying the above rationale might concern costspreading. In most joint business enterprises, this is as possible as in strict employer/employee relationships, and insurance is also possible. But sometimes a joint enterprise is found even where the activity is not a business one, that is, no financial gain is expected. Still, given that the activity is a joint one of a few people and the harmful conduct was to promote the common purpose, vicarious liability is probably acceptable. It is then quite close to personal liability. It is like the joint responsibility of the members of a sports team; if one member makes a mistake, they will all suffer the results – a loss.

(5-8) The principle of vicarious liability: persons should be liable for the torts committed in furtherance of their activities by their employees and agents, and by people engaged with them in joint enterprises. This principle could include others' driving one's automobile with consent, but the principle of compensation rationale has to be stretched to do so. Even less than in the other cases, the automobile's use is not one's activity. But ownership of the instrument used in an activity plus consent to it makes the activity close to a joint one. One can always avoid liabilty by refusing consent. Moreover, one can spread the cost by insurance. This is undoubtedly the basic reason; attaching the requirement of insurance to ownership rather than driving is easier to administer. Alternatively, one might justify liability of owners of automobiles by an analogy to dangerous activities considered in the next section.

The other area in which vicarious liability might be imposed is the family. Early imposition of vicarious liability on owners of automobiles was sometimes based on a family purpose involved in its use by other members of the family (Christie 1983, 345; see Prosser and Keeton 1984, 524-27). At one time men were liable for their wives' torts, but this did not actually amount to vicarious liability, since husband and wife were considered one person and husbands had control of all the property. Now that more rational principles govern the marital relation and ownership, this reason cannot apply. Some people also contend that parents should be liable for the torts of their children. Child raising is an activity of the parents, but unless the parents were negligent in supervising the child, it is doubtful that they could have conducted the activity without harm. Insurance would permit them to spread the risk, but victims can obtain insurance as well.

5.2.6. Abnormally dangerous activities. Unlike vicarious liability, in the other situations using strict liability, no one need intentionally or negligently cause harm. One class of such strict liability torts pertains to abnormally dangerous activities. In this area, while the person does intentionally engage in the activity, the specific harm causing act need not be intentional. The focus is on the nature of the activity, its dangerousness, as opposed to the manner of carrying on the activity, which is the focus of negligence (Fleming 1968, 159). Among the activities included in this species of strict liability are keeping wild animals, keeping dynamite, blasting, and flying airplanes that crash and cause damage on the ground. The liability is limited to the kind of harm which makes the activity dangerous, for example, being bitten by a lion (Rest. 2d Torts § 519(2)).

Strict liability for wild animals is an ancient part of the common law. A main source for strict liability for other activities is *Rylands v. Fletcher* (3 L.R.-E. & I. App. 330 (H.L. 1868)). Without negligence on their part, the defendants constructed a water reservoir on their land. When it was being filled, the water forced through mine shafts below the reservoir and flooded the connecting mine of a neighbor. Their Lordships basically adopted the position of Judge Blackburn when the case was previously considered in the Exchequer Chamber. He claimed that people who for their own purpose bring or collect and keep something on their land that would cause damage were it to escape do so at their own peril (*Fletcher v. Rylands*, 1 L.R.-Ex. 265 (1866)). However, Lord Cairns distinguished between natural and unnatural uses ("users") of the land, and courts have subsequently had much difficulty distinguishing them. It would probably be better to adopt the American concept of abnormally dangerous activities (Linden 1977b, 339).

(5-9) The principle of abnormally dangerous activities: persons should be strictly liable for physical harm if it results from a type of cause making their activities abnormally dangerous. This principle is acceptable, because it balances the freedom of defendants to engage in such activities (which are often socially useful) with concern for the well-being of others exposed to extra risk (see Keeton 1959, esp. 418-19, 427-29). As a plaintiff, one has

no reason unknowingly to accept the costs of someone else's abnormally dangerous activities; but given that the activities are socially useful, one could accept the risks if one would be compensated. As a defendant, one is not forbidden to engage in such useful activities, provided one accepts liability for the damage that one causes others. Most abnormally dangerous activities are carried on by persons or companies for a profit. They can therefore spread the costs of damage among those who purchase their products or services. The limitation on the extent of injuries for which one is strictly liable is in effect a concern with foreseeability and justified for the reasons given for so limiting liability for negligence (5.2.3).

The difficult problem with this principle is determining what conduct is abnormally dangerous. The *Restatement (Second) of Torts* (§ 520 and Comment 1) lists a variety of factors, such as degree of risk of harm, extent of harm, inability to eliminate the risk, and so on, and states that it is a matter for the court to determine whether an activity is abnormally dangerous. One factor is whether the activity is uncommon, which is little improvement over the natural use criterion. Clearly, keeping lions is uncommon in Ontario but perhaps not in parts of Africa. Many other situations are quite debatable. Moreover, why should it matter that many people in the area carry on dangerous activities? Another factor is whether an activity's value is outweighed by its dangerousness. An alternative approach to the *Restatement*'s is to use only dangerousness as a test and let it be determined by a jury. However, as there are apt to be many difficult borderline cases, this approach could create much uncertainty as to what activities are included. If judges make the determination as a matter of law, then although the classification of a new activity will be uncertain, due to stare decisis the status of activities adjudicated in previous cases will be fairly certain. Consequently, if decisions of abnormal dangerousness are legal ones for judges, dangerousness can be the test – the amount of harm times its probability.

5.2.7. *Products liability.* The last situation using strict liability pertains to products. In the United States, manufacturers are strictly liable for damage caused by defects in their products. In England and Canada, no such strict liability in tort exists (Clerk and Lindsell 1982, § 11-25; Linden 1977a, 495). To sue manufacturers of defective products in tort, one must prove negligence. The retailer is strictly liable under a contractual warranty for the fitness of the product for use, and if found liable, a retailer can then sue the manufacturer on the same basis (see Fleming 1968, 159). But since contractual warranties can be limited, the American strict liability tort is preferable. It increases the likelihood of compensation to injured persons and decreases transaction (direct procedural) costs for courts and retailers. Courts are spared one court case, and retailers two of them. People have no reason, as possible retailers, to expose themselves to this aggravation and expense. A Royal Commission has recommended the imposition of manufacturers' strict liability in tort for death and personal injuries resulting from defective products (G.B.R.C. 1978, 1, par. 1236). Presumably, the recommendation did not extend to property damage because that was beyond the scope of the inquiry.

(5-10) The principle of products liability: persons who manufacture or modify and sell defective products should be liable for physical harm from the foreseeable reasonable use of the products caused by the defects. This principle differs from that recommeded by the *Restatement (Second) of Torts* (§ 402A). The *Restatement* principle applies to anyone in the business of selling such a product. This makes retailers liable for products, even if they receive them from manufacturers in sealed containers. Such a principle does apply and makes sense with the system of contractual warranties in England. However, it is not necessary for tort law. As a practical matter, most suits are against manufacturers. An appeal to the special responsibility of persons supplying goods for the safety of the goods is not helpful, for the issue is whether such a responsibility should be recognized. The principle of economic deterrence is not furthered by imposing liability on retailers who sell goods in closed containers or otherwise do not modify them, for they are not the cheapest risk avoiders as they do not control the production. Nor does the principle of compensation apply, for retailers could not have conducted their activity without causing harm and they are much less able than manufacturers to spread costs. Our principle of products liability does apply if the retailer makes any changes in the product. Moreover, a negligence tort should be available if the retailer knows of a defect and negligently fails to warn of it.

Foreseeability of harm underlies several aspects of this principle. First, liability is limited to harm from foreseeable use of the product. To extend liability to all harm resulting from use of the product would place manufacturers at the whim of purchasers. For example, a standard, unreal, academic example, is the person who uses a power lawn mower to trim a hedge and cuts off a hand. Granted, manufacturers could spread the loss by passing it on in the cost of the product, but one has no reason to accept extra costs resulting from the unreasonable actions of fellow citizens. One would, of course, receive similar compensation for one's own unreasonable conduct, but that is something one can control and reduce and insure against if one wants. Thus, the harm should result from the normal or reasonable use of the product.

A second aspect related to foreseeability is that the harm stem from an unusual element in the product, a defect, and not something normally inherent in such products. A defect is something that renders a product less safe than a reasonable consumer would expect when used reasonably (cf. G.B.R.C. 1978, par. 1237; Rest. 2d Torts § 402A Comment g; *Barker v. Lull Eng'g Co*, 20 Cal. 3d 413, 143 Cal. Rptr. 225, 573 P.2d 443 (1978)). An example of this consideration arises in suits for cancer caused by smoking. If a person smoked before it was known that doing so might cause cancer, the manufacturer is not liable for a defect. Normal cigarettes had this result, and the manufacturer could not foresee such harm (*Lartigue v. R. J. Reynolds Tobacco Co.*, 317 F.2d 19 (5th Cir. 1963)). Even now that cancer is foreseeable, the carcinogenic effects of cigarettes are still not a defect but a normal feature of the product. Defectiveness is not the same as foreseeability. Also, the consumer can foresee the risk and assume it (see 5.3.1).

It is known that things ingested into the body (food and drugs) and applied to its surface are likely to cause illness. One might thus claim that manufacturers of such products should be liable for any personal injury that results from their use. Such a claim would go too far; many drugs have harmful side-effects, but their likely benefits outweigh their likely harm. To place liability for all resulting harm on manufacturers might increase the costs of a drug so much that it is uneconomical to produce. The costs are spread only among users of the drug, and in some cases that is a limited market. Indeed, several manufacturers of the DPT vaccine ceased to make the product because their liability costs made it unprofitable; there was then a shortage in some areas; yet, this vaccine is one of the most socially useful.

Moreover, one again faces the problem of special susceptibility. Most harmful reactions to drugs are due to overuse or special susceptibility of a small segment of the population. Often one does not know that one is susceptible. The best that can be done is to warn people and physicians that the drug is not safe for people with certain conditions or susceptibilities. Obviously, no warning should be required if the manufacturer has no reason to suppose that the product would cause harm (*Woodill v. Parke Davis & Co.*, 79 Ill. 2d 26, 37 Ill. Dec. 304, 402 N.E.2d 194 (1980)). How could one frame a warning of an unknown risk? One could only warn that the product might have unknown hazards, but that is true of any product. Food is slightly different. It is not dangerous to normal persons, although some people are susceptible to harm from certain foods. Thus, food processors can be required to assure that if the food is consumed in reasonable quantities it is not harmful in any known respect to normal persons. Ingestion of gross quantities of any substance, even water, can be harmful.

One might contend that manufacturers do not know that a particular product, say, the contents of a bottle of soda, is defective. Consequently, they are held liable when the defect is not foreseeable. However, they do know that their statistical sampling quality control procedures will not find all defective products. They can foresee that a percentage of their products will be defective. This makes the situation like negligence in that more care could be taken; that is, stricter quality control and checks could be instituted. But often the extra quality control is not reasonable, because the added expense is not worthwhile in terms of the number of defective items found. In negligence, this would imply that the risk was reasonable and no liability would result. The primary reason for products liability is to assure victims of compensation. It also has an indirect deterrent effect. Manufacturers will only know that further quality control is unreasonable if they know the costs of accidents resulting from undetected defects, and they will be more apt to know and attend to this if the costs are brought home to them. Consequently, products liability both ensures compensation to victims and helps ensure that accident rates are reduced to an economically reasonable level.

The final aspect of foreseeability concerns the design of products. The discussion so far has concerned only defects in products, that is, aberrations from the normal. But products can be built that are simply not as safe as they might be. The issues are whether there should be liability for defective design, and if so, what the standard should be – negligence or strict liability. The first issue is rather easily answered; people have as much reason to be compensated for injuries resulting from poorly designed products as from defectively manufactured ones.

The difficult issue is what the standard of defective design should be. One court has claimed that really no difference exists between a strict liability and a negligence standard in design of products, it being reasonable care in either case (*Jones v. Hutchinson Mfg., Inc.*, 502 S.W.2d 66 (Ky. 1973)). This is a mistake. Strict liability could involve liability for any foreseeable harm that might result from the design, whereas a negligence standard would impose liability only if it were unreasonable to design a product with the possibility of that type of harm. Some injuries are foreseeable even from reasonably designed products.

Engineers claim that sometimes making a product safe decreases its reliability or effectiveness. For example, a thermostat to cut off an electric popcorn popper if the temperature gets too high will increase safety; but if the thermostat is defective, the popper will shut off even when operating normally. Similarly, rubber or plastic pads at the back of power lawn mowers to prevent injury to feet and legs also make them less easy to pull in reverse when mowing under bushes. People do not necessarily want or expect a completely safe product design; they will rationally trade safety for efficiency or reliability. A full strict liability standard would discourage such reasonable trade-offs.

These considerations do not settle the issue, for one might still have good reasons to hold manufacturers liable for injuries resulting from even reasonable designs. One of the reasons for holding manufacturers liable for defective products despite reasonable quality control is the indirect deterrent effect in providing manufacturers information better to adjust the quality control. This reason does not apply as stongly in product design, because manufacturers will not know the value to place on reliability and efficiency. Some indication of this value can come from sales, but often the most important factor in sales is price. Increased sales might be obtained by designing an inexpensive but unsafe product. Strict liability will pass the costs for all design related injuries to the manufacturer, but not the considerations of efficiency and reliability.

Consequently, the standard for design should be the reasonable balance of risk of harm with the cost, reliability, and efficiency of the product. This judgment should be one for the fact finder, preferably a jury, since the aim is to have a design which makes the balance as a reasonable consumer would. Moreover, this judgment should be based on the information available at the time of design. The California Supreme Court has basically adopted this test, but it permits the jury to use hindsignt (*Barker v. Lull Eng'g Co.*, 20 Cal. 3d 413, 143 Cal. Rptr. 225, 573 P.2d 443 (1978)). This seems to imply that the jury can use information beyond that available to the designer at the time. One might as well let the jury consider subsequent developments in new materials that would make the product more safe. Either requirement would hold the manufacturer to a standard it could not possibly meet and amounts to making the manufacturer an insurer. As people can purchase their own accident insurance if they wish, there is no reason to make the manufacturer insure them. The resulting standard is to design the product to be as safe as reasonably possible. Although close to a negligence standard, it is somewhat stronger. It implies a duty to obtain all available information that might be relevant as well as reasonable testing. Negligent failure to obtain such information or to test, as well as negligent design with all information available would be grounds for liability.

Finally, because strict liability imposes costs on defendants which they could not reasonably have acted to avoid, only the most central interests should be protected by it. The primary interest is thus personal injury. The bulk of strict liability law concerns this. However, damage to property can also be included. The interests in reputation, privacy, and freedom are not likely to be affected by the type of conduct considered. Nervous shock and economic loss should depend on individual personal or property injury. Throughout, we have spoken of 'physical harm', meaning thereby 'physical injury to person or property'.

DEFENSES

5.3.0. *Introduction.* The theoretically central defenses in tort law relate to the duty or causation element of the plaintiff's tort action. That is, they contend either that the defendant had no duty to the plaintiff or that the defendant did not cause the injury. The first set of defenses considered are based on consent and deny that the defendant had a duty. The second set all relate to causation. We then consider a mixed group of defenses under the heading "Plaintiff's Responsibility." Some of them pertain to the plaintiff causing the injury, and others to the plaintiff being responsible for the injury even though he or she did not cause it. These latter essentially deny the defendant's duty. 'Immunities' are special claims that the defendant is free from tort liability, and 'privileges' exempt defendants from tort duties for the conduct in question.

5.3.1. *Consent.* An ancient tort law maxim is *volenti non fit injuria* – a person cannot be voluntarily injured. This maxim must be used carefully, for it has different rationales for different types of torts. It is most at home in intentional torts. For example, the duty underlying battery is not to touch a person without consent. A surgeon does not violate the duty or commit battery on a patient who consents to an operation. The same consideration underlies intentional injury to property and to privacy, for lack of consent is part of the respective duties. Presumably, no one would consent to having his or her reputation falsely besmirched, but a person might have consented to publication, for example, read and approved an article about him or her. The requirement of consent gives people control over who touches them, uses their property, and has or publishes information about them; such events can occur or not as they wish.

In negligence law, consent has usually gone under the name of assumption of risk or *volenti*. Its basis is somewhat different from that of consent in intentional torts. As we noted in discussing required contractual conditions (4.3.2), reasonable persons would not contractually agree to others negligently injuring them unless they received something in return. And no one would consent to be negligently injured (Fleming 1968, 144). In assuming risk, one does not imply that others should be negligent or even suggest that one does not want them to take care; instead, one waives the legal duty to compensate for any injury that might ensue. Thus, the other person has no legal duty to one, although a moral duty may remain. Such a waiver might be given because one particularly wants to engage in some activity. For example, a person might want to participate in the pit area of a demolition derby (*LaFrenz v. Lake County Fair Board*, 172 Ind. App. 389, 360 N.E.2d 605 (Ct. App. 1977)).

If a person clearly, expressly, and voluntarily assumes risks, as by signing a clear written release, there is no problem. Difficulties arise when the assumption is inferred from the circumstances. Historically, the common law used assumption of risk in ways that one could not rationally accept. The most notorious use was the 'fellow servant rule' that in taking a job one consented to possible injury by fellow employees. This rule illustrates the difficulties that can ensue when the law implies consent. People have no reason to accept a rule depriving them of compensation for injuries unless they actually, knowingly, and freely consent. Consequently, defendants should be required to show that an individual plaintiff was aware of the risks ('informed') and voluntarily and actually consented to them. It follows that consent cannot be found if there is compulsion, private necessity, infancy, or insanity, because the consent is either not free or the person is incapable of consent (cf. Epstein 1980a, 104 and 105).

Courts have become very reluctant to find assumption of risk (Linden 1977a, 427), and some American jurisdictions have abolished it as a defense distinct from contributory negligence (see 5.3.3). The primary reasons for this trend are the historical misuse of the doctrine, the development of 'comparative negligence' apportioning losses between negligent defendants and negligent plaintiffs, and conceptual confusion. For example, in *Blackburn v. Dorta* (348 So.2d 287 (Fla. 1977)), the Florida Supreme Court dissolved assumption of risk as distinct from other rules. It argued that express assumption of risk is contractual and so not a matter of tort law. What it called primary-implied assumption of risk indicates that there is no duty, and the court rejected it because it was the basis of the fellow servant rule. So far, one might agree, provided that releases are contracts and still acceptable and that many of the factors involved in assumption of risk are considered in determining whether there is a duty. But the court went on to reject what it called secondary-implied assumption of risk. Such risk could be reasonable or unreasonable. The court's example of reasonable risk was running into a burning building to save a child, and it claimed liability should apply in such cases. Unreasonable assumption of risk, the court said, amounts to negligence by the plaintiff and should be apportioned under comparative negligence.

Both of these last arguments are unpersuasive. First, most jurisdictions would not apply assumption of risk to rescuers, for rescues are foreseeable consequences of the original negligence. Moreover, there are situations in which one might reasonably assume risk. Suppose one needs to get someplace quickly and borrows the only available car knowing that its brakes are bad. Should the owner be liable to the borrower for an accident due to the bad brakes? Such situations simply are ones in which risks are accepted in return for whatever benefit makes doing so reasonable. In short, as a reasonable person, one would prefer having the benefit and waiving liability to not having the benefit. Of course, as a potential defendant, one could accept not being liable.

Second, unreasonable assumption of the risk is not the same as plaintiff negligence. The mental state is different, for one who assumes a risk must be aware of it, whereas a negligent plaintiff does not advert to the risk. Moreover, assumption of risk removes all liability of the other party, whereas with plaintiff negligence it merely decreases it by the proportional degree of fault. Nonetheless, there is a core of truth in the idea that implied unreasonable assumption of risk is similar to contributory negligence, namely, some courts use an objective standard for awareness of risk – would a reasonable person have been aware of the risk? Instead, a subjective standard should be used – was this plaintiff aware of the risk? One might contend that there still could not be unreasonable assumption of the risk, for if it is unreasonable, a person must not have appreciated the risk or he or she would not have so acted. This claim is false. It assumes that people cannot act unreasonably, that if people have knowledge of unreasonable risks, they will not assume them. Plato held such a view, but since Aristotle it has been recognized as incorrect.

Consent as a defense to strict liability should be similar to that for negligence, that is, based on clear evidence of informed and voluntary consent. Warning labels on cigarette packages are an example of consent in strict liability. Persons are forewarned that smoking can be hazardous to their health, and purchase of cigarettes can be construed as consent to the risks. However, one must be cautious about the use of warning labels as establishing consent. Mere knowledge of risks is not sufficient for consent or assumption of risk (Epstein 1980a, 101). Drugs and cosmetics are often covered with warning labels about possible risks and what constitutes their appropriate use. The warnings become treated like fine print in contracts. Few people read them all. Thus, reasonable limits should be placed on the ability of persons to exempt themselves from strict liability by written warning of risks.

Prescription drugs are an especial problem, because often only physicians receive warnings about their use and they might not know whether patients have contraindicative conditions. Despite the imposition of liability on drug companies for failure to warn patients (*Davis v. Wyeth Laboratories, Inc.*, 399 F2d 121 (9th Cir. 1968)), drug companies cannot ensure that physicians or pharmacists pass information to patients. The solution is to develop package inserts or handouts that pharmacists and physicians can give to patients. This solution still assumes that people will read them, but this is more likely as people become increasingly concerned about the effects of drugs and food additives. In food products, as we have seen (5.2.7), warning labels are simply not acceptable. The food must be safe for normal persons. Listing the ingredients on the label is one thing, warning labels are another. Listing ingredients allows persons sensitive to certain foods, such as diabetics to sugar, to take precautions.

(5-11) The principle of consent: persons should not be liable for harms caused to people who knowingly and voluntarily consent to the risks of the harms. This defense should be available for all torts. 'Harm' should here be understood to include consented to touchings and so on, although these are not legal harms in the sense of resulting from violations of a duty and by the principle people are not liable for causing them. Moreover, 'the harms' means those from a type of cause as we discussed in considering the scope of negligence (5.2.3). Proof of actual knowledge of risk of harm should be required for

all situations except warnings in products liability. Even there, the warning should be designed to come to the attention of a reasonable person.

5.3.2. *Causation*. The law standardly requires that to be liable a defendant's conduct must cause the plaintiff's injury, and it is also required by our principles of intentional torts (invasions of interests), foreseeability, abnormally dangerous activities, and products liability. At one level, this is not as important a factor as one might expect, because the law merely requires that the harm would not have occurred *but for* the defendant's conduct. That is, the plaintiff need only show that the harm would not have occurred had the defendant acted differently. Although this "but for" causation is necessary, it is insufficient to establish the causal element for liability. Before considering what else is necessary, it is useful to consider omissions.

It is often said that one is not liable in tort for omissions unless one has a duty to act. If one does have a duty to act, then the failure to do so is a cause of subsequent injury. For example, employers have a duty reasonably to assist employees in grave danger (Rest. 2d Torts § 314B). Consequently, if they fail to do so, they cause the injuries that employees would not have suffered had assistance been given. According to the common law, strangers have no duty to assist or rescue people in distress, even when they can easily do so. Sometimes this position is argued for on the ground that one's failure to rescue a stranger is not a cause of ensuing harm (Benditt 1983, 216-20).

All of this might well appear confusing. If Gibson has a duty to rescue Hamlin, then her failure to do so is a cause of his injury. But, it is said, one cannot impose such a duty on Gibson, because in the absence of such a duty her failure to rescue is not a cause of Hamlin's injury. In short, if Gibson has a duty, her conduct causes Hamlin's injury; if she does not have a duty, her conduct does not cause Hamlin's injury, and so there is no basis to impose a duty to rescue. However, regardless of Gibson's duty, Hamlin's injury would not have occurred had Gibson rescued him, so the but for condition is met. Consequently, causation has nothing to do with whether or not the duty should be imposed on Gibson. The causation language is merely an obscure and confusing way of making the conclusory statement that Gibson does or does not, did or did not, have a duty to rescue.

The fundamental point is that omissions are not, legally, a significant bar to causation. All sorts of omissions are the basis of tort liability, for example, failure to throw a train switch or to signal a turn while driving.

It might be said that these omissions all occur as an aspect of doing something else and constitute doing it negligently. To uphold this claim, one must make failure to rescue an employee an aspect of employing, and failure to rescue one's child an aspect of parenting. But being an employer or parent is not an act, and one might as well say that failing to rescue a stranger is an aspect of being a citizen or fellow human being. The issue that should be focused on is whether good reasons exist for imposing a duty. Absence of causation is often short-hand for the claim that there are not good reasons, but causation language simply creates confusion. It is more perspicuous simply to argue that there are not sufficiently good reasons to impose a duty.

There are no good reasons to accept principles about 'proximate causes' or injuries that are 'too remote'. Courts often say that before there can be liability, a defendant's conduct must be a proximate cause of a plaintiff's injury, and if it is not, the injury is too remote. About the only specific meaning that can be attached to these expressions is that the court does not think the defendant ought to have to compensate. The substantive point that underlies much, but not all of this language, is simply that the injury was not foreseeable. As we have seen (5.2.3), there are good reasons to limit liability to foreseeable harm. Although the concept of foreseeability is not easy to apply, it is surely clearer than speaking as though there were two types of causes – proximate and remote. It also focuses the discussion on an element that is clearly relevant to justifying liability. However, in considering negligent conduct causing economic loss, we did claim that one should not be liable even for all foreseeable economic loss (5.2.4). The argument, however, did not rest on considerations of causation, but on policy considerations such as the burden of liability and who best bears the risk. Proximate causation language misfocuses the issue and is best avoided.

In some cases, the but for concept of causation can lead to problems. Suppose Ihnen and Jevon each negligently start a fire, the two fires join and burn down Kelly's barn, but either fire alone would have done so. In this case, neither Ihnen's nor Jevon's conduct is a but for cause of the loss of Kelly's barn, for it is not true that the barn would not have burned but for the conduct of either alone. This type of 'overdetermination' shows that causes are not necessary conditions for events. Rather, they are better viewed as necessary elements of a set of conditions that are jointly sufficient for an event. Ihnen's conduct was a necessary element of a set of conditions sufficient to burn Kelly's barn. The same is true of Jevon's conduct. When there is only one set of operative sufficient conditions, a necessary element of jointly sufficient conditions is also a but for condition. However, when there are two or more such conditions, it is not. In these latter situations, courts often then ask whether the defendant's conduct was a substantial factor in the plaintiff's injury. It would be better to ask whether it was a necessary element in a set of conditions sufficient to produce the plaintiff's loss, but the legal results are likely to be the same on either test, namely, both actors caused the injury. *(5-12) The principle of causation: persons should be liable for all foreseeable harm that occurred because an aspect of their conduct contrary to duty was a necessary element of a set of conditions jointly sufficient to bring about the harm.* The phrase 'aspect of one's conduct contrary to duty' is meant to include the defect of a product, even though that is not strictly an aspect of conduct.

With this clarification of the concept of causation, we can rather quickly arrive at reasonable solutions for a number of problems that have vexed courts. First, for liability, the harm must result from the aspect of the defendant's conduct that was negligent. We have already accounted for this in the principles of foreseeability, abnormally dangerous activities, and products liability by requiring that the harm result from foreseeable or dangerous kinds of causes or the product defect. The same applies when it is claimed that the injury was caused by the plaintiff. An example is a person not wearing a seat-belt injured in an automobile accident. If there is no evidence that lack of wearing a seat-belt contributed to the injuries, then even if failure to wear a seat-belt is negligence, it did not cause injury (*Bentzler v. Braun*, 34 Wis.2d 362, 149 N.W.2d 626 (1967)).

Second, an intervening factor or cause should not bar liability if it was foreseeable. Of course, if the intervening factor and not the defendant's conduct caused the injury, then the defendant should not be liable. This would be the case, for example, where a person negligently starts a fire which goes out but lightning starts another that consumes the plaintiff's barn. However, so long as the defendant's conduct was a cause of the harm and the intervening factor was foreseeable, then the defendant should be liable even if the intervening factor is also a cause. This applies even to voluntary acts of others that would not have occurred but for the defendant's conduct. For example, one can foresee that others might try to rescue someone in danger or that doctors will render medical treatment. A physician would not have rendered care but for the plaintiff being injured. So, even if a physician negligently provides care, the defendant should be liable, although the physician should also be liable for the aggravation of the injury he or she negligently causes. Medical mistakes, whether or not negligent, are a foreseeable result of injury.

Third, in some situations only one of several parties in fact caused the damage, but the plaintiff cannot reasonably show which. This might occur, for example, when two hunters both shoot negligently and it cannot be determined which hit the plaintiff (*Summers v. Tice*, 33 Cal. 2d 80, 199 P.2d 1 (1948); *Cook v. Lewis*, 1951 S.C.R. 830). More complex situations arise when several manufacturers are negligent in marketing a product, the plaintiff is injured by such a product, but one cannot determine which firm manufactured the specific product used by the plaintiff (*Abel v. Eli Lilly and Co.*, 94 Mich. App. 59, 289 N.W.2d 20 (Mich. Ct. App. 1980)). In such cases, the plaintiff can prove all of the elements of a case except actual causation against all the defendants. As a plaintiff, one could certainly accept holding them all liable. As a defendant, it would be more difficult to accept that result. One would certainly not agree if one could prove that one did not cause the harm. Even if one could not, one would prefer no liability. However, given that one might be plaintiff or defendant and that one must accept a rule for all cases, then one could accept liability of all defendants who could not prove they did not cause the harm, provided damages were fairly apportioned among them.

Some people worry that acceptance of such a basis for liability might extend too far (Thomson 1984, 127-33; see Stening 1985). Suppose there are two cab companies in town, Red and Green, with Red having 60% of the cabs. Further suppose that a color blind pedestrian is hit by a cab at night but unable to distinguish the color and no other evidence is available as to which cab hit the pedestrian. Might Red Cab be held liable on the ground that since it operates more than half the cabs, it is more probable than not that one of its cabs hit the person? However, this hypothetical case differs significantly from the type discussed above. Here, the statistical evidence is used not only to establish causation, but also negligence. There is no independent evidence that both Red and Green Cab Companies were negligent towards the plaintiff.

Fourth, the possible apportionment of damages arises in several different types of situations. One is that just considered in which one of several negligent persons caused the harm. A slightly more complicated situation is where two or more persons negligently cause harm to another, but it is impossible to determine how much of the harm is caused by each. For example, Linton might cause Medlin to break a leg or sustain back injury, and subsequently Norton also break Medlin's leg or cause back injury (*Loui v. Oakley*, 50 Hawaii 260, 438 P.2d 393 (1968) (broken leg); *Watts v. Smith*, 375 Mich. 120, 134 N.W.2d 194 (1965) (back injury)). The last type of situation is one of overdetermination, for example, where Ihnen and Jevon both start fires and each is sufficient to burn Kelly's barn.

An acceptable apportionment of damages would be on the basis of the probability that one caused the harm. Usually that will involve an equal division of the damages; in overdetermination situations, the parties are equally likely to have caused the harm, so the division should be equal. In situations of several manufacturers of a defective product, the probability of causing the specific harm should be based on the share of the market of each manufacturer (*Sindell v. Abbott Laboratories*, 26 Cal. 3d 588, 163 Cal. Rptr. 132, 607 P.2d 924 (1980); see also Thomson 1984, 120-24; Epstein 1985, 260-62). The market share division is acceptable, because averaged over all cases it makes one liable for the amount of damages that one would probably have had to pay were there perfect information, that is, one could determine whose product caused each injury. Thus, it better achieves the aim of economic deterrence. This result is also supported by the principle of compensation, since the companies could have conducted their activities without producing the harms (nonnegligently) and can spread the costs.

5.3.3. *Plaintiff's responsibility.* Except for some variation for intervening causes, the causation defenses apply to all types of torts. Some defenses in this section are restricted to specific types of torts. Like the consent defenses, they all have in common the claim that the injury is in some sense the plaintiff's, not the defendant's, responsibility.

The first such defense applies to negligence torts and contends the plaintiff negligently caused part or all of the injury. Such a defense makes little sense for intentional torts, for the plaintiff is not likely to injure her or himself in the respects that are the focus of intentional torts. In products liability torts, the plaintiff's negligence is effectively taken into account by the requirement that the injury result from reasonable use; that is, manufacturers are not liable if plaintiffs unreasonably use products.

There is no reason to treat the negligence of the plaintiff any differently from other multiple cause cases (see Fleming 1968, 118). That is, plaintiffs should be responsible for the amount of injury they cause themselves. However, the common law used the principle of 'contributory negligence', which held that plaintiffs who negligently contributed to their injuries were not entitled to recover anything. This principle obviously does not further the aim of compensating victims. Nor does it further economic deterrence, as defendants are not liable even though they caused most of the damage.

A better but still inadequate principle is 'partial comparative' negligence. By this principle, so long as a plaintiff was not responsible for more than half of the harm, the plaintiff can recover for the portion attributable to the defendant. However, if the plaintiff was responsible for more than half the damage, the plaintiff cannot recover anything. (One version of partial comparative negligence permits plaintiffs to recover when they are responsible for exactly half the harm, but another version does not.) The same objections that apply to contributory negligence apply to the denial of any recovery if the plaintiff is more than half responsible; compensation is not furthered as much as possible, and defendants are not sufficiently deterred. Consequently, the acceptable principle is that of 'pure comparative negligence' which simply apportions the total damages between the parties in proportion to their responsibility.

The West Virginia Supreme Court has argued that partial comparative negligence is preferable to pure (*Bradley v. Appalachian Power Co.*, 256 S.E.2d 879 (W. Va. 1979)). The claim is that with pure comparative negligence plaintiffs who are less than fifty percent responsible will be deterred from suing. For example, suppose Orr has $20,000 damages and Page has $800,000 damages, and Orr was ten percent responsible while Page was ninety percent responsible. Orr would not sue, because she would recover only $18,000 and Page would counterclaim with Orr liable for $80,000. Orr would thus lose $62,000. But, of course, if Orr does not sue, Page probably will, and it would be foolish for Orr not to counterclaim. Moreover, partial comparative negligence can have the same results. Suppose Orr, Page, and Quaker are involved in a three party accident with equal responsibility. Suppose Orr and Page have $10,000 damages each, while Quaker has $100,000 damages. As Quaker's responsibility is less than half, Quaker can sue both Orr and Page for one third each of her damages, that is, $33,333 each, and they can counterclaim for only $3,333.

A difficult issue that courts and legislatures have generally ignored is the basis on which liability should be apportioned. In discussing multiple tortfeasors in the previous section, we said damages should be in proportion to the probability that one caused harm. But here we have said they should be in proportion to responsibility. Several different bases are possible – negligence, fault, causation, or responsibility. 'Fault', which is a commonly used term, is ambiguous between negligence, causation, and a combination of them. Causation alone is not acceptable. It has been suggested that negligence should be ignored and costs split on the basis of the force applied by each party (Epstein 1980a, 90). In a two car accident, each party would be liable for the proportion of the mass times the velocity of his or her car to the sum of that for the two automobiles. One has no reason to accept such a principle. Besides the unacceptability of strict liability for such accidents, it has other unacceptable implications. For example, it implies that people driving smaller automobiles would be liable for a smaller share of damages than people driving large ones, even though in at least some cases smaller automobiles expose people to greater risks of personal injury and therefore greater damages.

Nor does it seem logically possible to combine degree of negligence and causation into one criterion. Suppose as calculated above Ralston causes sixty percent of the damage and Sanford forty percent, but Sanford's negligence is greater than Ralston's in the same proportions. One might simply add the percentages of causation and fault and divide by two. But does it make sense to add percentages of fault and causation? It is like adding apples and air pressures.

If negligence were the basis, it would still have to be negligence that in fact contributed to the injury. A failure to signal a turn does not make a plaintiff liable for part of the costs of an accident if it did not causally contribute to the accident. It is also often difficult to determine which damages are due to which cause. Moreover, by hypothesis both parties are negligent, and it is also often difficult to distinguish degrees of negligence. Logically, it seems that one must treat all negligence alike and simply consider, when possible, causal contribution. Consequently, juries and judges using comparative negligence probably do make some mixture of causal contribution and degree of negligence, however illogical such a combination might be. One can, however, accept this practice, for its practical effect is that the division is according to what reasonable people (jury or judge) consider fair in view of all the circumstances.

(5-13) The principle of apportionment: parties should ultimately be liable for damages in proportion to their responsibility for the harm. This principle is as much a principle for damages as liability or defenses. The argument in the previous section to apportion damages in proportion to the probability that a party caused it was based on the assumption of equal negligence or products liability. Consequently, when that assumption applies, the only element of responsibility that can vary is probability of causation. The principle of apportionment states that "parties should ultimately be liable" to leave open the possibility of a party being held to pay all damages and

then obtain contribution from others. It also leaves unanswered the question of what to do when one party is unable to pay its share. (On these points, see generally Uniform Comparative Fault Act 1979; Klar 1977, 145-65.)

The defenses of persons and property also arise in criminal law where they have been more thoroughly analyzed. Consequently, here we only briefly sketch them, leaving a fuller discussion to the next chapter (6.3.5 and 6.3.6). Defense of persons – self or others – primarily applies to assault and battery, although it also applies to negligent contact (Prosser and Keeton 1984, 124). One may use reasonable force to protect oneself from what one reasonably believes to be danger (Linden 1977a, 63-64; Prosser and Keeton 1984, 124-25). One may not use more force than a reasonable person would think necessary. Similarly, one should be able to use reasonable force when one reasonably believes it necessary to protect other persons (Linden 1977a, 68-69; Prosser and Keeton 1984, 129-31). In effect, this defense claims that the plaintiff is responsible, because of the threat he or she created to the defendant or others. Any claim that would suffice as a defense in criminal law should suffice in tort law. One might think that because the penalty to the defendant is less in tort than criminal law (damages rather than imprisonment), one should restrict the defense more in tort law. However, the argument for these defenses is that one has no reason to accept greater limitations on protecting oneself. Consequently, one has no reason to pay, by way of damages, for protecting oneself or others.

Similar considerations apply to the defense of property (Prosser and Keeton 1984, 131-37). What force is reasonable in defense of property differs from that for defense of persons, because property is not as valuable as persons. The defense in tort law should be as broad as that in criminal. Reasonable force may also be used to recapture personal property immediately after it has been wrongly removed from one's possession. Unless one has just been dispossessed of real property, recourse to the courts is preferable as the dwelling or land will not be moved away (Prosser and Keeton 1984, 144-45). Recovery of stolen property should also be a defense to trespass on the land of someone who did not steal it, provided one does not injure the innocent person's property. Presumably, one could otherwise use the law to recover it.

Historically, that the plaintiff was a trespasser on land was also a defense of the occupier to an action for negligent injury. Although the defense is based on an absence of duty (Seavy 1942, 98), it did generally fit the

prevailing contributory negligence principle. As the trespasser was supposedly at fault since it was an intentional tort, he or she was guilty of
contributory negligence in any negligence action. Of course, as we noted
(5.2.1), the classical doctrine did not really make trespass an intentional
tort, since it did not require knowledge (or even negligent ignorance) that
the land belonged to another. Similarly, people on the property with consent were divided into 'licensees' and 'invitees' toward whom different
duties were owed. In England, the distinction between licensees and invitees was abolished by the Occupiers' Liability Act 1957. In America,
these doctrines were chipped away over time by various exceptions. Today,
in most jurisdictions, they have been substantially abolished.

   The primary choice of acceptable principles is between occupiers having
the same duty to all persons on their land and their having different duties
to trespassers and others. By the latter approach, a negligence duty of
reasonable care would apply to all persons on the land with permission, but
not to trespassers, thus limiting liability to trespassers to intentional and
reckless injury (see *Mounsey v. Ellard*, 363 Mass. 693, 297 N.E.2d 43
(1973)). For people on one's property with permission, whether actual or
implied, one would be required to ensure that places they are likely to go
are safe and to give warning, when one has a chance, of unobvious dangers.
One can foresee that mail carriers and others are likely to use sidewalks
and steps to the front door, so there is a duty to keep these reasonably safe,
including removing snow and ice within a reasonable time. Immediately
after a snow fall or ice storm, anyone using the sidewalks or steps should
expect slippery patches. Reasonably prudent persons would take such
steps for their own protection, so it is reasonable to make them liable to
others for failure to do so. In effect, the requirements are those that
reasonable people would ordinarily expect of others and provide themselves.

   The question is whether occupiers should also have a duty of reasonable
care towards trespassers. Trespassing is no longer considered such a major
fault that it should deprive one of all protection. The House of Lords has
recognized that some duties of care should extend to trespassers (*British
Rys. Bd. v. Herrington*, 1972 A.C. 877), and this has now been recognized
in several other common-law jurisdictions (Clerk and Lindsell 1982, § 12-
51) and by exceptions in many American jurisdictions. However, occupiers
cannot foresee all the difficulties that trespassers might get into, simply
because they cannot foresee all trespassing. Consequently, they should be
required to take precautions against trespassers being injured by highly

dangerous things – railroad roundtables, high voltage power lines, poisonous water, and so forth, whether or not created by the occupier (cf. Epstein 1980a, 121). In short, they should at least be required to take reasonable precautions with inherently or abnormally dangerous things. As a trespasser, one would obviously want such care. As an occupier, it does not impose any extraordinary burdens, only those precautions a reasonable person would take anyway. Consequently, a separate standard for trespassers is not required, only the application of the usual elements of negligence to the circumstances (*Rowland v. Christian*, 69 Cal. 2d 108, 70 Cal. Rptr. 97, 443 P.2d 561 (1968); *Scurti v. City of New York*, 40 N.Y.2d 433, 387 N.Y.S.2d 55, 354 N.E.2d 794 (1976)). *(5-14) The principle of occupiers: for purposes of assessing their liability to entrants on their land, occupiers of real property should be treated the same as other actors.* In effect, this principle abolishes the defenses of trespass and invitee.

5.3.4. *Immunities and Privileges.* Immunities exempt classes of persons from tort liability. The dominant remaining immunity, unless one counts that of occupiers of land, is that of government. Often the law distinguishes various levels of government, granting a greater immunity at the national and state or provincial level than at local levels. Distinctions are also sometimes drawn between governmental and 'proprietary' functions (those private entities might also fulfill). Here we consider only a general immunity and assume that for governmental immunity negligence is not applicable unless officials exceed the bounds of their discretion.

Three main arguments have been given for governmental immunity (see *Mayle v. Pennsylvania Dep't of Highways*, 479 Pa. 384, 388 A.2d 709 (1978)). One is that the king can do no wrong, so the government cannot not be at fault. Today this is known to be sheer poppycock. A second is the fear of bankruptcy of governmental units. At the state and national level, bankruptcy is more likely to result from improvident legislative spending than from tort liability. At the local level, however, it could be a problem. A small town or village subject to a large tort claim could be forced to the verge of bankruptcy. But it is not apparent that there is a greater reason to protect small governmental units from bankruptcy than private individuals or organizations. The third argument is that the floodgates of litigation will be opened; the courts will drown in cases against the government. This argument is always the last ditch stand against broadening liability, but when it has occurred, courts have always managed to swim rather than sink, and usually in shallow water at that.

The so-called liability insurance crisis in the United States is not really relevant here. In some places, local governments have found the cost of insurance too great and simply closed facilities. But the problem is not an overburdening of courts or restricted to governments. Instead, it results, at least in part, from a broadening of the scope of liability generally and an increase in the size of awards (United States 1986, 2). Retaining a governmental immunity will not solve the problem, and if the problem is solved, then the governmental burden should be no greater than for others.

The central argument for governmental liability rests on the deterrent and compensation aims of tort law. Tort liability will probably have as much deterrent effect on the government as any corporation. The effect of governmental immunity is to deny persons compensation due to the irrelevant feature of the tortfeasor's employer. If one treats a tort claim as the property it is, then the immunity is contrary to the principle of social burdens (3-7), for the harmed person suffers a grossly unequal burden for the production of public benefits (see 3.1.2). The government can spread the cost among all the beneficiaries, and thus meets the conditions of the principle of compensation. Consequently, a general governmental immunity is not acceptable (see also Epstein 1985, 42).

Most other immunities are justifiably extinct or on their way to extinction. One was interspousal immunity. To a large extent, it developed from the position unjustifiably accorded married women by the common law. Their husbands had legal authority to exercise their rights, so if a woman wanted to sue her husband, he would have to bring the action; any duty would be owed to himself, so he could waive it. The same applied *mutatis mutandis* should he want to sue her. A related parent-child immunity developed in the United States. It, like the spousal immunity, was argued for on the grounds of protecting family harmony, as well as not interfering with parental care. To state the grounds on which children sued their parents in the cases in which the immunity arose is sufficient to discredit these reasons – illegal imprisonment in an insane asylum (*Hewlett v. George*, 68 Miss. 703, 9 So. 885 (1891)), cruel and unusual treatment (*McKelvey v. McKelvey*, 111 Tenn. 388, 77 S.W. 664 (1903)), and rape by the father (*Roller v. Roller*, 37 Wash. 242, 79 P. 788 (1905)). These situations may have been redressable under other legal forms, but that does not necessarily support denial of this form of relief.

The charitable immunity was another U.S. invention on the ground that beneficiaries should not sue their benefactors, but of course, not everyone injured by a charity is a beneficiary of it. Even injured beneficiaries might well complain that with benefactors like that they do not need enemies. *(5-15) The principle of immunities: no general immunity should be recognized.*

One might wonder whether an immunity should be granted to children and the mentally abnormal. In criminal law they are excused, so why not in tort law? The answer is complex. First, they do have some exemption. If they cannot form the intent for an intentional tort, they cannot be held liable for it. However, the intent requirement is often such that children and mentally abnormal persons can meet it. Second, the mental element requirement in tort law is not as strict as in criminal law. Negligence is not an appropriate basis for criminal responsibility (see 6.2.2). Mentally abnormal people and children do often meet the standard of negligence, even though our principle of that standard grants a limited duty allowing for age and experience. Third, the arguments given for an objective standard (5.2.2) apply to mentally abnormal persons; they are simply the largest class of adults who are not likely to be personally capable of conforming to the negligence standard. In short, any argument for an objective standard of negligence is an argument against an immunity, as opposed to a limited duty, for mentally abnormal persons. Fourth, in strict liability torts, no mental element is required. As the primary basis for excusing children and mentally abnormal persons from tort liability rests on the mental element, if it is not required, the basis for excuse or immunity does not exist. Finally, as children and mentally abnormal persons sometimes have assets, the aim of compensation is furthered by denying them an immunity.

Privileges, unlike immunities, do not excuse persons from liability for tortious conduct; they only excuse specific conduct. The underlying rationale is that there is no duty to avoid the specific conduct. A complex privilege of legislative authority can be claimed in strict liability torts (see Linden 1977a, 465-67). Courts usually require the legislation clearly to authorize (not merely permit) the activity and limit the privilege to harm which is a necessary or inevitable result of the activity. If the defendant has been negligent, liability will be imposed. One might try to base this privilege on indirect consent through one's representatives, but our argument for the principle of consent required knowing and actual consent. Nonetheless, one would agree that if a legislature has clearly ordered an activity, then strict liability should not follow. Presumably, if the activity is authorized, then the legislature wanted it to occur. If it is desirable that all persons injured by it be compensated, then the legislature should be prepared to foot the bill. As the legislature authorized the activity in the public interest, then the public should bear costs its agent could not have avoided by reasonable care. Presumably, however, the legislature does not authorize negligence any more than an ordinary individual consents to people not taking reasonable care.

Other privileges worth remarking pertain to defamation (see generally Prosser and Keeton, 1984, 824-39). They require that the publication be made in a reasonable manner and for a legitimate purpose. They are justified on the basis of the value of the purpose to the public or to the private individuals involved. To further a court's search for truth, people appearing in court have a privilege. Of course, a witness who knowingly tells something false about another person is guilty of perjury. Likewise, to further public discussion, legislators have a privilege in legislative proceedings. In some contexts, private individuals also have a privilege if the information is given in good faith, for example, informing a woman about the character of her intended husband or providing a reference to a prospective employer. In both situations, the interests of the recipient of the information justify the privilege, which implies that the disclosure should be limited to persons who plausibly have such an interest, not, say, the friends of a prospective bride.

The final defense considered is necessity. In public necessity, the peril is to the community at large. Here it is generally held that compensation is not required. For example, compensation was not due when a private house was destroyed to prevent a fire spreading to the rest of the town (*Surocco v. Geary*, 3 Cal. 69 (1853)). The argument can be made that the plaintiff's house would have been destroyed anyway. But sometimes the property would not have been damaged in any case. As the public benefits and can spread the cost among all those who gain, it is reasonable to require public compensation (cf. Fleming 1968, 189). Indeed, all the arguments above against governmental immunity apply here as well. Thus, public necessity should not be recognized as a defense, at least when the harm would not have otherwise occurred.

The privilege of private necessity has caused many commentators difficulty (Bohlen 1926; Coleman 1983, 74-89; Fletcher 1983, 104-6 and 120-22). The problem is less difficult from our perspective. The question is: Under what conditions would one accept people committing otherwise tortious actions to save themselves or their property from peril? The usual cases involve trespass or damage to real property, for example, fastening one's boat during a storm (*Ploof v. Putnam*, 81 Vt. 471, 71 A. 188 (1908)). The most acceptable rule would permit the use of such property provided compensation is paid for any damage (*Vincent v. Lake Erie Transp. Co.*, 100

Minn. 456, 124 N.W. 221 (1910); but see *Manor & Co. Ltd. v. M.V. 'Sir John Crosbie'*, 52 D.L.R.2d 48 (Nfld. 1965), *aff'd sub nom. Munn & Co. v. 'Sir John Crosbie'*, [1967] 1 Ex. 94 (negligence action denied)). As a person in peril or with property in peril, one can be protected at a lesser cost than should the loss occur. As a property owner not in peril, one loses nothing if compensation is paid. Thus, no one loses and some avoid an even greater loss.

REMEDIES

5.4.0. *Introduction.* The primary remedy in tort law, as in contract law, is money damages. Difficulties arise because damages might not fully or properly compensate for some injuries, especially those to reputation and privacy, and the pain and suffering from personal injury. Nonetheless, courts do attempt to calculate some monetary value and award it. As in contract law, in some situations monetary damages do not seem appropriate. An 'injunction' is then issued ordering the defendant to cease doing something or to do something. Injunctions are granted mostly in cases of continuing torts of nuisance.

5.4.1. *Damages.* As we have seen (5.0), tort law is concerned with minus sum interactions in which the plaintiff has suffered a loss. The point is to make up the loss, not, as in contract, to make the plaintiff better off, for the defendant has not agreed to an interaction from which the plaintiff could expect to benefit. *(5-16) The principle of tort damages: damages should include all a party's actual losses that constitute foreseeable harm.* Foreseeable harm is the type of harm designated by the principles of foreseeability and products liability. For purposes of damages, the foreseeability condition also applies to intentional torts. The principle of tort damages will usually place the plaintiff in the position he or she would have been in but for the defendant's violation of a duty. It will not always do so, because some losses might occur that a reasonable person in the defendant's position would not foresee as resulting from the conduct. However, these losses are not the defendant's responsibility. All of our arguments for restricting the scope of duties to foreseeable harms amounted to arguments to exclude these losses from damages.

As in contract law (4.4.3), a plaintiff should mitigate damages. It is unacceptable to allow a plaintiff to fail to take reasonable steps to prevent the loss increasing. The main difficulty about mitigation arises in personal injury cases where the injured person has minority views about medical treatment. In *Lange v. Hoyt* (114 Conn. 590, 159 A. 575 (1932)), the defendant claimed that the Christian Scientist mother of an injured minor child delayed consenting to an operation that might have prevented a permanent handicap. The court rejected the claim and held that allowance must be made for differences of opinion about reasonable medical care. In such a case, a mother's negligence should not be attributed to a minor child; that would amount to vicarious liability for contributory negligence. If a mother were negligent and the family immunity abolished, the child should have a claim against its mother.

The primary exception to the damages principle in the law concerns 'punitive' or 'exemplary' damages which are not based on a plaintiff's loss. Canadian courts are probably more generous in awarding punitive damages than American courts, and English courts rarely award them (Fridman 1978, 249-50). American courts might allow punitive damages if the defendant's conduct was "malicious," "wanton," or "oppressive" (Christie 1983, 705). English courts award them only for outrageous acts of government employees or when the conduct was calculated to make a profit even if damages were paid (*Rookes v. Barnard*, 1964 A.C. 1129, 1226; Clerk and Lindsell 1982, § 5-37). However, 'aggravated' damages can be awarded when the manner of the defendant's conduct involves special insult to the plaintiff (Clerk and Lindsell 1982, § 5-36). Statutes also sometimes authorize damages in excess of actual losses; for example, in the United States, treble damages are authorized for some violations of the antitrust law. For present purposes, these damages can also be considered punitive – in excess of actual loss.

Generally, punitive damages cannot be justified by the principles of retribution, economic deterrence, or compensation. The principle of civil retribution requires that reparations be made, and reparations are to repair the loss. The compensation principle is to compensate for the loss, so it will not support greater damages than needed to make up the loss. Economic deterrence also usually involves no more than compensation for losses, because awards of greater damages would lead defendants to put more effort into prevention than is economically appropriate.

Nonetheless, there are a few situations in which the deterrence or retributive principles might justify damages in excess of actual loss. The clearest one is where the defendant will gain unless penalized. For example, a photographer might invade the privacy of a famous person, take pictures, and subsequently sell them to a sensational weekly paper for a large sum. Unless the defendant pays a sum at least equal to that received, the deterrence will be inadequate. One might also argue that the plaintiff could have arranged to have the pictures taken and charged for them, so in effect it is a loss to the plaintiff. But this argument might not always be available.

This type of case raises a question about the adequacy of our description of tort law as only concerned with an after the fact view of interactions as minus sum ones (5.0). Here, one might say, one has unjust enrichment based on wrongful gain. There are several possible replies to this objection. First, one can claim that the case should be classified as one of quasi-contract or restitution, not torts. Second, the interaction might have been a minus sum one, because the plaintiff might not have voluntarily agreed to the photographs for the amount the photographer obtained. If so, then the plaintiff lost more than the photographer gained. Third, the essence of the action, what makes the "gain" wrongful, is the invasion of the privacy of the plaintiff, which is a loss. In short, the unjustness of unjust enrichment is always based on the violation of a duty to a person – invasion of privacy, failure to disclose, and so on. Thus, one needs to distinguish the basis for the action and the principles for awarding damages.

The other type of situation in which greater damages can be justified are those in which English courts award aggravated damages. It is especially difficult to place a monetary value on affront or insult. Indeed, just such a situation was involved in *Fisher v. Carrousel Motor Hotel, Inc.* (424 S.W.2d 627 (Tex. 1967)) which we discussed in connection with the retributive principle (5.1.1). It will be recalled that the motel's employee snatched a plate from the hand of a black patron and shouted that blacks could not be served. The same consideration applies to some situations in which 'nominal' damages (small amounts not based on actual loss) are awarded. Nominal damages are primarily awarded for trespass and defamation. As we have suggested that trespass require knowledge that one does not have consent, we can also view it as an affront to the plaintiff's property rights. This view is not appropriate if, like the common law, such knowledge is not required. However, this basis for awards in excess of actual loss is limited to intentional, or at most reckless, torts.

Damages are sometimes classified as 'special' or 'general'. Historically this meant those that were dependent on the plaintiff's special situation or common to all similar plaintiffs. Today the distinction is primarily between those that can be calculated with reasonable accuracy (special), such as medical expenses, and those that are only roughly approximated (general), such as pain and suffering (Christie 1983, 675). General damages are also sometimes said to be presumed to occur due to the tort. The more crucial questions, however, concern the kinds of things for which one can be compensated and how amounts are determined. We briefly examine only a few of the many issues.

Most disputes center on damages for personal injury. Two 'heads' or categories of such damages are medical expense and services that one would have performed for oneself had one not been injured. Obviously, as these are losses or expenses a person would not have otherwise had, they should be included in damages. Expenses up to the time of judgment can be accurately calculated, whereas future expenses of these types must be estimated. An issue arises as to whether services for which the plaintiff did not pay should be included. For example, a plaintiff's wife might give up employment to nurse him (*Roach v. Yates*, [1938] 1 K.B. 256 (C.A.)). On the one hand, it is argued that the defendant should not have to pay for items the plaintiff did not pay for; the plaintiff suffers no actual loss and payment would be a net gain (see *Coyne v. Campbell*, 11 N.Y.2d 372, 230 N.Y.S.2d 1, 183 N.E.2d 891 (1962)). On the other hand, it is contended that the defendant should not reap the benefits of the plaintiff's ability to provide treatment or services without a direct cash payment. To do so would result in defendants paying less than the full cost of accidents and thus uneconomical deterrence. The latter argument has the better of it. Although a plaintiff should mitigate damages, obtaining services without direct payment does not mitigate damages, it only shifts them. Were friends or relatives to make a cash gift equivalent in value to the services, no one would contend it should decrease the defendant's payment. Moreover, often plaintiffs lack the funds to pay for services while waiting years for a final award. This is now clearly the rule in England (*Donnelly v. Joyce*, 1974 Q.B. 454 (C.A.)).

Lost income or earning capacity is another major head of damages. Three issues can be considered here – the basis for figuring lost income, taxation, and 'collateral' or other sources of funds – although the last is broader than lost income. One question about the basis is whether the award should be for lost capacity or only probable actual losses. For example, one might contend that housewives have no earnings, and although compensation should be given for services (such as a maid) to replace those a housewife cannot perform, no award should be made for lost earnings. However, as most housewives now reenter the labor force after children are grown or change from part-time to full time employment, this argument is unpersuasive. Thus, lost capacity appears to be the more acceptable basis. Another question has been whether the loss of earnings should be based on the life expectancy of the person before injury (American rule) or after injury (traditional English rule). The American rule is the appropriate one, because it uses what the plaintiff has actually lost and to deny that compensation would deprive the plaintiff's dependents of a source of income. England has now also adopted this position, but subtracts an amount for the plaintiff's living expenses during the "lost years" (*Pickett v. British Rail Eng'g Ltd.*, 1980 A.C. 136).

A major issue has been the extent to which taxation should be taken into account. Given that the aim is to compensate for actual losses, taxation should be taken into account. There are three central respects in which taxes are relevant. First, a plaintiff's gross income would be subject to income taxes, so the appropriate amount is net or after tax income (*Norfolk & Western R.R. v. Liepelt*, 444 U.S. 490 (1980); *British Transp. Comm'n v. Gourley*, 1956 A.C. 185). Second, damage awards are not usually taxable, so no allowance should be made for taxes when that is the case. Third, income from invested awards is usually taxable, so one should take that into consideration. In 'lump sum' awards (full amount now for past and future expenses and income), the idea is to provide an amount that will be equal to what the plaintiff would have earned. If one discounts for taxes in figuring lost income, one must also add for taxes in determining the future value of income from the award. Each of these considerations is simply to make the award equal to what the plaintiff actually loses.

The third issue is collateral benefits, as from accident or disability insurance, pensions, and so forth. The general American rule is that collateral benefits are not to be taken into account. The English position is less clear (Clerk and Lindsell 1982, § 5-20). Nonetheless, in both, some sources are considered and some are not. The central question is how to distinguish between those that should and should not be considered. One basis for distinction is whether or not the plaintiff paid for or contributed to the plan from which the funds come. Thus, if one paid for accident insurance, that should not be deducted, but funds from noncontributory government plans should be. Another basis for distinction is whether the purpose is to provide a benefit irrespective of a right to recover. On this basis, some noncontributory government plans might be deemed to confer a benefit irrespective of rights to recovery.

Keeping in mind the principle of compensating for actual loss, some elements of this dispute are resolvable. First, if the purpose is to provide a benefit irrespective of rights to recover, then it should not be deducted any more than a Christmas gift from a friend. Unfortunately, legislation often fails to make clear whether this is the purpose. Second, if a plaintiff had merely contributed to a savings account for a rainy day, it would be clear that the funds should not offset the award. The insurance aspect of most plans merely makes this more complex. In effect, through insurance a number of persons all contribute to a savings account to provide for any of them that needs it due to specified causes. The payments to the plaintiff are merely the return on an investment; there would be no windfall gain should the defendant be 'judgment proof' (unable to pay) or the person never be injured.

However, despite the original theory, social security in the United States is not an insurance scheme; it is a pay-as-you-go system in which current contributions are for current recipients. If an injured person is permitted to keep such payments in addition to full compensation, it is at the expense of current contributors. There is no justification for such a windfall to the injured person. However, an offset to the amount the defendant pays would be a windfall to the defendant. Viewed from the perspectives of all persons – plaintiff, defendant, and other contributors to social security, the acceptable rule would be not to pay social security or to have the defendant reimburse the social security fund. This applies only to disability payments, not ordinary retirement payments, which the injured person should be permitted to keep and which should not be an offset (see 4.4.3).

A major area of controversy concerns damages for pain and suffering and/or loss of 'amenities'. English courts distinguish loss of amenity or capacity from pain and suffering, although often the two are lumped together (see generally Clerk and Lindsell 1982, § 5-24). Loss of amenity is supposed to be for the loss of ability to engage in activities. Although the courts start from a schedule based on the kind of injury, variations are made for the significance of loss to the plaintiff. Loss of a leg, for example, is more significant to a person who regularly engages in sports than to a sedentary scholar. Often such differences show up in lost income; a baseball player who loses a leg will suffer a greater loss of income than a scholar, who should be able to carry on with his or her usual work. But the differences do not always affect income.

A question is whether loss of amenities is different from pain and suffering. The House of Lords has held that it is and that it is an appropriate award even when the plaintiff is in a coma, although an award for pain and suffering would not then be (*H. West & Son v. Shephard*, 1964 A.C. 326; see also *Regina v. Jennings*, 1966 S.C.R. 532). In the United States, such an award is unlikely to be made (Christie 1983, 699). It is difficult to see how the loss of amenities or capacity can refer to anything other than loss of enjoyment of life, and that is included in pain and suffering. Consequently, loss of amenities is not an acceptable head of damages.

This leaves pain and suffering as the central category. Obviously, the value of pain and suffering is not at all accurately calculable. It is often difficult to determine how much pain plaintiffs in fact suffer (they are inclined to exaggeration), and then it is unclear how money would compensate for it. Also, there can be great variability in awards for plausibly similar amounts of pain and suffering, depending in part on the eloquence of the plaintiff's lawyer and the plaintiff's acting ability. Awards for pain and suffering in the United States are generally higher than those in England, perhaps in part to cover the costs of legal fees (Fleming 1968, 127), but this merely confuses two distinct issues. One might suggest abolishing pain and suffering as a head of damage, but people do suffer as a result of personal injury, although with modern drugs actual pain should be much less than previously. Suffering is a loss or detriment caused by defendants. Thus, some compensation for it is acceptable.

The primary problems in the United States concern the great and unjustifiable variations between cases and the large amounts often awarded. In England, almost all tort actions are tried without a jury, and the judges tend to impose more uniform awards than do U.S. juries. Thus, one modification would be to have judges rather than juries determine damages (Fleming 1968, 130). Neither plaintiffs nor defendants have reasons to find the current disparity in the United States acceptable. The large amounts of awards in the United States have contributed to the so-called insurance liability crisis. For example, in a ten year period, in Cook County Illinois average punitive damage awards increased from $40,000 to $1,152,174 (United States 1986, 3). In recent years, some attempts have been made to place a cap on awards for pain and suffering, especially in medical malpractice cases, but also more generally. For example, in 1986 the Florida legislature passed a law capping awards for pain and suffering at $450,000 ("Lawmakers" 1986). The federal administration has considered limiting products liability awards for pain and suffering, mental anguish, emotional distress and punitive damages to $100,000 ("Reagan Proposal" 1986). The best solution, as in the English treatment of amenities, would be a schedule of amounts for various types of injuries with some variation allowed. This would both provide uniformity and control the amounts.

Damages for death should be calculated on the same basis as personal injury. Dependants might also be allowed to sue in their own right for what the deceased would normally have contributed in financial support, unless this money is recovered by the estate. A problem concerns compensation for the death of children and others not in the labor market (Prosser and Keeton 1984, 952-53; Christie 1983, 720). In the past, parents were compensated for the lost income of their children. But in modern society, children are not likely to work and contribute any income while at home. Consequently, courts recognize other factors, such as loss of companionship, which is as speculative as pain and suffering. An alternative would be to compensate parents for the cost of raising the child (which might be viewed as the replacement cost). In a sense, parents have not lost all that they have spent, since they have had the enjoyment of the child, yet they have lost future enjoyment. As raising a child to the age of eighteen now costs well over $100,000 in the United States, this could amount to a significant sum. It would value all children of the same age virtually the same, thus promoting uniformity. However, compensation for the death of young children would be much less than that for older ones.

Figuring the amount of award for damages to property is much easier than for personal injury. It should be the lesser of (1) the market value at the time of harm, (2) the market value less salvage, or (3) the cost of repair. This will replace the actual loss. In one type of situation this might be unfair. Suppose Tolar converts Umstead's property to his own use, and the market value of the property increases significantly. Then Tolar will be able to compensate Umstead for the value at the time of conversion and still make a profit. Often, Umstead will be able to sue in quasi-contract or restitution and recover the amount of the later sale (Williams and Hepple 1976, 20). If not, then this is an appropriate case for penal damages.

One specifically calculable category of damages is especially contentious, namely, legal fees. We do not explore this matter in detail. In England and Canada, a successful plaintiff is usually awarded legal fees. In the United States, this is not usually done and a successful plaintiff must pay out of the award received. As we noted, covering legal fees is often a reason for high awards for pain and suffering. The chief argument for awarding legal fees is that otherwise the plaintiff is not fully compensated, since attorney fees can be as high as forty percent or more of the award. The chief arguments against awarding legal fees are (1) that many people with deserving cases do not have the money to hire lawyers and pursue suits or to pay both legal fees if they lose, and (2) that often defendants have good reasons for thinking they are not liable, so justice does not require defendants to pay for asserting what they plausibly take to be their rights. Our principle of legal assistance (2-12) in 2.3.3 would solve the problem of people in personal injury cases being unable to afford to sue. Given such aid, award of legal costs in the judge's discretion would be acceptable. Judges should actually use discretion and not, as in England, routinely award legal fees. A judge might do so when to discourage lawsuits a defendant, like the Canadian Medical Protective Association, contests all cases no matter how deserving.

5.4.2. *Injunctions.* Historically, like specific performance in contract (4.4.4), injunctions were an equitable remedy and not available in the common law where only money damages could be awarded. Injunctions were issued only when damages were found inadequate. However, like specific performance of a contract for the sale of land, injunctions are, with some exceptions, granted whenever they can stop present or future tortious conduct (Williams and Hepple 1976, 62-3). This principle is acceptable. *(5-17) The principle of injunctions: injunctions should be granted whenever they can stop tortious conduct.* A plaintiff would prefer to avoid a loss rather than suffer one and be compensated. In economic theory, persons are not adequately compensated unless they are indifferent between the injury and compensation. However, legal awards are rarely fully compensatory in that sense. Normally, a defendant will not gain by committing a tortious act and having to pay compensation. In negligence and nuisance, if the benefit to the defendant is greater than the risk to the plaintiff, the conduct is reasonable and so not tortious. Moreover, we have found penal damages appropriate when the defendant's conduct is calculated to make a gain after paying compensation.

The chief exception to this principle is a certain type of nuisance case. Injunctions are often issued in nuisance cases, for example, to prohibit a factory from continuing pollution of a stream. Damages would not normally be useful, because the pollution would persist and a new action would arise. However, earlier (5.2.4) we found that liability for nuisance should sometimes exist even when the benefit of the defendant's conduct outweighs the disadvantage to the plaintiff. The argument was that if costs could be spread, then the compensation principle justified payment for a loss. Consider the situation in *Boomer v. Atlantic Cement Co.* (26 N.Y.2d 219, 309 N.Y.S.2d 312, 257 N.E.2d 870 (1970)). People living in the neighborhood of the defendant's cement plant sued for damages for past, and an injunction to prevent future, dirt, smoke, and vibrations coming from the plant. If an injunction were granted, Atlantic would have to close its plant at significant cost and put many people out of work. The benefit of the defendant's conduct outweighed the harm to the plantiffs, so the conduct was reasonable. Yet, the defendant's conduct was a nuisance in the ordinary nonlegal sense.

The award of damages in such cases is not a completely happy outcome. Without an injunction, the people living in the neighborhood would have continual suits. The actual award of permanent damages meant that people in the neighborhood were practically forced to sell their rights to be free of the nuisance. Although this result seems unfair, it is not too different from other sorts of cases. If a motorist runs into one's automobile and demolishes it, one has in fact been forced to sell it. The main similarity is with public takings (3.3.5). Compensation for government actions is due, according to our principle of takings (3-15), on the basis of the extent to which individual property is singled out, the owners had no reason to expect limitations on it, and property rights are curtailed. In these nuisance cases, plaintiffs are singled out in that only a limited number in proximity to the source are affected. They had no reason to expect the problem (did not come to the nuisance), and the invasion of interest is significant. Moreover, in *Boomer* there is a significant public benefit.

The significance of not expecting the nuisance can be seen in *Spur Indus., Inc. v. Del E. Webb Dev. Co.* (108 Ariz. 178, 494 P.2d 700 (1972)). In 1956, the original defendant, Spur Industries, established a feedlot fifteen miles outside of Phoenix. Subsequently, Del Webb bought a large amount of land and began a residential development. By 1967, Webb had expanded to within 500 feet of the feedlot. Webb had thus brought people to the odors of the feedlot. Here we have incompatible private uses of land. The court granted Webb a permanent injunction against the feedlot, but since Webb had brought people to the "nuisance," it was required to compensate Spur for the reasonable costs of moving or shutting down. This is *Boomer* in reverse. In effect, the residential area was what might be called a reverse nuisance to Spur and Webb had to compensate Spur, spreading the costs over the homeowners (or the profits Webb had made from them). The same result should have occurred had the city (Sun City) incorporated the land and zoned the feedlot out of existence (but see Epstein 1985, 118-20).

BEYOND TORT LAW

5.5.0. *Introduction.* The preceding analysis of principles of tort law has assumed that principles are to be used by courts in adjudicating cases brought to them by the parties to a dispute. In the rest of this chapter we drop that assumption. We briefly consider whether litigation is the best way to handle the matters addressed in tort law. The point is not so much to argue against extant tort law – others have done so at great length – as to emphasize that there are alternative approaches to many problems addressed by courts. Rationally, besides considering the principles courts should use to handle cases, one should also ask whether it is best to approach the problems by judicially applied law. This question brings out the general limits adjudicatory procedure places on substantive laws.

5.5.1. *Inadequacies.* To consider whether tort law is an appropriate approach to problems, one should test it against its aims. However, the aims at the beginning of this chapter were formulated on the assumption that courts were dealing with two or at least a few parties. Thus, in the arguments one had to consider that one might be plaintiff or defendant. When one drops the assumption that resolutions are limited to the parties in an interaction, broader aims emerge. Economic deterrence was justified as allocating the loss between parties so as best to deter, but there are other ways to deter conduct than by allocating losses, for example, criminal penalties. The principle of compensation was limited by similar considerations, although we did allow for possible cost spreading. Without those limiting assumptions, one would reasonably seek the most economical method of deterring accident-causing conduct and compensating for all or most significant harm. Thus, we should test tort law against these broader aims.

The extant tort law is not a significant deterrent. First, the widespread existence of insurance decreases the deterrent effect. Defendants do not bear the full costs of the harm for which they are liable, so their economic calculations about risk taking are distorted. Even if higher insurance rates are imposed on people who have accidents, the time lag between an accident and higher rates weakens the deterrent effect (Williams and Hepple 1976, 148). "[I]n fact it is a demonstrable truth – that our combined tort-insurance system imposes costs on accident victims (negligent or even innocent) far more frequently and more heavily than it imposes costs on negligent tortfeasors" (Atiyah 1980, 288). The various subgoals of economic deterrence, such as reducing the number of accidents and reducing the social costs afterwards as by cost spreading, are not fully consistent (Calabresi 1970a, 29). Second, especially with comparative negligence, it is often not clear until after the court case who was liable for how much (Epstein 1980b, 786). If one does not know whether one will be liable, the incentive to take precautions is weakened. Third, factors other than liability may be much more important in preventing accidents (Epstein 1980b, 784-85; see Blum and Kalven 1970, 237). A stop light might prevent many automobile accidents at a dangerous intersection.

In truth, criminal law enforcement, surveillance of industrial operations by public inspectors, the pressure exerted by insurance companies in educational safety campaigns and adjustment of premiums in the light of the insured's safety record, and not least the psychological truism that the human instinct for self-preservation constitutes probably the most formidable antidote to the wanton creation of hazards – all these are much more effective agents for the promotion of accident prevention than the law of torts could ever hope to be (Fleming 1968, 14).

Thus, tort law as analyzed earlier in this chapter is not highly effective in preventing or deterring accidents.

Nor is tort law effective in achieving compensation. First, the compensation is often inadequate. In automobile accidents under a negligence system, the most severely injured are underpaid, although those with minor injuries are often overpaid (Keeton and Keeton 1971, 458). Second, many people are not compensated at all. It has been estimated that in England only 6.5 percent of people injured in accidents receive tort compensation – 10.5 percent of those injured at work, 25 percent of those injured on the road, and only 1.5 percent of people injured elsewhere (Atiyah 1980, 277 and 286, citing G.B.R.C. 1978, 1, 24 and 2, 19). Third, some scholars contend that the application of tort principles such as negligence results in inconsistent rules and decisions (Glassbeek and Hasson 1977, 402-10). Further, whether one is compensated can depend on the whim of a jury member or the competence of a lawyer. Fourth, even our principles do not support compensation in many cases that are similar from the injured person's viewpoint. Products liability will compensate one for injuries from defective products even though the accident is not anyone's fault, but even it will not compensate one for injuries from products that simply wear out or injuries from other sources, such as falling trees, that are not even indirectly caused by persons. Fifth, the insurance system that provides payment for most tort injuries is highly inefficient. Only about one-third to one-half the money paid in premiums is paid out in damages (United States 1986, 2; Keeton and Keeton 1971, 458). It has been estimated that in one period in England £170 million were spent on administration, £130 million paid for pain and suffering, and only £65 to 70 million paid for actual pecuniary loss (Atiyah 1980, 292). If administrative costs were only 10 percent of the amount paid out, four accident victims could be compensated for every one under the existing system.

In 1967, the New Zealand Royal Commission of Inquiry into Compensation for Personal Injury summarized its findings about the tort action as follows:

(1) The adversary system hinders the rehabilitation of injured persons after accidents and can play no effective part beforehand in preventing them.

(2) The fault principle cannot logically be used to justify the common law remedy and is erratic and capricious in operation.

(3) The remedy itself produces a complete indemnity for a relatively tiny group of injured persons; something less (often greatly less) for a small group of injured persons; for all the rest it can do nothing.

(4) As a system it is cumbersome and inefficient; and it is extravagant in operation to the point of absorbing for administration and other charges as much as $40 for every $60 paid over to successful claimants.

(5) The common law remedy has performed a useful function in the past, but it has been increasingly unable to grapple with the present needs of society and something better should now be found. (N.Z.R.C. 1967, 178.)

Moreover, the common-law tort system is being gradually eroded by other social mechanisms. Workers' compensation was introduced to provide remedies where none or limited ones were available before. In almost all industrialized countries, it has simply replaced tort law for accidents at work. In much of the United States, no-fault automobile insurance has replaced the tort law system, at least for minor damages. In Canada and England, national health insurance now covers the costs of medical treatment, so that item of damages is not important. One of these days, even the United States will recognize that the health of its citizens is a social responsibility and provide national health insurance; it already does so for the elderly and very poor. Many people now purchase their own insurance to compensate them for accidental injuries.

Finally, the so-called liability insurance crisis in the United States is further evidence of the breakdown of the tort law. One might object that this crisis, in fact, is due to departure from the traditional tort law. Indeed, a major recommendation has been a return to traditional fault-based tort law – reduction or elimination of strict liability (United States 1986, 4). However, this and other recommendations amount to decreasing liability and amounts one can recover under extant tort law. Instead of furthering the aim of compensation, they hinder it. Moreover, to the extent economic deterrence is effective, they also hinder its achievement.

5.5.2. Alternatives. Even if the extant tort system or one modified to fit our principles has defects, it must be compared with the possible alternatives. There are basically three alternatives (Epstein 1980b, 776): changing from negligence to strict liability in all or most cases, abolishing tort law and putting nothing in its place (which will be called no-liability), and replacing tort law with no-fault insurance. As noted above, workers' compensation has implemented a no-fault system for accidents at work.

Most of the discussion in the United States occurred during the second half of the 1960s and the first half of the 1970s and concerned no-fault insurance versus negligence liability for automobile accidents. The general concerns were to preserve the alleged justice of fault-based tort liability and the deterrence ability of alternative systems (see Blum and Kalven 1965; Calabresi 1970b; Blum and Kalven 1970; Calabresi 1970a). Our discussion above has indicated that tort law is not an effective deterrent. The justice argument also fails to support tort law. The retributive aim does not support most torts, and morality and justice do not support the broad, objective standard of negligence (see Coleman 1975).

Nonetheless, strict liability for automobile accidents has recently been advocated by Richard Epstein (1980b), and it is worthwhile briefly considering the arguments for it or no-liability versus a no-fault system. Epstein compares the systems in three respects – administrative costs, incentive effects (deterrence), and equity. He recognizes that no-fault has fewer administrative costs than strict liability, although of course no-liability has the fewest, namely, none. He claims that strict liability is slightly preferable to no-fault in incentive effects, but he recognizes that a system of liability is not likely to be very influential. However, he does not clearly consider the effects of insurance on a strict liability system. If insurance is allowed, then almost all the deterrent effect of strict liability is likely to disappear, especially when those who are liable might not have been at fault. People will have no reason to believe that they might reasonably have acted differently and so take precautions.

Epstein's main reasons for preferring strict liability pertain to equity. First, he claims it provides a more legitimate ground for compulsory insurance. It is legitimate to require people to insure for harm caused others, but requiring them to insure themselves is paternalistic (Epstein 1980b, 791). There are two possible responses to this claim. Compulsory no-fault insurance might be justified on public good rather than páternalistic grounds (for analysis of public good see Bayles 1978, 157-59). Alternatively, a no-fault system need not require first party insurance. However, if people did not insure themselves, one would have to let them suffer. Because no developed Western country does let impoverished people suffer without medical care, food, and housing, compulsory insurance is a public good, and thus one returns to the first response. One should note that with a no-liability system, reasonable people would obtain first party no-fault insurance. Consequently, a no-liability system essentially turns into a no-fault one.

Epstein's second argument against no-fault automobile insurance is that there is no rational basis for limiting it to automobile accidents (1980b, 788). He also contends that although many persons are not compensated by the extant tort system, most accident victims are compensated from some source or other – accident insurance, disability insurance, and so forth. But these arguments are only valid against instituting no-fault automobile insurance alone. They in fact support a comprehensive no-fault insurance system. Such a system does not try to distinguish between automobile accidents and others, and it combines the multiplicity of sources of compensation into one rational system providing compensation for all injuries. By also limiting amounts for pain and suffering and loss of income, it is also not signficantly more expensive than what is otherwise spent. Thus, the alleged high cost of compensating for all injuries does not become a major problem.

Just such a plan has been adopted in New Zealand. The plan emanated from a Royal Commission report (N.Z.R.C. 1967). According to the plan, workers' compensation, automobile insurance, and social security disability programs were to be rolled into one large system. Compensation for accidental personal injury was to be paid no matter the cause. By combining all the insurance premiums and other monies then spent on accidents, proportionately little more would be needed to cover all accidents. Thus, the aim of compensation would be achieved for all personal injury. Deterrence was to be pursued in other ways, in particular by a special department set up to promote safety (N.Z.R.C. 1967, 184). The proposal was limited to personal injury from accidents. Although the Commission saw no logical reason why it should not extend to illness and disease as well, it did not do so for practical reasons (N.Z.R.C. 1967, 26). A similar proposal in Australia included illness and disease (Luntz 1975, par. 1.204).

The plan has generally been implemented (see G.B.R.C. 1978, 3, pars. 861-90). At first, the scheme was limited to wage earners and persons injured on highways, but it was soon extended to everyone (G.B.R.C. 1978, 3, pars. 859-60). The system is financed by three funds – one for wage earners financed by a tax on employers and the self-employed, one for automobile accidents financed by levies on motor vehicles (and driver's licenses if necessary), and a supplemental scheme for others financed from general revenues. Compensation includes eighty percent of lost pre-tax earnings up to a ceiling; medical and other reasonable expenses; and limited lump sum amounts for bodily impairment and loss of amenities, pain and suffering, and so on. Although expectably there were some problems in the first year or so, none of them were major (see G.B.R.C. 1978, 3, pars. 902-23).

Individuals have good reasons to support adoption of such a scheme, including compensation for disease and illness. First, it obviously fulfills the general compensation aim much better than the tort system. Since personal injury and illness are significant impairments of one's capacities for achieving one's aims in life, they are undesirable. One reasonably wants to be protected from them and their detrimental effects as much as reasonably possible. The system amounts to a form of universal insurance against personal injury and illness. Second, deterrence can be achieved as well or better in other ways, so nothing need be lost in fulfilling the aim of deterrence. Indeed, separating the two aims might make it easier to pursue deterrence.

However, it might be objected, the New Zealand system is limited to personal injury and that has been the emphasis of the preceding arguments. Property damage also occurs in conjunction with much personal injury. Consequently, tort cases will still be necessary whenever property damage occurs with personal injury. In contrast, most no-fault automobile insurance systems also include property damage, at least up to some amount. A New Zealand type personal injury scheme only decreases the amount of damages that can be collected when property damage also occurs. Moreover, property damage occurs independently of personal injury, and the tort system will still be necessary for those accidents.

There are two possible responses to this objection. The first and more moderate is simply to note that elimination of personal injury claims will likely reduce the number of tort cases. Besides the cases which involve only personal injury, fewer court cases involving both personal injury and property damage are likely. People might be more willing to settle when only property damage is to be recovered. The amount of damages is more easily fixed than when pain and suffering and other general damages are involved. And with lower amounts at stake, people have more reason to settle out of court and avoid large legal expenses.

A more radical response is to suggest a system of universal no-fault property insurance. There is no readily apparent reason why no-fault property insurance could not be established. Indeed, to a large extent it already exists. Most real property is insured. Businesses either are self-insurers passing on costs to customers or have other insurance. Most homes are mortgaged with the lenders requiring insurance against significant damage. Reasonable homeowners without mortgages also insure. In short, as most real property is already insured one way or another, all that is necessary is to convert to a universal no-fault insurance. This could be done through the property tax system or simply requiring evidence of insurance. There are, of course, issues about rates, but these arise with private insurance as well.

This leaves personal property. Intangible personal property cannot suffer physical harm, and many savings accounts are insured through the government. Many no-fault automobile insurance plans include limited property damage. That could easily be extended. Most homeowners' or renters' insurance policies cover personal goods, although insurance against theft can be expensive or require a high deductible. Unlike insurance for real property and personal injury, there is no easy way to have a government system, but a government system is certainly not necessary (and perhaps not desirable) for real property, only a requirement of insurance. Nor is it immediately obvious how one might simply enforce compulsory universal personal property insurance other than for automobiles. However, if tort liability were abolished and automobiles covered, individuals would have a good reason to obtain insurance for their other personal goods.

Abolition of tort remedies and implementation of a comprehensive personal injury scheme, compulsory no-fault insurance for real property and automobiles, and consequent individual purchase of no-fault insurance for other personal goods, would leave little for the tort law system. Primarily, only nuisance and a few intentional torts are left. Many intentional torts also amount to crimes – assault and battery, conversion of property, and fraud – so deterrence is already provided and the no-fault systems would cover compensation. However, tort actions for assault and battery might be more effective than criminal enforcement, at least for less serious cases (Williams and Hepple 1976, 172-3). Defamation, invasion of privacy, nuisance, and some economic torts (misrepresentation) would not be covered by the personal injury and property insurance schemes or criminal law. With these few exceptions, the tort law system could be abolished, and its aims better achieved, by a system of insurance and various independent deterrence mechanisms outside the limiting framework of legal adjudication. The common-law legal framework is not always the best, and there appear to be good reasons for abandoning it for most torts. Yet, the failure of a comprehensive no-fault plan to even be on the agenda for discussion in the alleged liability insurance crisis in the United States may show the pervasiveness of the assumption of the common-law adjudicatory framework as much as the conservative temper of the times.

CHAPTER 6

CRIMINAL LAW

INTRODUCTION

6.0. When ordinary citizens think of law, they usually think of criminal law. Yet, except for minor traffic offenses, most people will not be directly involved as a party in a criminal case, but many will be involved as a party in a tort, contract, or divorce case. Criminal law perhaps dominates thought due to its relation to core values – security of person and property – and the social ubiquity of law enforcement officers.

In Chapter 3, we accepted the principles of stability (3-4) and transferability (3-3) of property, and the latter was also important for the analysis of contracts. Our earlier focus on the principle of stability was on stability of legal title to property, but the principle also includes stability of possession. The principle of transferability states that involuntary transfers should be prohibited. Some effect was given to this clause of the principle by holding that contracts procurred by duress and undue influence are voidable (4.3.7). To the concern for property, the last chapter added a concern for interests in the person – bodily and mental integrity, privacy, and reputation.

When these principles and interests are unjustifiably infringed, the primary civil law response is to restore persons to the positions they were in; this is clearly the aim of rescission of contracts and tort damages. Such restoration does not necessarily provide security of person and property. Security consists not only of avoidance of harm but also avoidance of threat of harm (see Bayles 1980, 28-29, for a more detailed analysis). Insecurity is an undesirable situation even if the harm or loss never eventuates; the fear of loss can be unsettling and most people act to reduce it. Although one aim of tort law is economic deterrence, for a variety of reasons tort law is not always effective at preventing harm (see Posner 1985, 1201-05). Moreover, when we dropped the assumption that the aims of tort law were to be accomplished solely by adjudication of cases, an alternative social insurance system was clearly preferable for compensation, and other mechanisms were needed to deter and prevent harmful conduct.

Criminal law, like tort law, concerns interactions that are in fact minus sum ones. Those crimes involving involuntary transfers of property or services are all strictly economic minus sum interactions (Posner 1985, 1195-96). However, the criminal law perspective is broader than the parties immediately involved. For example, bribery and antitrust agreements can be plus sum interactions for the parties directly involved; they are minus sum ones only when one also includes the interests of the public.

The distinctive features of criminal law are strict prohibitions of actions and imposition of harms (possibility of imprisonment) on offenders. Unlike tort law, criminal law is not concerned with compensation or reparations to victims. Instead, it imposes harms on perpetrators. Although from the standpoint of the defendant tort damages are similar to fines in that money is paid, fines are not paid to individual victims. The distinctive aspect of the criminal law response is imprisonment. Consequently, we assume that the criminal law involves the possibility of incarceration. This assumption excludes many regulatory offenses from criminal law (see L.R.C.C. 1974, 38). Criminal law differs from tort law in another respect. Most tort law duties do not flatly prohibit activities, they only require that one conduct them carefully or that compensation be paid should anyone be injured. (The primary exceptions are intentional and nuisance torts.) Criminal law duties do flatly prohibit actions – murder, assault and battery, theft, robbery, and so on. The point is to prevent their occurrence.

AIMS

6.1.0. *Introduction.* Over the centuries a variety of normative aims have been suggested for legal punishment and thus implicitly for the criminal law through which legal punishment is administered. However, the aims of the criminal law should be kept distinct from issues of sentencing – what specifically should be done with offenders after they have been found guilty. At this point, we are concerned with the former and assume only that punishment involves the possibility of imprisonment.

Among the normative aims that have been suggested for punishment, the following are the more important: to deter people from criminal acts (deterrence), to requite wrongdoing (retribution), to reform offenders (reform or rehabilitation), and to condemn conduct contrary to social values ('denunciation'). Another possible aim, to educate people about social values, is closely related to denunciation, for education is often achieved by condemning conduct contrary to the values. What the prohibited conduct or specific social values should be is discussed below (6.2.3). Here we simply refer to criminal acts or conduct.

6.1.1. *Deterrence*. Traditional accounts of deterrence have confused the aim of criminal law with a method of achieving that aim (cf. Van den Haag 1986, 105). In part, this confusion has resulted from discussing the aim of punishment rather than criminal law generally. The purpose of criminal law is to prevent the occurrence of criminal acts (see also Posner 1985, 1215). Punishment helps achieve this aim in three ways. First, by 'specific deterrence' persons who are punished are deterred by fear of further punishment from performing future criminal acts. Second, by 'general deterrence' punishment deters others from committing criminal acts out of fear of being similarly punished. Third, some forms of punishment (imprisonment and capital punishment) 'incapacitate' offenders. While in prison, offenders cannot commit many crimes (at least against nonprisoners). It is important to realize that other aspects of the criminal law besides punishment might help prevent criminal acts, and punishment itself might help prevent crime in other ways than these traditional three.

Moral and practical objections are made to the prevention by deterrence aim. One moral objection is that innocent persons might be punished. If a rash of crimes occurs, others might be deterred were a prosecutor to secure a conviction by withholding evidence of a defendant's innocence. So long as most people do not know that the defendant is innocent, they might refrain from similar crimes for fear of being punished. Even if punishing innocent persons is rarely likely to be an effective deterrent, excessive punishment might be. Judges sometimes give heavy sentences to set an example and deter others in the community. More likely, the punishment for certain crimes might be set excessively high. For example, ten years imprisonment for first offenses of drunk driving might deter it more effectively than current sentences. (The Florida legislature has just enacted a maximum penalty of five years for persons with four or more convictions of driving under the influence ("Drunken driving" 1986).)

One has good reasons not to accept a criminal law system that deliberately punishes innocent persons. One seeks to prevent criminal acts to provide security from harm. If innocent persons are knowingly punished, one cannot avoid the harm of punishment by avoiding criminal acts. One will always be at risk of punishment, so the threat of harm and insecurity is always present. The very system designed to provide security would increase it. *(6-1) The principle of innocence: a person innocent of a criminal act should not be punished for it.*

It might be objected that this reasoning does not apply if punishment of the innocent is rare. The security provided by the extra deterrence might be much greater than the insecurity produced by rare punishment of innocent persons. Consequently, although one has good reasons inherent in the aim of prevention to reject a system that regularly punishes the innocent, one might find acceptable a system that occasionally does so.

This objection confuses a true claim and a false one. Security is increased by a criminal law system that occasionally punishes innocent persons, because it is impossible to eliminate mistakes. The only way to be sure not to punish an innocent person is not to punish anyone. It does not follow that one can accept a principle that permits courts or other officials knowingly punishing innocent persons. Even if a principle only permitted officials to punish innocent persons in exceptional situations, one would never be sure that officials might not mistakenly think the present situation was such an exception. The underlying problem is that occasional knowing punishment of the innocent would work only if it were secret or secretly applied, but legal principles cannot be secret. Consequently, even many critics of deterrence (or a utilitarian basis for it) recognize that it will not permit deliberate punishment of innocent persons (Dworkin 1985, 79-80). Consequently, the principle of innocence supports a rule against knowingly punishing innocent persons, and it also provides a reason against even mistaken punishment of innocent persons, although like any other principle, it can be outweighed by others.

Surely if criminal law does prevent criminal acts, that is a good rather than bad result. If, consistent with other aims, the criminal law can effectively prevent criminal acts, that is an aim worth pursuing. If one has good reasons for thinking that criminal acts are undesirable, then one has good reasons for thinking it better that there be fewer rather than more of them and thus for prevention to be one aim of criminal law (L.R.C.C. 1974, 5). Indeed, criminal law can provide security only if it contributes to there being fewer rather than more criminal acts, that is, prevents them. *(6-2) The principle of prevention: criminal acts should be prevented.* The moral objection to deterrence based on the principle of innocence does not show that prevention is not an aim of criminal law. At most, it shows that it is not acceptable as the sole aim. Acceptance of the principle of innocence as an aim at least partly remedies this objection. Whether a principle regarding excessive punishment is also appropriate is considered below (6.1.2).

At this point a practical objection to the aim of prevention arises. It is that the criminal law does not in fact deter people from criminal acts. Proponents of this objection frequently cite 'recidivism' rates (rates of repeat offenders) and appeal to the many cases of homicide and assault that are committed in the heat of passion. These latter offenders, it is suggested, do not think of possible criminal sanctions before killing or striking their victims.

Although this objection rests on empirical grounds and can be affirmed or refuted only by empirical studies, it appears to involve the fallacy of hasty generalization. It generalizes from certain crimes or offenders to all crimes and offenders. There is evidence that changes in criminal laws decrease (or increase) certain types of conduct. A simple example is the change in legal highway speed limits. (Although the sanction does not involve imprisonment as we require of criminal laws, it illustrates the point.) When the law in the United States was changed from a maximum of seventy to fifty-five miles per hour, people did drive slower. Granted, the average speed on the highways might be more than fifty-five miles per hour and has increased in recent years, it is still slower than it was previously. Although some crimes are committed in the heat of passion, others are more rationally planned, such as fraud on income tax returns or medicaid reimbursements. Even if the criminal law does not deter the former, it might deter the latter (see *United States v. Bergman*, 416 F. Supp. 496 (S.D.N.Y. 1976)); and there is evidence that it does. The criminal law might even prevent some crimes committed in the heat of passion. For the objection to be true, no more assaults and homicides would have to occur even if there were no criminal laws prohibiting such conduct. No government is likely to provide the ultimate experiment by abolishing its laws against assault and homicide, but it seems implausible that the rates of such acts would not increase were the relevant laws repealed.

A few other points should be noted about the practical objection. First, the preventive aim does not require that criminal prohibition be the sole reason people refrain from criminal acts. Indeed, many people would refrain from them without criminal prohibition. But that there are multiple reasons or causes does not imply that criminal prohibition is not one and worth having. Second, general deterrence might not stem from individual criminal sanctions. That is, whether a specific offender receives a criminal sanction might have no or negligible effect on crime rates. General deterrence more likely stems from the pattern of enforcement. The probability of being punished is an important psychological component of deterrence, but it depends on perceived statistical rates of punishment, not individual instances. Nonetheless, individual instances constitute the statistical rates. So punishment in individual cases may be justified even though there is not likely to be any specific deterrence. In *Regina v. Jones* (1956 Ont. W.N. 396, 115 C.C.C. 273), the court probably went too far in imposing an eighteen months sentence for three charges of indecent assault on children on general deterrence grounds, when it admitted that the defendant was unlikely to repeat the crime, imprisonment would be detrimental to the defendant's psychiatric condition, and true sexual perverts would not be deterred. Third, within certain limits, even statistical rates of conviction and punishment might not be important for general deterrence. A threshold might exist, and as long as more than a certain percentage of criminal acts are punished, crime rates might remain fairly constant. Thus, it is probably the general system of criminal law enforcement that deters criminal acts. (For a good discussion of deterrence, see Gross 1979, ch. 9.)

6.1.2. *Retribution.* There are strong and weak versions of the retributive aim of punishment. The strong version stems from Immanual Kant ([1797] 1965, 99-106) and is not advocated by many people today. According to it, criminal punishment is requital for wrongdoing. Justice requires that the same rules apply to everyone. If someone violates a rule of the criminal law, then that person has an unjust advantage over others, and justice requires that this wrong be requited or expiated by punishment (see also Galligan 1981, 157). No one can justly be used as a mere means to the well-being of others, for example, though innocent being punished to deter others. Finally, justice requires that the punishment be equal to the wrong done; were it greater, the person would to that extent receive more punishment than deserved and be used as a means for others; were it less, the wrong would not be requited and the person still have an unjust advantage.

The strong version of retributivism implies that punishment ought to be imposed even though no good, for example, deterrence, would result other than requital of wrongdoing. Many people claim that this amounts to the view that two wrongs make a right, that the addition of punishment to the wrong committed makes a right. However, strong retributivists deny that the punishment is a wrong. Our question is whether one has reason to accept systematically imposing punishment regardless of whether good would come from it. One does not. To do so would risk being punished oneself when no good would result. Although one could accept a system in which the potential benefits of security outweighed the potential harms of punishment, one has no reason to accept a system in which one might only lose. In the former, one risks loss for a greater chance of benefit. In the latter, loss or harm is imposed without any concern for an offsetting benefit.

One might object that this argument overlooks one possible benefit, namely, the satisfaction of vengeance or resentment should one be a victim. Vengeance, however, is not a rational sentiment, for it is simply a desire to inflict harm on those who have harmed one. Its practical effect is merely to increase the amount of harm in society. Of course, not everyone in a society is rational, and all of us are irrational at times. Thus, people, including oneself, might feel vengeance. Although one might rationally accept a system that allows persons to act on irrational sentiments when only the actors might be harmed, one could not accept it when others (including oneself) might be harmed. One surely would not design a legal system that encourages vengeance. Indeed, one reading of the historical development of criminal law is as a gradual substitution of a reasonable public system of punishment for private vengeance. Consequently, one cannot rationally accept criminal laws imposing punishment merely to satisfy irrational desires for vengeance.

Resentment differs from vengeance; it is a sentiment of disapprobation directed towards a person who has wronged one. It is not irrational and has good consequences, for example, reinforcing self-respect and inhibitions to such conduct. Punishment can assuage resentment by preventing the other person having wronged one with impunity. However, the mere assuaging of resentment does not outweigh the harm of imprisonment. Consequently, a system that traded the possibility of imprisonment for the mere assuaging of resentment would not be a rational one. Although more good than assuaging resentment is needed to justify punishment, assuaging resentment is a benefit that can be taken into account.

Weak retributivism has two basic principles. (1) Only persons who have committed criminal acts may be punished. (2) Punishment is permissible only in proportion to the wrong done. The first principle prohibits punishing innocent persons and is therefore already covered by the principle of innocence, although we did not argue for that principle on retributive grounds. Actually, the first principle is otiose in weak retributivism, for its point is included in the second one, the principle of proportionality. If a person has committed no crime or wrong, then no punishment can be proportional to it. Weak retributivism's principle of proportionality differs from Kant's strong retributivism by not requiring, only permitting, punishment that is proportional to the wrong done.

Weak retributivism cannot provide a reason for having a system of criminal law and punishment. It only states that it is permissible to punish people in proportion to the wrong they have done, not that one should or that there is a reason to do so. Hence, because one needs a reason to impose punishment, it is not a substitute for prevention as an aim of the criminal law. Nevertheless, many people think that weak retributivism, or at least the principle of proportionality, can provide a secondary aim limiting the pursuit of deterrence (Hart 1968, 11-13). Indeed, when deterrence is said to justify excessive punishment, that means punishment in excess of that permitted by the Kantian principle of punishment equal to the wrong done or the principle of proportionality.

We need then to consider whether a principle of Kantian equality or of proportionality of punishment is acceptable to avoid imposition of excessive punishment in the pursuit of deterrence. With the Kantian equality principle, it is often impossible to determine a punishment equal to a crime. Although capital punishment might be equal to murder, what punishment would be equal to rape? Even Kant recognized that the letter of equality was not possible, only the spirit. In that spirit, he recommended castration as the appropriate punishment for rape (Kant [1797] 1965, 132-33; but see Davis 1984 (rape equal to ordinary battery)). Thus, Kant's principle might better be called one of equivalence. Yet, one needs some basis for determining when a punishment is equivalent to the wrong done.

A contemporary approach, which draws on the natural rights tradition, is to determine equivalence by the rights violated by criminal acts (Goldman 1979, 43-46). In violating rights, one forfeits those same rights or an equivalent set. Punishment cannot be more than what would be equivalent on some average preference scale. Such an equivalence places a severe limit on deterrence, because to deter, the expected punishment (probability times amount) must be greater than the expected gain from a criminal act (see Posner 1985, 1201). If the amount can be no more than the wrong done and must be discounted by the probability of being convicted, then theft becomes a lucrative enterprise (one will lose no more than one gains and might not lose at all).

This view is surely unacceptable. Its standard for punishment is that of compensation, although there is no transfer to the victim. Granted, people who commit criminal acts cannot complain about that amount of punishment, but it does not follow that they could complain about more punishment. The question concerns principles for a system of punishment. One could accept a system as long as the total harms avoided by prevention are greater than the total harms of punishment. Such a system can involve inflicting more harm in punishment of individual offenders than they caused by their criminal acts. The acceptability of the system is increased if one can avoid committing criminal acts and thus suffering any punishment (see 6.2.1 and 6.2.2). It will not do here to reply that even the ability to avoid punishment will not justify "excessive punishment" (Goldman 1979, 55). Nothing will justify excessive punishment, because by definition excessive punishment is not justifiable. The question is whether punishment inflicting more harm in individual cases than caused by the criminal act is justifiable, and the ability to avoid punishment by avoiding criminal acts does make it more acceptable (see also Alexander 1980, 221 n. 18).

The principle of proportionality avoids these problems of equivalence. The basic notion of proportionality is that crimes and punishments be ranked by their undesirability, and the more severe punishments reserved for the more serious crimes. Unfortunately, the principle of proportionality, at least as a principle independent of preventive concerns, is of no use. There are two ways in which punishment might be said to be disproportional and thus excessive. First, a particular defendant might be punished more than other similar persons who have committed similar crimes – exemplary punishment. The complaint here is of a disproportion between the punishment given this offender and that given similar offenders, not between this punishment and this crime. One person is singled out for extra punishment for reasons independent of that person's conduct. This problem is one of fairness in the administration of justice, of equal application of the law, and is not peculiar to criminal punishment.

Second, punishment might be said to be disproportional because a whole class of conduct has a severe punishment applied to it, say, ten years imprisonment for drunk driving. To apply the principle of proportionality to this type of situation, one must be able to rank crimes by the wrong done. The principle of proportionality cannot assist in developing this ranking, because it presupposes such a ranking. Nor can it help in matching the punishment to crimes, that is, in specifying how much punishment is proportional. For example, suppose one has all the crimes ranked in order of wrongness with deliberate homicide as the most serious. The principle of proportionality will not tell one whether deliberate homicide should be punishable by death, life imprisonment without parole, twenty-five years imprisonment, or what (Bedau 1985, 102-3; Brandt 1985, 188). Only an equivalence principle could do that.

Nonetheless, a greatly weakened principle of proportionality remains. *(6-3) The principle of proportionality: the severity of punishments should be proportional to the seriousness of crimes.* This principle excludes assigning a greater punishment to a less serious crime than one assigns to a more serious one. For example, one cannot assign a greater punishment to a lesser included offense than the primary offense. This sort of proportionality can be and often has been justified on preventive grounds (see also Posner 1985, 1207). If similar punishments are given for crimes that differ in their seriousness, say, petty theft and bank robbery, then criminals have no reason to refrain from the more serious. One might as well rob a bank as steal a few dollars unless detection and conviction rates differ significantly, since their punishment will be the same. This point lies behind a frequent objection to the abolition of capital punishment, namely, that it provides no deterrent to persons serving life sentences. Consequently, the prevention aim can account for the justifiable core of the principle of proportionality. There is a sense in which this principle of proportionality does not prevent excessive punishment, namely, punishment could be more than necessary for deterrence. However, that is contrary to the idea that some good will come from it, and it is excluded by the principle of least drastic alternative (6-7) developed in 6.2.2.

6.1.3. *Reform and denunciation.* The aims of reform and denunciation can be dealt with quickly. As an overall aim of criminal law, reform would imply that people be "punished" whether or not they had committed criminal acts. If people are disposed to commit criminal acts, then the law should intervene to reform them. Given the current ability to predict criminal conduct, one could not rationally risk such possible restraints on freedom. Undoubtedly many people who had not and would not commit crimes would fall into the clutches of the criminal law. Pursuit of a full-blown reform aim would decrease rather than increase security. If one claims that the aim is reform only of those who commit criminal acts, one is committed to preventing recidivism but not first offenses. Consequently, no one should suffer reform or rehabilitation unless there are other reasons for imprisonment (*United States v. Bergman*, 416 F. Supp. 496 (S.D.N.Y. 1976)).

Reform is surely a sensible aim in conjunction with prevention. If criminals are reformed, they will not commit crimes in the future. Thus reform will help ensure that fewer rather than more criminal acts occur. The difference between reform and specific deterrence lies in the motive for not committing crimes. Specific deterrence involves a desire to avoid future punishment, while reform removes the desire to commit criminal acts. Obviously, reform is preferable; it will be effective when specific deterrence might not be because a person thinks detection and conviction unlikely. Consequently, reform provides more security than specific deterrence. *(6-4) The principle of reform: reform of offenders should be sought in sentencing and correctional programs.*

Denunciation is not so much an independent aim as one method by which prevention can be achieved. The point of denouncing wrongdoing, thereby attaching a stigma to the convicted person and bolstering social values (educative effect), is at least to confirm law abiding denizens in their conduct. If denunciation had no effect on the incidence of criminal acts, what would be its point? But denunciation alone would not support a criminal law system that imposed punishment. A court's judgment that a person is guilty of a crime constitutes denunciation (Walker 1981, 112). At best, punishment only shows that the denunciation is serious, but seriousness can be shown in other ways.

Nonetheless, the denunciation view indicates that much prevention is not to be found in specific instances of punishment but a general upholding of standards of behavior so that most people do not even contemplate committing criminal acts. It is an element of indirect prevention. Even the Law Reform Commission of Canada, which generally espouses a denunciatory aim for criminal law (L.R.C.C. 1979a, 5, 16), recognizes that denunciation by punishment indirectly protects people (L.R.C.C. 1979a, 27). Although the actual effect of denunciation in preventing criminal acts is unknown, it is a permissible consideration. In developing criminal law, it is reasonable to try to increase rather than decrease the effect of denunciation in preventing criminal conduct. One need not go so far as to oppose leniency when it is justifiable on other grounds in the hope that its denial will increase the denunciatory effect. *(6-5) The principle of denunciation: a denunciatory effect in preventing criminal acts should be fostered.*

A major factor in the denunciation principle is the ethical culpability of the conduct. Although it is often said that denunciation supports the social values underlying the law, it is likely to do so only when conduct contrary to those values is ethically culpable in the sense explicated in conjunction with the principle of civil retribution (5-1) in 5.1.1. Not all events contrary to values are condemned, only actions knowingly contrary to those values.

For a denunciatory effect, condemnation must appeal to people's strong sentiments of disapprobation, and these are largely restricted to ethically culpable conduct. Most people do not consider technical violations of regulations and laws, especially strict liability offenses, as tainting an offender's character.

In conclusion, the primary aim of the criminal law is to provide security of persons and property by preventing criminal acts that threaten or violate them. This implies that prevention is a necessary aim of criminal law. Besides deterrence, such prevention can also be bolstered by emphatic denunciation of criminal conduct supporting people's inclinations to refrain from it. However, punishment of innocent persons should be avoided; they should never knowingly be punished. Punishments for crimes should be proportional to their seriousness. In corrections, reform is another acceptable aim. Although it includes somewhat more than the above aims, the following statement of the purpose of the criminal law by the Government of Canada generally captures our argument:

> The purpose of the criminal law is to contribute to the maintenance of a just, peaceful and safe society through the establishment of a system of prohibitions, sanctions and procedures to deal fairly and appropriately with culpable conduct that causes or threatens serious harm to individuals or society. (Canada 1982, 52.)

CRIMINAL ACTS

6.2.0. *Introduction.* In analyzing criminal acts, we are implicitly specifying the scope of criminal law duties, just as we were in analyzing torts as intentional, negligent, and so on. As in the previous chapter, we do not specify particular duties or crimes. Instead, we restrict the discussion to general features of criminal conduct. Standard criminal liability requires an act done with a particular mental state that produces harm. After examining the conditions of act, mental element, and harm, we examine crimes in which the harm does not occur or primarily results from another person's conduct.

6.2.1. *Voluntary conduct.* The common law restricts criminal acts to voluntary conduct, that is, conduct a person has the capacity to engage in or not. *(6-6) The principle of voluntary conduct: only voluntary conduct should be criminal.* Conduct includes acts, omissions, and some 'states of being' such as being in possession of stolen property. The requirement of voluntariness here is a minimal one – the ability for alternative conduct. That behavior would be difficult or unreasonable in the circumstances is not excluded by this principle. One must be unable to do otherwise even if one so chooses. The requirement does exclude such behavior as involuntary muscular contractions, failures to act when one could not have done so, and states of being one cannot immediately terminate. Security would be decreased were involuntary behavior and states made criminal. The criminal law cannot prevent such behavior. Were involuntary conduct criminal, one would be unable to avoid the harm of punishment and so less secure.

One might contend that making some involuntary behavior or states criminal might increase security by deterring others from falsely claiming that their behavior was involuntary. However, to increase security, one would have to show that the number of people who would be deterred from criminal conduct by being unable to make such false defenses is greater than the number who would be punished for involuntarily behaving that way. Otherwise, one would impose more harm than one would prevent. The claim has no plausibility for behavior that is usually involuntary, for example, sneezing. It is more plausible for behavior that is usually voluntary but can be involuntary. Still, one must show that courts are unable accurately to identify involuntary behavior. Even if this were true, which is doubtful, it might not have much effect on prevention. Surely, a potential criminal will be better advised to try to avoid detection than to try to make his or her conduct appear involuntary (see also Brandt 1985, 192-93). In any case, one would still not need to prohibit a defense of involuntary behavior, only place a heavy burden of proof on the defendant.

Because the law only proscribes conduct that is usually voluntary, few cases involve the issue. An example is *Kilbride v. Lake* (1962 N.Z.L.R. 590 (N.Z. Sup. Ct. 1961)) in which the defendant had been convicted of not displaying a warrant of fitness on the windshield of a car on the road. The defendant had parked the car with such a warrant and gone to conduct some business. When he returned, the warrant was gone and he had received a notice of an offense. The court held that the conviction violated the requirement of voluntary conduct, because the defendant could not have avoided the offense. The warrant was removed by some cause beyond his control and knowledge. However, such a defense was not recognized in an English case. The defendant there was a French citizen whose permission to be in England was cancelled by immigration authorities. The defendant went to Ireland but was deported back to England, at which point the defendant was charged and convicted of being in England without permission (*Rex v. Larsonneur*, 24 Crim. App. 74 (Crim. App. 1933)). Because it believes most cases of involuntary conduct involve 'automatism' (unconscious conduct) or compulsion, the Law Reform Commission of Canada has recommeded not having a specific requirement of voluntary conduct but simply covering it under those defenses (L.R.C.C. 1982, 19). However, that approach would fail to provide a defense in a case like *Kilbride*.

The *Kilbride* case involves an involuntary omission. Conduct includes omissions when there is a legal duty to act (M.P.C. § 2.01(3); LaFave and Scott 1972, 182). Sometimes courts strain to find acts. In *Fagan v. Commissioner of Metropolitan Police* ([1969] 1 Q.B. 439 (Q.B. Div'l Ct.)), a police constable directed the defendant to park near the curb and the car's wheel went onto the constable's foot. The constable told him to drive off the foot, but the defendant turned off the motor. After further requests, the defendant drove off the constable's foot. The defendant was convicted of assault. The problem is that criminal assault of the sort in question requires an intentional bodily contact. The defendant contended that he did not intend to drive onto the constable's foot, so that did not constitute assault. After that, there was only an omission to remove the car, not an act. In upholding the conviction, the court claimed that after the car was on the foot there was indirect bodily contact through the car and an act when he switched off the engine. Although one may find the defendant's conduct reprehensible, as the dissent noted, the court surely exceeded the bounds of legitimate construction of an act; and as the defendant had no legal duty to remove the car (and complied if there were, albeit slowly), the conviction should have been reversed.

The distinction between voluntary and involuntary states of being is not generally recognized in the literature. The U.S. Supreme Court confronted the issue of punishment for involuntary states of being in a case involving the conviction of a man for being addicted to the use of narcotics (*Robinson v. California*, 370 U.S. 660 (1962)). The Court held that such a criminal law imposes cruel and unusual punishment. It reasoned by analogy to a disease (or perhaps thought addiction is a disease). It also suggested that alternative methods of dealing with addicts, such as compulsory treatment, were available.

Why would it be wrong to make having a disease a crime? One reason might be that people have no control over whether they contract a disease, that is, get it involuntarily. But that is not true of all diseases, for example,

venereal diseases; besides, people might have some control over becoming
addicts. Rather, the point is that one cannot voluntarily and immediately
escape the state of being an addict. Although one might voluntarily undergo
a course of treatment curing one of addiction, alcoholism, or some disease,
one cannot immediately accomplish a cure. This point is implicitly recognized in the Model Penal Code where it misleadingly defines possession as
an act if the person knew of the possession "for a sufficient period to have
been able to terminate his possession" (§ 2.01(4)). The ability to voluntarily
and quickly terminate a state of being by an act justifies making it criminal,
but it does not make it an act.

Normally, by a simple voluntary act one can dispose of stolen goods or
narcotics in one's possession. However, some narcotics possession laws do
not allow for this condition. For example, in *People v. Valot* (33 Mich. Ap.
49, 189 N.W.2d 873 (Mich. Ct. App. 1971)), the defendant was found along
with others sleeping in a motel room registered in his name, and marijuana
was also found in the room. The defendant claimed that others had brought
the marijuana in after he had gone to sleep. The court claimed that the
marijuana was under the defendant's control. If the facts were as the
defendant claimed, then it should be considered involuntary possession, for
he had no ability to terminate possession by a simple act. However, there
was evidence that the defendant's version might not be true. Interestingly,
statutes that make it a crime to be in the presence of drugs rather than have
them in one's control better meet the voluntariness condition. Unless a
person is paralyzed or otherwise unable to leave a room, apartment, or
building, the person can simply leave a place where drugs are present.

6.2.2. *Mental elements.* Further requirements than voluntary conduct must
be met before conduct is justifiably made criminal. 'Mens rea' or a mental
element is also required. A variety of different mental elements are possible
and have been used. The Model Penal Code approach best explicates them
(§ 2.02(2)). The possible ones are as follows: a person can be required to
act purposely, knowingly, recklessly, negligently, or without any of these
(strict liability). The concepts of purposely and knowingly distinguish two
different conditions described as 'intent' in tort law and most common-law
criminal law. To act knowingly, one must be aware of a circumstance or
that a consequence is practically certain to result. To act purposely, one
need not be certain that a result will occur, but one must desire or hope
that it will or that a circumstance exists.

The definitions of recklessness and negligence are basically the same as in tort law. To act recklessly is to be aware of and disregard "a substantial and unjustifiable risk" that a circumstance exists or consequence will result. The Model Penal Code defines 'unjustifiable' as great deviation from the conduct a law abiding person would observe (§ 2.02(2)(c)). To act negligently is to fail to be aware of such a risk when one should. The standard is objective in that one need not be aware of risks (LaFave and Scott 1972, 211). The last possibility is that no mental element of the above types is required; such crimes are usually called strict liability offenses.

The distinction between recklessness and negligence is often hard to discern in the cases. For example, in *Commonwealth v. Welansky* (316 Mass. 383, 55 N.E.2d 902 (1944)), Welansky was convicted of involuntary manslaughter involving recklessness for failure to provide sufficient fire exits in a nightclub that burned with many resultant deaths. The court claimed that recklessness involves knowing facts that would lead a reasonable person to know of danger and choosing to run the risk, even though one did not realize the danger. In short, while one must be aware of facts creating a risk, one need not be aware of the danger (see Hall 1960, 131-32). But one cannot choose to run a risk of danger if one is not aware of danger. Similarly, in *State v. Cushman* (133 Vt. 121, 329 A.2d 648 (1974)), the defendant was convicted of recklessly placing another in danger of death or serious bodily injury for pointing a gun that he believed to be unloaded at a police officer. The Vermont statute in question presumed recklessness when a person knowingly pointed a firearm at another whether or not the person believed it was loaded. These cases depart from the use of 'recklessness' here. One must actually be aware of danger, although the circumstances can be such that a judge or jury can infer awareness. However, 'wilful blindness' is not accepted as equivalent to recklessness (cf. L.R.C.C. 1982, 27).

The central question is which of these mental elements should be used for crimes. Everyone agrees that purposely, knowingly, and recklessly causing harm can be crimes; the dispute concerns strict liability and negligence. There are three commonly offered reasons for restricted mens rea, that is, limiting criminal liability to the first three mental elements and excluding negligence and strict liability. First, at the time of acting, people cannot avoid acts of negligence and strict liability, so criminal liability for them subjects people to the risk of punishment for conduct they cannot avoid at the time of acting. Much criminal harm – hitting persons and damaging property – can occur in the course of many activities. If people

could be convicted for doing so negligently or without any mental requirement, they would be at risk of punishment that they could not avoid. This
risk would greatly increase insecurity. Second, and related to the first,
because people cannot avoid acts of negligence and strict liability at the
time of acting, criminal sanctions are unable to deter them at the time of
acting. If the conduct cannot be prevented, criminalization will not contribute to security. Third, the denunciatory aim of criminal law requires that
the conduct be ethically culpable. However, people are not morally blamed
for behavior they could not avoid. Consequently, negligence and strict
liability should not be criminal conduct. A variation on this last argument
emphasizes that moral blame attaches to defects of character or motivation
(Bayles 1982a; Brandt 1985). If a person acts purposely, knowingly, or
recklessly one can infer that the person lacks proper motivation to avoid
harm. But if a person acts negligently or with strict liability, one cannot
make that inference.

    These reasons have been challenged with respect to both negligence and
strict liability offenses. Two general reasons can be given for holding that
they do not apply to strict liability offenses. First, strict liability offenses
might promote security by deterring people from engaging in types of
activity, as opposed to specific acts, that can have harmful consequences.
The punishments are usually light – fines or short jail terms – and great
harm can be caused, such as that from selling impure drugs (see *United
States v. Dotterweich*, 320 U.S. 277 (1943)). Second, sometimes it is very
difficult to obtain evidence of a person's mental state and so obtain convictions.

    These arguments are not persuasive. The argument from the difficulty of
obtaining evidence implicitly assumes that only persons with one of the
other mental elements should be convicted. If a court can determine that
a defendant had one of the other mental states, strict liability is not needed.
If a court knows that the defendant did not have one of the other mental
states, then by the assumption punishment cannot be justified. Hence, the
argument can only justify convictions if a court cannot determine whether
a defendant had one of the other mental states. In the absence of evidence,
one has no more reason for assuming the defendant did rather than did not,
so one has no basis to assume conviction rather than acquital is appropriate.

    The first argument is more plausible. It counters the first and second
arguments for restricted mens rea by claiming that, everything considered,
strict liability offenses can indeed increase security. Some types of activity,

such as driving and producing or distributing food and drugs, have the potential for great harm, and the punishment for strict liability offenses is usually light. Strict liability offenses can deter people who cannot be sure of avoiding harms from engaging in these activities. Thus, although people cannot be deterred from specific acts, some can be deterred from engaging in kinds of activities. The resulting decrease in harm might outweigh the increased harm in punishment.

There are several problems with this argument. One is that it shifts deterrence from the specific act to a type of activity. It is admitted that persons cannot at the time avoid the specific act, only the general activity. For example, in *The Queen v. Pierce Fisheries Ltd.* (12 D.L.R.3d 591 (Can. 1970)), the defendant was convicted of having twenty-six undersized lobsters in 50,000 to 60,000 pounds of lobsters, even though no one knew of the presence of the undersized lobsters and the employees had been instructed not to purchase them. The specific act could not be deterred. The only way Pierce Fisheries could avoid liability would be to cease dealing in lobsters. Consequently, the argument will not work for many types of acts prohibited in the criminal law, acts that can occur in almost any social activity. These are more general offenses that one might commit as a person rather than in special roles or activities (L.R.C.C. 1974, 3). To avoid bumping into others or destroying property, one would have to avoid all social activity and the costs to liberty would outweigh any gain in security.

Second, the argument does not avoid the concern with ethical blame and denunciation. People would still be denounced for acts that they could not avoid at the time of acting and that did not evince a defect of character or motivation. Third, the usual strict liability offenses concern conduct that differs from the 'core' offenses (see 6.2.3) in the criminal law. Society does not want to deter everyone from engaging in the activities for which strict liability offenses are usually created – driving, processing food, and producing drugs, but it does want to deter everyone from murder, battery, and theft. Fourth, we should exclude from consideration offenses for which the penalty is only a fine. These regulatory offenses are not the core criminal law.

The question, then, is whether incarceration is ever appropriate for strict liability offenses. Would it have been acceptable to jail the officers of Pierce Fisheries? In Canada in the early 1970s, imprisonment was available for seventy percent of strict liability offenses (L.R.C.C. 1974, 23). Since such punishment is undesirable, if security can be brought about by some less drastic method, then it should be used. *(6-7) The principle of the least drastic alternative: if the net benefits of noncriminal control of conduct are equal to or greater than those of criminal control, then the noncriminal method should be used.* Even if more instances of the harmful conduct occur, if a noncriminal approach imposes a significantly lesser penalty, then the net benefit will be greater with it than with the criminal law. By our method, one must assume that one has a chance of being either party (here a criminal defendant or a victim). Thus, one can expect to gain from using the least drastic alternative, and it is acceptable. It has not been shown that noncriminal approaches, such as tort liability, licensing and inspection, or simply prohibiting certain people from engaging in activities, will not have a greater net benefit than strict criminal liability.

Consequently, strict liability offenses should be banned from the criminal law (see *Morissette v. United States*, 342 U.S. 246 (1952) (implying intent in statutes involving common-law crimes); *Commonwealth v. Koczwara*, 397 Pa. 575, 155 A.2d 825 (1959) (rejecting vicarious liability involving imprisonment)). Strict liability cannot be justified for acts that are likely to occur in many different activities. It does not conform to the denunciatory aim of the criminal law. It deters people from socially valuable activities, and other less drastic measures are available to provide the security it might produce.

Except for regulatory offenses, little would be lost in the criminal law. The chief strict liability offenses in the Model Penal Code concern sexual intercourse or assault with a person below the age of ten (§ 213.6 (1)). This is a plausible place for a variation of the argument from evidence, namely, no evidence would be sufficient to convince a judge or jury that the defendant believed someone younger than ten was over the age of consent (sixteen or older). Essentially, the law makes an irrebuttable presumption of knowledge.

One might contend that negligence differs from strict liability, so even if the latter is unacceptable, it does not follow that negligence is. However, arguments have been given against permitting negligence offenses in the criminal law. The Law Reform Commission of Canada contends that criminal sanctions stigmatize or denounce wrongful conduct and that, therefore, a person must have meant to do the prohibited act (1979a, 22). Similarly, Jerome Hall contends that criminal liability should rest on the voluntary commission of a proscribed act (1960, 104, 133-34). Because one who acts negligently is not aware of the circumstances that make the act likely to cause the prohibited harm, in the circumstances the person cannot avoid it. Moreover, Hall contends, there is insufficient evidence to show that criminal sanctions of negligent conduct would deter (Hall 1960, 138-39).

These arguments are not completely persuasive. First, in ordinary life the claims that "I didn't mean to do it" and "I didn't stop to think" are not accepted as excuses (Hart 1968, 133). That is, people are blamed for some negligent acts. This point seems to undercut the Law Reform Commission's argument, because it shows that ordinary people do take negligent conduct to be wrong and blameworthy. Elsewhere the Law Reform Commission permits the possibility of a few negligence offenses (1979a, 28). Second, common sense supports the belief that sanctioning negligent conduct can make people more careful. Finally, Hall's argument about voluntary choice appeals to a principle of punishing only voluntary conduct. However, one must be very careful with the concept of a voluntary act. Our principle of voluntary conduct requires an act to be voluntary in the sense that one could do otherwise if one chose. Negligent acts are voluntary in this sense. Negligent actors can refrain from the conduct. Negligent actors lack awareness of the reason for refraining, not the ability to do so.

However, these replies are not devastating. Consider first the blameworthiness of negligent conduct. Not all blame is ethical blame. A negligent person should have been aware of the relevant circumstance or consequence. Thus, one can contend that it is really a prior act, that of not obtaining knowledge or awareness, for which the person is responsible and blameworthy. One should have stopped, looked, and listened (for example, a motorist at a stop sign). People can direct their attention to matters. However, at the time, the person might not have been consciously thinking that he or she should do so. Everyone is occasionally careless. This does not show a defect of character. Ethical blame attaches to persistent carelessness or negligence – that indicates a character trait, a careless person – not to individual acts of carelessness. Consequently, even though "I didn't think" is not an excuse, it does not follow that a person who commits a careless act is ethically blameworthy.

Moreover, the other arguments against strict liability need slight or no modification to apply to negligence. First, deterrence applies to types of activity rather than specific acts. Negligence differs from strict liability in that it attempts to deter the way activities are conducted, while strict liability attempts to deter particular persons from engaging in activities. Still, when applied to general harms, such as negligently striking people without their consent, the gain in decreased blows is likely to be outweighed by the loss of liberty necessary to avoid such conduct. Thus, like strict liability offenses, most criminal negligence offenses are regulatory of specific types of activities. Second, society does not want to prevent most activities criminal negligence concerns, only their being conducted carelessly. Third, it has not been shown that the harms cannot be reasonably avoided by other legal techniques, that is, that criminal law is the least drastic alternative.

The chief nonregulatory negligence offense is negligent homicide (M.P.C. § 210.4). The main point of such an offense is to control negligent driving resulting in death. By criminalizing negligent homicide, one might cause people to view driving more seriously and be more careful. This would largely result from the denunciatory and educative effect of punishment. Even here, however, negligent homicide need not be used. The central offense is reckless driving, not negligent driving. Consequently, the Law Reform Commission of Canada has suggested varying the severity of penalties for reckless driving depending on the resultant harm – no injury, bodily injury, death (1984, 59). Specifying the activity that is the cause of concern might increase the denunciatory and educative effect of the law. A similar argument could be made for the reckless use of firearms. Such a law, however, would not support conviction in cases such as *People v. Howk* (56 Cal. 2d 687, 16 Cal. Rptr. 370, 365 P.2d 426 (1961)). In that case, the defendant was convicted of involuntary manslaughter for lack of "due caution and circumspection" in selling a firearm to a person who had previously indicated he wanted to kill his girl friend. In any event, a general crime of negligent homicide is not necessary or acceptable.

(6-8) The principle of culpability: only purposeful, knowing, and reckless conduct should be criminal (see L.R.C.C. 1974, 19). One of these mental states should be required for each element of a crime (M.P.C. § 2.02(1)). Only with such a principle are criminal acts restricted to ethically culpable ones that indicate a defect of character and that one can avoid at the time of acting. Both negligence and strict liability would shift the time at which conduct could be avoided to some time prior to the act. Their application to acts that are likely to occur during many different activities would significantly decrease security. Even applied to specific types of activity, they are not intended to deter the activity but only specific people from engaging in it or the way the activity is conducted. It has not been shown that less drastic alternatives will not achieve the aim. Finally, they do not support the blameworthiness or ethical culpability involved in the denunciatory aim of criminal law.

6.2.3. *Core offenses.* One can, at least roughly, divide criminal conduct into core (or substantive) offenses and secondary offenses that are based on a relationship to core offenses. Secondary offenses are distinguished by the relationships they have to core offenses – attempting, soliciting, conspiring, and aiding others to commit them.

Before explicating the core offenses, we must consider one other general feature. A traditional principle is that of legality – no crime or punishment without an antecedent law (L.R.C.C. 1982, 11-13). One manifestation of this principle is the general disappearance of common-law crimes and their replacement by statutory offenses. A correlative principle is that one should be able to determine what conduct is prohibited. *(6-9) The principle of certainty: criminal laws should be simple, clear, and precise.* This principle is perhaps addressed to legislators more than courts, since most or all criminal law is statutory, but it is still relevant to courts in interpreting statutes.

The principle of certainty contains three different criteria. Criminal conduct should be precisely demarcated from noncriminal conduct. There will always be borderline cases when, due to unusual facts or the fuzzy borders of concepts, the distinction will not be easy, but these should be minimized. A law can precisely demarcate criminal from noncriminal conduct but still be so unclear that most people cannot understand it by themselves. The prolix language of many statutes perhaps precisely defines criminal conduct, but its unclarity deprives it of value to the ordinary citizen. Simplicity is not the same as clarity, although it can contribute to clarity. A rule with one exception is simpler than one with five, although all five exceptions might be clear. A simple law is more easily remembered than a complex, though clear and precise one. (For a good discussion of these factors in the context of theft law using 'certainty' instead of 'precision', see L.R.C.C. 1977, 3-9 and 54-63.)

The normative point is to reduce uncertainty. People want to avoid criminal sanctions, and this requires that they be able to tell whether their proposed conduct is criminal. Not only must the law precisely distinguish criminal from noncriminal conduct, but people must be able to know what it requires; it must be simple and clear. Of course, with uncertainty, they could avoid criminal sanctions by being cautious and forgoing any conduct that might possibly be criminal. But their liberty of action would be significantly decreased, and they have no reason to accept laws that do this unnecessarily. Although these reasons also apply to other fields of law, they are especially important for criminal law. The criminal law sanction is generally more undesirable than that in other fields. People are less likely to guide their conduct by considerations of tort liability than criminal liability, and in contract law, people draft their own duties or at least need not agree until the duties are clear.

The principle of certainty is expressed in various ways in the law. The most obvious example is the U.S. Supreme Court's void for vagueness doctrine which renders laws that do not clearly specify criminal conduct unconstitutional violations of due process (*Papachristou v. City of Jacksonville*, 405 U.S. 156 (1972) (vagrancy)). It is also found in the principles of plain meaning and narrow construction of statutes (*McBoyle v. United States*, 283 U.S. 25 (1931)). Offenses can be formulated simply, clearly, and precisely, although some trade-off must often be made between them. For example, the Model Penal Code takes the equivalent of six typewritten pages to set out various offenses of fraud, including tampering with records, deceptive business practices, and rigging contests (§§ 224.0 to 224.14). In contrast, the Law Reform Commission of Canada has proposed a law that takes a little over one page (1979b, 18-19). No reason exists to believe that the latter involves significantly more uncertainty than the former.

The question of what conduct should be criminal has been disputed for centuries, resulting in a voluminous literature (see Bayles 1978; Feinberg 1984; Feinberg 1985; Packer 1968). The preferable approach is to specify types of considerations that are good reasons for making conduct criminal. Among the considerations proposed are harm to others (individuals or the public), harm to the actor, offense to others, and the immorality of the conduct. We cannot here discuss the question in detail. It is generally agreed that the primary purpose of the criminal law is to prevent persons harming others. This purpose is especially dominant where, as we restrict it here, the laws have incarceration as a sanction. Harm caused by others and the possibility of it create insecurity. Whether any considerations other than causing harm to others are appropriate is much disputed, but as the offenses supported by these considerations are peripheral to traditional criminal law, we ignore them here.

Several elements can be involved in harm to others. Joel Feinberg has formulated the harm principle as follows:

It is always a good reason in support of penal legislation that it would probably be effective in preventing (eliminating, reducing) harm to persons other than the actor (the one prohibited from acting) *and* there is probably no other means that is equally effective at no greater cost to other values. (Feinberg 1984, 26.)

This formulation, as Feinberg notes, involves three elements. First, harm to others is a reason for proscribing conduct. Second, criminal law will be effective in preventing the harm. Third, criminal prohibition is, according to Feinberg, necessary to do so. Instead of combining these elements into one principle, we treat them as three distinct principles.

(6-10) The principle of harm: criminal law should primarily prohibit conduct in which the risk and gravity of harm to others is greater than the harm (loss of liberty, privacy, and so on) of enforcement. The underlying notion is that the criminal law should do more good (by preventing harm) than bad (harm from enforcement). Risk and gravity of harm are separately specified simply to remind one to consider both; ordinarily 'risk' means 'probability times amount'. To apply this principle, one must identify the harm, what or whom will be harmed, the gravity of the harm, the probability of the harm, the harm in the proposed criminal sanction, the frequency with which it will be imposed, and any other harms involved in detection of crimes. One must not consider individual cases, but the total instances of the harmful conduct and of instances of enforcement. Harm can be caused by investigations that do not result in convictions and sanctions, for example, at least the costs of investigation. If the harm of enforcement is worse than that prevented, then people do not have a good reason for making the conduct criminal. For example, sometimes criminal sanctions are imposed for late filing of forms to the government, which at most delays inconsequential government review or action. In these cases, the likely harm is less than that of criminal enforcement.

(6-11) The principle of effectiveness: a criminal law should deal effectively with the problem. If it cannot, there is insufficient reason for criminalization because the central problem will remain. One cannot expect criminal laws to eliminate the conduct in question completely, but they should at least keep it at a tolerable level. This principle is not quite the same as the harm principle. The harm principle would be satisfied if little harmful conduct were prevented, but even less harm resulted from enforcement, say, due to difficulties of detection. The principle of effectiveness would oppose such a law, because the chief problem remained.

At least three considerations pertain to effectiveness. First, people might not view the conduct as immoral. If they do not, the denunciatory aim of criminal law and its indirect preventive effect will not be achieved. If they do not view the prohibited conduct as seriously wrong, then they are not likely to take the law seriously and to comply with it. Some authors contend that accepted immorality is a necessary condition for making conduct criminal (Packer 1968, 261-64). The condition here is not that strong, only that it is a factor to be considered as affecting effectiveness. One reason for not making it a necessary condition is that society's morality lags behind developments in technology and understanding of the harmful effects of conduct. For example, the government might have good reason to impose criminal sanctions for certain polluting activities before most people in society view it as morally wrong.

Second, if there is significant social dissent from the law, then it is less likely to be effective. Indeed, it might bring the law into disrepute and do more harm than good. This consideration applies even if many people do think the conduct immoral, for example, prohibiting abortion. Third, it might be impossible to obtain evidence to enforce the law effectively without doing more harm than good. For example, laws prohibiting couples using contraceptives cannot be effectively enforced without gross violations of privacy that are worse than the alleged harm to be prevented (*Griswold v. Connecticut*, 381 U.S. 479 (1965); see also *Stanley v. Georgia*, 394 U.S. 557 (1969) (pornography in home); and *Ravin v. State*, 537 P.2d 494 (Alaska 1975) (marijuana for personal use in own home)). Thus, no law on these matters compatible with the principle of harm can be effective.

The third principle is that of the least drastic alternative formulated above (6.2.2). This principle is not quite the same as Feinberg's requirement of necessity – that there be no other means equally effective at no greater cost. The principle of the least drastic alternative does not require that other means be equally effective if the decrease in harm of enforcement is greater than the increase in harm from unprevented conduct. That is, it allows less effective means provided that the net benefit (harm prevented less harm of enforcement) is greater. Of course, the principle of effectiveness puts a lower limit on the amount of harm prevented; the noncriminal means must still reasonably deal with the problem.

It remains to indicate briefly the chief offenses that meet the principles of voluntary conduct, culpability, harm, effectiveness, and least drastic alternative. This primarily involves indicating the interests that are harmed by the prohibited conduct. The core offenses are those that threaten or violate security of person or property or the functioning of public institutions in ways that might significantly harm people. One group of offenses against the person protects bodily integrity from unwanted interference whether or not bodily injury results. People rationally desire control over their bodies, so unconsented to use of them is a significant harm. Besides the absence of actual harm, security also includes the absence of a significant threat of it. These offenses include common-law assault and sexual assault or rape as well as homicide and battery. Sexual assault or rape violates control over one's body regardless of whether physical injury occurs. Physical injury is only evidence of lack of consent, and absence of consent can be proven without it. We leave open whether sexual assault should be treated differently from assault and battery (see Davis 1984). Common-law assault involves intentionally causing the victim to fear bodily harm (LaFave and Scott 1972, 609 and 611-12). Another and smaller group of offenses against the person protects the interest in freedom. These offenses include kidnapping, false imprisonment, and criminal coercion. A few other offenses, such as wiretapping, protect privacy.

The core offenses against property are theft, robbery, blackmail, fraud, and arson. The Law Reform Commission of Canada claims that in each of the first four, persons are dishonestly deprived of property (1977, 17-19). It distinguishes between them as follows. In theft and robbery, the victim does not consent to the taking of the property; robbery is distinguished from theft by involving the use or threat of the immediate use of violence. In blackmail and fraud, the victim does consent to the taking of the property, but the offender unjustly manipulates the consent. In blackmail, the consent is produced by threats of harm – violence or injury to reputation. In fraud, victims are deceived into consenting to something to which they otherwise would not have consented. In arson, unlike the other four, the offender might not be obtaining personal benefit from the property. Nonetheless, the victim is deprived of its use, and often others are placed in jeopardy. Burning one's own building to collect insurance involves both arson and fraud against the insurance company.

The last broad category of core offenses is those that cause harm to the general public, especially by interfering with the functioning of public institutions. Rioting and disorderly conduct harm the general public. Not all public institutions are equally important. Particular emphasis is on the operation of the legal system. Thus, perjury and bribery of jurors and judges as well as interference with police officers raise the prospect of significant insecurity. A person might be unjustly convicted or lose a civil case. Bribery, of course, can pertain to activities of other government officials. There the harm is that public decisions will be made to the detriment of the people. Interferences that merely delay public decisions or activities, for example, late filing of forms, do not usually create a significant risk of harm to others. Consequently, they do not meet the principle of harm test for criminal offenses.

Most criminal codes also contain a miscellany of other offenses, such as bigamy, prostitution, public indecency, mutilation of corpses, and so forth. Many of these crimes do not meet the tests of the principles of harm, effectiveness, and least drastic alternative and should be abolished (but see Feinberg 1985). Even those that do meet these tests do not seriously threaten people's security. Given limited resources, they should not be major concerns of criminal justice systems (Packer 1968, 259-60).

6.2.4. *Inchoate offenses and accessories.* The 'inchoate' offenses of attempt, solicitation, and conspiracy are related to core offenses by being anticipations of core offenses without the harm actually occurring. Security would be greatly decreased if the law could intervene only after a harm had occurred. To prevent core offenses, it can be beneficial to punish conduct before the harm results; if one will be punished even if one does not complete the core offense, the risk of the conduct (and thus deterrence) is increased (see Posner 1985, 1217 (attempts)). However, the principle of a voluntary act requires that some act be taken toward the offense. Generally, this act should increase the risk of the core offense occurring. Because inchoate offenses are anticipatory of substantive offenses, the required mens rea is purposefulness; the actor's purpose is to commit an act constituting the core offense.

Perhaps the central inchoate offense is attempt. In attempting something, a person tries to do it or bring it about, and trying involves making something an object or goal – purposefulness. It has been argued that purposefulness is not necessary for all attempts (Williams 1965, 24-25). Suppose Allman and Bullock both spy a lost watch ahead on a path beside a cliff. As they both rush to get the watch, Allman pushes Bullock from the path knowing that should she fall over she will almost certainly be killed. Suppose, however, that Bullock grabs a small shrub and is thus saved from death. Allman, it is contended, should be and is guilty of attempted murder although he did not desire Bullock's death, only knew that it was practically certain. Moreover, the Model Penal Code gives this result. Although it generally requires purposefulness for an attempt, it does permit knowledge that a result will occur to constitute an attempt (§ 5.01(1)(b)). However, this exception to the requirement of purposefulness is not necessary (but see Robinson 1984, § 85(c) (awareness of substantial risk should suffice)). Allman's shoving Bullock over the cliff should constitute aggravated assault under the Model Penal Code (§ 2.11.1(2)(a)), and the punishment for aggravated assault is the same as that for attempted murder (§§ 2.1.1 and 5.05(1)). If, as we argue (6.4.2)) attempts should be punished less than successful crimes, then when knowledge rather than purpose is involved, there is almost always a lesser offense of which a person could be convicted or punishment is inappropriate.

Much dispute has concerned how close the act must be to the fulfillment of the crime. Shooting at and missing a person clearly suffices, but has one gone far enough in merely taking a weapon to a car with the intent to drive to a place to lie in wait for the intended victim? A normative approach establishes a test for such cases, although the facts necessary to meet the test vary from crime to crime and case to case. As the purpose of the criminal law is security, the act should create a significant risk of the harm (see also Posner 1985, 1218). If a significant risk exists that the person would commit a criminal act, there is sufficient conduct for an attempt. The act must be more than 'mere preparation', that is, acting with the intention of performing another act that is part of the crime; it must be an act in the attempt to do something (Hart 1983, 376). Probably the language of a 'substantial step' in the commission of the crime is as good as any other (M.P.C. § 5.01(2)).

Whether the person must be able to succeed is a highly debated point. The law traditionally distinguishes factually and legally impossible attempts. Factual impossibility does not excuse. Suppose, unknown to Cole, the gun he aims at Doty is not loaded. Still, Cole has manifested a purpose of committing a crime, and his conduct poses a threat to people. Were he to discover that the gun were unloaded, he would take steps to rectify the situation. Legally impossible attempts have not usually been considered crimes. For example, if Emory tries to smuggle a watch, thinking its importation is proscribed when it is not, then Emory is not guilty of a crime. The courts, however, have been greatly troubled by cases involving the receipt of stolen goods when the police have intercepted and had custody of the goods (*People v. Jaffe*, 185 N.Y. 497, 78 N.E. 169 (1906); *People v. Rojas*, 55 Cal. 2d 252, 10 Cal. Rptr. 465, 358 P.2d 921 (1961); *Haughton v. Smith*, 1975 A.C. 476). As the goods are not stolen, there would be no crime even if the person succeeded. Yet, when people purposely act to cause harm and the acts would create a significant risk of harm were the facts as the actors thought, security interests are threatened.

The resolution of the problem rests on the mental element being purpose. To determine whether some fact or circumstance is an element of a person's purpose, one should consider whether the person would have acted differently had he or she thought the circumstances were otherwise. If so, then they were part of the purpose. The underlying principle is that mistaken beliefs are relevant if they affect the incentive in acting (Fletcher 1978, 161). The point of the law is to promote security by preventing people with criminal purposes acting to further them. Emory would still have brought the watch into the country even had he believed it legal. The illegality was no part of his purpose. The receiver of stolen goods, however, would not act the same way if he or she knew the true facts – that the goods were in police custody. The status of the goods is relevant to the receiver's purpose, and this makes the person a threat (see also Bayles 1982a, 10-14; but see Richards 1979, 1441; Robinson 1984, § 85(d) (belief in circumstances that would constitute a crime should suffice regardless of purpose).

Solicitation is a simpler crime than attempt. It involves commanding, encouraging, or requesting another to perform a crime or to participate in a crime (M.P.C. § 5.02(1)). A simple example is asking another to commit murder for a fee. The purpose is the commission of the crime requested. The act is that of asking. If the actor does not really desire that the crime occur, then no solicitation has occurred. Thus, a vice officer who requests an act of prostitution is not guilty of solicitation. It makes no difference whether the other person agrees. The solicitor still poses a threat, for if the first person asked refuses, the solicitor is likely to ask another person to commit the crime.

Conspiracy is the most controversial of the inchoate crimes, because it has the greatest potential for abuse by prosecutors. The central elements are easily stated, namely, an agreement or combination of two or more persons to commit an unlawful act; sometimes an act in furtherance of that agreement is also required. If an act in furtherance of the conspiracy is required, it need not be as proximate to the crime as the substantial step in attempts. The reason is that the agreement is, like an act of solicitation, itself an act.

At this point, the problems start. First, there are difficulties over the mental requirement. Again, this should be purposefulness. The purpose should include all the elements of the crime. In *United States v. Feola* (420 U.S. 671 (1975)), the U.S. Supreme Court considered whether a conspiracy to assault a federal officer required knowing that the intended victim was a federal officer. The majority held that it did not, because the requirement that the victim be a federal officer is only for jurisdictional purposes – to make it a federal crime – and is not required for an attempt at the crime.

The dissent held that it is an element. The answer should depend on whether assaulting a federal officer is punished differently from assaulting a civilian on federal property. If it is, then it is not a purely jurisdictional element but designed specially to protect officers.

A second problem concerns whether both (or all) parties must have the purpose, although only one has to act. In *Regina v. O'Brien* ([1955] 2 D.L.R. 311 (Can.)), O'Brien and Tulley allegedly conspired to kidnap a woman. However, at trial Tulley testified that although he went with O'Brien to look for a house in which to keep the woman, he never intended to go through with the crime. He was out of work, broke, and leading O'Brien along for the advance payments O'Brien was giving him. As Tulley never had the purpose of kidnapping the woman, there were not two people with the requisite purpose, and the court held that O'Brien could not be convicted of conspiracy. Other courts and the Model Penal Code have held the contrary (*State v. St. Christopher*, 305 Minn. 226, 232 N.W.2d 798 (1975); M.P.C. § 5.03(1) and Comment 2). The central argument for this latter position is that a person exhibits a criminal purpose just as much as if the other party also shared it. This position, however, amounts to punishing people for thoughts. Moreover, a primary argument for making conspiracy a crime is that several people acting together are more dangerous than an individual acting alone (see also Posner 1985, 1218-19). That extra danger surely does not exist if there is no agreement. Besides, the unilateral situation can be covered by solicitation or perhaps attempt. O'Brien might have done enough to be guilty of attempted kidnapping.

Another problem concerns conspiracy to commit several crimes. The Model Penal Code holds that there is only one crime so long as the various crimes are part of the same conspiracy. However, the U.S. Supreme Court has held that persons can be convicted and sentenced for two separate counts of conspiracy resulting from one conspiracy to import and distribute marijuana, one for importing and another for distributing (*Albernaz v. United States*, 450 U.S. 333 (1981)). This anomalous result arose because Congress had enacted two different conspiracy sections, one for each crime. If conspiracy is a separate and distinct crime, then one act (agreement) should constitute only one crime. Otherwise, one makes all included crimes separate conspiracies.

Finally, complicity in a crime should involve helping another to commit a crime (or failing to try to prevent one when one has a duty to do so) with the purpose of assisting that person (see M.P.C. § 2.06(3)). There are three key elements – the criminal purpose, actual assistance, and the commission of a crime by another. Without them, the person does not present a threat to security. If a person does not intend to assist, for example, sells rubber gloves to another person who uses them in the commission of a crime, the seller poses no threat to society (but see Posner 1985, 1219 n. 47). Similarly, if a person does not in fact help, then the person is not a party to the crime. Finally, if no crime occurs, one cannot have assisted in it. However, if the principal's defense is merely an excuse or one of public policy, then complicity should be possible, for the offense occurred (see Robinson 1982, 278-81; Robinson 1984, § 37(a)).

These requirements are more strict than those usually found in the law. The reason is to prevent compounding of crimes (see generally Smith 1981). The danger is tying inchoate crimes and complicity together (compounding) to create crimes far from the harm to be prevented. We have already seen that the U.S. Supreme Court's interpretation of conspiracy can turn one act of conspiracy into two crimes. The Model Penal Code includes attempts in complicity – "aids or agrees or attempts to aid such other person in planning" or committing a crime (M.P.C. § 2.06(3)(a)(ii)). Thus, one is an accomplice if one attempts to help another plan a crime. Consequently, conspiring to attempt to help another plan a crime could be a crime (Smith 1981, 44). By the logic, one might also attempt to conspire to attempt....

All of this pursues prevention far beyond a point justifiable by the principles of harm, effectiveness, and least drastic alternative. By restricting complicity to actual assistance, we have made possible attempted complicity. This does not, in itself, place a limit on the compounding, for one could still conspire to attempt to aid. The harm and other principles require a limit to this compounding. *(6-12) The principle of inchoate offenses: inchoate offenses should involve the purpose to commit a substantive crime and should not be compounded.* This principle opposes criminal offenses of attempted solicitation or conspiracy, solicitation to attempt or conspire, and conspiring to attempt or solicit. Some of these combinations do not make sense anyway. It is unreasonable to solicit someone to attempt; at that point, one does not plan to fail. It is also doubtful that any inchoate offenses should survive the substantive crime. Attempts are merged in the completed crime, so one cannot be convicted of both murder and attempted murder. Only conspiracy survives as a separate crime. If people are convicted of the substantive crime, it is doubtful that they should also be convicted and punished for conspiring to commit it. As the preventive effect of doing so is unclear, we leave the issue unresolved.

DEFENSES

6.3.0. *Introduction.* In considering defenses, we assume that the defendant's external behavior was of a type prohibited by a criminal law. The concern is with defenses other than "I didn't do it; it was someone else" that might show that conviction and punishment are inappropriate. Some people are exempt from the criminal law. The clearest instance of this is very young children. At common law, children under the age of seven were completely exempt (Williams 1961, 814). The argument was that they lacked mens rea, but this argument is not satisfactory. As we saw (5.3.4), children can have the intent necessary for intentional torts which is the same as that for many crimes. As we shall discuss (6.3.2), a better reason is that children lack the capacity for rational control of their conduct necessary for responsibility. The major question is what age level should be used as a cut-off for nonresponsibility. The Law Reform Commission of Canada has suggested exempting everyone under twelve years of age, which seems more reasonable than seven (1982, 39-40). An alternative is to conclusively presume nonresponsibility below some age, have a rebuttable presumption for an age range such as twelve to eighteen, and a rebuttable presumption of responsibility or maturity over eighteen (Robinson 1984, § 175(e)). The latter approach is more compatible than the former with the variable capacity of young persons for rational choice and control (see 4.3.4).

Most defenses are based on the principles of culpability, voluntary act, and harm. Some defenses, such as many mistakes and intoxication indicate that a person lacked a requisite mental element (Williams 1965, 16 (mistake)). Other defenses, such as compulsion, indicate that no voluntary act was involved. One must be very careful in classifying such defenses not to confuse 'voluntary' as unable to act otherwise if one chooses with not having a reasonable alternative. These senses rest on different normative grounds. As we discuss below, although the defenses of duress and necessity were historically thought to rest on the voluntary act requirement, they depend on other considerations. Yet other defenses (justifications), such as self-defense, indicate that although usually acts of that sort cause harm, in the particular circumstances the principle of harm is not met and the act is not wrong. However, as we discuss in the next section, an additional and broader principle underlies some defenses.

6.3.1. *Mistake or ignorance.* The traditional common-law view is that a mistake of fact concerning an element of a crime is a defense, but ignorance or mistake of law is not, except perhaps for questions of private law, such as whether a piece of property belongs to one. This view bases the defense on the principle of culpability. A mistake of fact shows a lack of mens rea and is a defense, but a mistake or ignorance of law does not show lack of mens rea and is not a defense. One must have an appropriate mental state concerning a circumstance or consequence that is part of the definition of the prohibited conduct (Fletcher 1978, 696-97; Gross 1979, 259-62). If Foley is charged with selling alcohol on Sunday, it is irrelevant that she was mistaken about the month, but it is relevant that she was mistaken about the day of the week. If a person is mistaken about something that is part of the definition of an offense, the person lacks the requisite mental element and has a defense. As the definition of prohibited conduct does not include the fact that it is prohibited, mistake of law cannot provide a defense on this basis.

An issue is whether a mistake of fact must be reasonable. The principle of culpability requires that the defendant be aware of the risk of a result or have it as a conscious object; if the person lacks that awareness or purpose, then the mental element is lacking even if a reasonable person would have been aware of it. *Director of Public Prosecutions v. Morgan* (1976 A.C. 182), which reaffirmed that mistakes of fact need not be reasonable, has caused considerable discussion. Morgan met three servicemen in a bar, and while all were intoxicated invited them home to have intercourse with his wife. He told them that although she would resist, this was just one of her odd ways of enjoying intercourse. Despite her protestations and resistance, all three servicemen had intercourse with her. At trial they claimed that they believed Ms. Morgan consented to the intercourse. The House of Lords held that if they honestly believed that she consented, they should be acquitted, but that on the evidence no jury could find that they in fact believed that she consented.

One might argue that permitting unreasonable mistakes as defenses in such cases increases insecurity, because potential rapists know they can get off if they make a plausible claim that they believed the victim consented. There will be less deterrence. This argument is merely a particular application of the security argument for negligence as a basis for liability, because to require a reasonable belief is to require that persons not be negligent about information. However, it is at best uncertain that requiring a reasonable belief would increase security. First, the claim of unreasonable mistake must be plausible enough to raise a reasonable doubt for the jury or judge. For a jury to find that the accused believed the woman consented, the accused will probably have to present either a plausible reason for so believing or some other extenuating feature, such as drunkeness. That is, the reasonableness of a belief is important evidence that one actually so believed (see Gross 1979, 262-64). Second, the more likely type of case for a mistake is one in which a woman does not clearly evidence lack of consent. If defenses are successful in some of these cases, rapists might not be much encouraged. It is unlikely that, at the time of acting, a rapist calculates the possibility of a false defense as opposed to overall conviction and punishment rates (see also Brandt 1985, 192-93). These uncertain gains in security do not outweigh the certain harm of increased punishments. If the security argument for reasonableness of belief will not work for rape cases, it is implausible that it will work for others.

A second issue of mistake of fact is whether the defendant must have been 'innocent'. This issue arises when what the defendant thought he or she was doing is still a crime. The answer largely stems from a point developed in discussing impossible attempts (6.2.4). In those cases, although the actor cannot succeed, he or she is trying to do something harmful and thus poses a threat. A similar consideration applies when on the defendant's mistaken view of the facts the conduct is a crime (see M.P.C. § 2.04(2)). The person evidences a defect of character. If what the person thinks he or she is doing is a lesser included offense, then the person had the mental element for that offense. The chief difference between mistakes resulting in culpability for lesser offenses and interrupted impossible attempts is that the mistaken defendant actually commits an offense, so one need not worry whether the defendant would have gone ahead with the crime. However, the Model Penal Code does not seem to recognize the possibility that the offense the defendant mistakenly thought he or she was committing was a more serious one. It might be better to only allow conviction if the crime was an equivalent or lesser one (Robinson 1984, § 62(c)).

Although the principle of culpability will not usually provide a basis for a defense of mistake of law, because the illegality of conduct is not part of the definition of the conduct, it can provide a basis for some mistakes that are a blend of law and fact. If a person mistakenly thinks some item is his or her property, then that person lacks the necessary mental requirement for theft, namely, to appropriate the property of another. Whether something is the property of one person or another involves a judgment applying law to a particular fact situation.

One might think that the principle of denunciation can support a defense of mistake of law. If persons mistakenly believe that conduct is not criminal, then they are innocent and punishment is inappropriate. But this argument uses the wrong sense of 'innocent'. For criminal liability, people need not believe that their conduct is immoral, because some conduct might justifiably be made criminal although it is not commonly thought to be immoral (see 6.2.3). To claim a person who does not know conduct is illegal is innocent amounts to holding that the conduct's illegality is part of the crime's definition, which it cannot be. Either the statute would presuppose what it is establishing – that the conduct is illegal – or it would redundantly make it illegal to commit otherwise illegal acts. Moreover, allowing a defense of ignorance of the law would encourage such ignorance. The result would be greater insecurity.

Nonetheless, there is a normative basis for a defense of mistake or ignorance of law, not as showing a lack of mens rea but as an excuse showing the person was not responsible (cf. Robinson 1982, 224; Robinson 1984, § 25(b)(s)). *(6-13) The principle of reasonable opportunity: persons should not be criminally liable for acts if at the time of acting they lack a reasonable opportunity to conform to the law* (see L.R.C.C. 1974, 6). This principle goes beyond those of a voluntary act and culpability but rests on a consideration involved in their justification. An argument for those principles was that one reasonably wants to avoid punishment, and that if one's behavior was not voluntary or one was not aware of dangers at the time of acting, one could not conform to the law and so avoid punishment. But an act might be voluntary and a person aware of what he or she is doing, and the person still not have a reasonable opportunity to conform to the law – to avoid the act (Hart 1968, 152-3, 181, 191, and 201). If so, then imposition of punishment would not significantly increase security. If persons cannot reasonably avoid an act, they cannot be reasonably deterred from it at the time of acting. Moreover, the denunciation principle would also not pertain. People who lack a reasonable opportunity to avoid conduct are not ethically blameworthy. Usually, their conduct does not evince a defect of character. Even when it does, inability to rationally or reasonably control its manifestation blocks ethical blame. Arguments against this principle take the same form as those for negligence and strict liability and are subject to the same replies.

If one cannot reasonably discover that conduct is illegal or has been told by an authority (judge or administrative officer) that it is legal, then one does not have a reasonable opportunity to avoid criminal liability. An acute example is provided by *Regina v. Campbell and Mlynarchuk* (10 C.C.C.2d 26 (Alta. Dist. Ct. 1972)). The defendant Campbell was charged with engaging in an immoral performance, namely, dancing nude. One of her defenses was that she had refused to do so until being informed that in a similar case a superior court judge had ruled that nude dancing is not illegal. Unfortunately for Ms. Campbell, by the time her case came to trial, the other case had been reversed on appeal. Consequently, it was held that she, like the lower court judge, had made a mistake of law, which was not a defense. The irony is that on further appeal, the appellate decision in the other case was reversed, that is, Ms. Campbell and the lower court judge were correct about the law (*Johnson v. The Queen*, 13 C.C.C.2d 402 (Can. 1973)).

The Model Penal Code permits a defense of ignorance of law when the law has not reasonably been made available or the person relies on an official statement of law (§ 2.04(3)). However, the first condition is perhaps too weak. Simple inability reasonably to discover that conduct is criminal should not be a defense. To promote security, people should be encouraged to try to discover the law. The Model Penal Code does not clearly require that one have so tried. The Law Reform Commission of Canada recommends simply requiring that the mistake be reasonable (1982, 82). Arguably, this does require an attempt to find out the law, because a mistake is not reasonble if one does not try to ascertain the truth.

However, there must be a reasonable basis for thinking conduct might be criminal. For example, a Los Angeles ordinance made it a crime for persons previously convicted of a felony to be in the city for more than five days without registering, and made each day a separate crime. A previously convicted felon not on parole would have no reasonable basis for thinking it necessary to register merely to be in Los Angeles (*Lambert v. California*, 355 U.S. 225 (1957) (reversing conviction on due process grounds); see also *United States v. Mancuso*, 420 F.2d 556 (2d Cir. 1970) (persons previously convicted of drug offense must register with customs on leaving and entering the country)). In contrast, most businesspersons do have reason to think that laws, even criminal laws, might pertain to their conduct and that they should investigate the possibility.

One might plausibly contend that in an ideal or completely justifiable criminal system, ignorance of the law would not be a needed defense. All of the above cases involve conduct that arguably should not be crimes. The harm, effectiveness, and least drastic alternative principles would not justify making the conduct criminal. Nonetheless, even in a wholly justifiable system, occasions might still exist for a defense of ignorance of law. *United States v. Barker* (546 F.2d 940 (D.C. Cir. 1976)) reversed convictions of two Watergate "footsoldiers" for conspiring to violate Dr. Fielding's constitutional rights by an unlawful search of his office. The court held that they should have been permitted to show that they had a defense of a good faith reasonable reliance on the apparent authority to enter. The defendants had relied on the authority of E. Howard Hunt, an employee of the White House, that the search was authorized for national security.

6.3.2. *Mental abnormality.* The insanity defense is not frequently raised and is often unsuccessful (Bazelon 1984, 263; Morris 1982, 59). Yet it is certainly the most controversial defense and has probably had as much written about it as all the others combined. A variety of issues surround mentally abnormal offenders, and much of the controversy and discussion confuses them. Mental abnormality has been considered by the criminal law in three main ways: affecting a person's capacity to be tried, affecting a person's liability for conduct (as a defense), and affecting the disposition of a person (punishment, psychiatric treatment). Much confusion stems from mixing either of the first two matters with the last.

Our concern here is solely with mental abnormality as affecting a person's liability for past behavior. Three major questions concern mental abnormality as a defense to liability: (1) Should it be the basis for a separate defense? (2) If so, under what conditions? What is the test? (3) Who should have what burden of proof? These questions should be sharply distinguished from questions of disposition. People who were not responsible for their conduct might be detained or released (see A.B.A. 1984, Standards 7-7.1, 7-7.3, 7-7.4, and 7-7.6). Moreover, people who were responsible but are mentally abnormal should perhaps not be imprisoned but provided psychiatric treatment on an in-patient or out-patient basis.

The abolitionist stance is that mental abnormality should not be a separate defense. Mental abnormality is relevant when, but only when, it shows that a person did not perform a voluntary act (for example, involuntary movements during an epileptic seizure) or lacked the requisite mens rea. The argument for recognizing mental abnormality to this extent is the same as that for the voluntary act and culpability requirements. An objection to permitting mental abnormality to negative mens rea is that an acquitee would not be automatically committed to a hospital like most acquitees by reason of insanity (Williams 1965, 112). This objection, however, mixes considerations of liability and disposition. Arguments for limiting mental abnormality to showing lack of mens rea are basically arguments against a broader defense and are considered below. Any separate insanity defense must then apply when a defendant's conduct was both voluntary and culpable.

Even though some doubt exists that the precise wording of the test of insanity as a defense has much practical significance (Sales and Hafemeister 1984, 266; but see A.B.A. 1984, Commentary 332; Slobogin 1985, 521-22), it is useful to consider justification of the defense in the context of various tests. The most famous case involving insanity, from which the usual test governing the defense for over a century sprang, was that of Daniel M'Naghten. Thinking he was the subject of a tory plot, M'Naghten attempted to kill the British Prime Minister Peel but killed Peel's secretary by mistake. The rule established in that case is as follows:

[I]t must be clearly proved that, at the time of committing the act, the accused was labouring under such a defect of reason, from disease of the mind, as not to know the nature and quality of the act he was doing, or, if he did know it, that he did not know he was doing what was wrong. (*M'Naghten's Case*, 8 Eng. Rep. 718, 722, (H.L. 1843).)

The first part of the test, that the accused does not know the nature and quality of the act, simply indicates a lack of the requisite mental element. If an accused did not know what he or she was doing, then he or she could not have done it knowingly. Why an accused should know that the act is wrong is unclear. The Lords stated that if the test were put in terms of the law, a jury might become confused and think that actual knowledge of the law is essential for a conviction, which it is not. In any case, M'Naghten did know that he was attempting to kill the Prime Minister, that the law forbade it, and that most people thought it morally wrong (Fingarette 1972, 139). Consequently, even by the test formulated in reference to M'Naghten, he should have been convicted. Nonetheless, there was overwhelming and uncontradicted testimony that he was suffering from "what today would be described as delusions of persecution symptomatic of paranoid schizophrenia" (A.P.A. 1983, 142).

In the United States during the 1960s and 1970s, the chief competing test for insanity was that of the Model Penal Code.

A person is not responsible for criminal conduct if at the time of such conduct as a result of mental disease or defect he lacks substantial capacity either to appreciate the criminality [wrongfulness] of his conduct or to conform his conduct to the requirements of law. (M.P.C. § 4.01(1).)

This test varies from the M'Naghten one in several respects. First, it drops the "nature and quality of the act" consideration, essentially covering it under another provision allowing mental abnormality to negate mens rea (M.P.C. § 4.02(1)). Second, it includes both mental disease and defect, thus incorporating mental retardation along with mental illness. Third, it uses 'appreciate' instead of 'know' to permit emotional or conative considerations as well as cognitive ones. Fourth, it is stated in terms of 'substantial capacity' to allow for degrees of incapacity. Fifth, it adds a new condition – lack of capacity to conform to the law (control one's behavior) even if one appreciates its wrongfulness.

During this period, the trend was for the Model Penal Code test to replace the M'Naghten test. However, during the early 1980s, the trend has been to return to a modified M'Naghten test. In 1983, the American Bar Association and the American Psychiatric Association threw their support to a restricted version of the first clause of the Model Penal Code test, which amounts to a modified M'Naghten test (A.B.A. 1983, 136; A.P.A. 1983, 145). Besides dropping the capacity to conform clause, they would also substitute 'unable' for 'lacks substantial capacity'.

A person is not responsible for criminal conduct if, at the time of such conduct, and as a result of mental disease or defect, that person was unable to appreciate the wrongfulness of such conduct. (A.B.A. 1984, Standard 7-6.1(a).)

The American Psychiatric Association also recommended that any mental abnormality must be serious. The American Bar Association did not go quite that far, only recommending that the condition must have "substantially affected the mental or emotional processes of the defendant" (A.B.A. 1984, Standard 7-6.1(b)(ii)). In 1984, Congress amended the federal criminal code to use a M'Naghten type test incorporating the American Psychiatric Association's recommendation that the condition be serious. A person has a defense if "as a result of a severe mental disease or defect, [he] was unable to appreciate the nature and quality or the wrongfulness of his acts" (Insanity Defense Reform Act of 1984, Pub. L. No. 98-473, § 402(a), 98 Stat. 2057 (1984) (to be codified at 18 U.S.C. § 20(a))).

The central decision about these alternative tests depends on the reasons for recognizing an insanity defense. If mental abnormality prevents a person fulfilling the requirements of culpability, then that person should not be liable, but that is covered by the usual requirement of culpability (Robinson 1984, § 173(e)(3)). Consequently, a test should not refer to a person knowing or appreciating the nature and quality of his or her act (but see Robinson 1984, §§ 173(a) and (e)(3) (retaining perception of nature and consequences of act primarily for negligence and strict liability crimes)). It is redundant, and if the burden of proof for the insanity defense differs from that for mens rea, it will confuse matters (see also A.B.A. 1984, Standard 7-6.9(b) (not relieving state of responsibility to prove mental state required for offense)).

The justification of the insanity defense rests on the principle of reasonable opportunity. The Model Penal Code test encapsulates two broad reasons why a person might not be able reasonably to avoid conduct. One is a lack of ability to appreciate that what one is doing is wrong. The other is an inability to conform or restrain oneself. While we have used 'inability', this does not imply preference for that terminology over 'substantial capacity'. If one lacks substantial capacity, then one does not have a reasonable opportunity.

A number of objections have been made to the control wing of the Model Penal Code test. The American Psychiatric Association contends that it is difficult to distinguish between persons who could not conform and who merely did not conform, and that most persons who cannot conform also fail to appreciate the wrongfulness of their conduct (A.P.A. 1983, 145). Following traditional psychiatric methodology, no scientific evidence is given for these claims, and there does not appear to be any such evidence (Sales and Hafemeister 1984, 271). Moreover, the difficulty of a distinction, or its lack of objectivity or scientific basis (A.B.A. 1983, 138; see also A.B.A. 1984, Commentary 330), is surely not to the point. These criticisms assume that the issue is a scientific one for psychiatrists to resolve rather than a moral one for juries. Even if most persons who could not conform also could not appreciate the wrongfulness of their conduct, that does not justify punishing the few who can appreciate it but not conform.

It is further claimed that the control wing creates "a significant risk of 'moral mistakes'"; more "'morally correct'" decisions are likely with the cognitive test alone (A.B.A. 1984, Commentary 329). Unfortunately, the concept of a moral mistake is not defined. It has been suggested that moral mistakes occur when a jury decision does not conform to that of the general public (Wexler 1985, 541). If this is the meaning of 'moral mistake', then it should be ignored. Presumably, the jury has heard more detailed evidence than the general public, and better informed reasonable persons are more likely to be correct than less informed ones. In short, the moral mistake is that of the general public, and the correction is better education and information for the general public, not denial of an otherwise justifiable defense.

However, a moral mistake might better be taken to mean an error – finding guilty when innocent or innocent when guilty. If that is the meaning, then a mere assertion that fewer mistakes occur under the cognitive test alone is not conclusive. One must also weight the errors by the moral error cost (see 2.1.2). Presumably, given the principle of innocence, it is better to make errors not convicting the guilty than convicting the innocent. Presumably, a test involving both cognitive and control elements will acquit more innocent persons than one having only a cognitive element. Consequently, one must show that with a control wing too many guilty persons will be acquitted to justify not convicting the few innocent persons who would not be acquitted with a cognitive wing alone.

Does the principle of prevention override the control test? Although insecurity is increased if mentally abnormal persons who cannot reasonably avoid their behavior are permitted lose, this claim does not justify criminal punishment. It mixes the issues of liability and disposition. Security can justify restraining or confining persons and/or compulsory treatment (*Jones v. United States*, 463 U.S. 354 (1983)), but it does not justify convicting and punishing them. The American Bar Association has recommended standards that provide for special confinement procedures for insanity acquitees of crimes risking death and serious bodily injury (A.B.A. 1984, Standards 7-7.3 to 7-7.11). Moreover, one could even make those procedures stronger (Wexler 1985, 555-60).

Abolitionists object to both wings of the Model Penal Code test. One of the most articulate opponents of the insanity defense is Norval Morris. His primary objection is that it draws a sharp line between the guilty and the innocent when in fact there is a continuum (Morris 1982, 64). This is correct, but it is not the only place the law makes such sharp distinctions. They also arise whenever reasonableness of beliefs or conduct is in question, as in mistakes about justifications. That a distinction is blurred rather than sharp is not a reason for failing to make it at all. Despite his general protests against doing so, Morris also seems to confuse criminal liability and disposition, because he goes on to say that the defense does not pick out those prisoners "most in need of psychiatric treatment." Again, this might well be correct, but that is not and should not be its function. Moreover, allowing a defense going to mens rea, as Morris does, might also fail to designate those most needing psychiatric treatment. Morris's other points are merely that mental abnormality can go to issues of mens rea and that 'diminished responsibility' could be added for homicide cases. We have already recognized the former, and below we contend that diminished responsibility is not needed if the insanity defense is recognized.

Perhaps the most telling response to both abolitionists and those who support only the wrongness test is one of consistency. There does not seem to be a consistent, principled basis for exempting children and yet rejecting the broader Model Penal Code defense. Why are children exempt? An abolitionist cannot plausibly claim that it is because they lack mens rea. Children have the requisite intent for intentional torts, and that intent (knowledge) covers many crimes. One can argue that some children, especially the very young, cannot appreciate the wrongfulness of their conduct (see Robinson 1984, § 175(d)(3)). But when one deals with children ten years or so old, even that argument appears weak. They seem to lack substantial capacity to conform to the law. The Law Reform Commission of Canada recognizes this factor, because one of its proposals is to exempt twelve and thirteen year olds unless they can appreciate the wrongfulness of their conduct and have "substantial capacity to conform to . . . the law" (1982, 40). Children lack the ability to forgo short-term benefits to avoid long-term losses or to obtain long-term gains. This is not the same as inability to appreciate the wrongfulness of conduct, unless one gives 'appreciate' a weight it cannot bear (essentially include lack of control in 'appreciate'). Moreover, this same lack of capacity is evidenced by mentally retarded persons, who are also included in the insanity defense. Indeed, mentally retarded persons are developmentally delayed, that is, they are like children. Thus, the principle that exempts children must also exempt mentally retarded persons.

Consistent with the principle of reasonable opportunity, one might collapse both wings of the Model Penal Code test into one – the lack of capacity rationally or reasonably to conform to the law. If one lacks capacity to conform, then one lacks an opportunity (in a broad sense) to do so. If one cannot appreciate the wrongfulness of conduct, then one cannot reasonably refrain from it; one does not have a reason to do so. Moreover, if one cannot rationally control behavior – compulsive behavior – one cannot reasonably conform. However, for emphasis, both conditions are explicit in our principle. *(6-14) The principle of mental abnormality: persons should not be criminally liable if, at the time of acting, due to mental disease or defect, they lack the capacity to appreciate the wrongfulness of their conduct or to conform to the law* (see also N.C.I.D. 1983, 3, 36).

The question remains whether, and if so why, Daniel M'Naghten and others like him should be able to invoke the defense. M'Naghten knew that his conduct was criminal and that most people thought it morally wrong. The answer partly lies in the notion of 'appreciate'. While M'Naghten knew that the conduct was wrong, he did not appreciate it as something to be avoided. One might object that the same is true of most criminals; they know the conduct is criminal but are not thereby motivated to avoid it. Although this is true, there is a difference. By the test, the reason for the lack of appreciation must be due to a mental disease or defect. Although it has been suggested that all criminals suffer from a personality disorder, that is a very dubious proposition. Moreover, someone like M'Naghten cannot by the usual processes of reasoning avoid concluding that there is a plot against him. That is, mentally ill persons suffer from an inability to perceive reality and reason from its correct perception to the appropriate conclusions. Consequently, they lack the capacity and opportunity reasonably to conform to the law.

The burden of proof in an insanity defense should fall on the defendant. For the defense to apply, there is a voluntary act and the requisite mental culpability. People are presumed to be sane, and the defendant is arguing that he or she is an exception to that presumption. Consequently, the defendant should have to prove this claim. Nonetheless, jury instructions must be carefully made, because evidence of mental abnormality can go either to lack of mens rea or to the insanity defense. The prosecution must prove beyond a reasonable doubt that the defendant had the requisite mens rea; only if the jury is convinced of that, as would be likely with M'Naghten, should it consider whether despite that intention the defendant proved by a preponderance of the evidence that he or she could not appreciate the wrongfulness of the conduct or could not conform (see A.B.A. 1984, Standard 7-6.9(b)(ii)). The U.S. Congress has imposed a higher standard of persuasion even for the narrow test of inability to appreciate wrongfulness (Insanity Defense Reform Act of 1984, Pub. L. No. 98-473, § 402(a), 98 Stat. 2057 (1984) (to be codified as 18 U.S.C. § 20 (b)). However, given the strong presumption of sanity that must in fact be overcome, there is no reason to treat the insanity defense differently in this respect from any other affirmative defense (see N.C.I.D. 1983, 3, 35-36).

Two other methods of considering mental abnormality can be briefly considered. One is an additional verdict of guilty but mentally ill. The aims of that verdict are to reduce the number of insanity acquitees (providing social protection) and to direct a defendant to psychiatric treatment. One has good reasons to reject this additional possible verdict (A.B.A. 1984, Standard 7-6.10; Fentiman 1985; Note 1983; Morris 1982, 83-87; Slobogin 1985). First, it confuses the issues of liability and disposition. Juries might convict people rather than find they have an insanity defense, because they want to be sure the person is confined and treated. But as noted before, a person's nonresponsibility and nonliability do not imply society does not need protection. The protection should simply come from another part of law. Second, juries are not competent to determine whether a person needs psychiatric treatment. One cannot reasonably accept having a jury of laypersons determine whether one should receive psychiatric treatment. Third, it can be and perhaps is being used to sanction criminal behavior. Sex offenders might use it to escape the denunciatory force of conviction (N.C.I.D. 1983, 33). Fourth, in practice, it has contributed to an increase in insanity pleas and might not have reduced significantly the number of acquitals (Slobogin 1985, 506-10). Fifth, it has not in fact resulted in longer confinement (Slobogin 1985, 511). Sixth, persons convicted under this verdict probably do not in fact receive more psychiatric treatment (Fentiman 1985, 629-30; Slobogin 1985, 512-15).

The other method is to adopt a defense of diminished responsibility as England has done for capital crimes or 'diminished capacity' as developed by some American courts. The latter is not significantly different from mental abnormality indicating that a defendant did not have one mental state, say, purposefulness, but had another, recklessness, rendering him or her guilty of a lesser offense, manslaughter rather than murder (LaFave and Scott, 1972, 325-32). That is already covered. The English version permits a reduction of murder to manslaughter if mental abnormality "substantially impaired" the defendant's "responsibility" for the offense (Homicide Act 1957 § 2(1); Morris 1982, 68; Williams 1978, 622-30). It's virtue is that it allows for recognition of degrees of incapacity to conform; it's vice is that it is restricted to homicide cases. Mental abnormality is not relevant only to homicide, nor is it likely to be pleaded primarily in homicide cases (N.C.I.D. 1983, 251; Sales and Hafemeister 1984, 256). Given an insanity defense that allows for lack of capacity to conform to the law and the separation of the questions of liability and disposition, one has no strong reason to accept this additional defense.

6.3.3. *Intoxication*. The defense of intoxication has caused courts and drafters of criminal codes much agony. Although intoxication need not be due to alcohol, our discussion focuses on alcoholic intoxication because it is the form most frequently before courts. The basic reason for the agony is that the defense seems to bring the principle of culpability into conflict with the principle of prevention. If a person is too intoxicated to have a required mental element for a crime, then the principle of culpability implies that the person should not be convicted. Yet, violent criminal behavior while drunk creates much social harm and insecurity which the law might prevent.

Two main approaches have been suggested or used to resolve this conflict (Fletcher 1978, 846-52; L.R.C.C. 1982, 54-63). The usual common-law approach distinguishes between 'specific intent' or purpose and 'general intent' or knowledge and recklessness (*Director of Public Prosecutions v. Beard*, 1920 A.C. 479; but *Beard* did not limit the intoxication defense to specific intent, see at 504 and Williams 1965, 43). Intoxication negating specific intent is a defense, but intoxication negating general intent is not (perhaps because it is thought that no one can be so drunk as to lack general intent). The absence of specific intent usually lowers the crime to a lesser one, so the person is not completely exonerated. This resolution is not very apt, for courts have been left to dispute whether crimes such as rape require a specific intent (see, for example, *Regina v. Vandervoort*, 1961 Ont. W.N. 141; *Regina v. Boucher et al.*, 40 W.W.R. 663 (B.C. 1963); and *Leary v. The Queen*, 74 D.L.R.3d 103 (Can. 1977)). The common law also sometimes allows a defense if intoxication was involuntary.

The second approach is to allow a defense if a person lacks a requisite mental element by reason of intoxication, but then convict the person for an offense of criminal intoxication. The crime is becoming intoxicated, and the voluntary act principle is not violated, because drinking is the act. The only defense to this latter charge would be that the intoxication was involuntary. The underlying principle is that the defendant is responsible or culpable for becoming intoxicated. This approach has the advantages of certainty and simplicity, which the first approach sorely lacks. Yet by its rationale, there is no reason to require that the defendant have committed an otherwise criminal act (Fletcher 1978, 848). Alternatively, one might institute negligence crimes and convict for them (Fingarette and Hasse 1979, 245-47), but we have rejected negligence offenses.

Three points about intoxication as a defense are clear. First, the specific/general intent distinction should be abandoned (M.P.C. § 208; *The Queen v. O'Connor*, 54 Austl. L.J.R. 349 (Austl. 1980)). Not even judges can agree which crimes involve specific intent. Moreover, the same reason applies to allowing the defense in either case, namely, lack of a requisite mental element. Second, and more controversially, the distinction between voluntary and involuntary intoxication is irrelevant. Usually, a complete or broader defense is allowed for involuntary than voluntary intoxication. But like negligent homicide, restricting voluntary intoxication as a defense turns an earlier venial sin into a later mortal sin (see also Robinson 1984, § 162(b)(2)). Voluntary intoxication, which is not a crime, is made the culpable element in such crimes as rape and assault. Third, if when the intoxication is induced a person has culpability for the subsequent offense, then the person can be held liable (see Robinson 1984, §§ 162(d)(3) and (4)). For example, if a person repetitively becomes intoxicated and commits acts that would be crimes but for the intoxication, then the person might be charged with reckless endangerment. By becoming intoxicated, such a person knowingly creates a danger to others (see also Brandt 1985, 181). The same would apply to another who, aware of the person's tendencies, caused the person to become intoxicated.

These points leave open whether there should be a separate crime of criminal intoxication for nonrepetitive offenders who successfully present a defense of intoxication. As we handled reckless driving and homicide in 6.2.2, we can also assign greater penalties to drunk driving that results in injury or death. Consequently, one is primarily left with assaults and rape. Even here, a separate offense of criminal intoxication is not necessary. The common law has generally claimed that assault is an offense of general intent for which intoxication is not a defense. The point, however, is that intoxication does not prevent one knowing that one is striking another or using a dangerous weapon. That is, drunkenness simply does not, except perhaps in the most extreme cases, negate the mental element (see *State v. Stasio*, 78 N.J. 467, 396 A.2d 1129 (1979) (Handler, J., concurring)). In rape and sexual assault, intoxication might prevent a person from knowing that the other person does not consent, but that is doubtful. Usually, a person simply intends to have intercourse regardless of the other person's consent. Moreover, if a person is too drunk to recognize obvious facts indicating lack of consent, that person is also probably too drunk to believe the victim does consent, and without such a sincere belief, there is no defense of mistake (Williams 1965, 49). In sum, a close examination of cases indicates that intoxication rarely prevents people having the requisite mental element, so a crime of criminal intoxication is not needed for security.

One might contend that an even broader defense, like the insanity defense, should be allowed for intoxication. The Model Penal Code and some states allow it for involuntary intoxication (M.P.C. § 2.08(4); *Torres v. State*, 585 S.W.2d 746, 749 (Tex. 1979); cf. Fingarette and Hasse 1979, 200-02). At this point, some of the arguments about the insanity defense have weight. First, alcohol reduces inhibitions, that is, makes one less able to conform to the law. Thus, the possibility of harm is increased if a broader defense is allowed; alcohol use, unlike mental abnormality, is involved in a large number of crimes. Second, deciding whether a person could not reasonably conform or merely did not do so becomes much more difficult, in part because one is dealing with a temporary condition relatively impervious to later analysis. Consequently, the principle of prevention reasonably outweighs the principle of reasonable opportunity here.

But prevention does not override lack of culpability, because the principle of culpability is plausibly stronger than that of reasonable opportunity – it concerns core cases. Put another way, if intoxication results in the absence of voluntary acts or mens rea, two principles oppose liability – that of voluntary act or culpability and that of reasonable opportunity. Whereas if intoxication deprives a person of the capacity to appreciate wrongfulness or to conform to the law but not to act voluntarily or to have mens rea, only the principle of reasonable opportunity opposes liability. *(6-15) The principle of intoxication: persons should not be criminally liable by reason of intoxication, if, and only if, at the time of acting, intoxication negates a voluntary act or a mental element of the offense.*

6.3.4. *Lesser evils.* The defenses of duress, necessity, and choice of evils appear to be based on the requirement of a voluntary act, but this appearance is deceptive. The voluntary act requirement does pertain when a person is physically compelled. An example would be a stronger person grasping one's arm and hand with a knife in it and by superior physical force moving it them to stab someone. The movement of one's arm is no more voluntary than the contraction of one's heart muscle. A similar consideration applies to omissions when it is physically impossible to act. Rather than a separate defense, such compulsion is simply an instance of failure to meet the voluntary act requirement.

The defenses of duress, necessity, and choice of evils are signficantly different. With each defense, the person could act otherwise. In duress, someone threatens the actor or others with harm if the actor does not perform an act. In *Regina v. Hudson and Taylor* (56 Crim. App. 1 (C.A. 1971)), two teenage girls were threatened with stabbing if they testified at a trial, and the threatener sat in the courtroom when they testified. Their defense of duress to a subsequent charge of perjury was accepted. As they were physically capable of telling the truth, duress cannot rest on the voluntary act requirement. By the principle of reasonable opportunity, the normative question is whether the person could reasonably avoid acting. Duress is usually unavailable if the conduct seriously endangers the life or violates the bodily integrity of another (see LaFave and Scott 1972, 375-76; L.R.C.C. 1982, 87; but see *Director of Public Prosecutions for Northern Ireland v. Lynch*, [1975] A.C. 653 (duress available for accessory to murder)). Sometimes it is also required that a person not be responsible for getting into the situation (LaFave and Scott 1972, 376). On one version of necessity, a person has a defense if, due to circumstances other than threat by someone, the person acts to avoid immediate harm to persons or property, the harm is substantially greater than that of the offense, and it could not have been effectively avoided by less drastic means (L.R.C.C. 1982, 96; see also LaFave and Scott 1972, 381). The choice of evils defense is quite similar. The harm done is less than that avoided, and the person is not responsible for bringing about the situation requiring the choice (see M.P.C. § 3.02; Robinson 1984, § 124(a)).

There are significant variations on these defenses, especially duress, which has a quite distinct version. We shall elucidate a common approach reducing them to one defense, that of lesser evils, and at the end of the section briefly consider another version of duress. One common element of these defenses is that the harm of the act be less than that likely to occur should it not be performed. The defense of duress does not make this point explicit, but it is implicit. Duress must involve a threat of death or serious bodily injury, and that would ordinarily be a greater harm than property damage. Moreover, it is not taken to justify intentionally killing another, where the harm caused is arguably equal to or greater than that threatened. Whether the situation results from threats of another (duress) or other circumstances (necessity, choice of evils) is normatively irrelevant. Thus, a defense of lesser evils will capture most if not all of what is included in duress and necessity.

The principles of prevention and harm provide the basic justification; more harm is prevented than caused. It is unreasonable to choose the greater rather than the lesser harm, so the actor does not have a reasonable opportunity to avoid the conduct. The claim is that it is better, everything considered, to "break the law." For this to be true, the exception must be based on the same principles that justify criminal laws. In particular, the principles of harm and least drastic alternative must be fulfilled. The harm avoided must be greater than that caused, and there must not be a less drastic alternative.

A requirement that the actor not be responsible for getting into the situation might appear to follow from the reasonable opportunity principle. If a person is responsible for the situation, then he or she had a reasonable opportunity to avoid the conduct by avoiding the situation. However, this requirement shifts the opportunity to avoid an act from the time of its performance to some prior time and is therefore unacceptable. This situation can be handled similarly to becoming intoxicated. The person is liable for any offense committed in causing or bringing about the circumstances giving rise to the defense (Robinson 1984, § 123(c)). Sometimes that will support conviction for a lesser offense, for example, reckless endangerment. Theoretically, if the person brought about the situation in order to have a defense, it could include the subsequent harm caused, for the person would act purposely with respect to it. One could not create a general offense similar to criminal intoxication, such as recklessly creating the possibility of wrongdoing, without too much uncertainty to satisfy the principle of certainty.

Some types of acts or choices might seem never to be justifiable or acceptable. Legally, duress is not accepted as a defense for conduct seriously endangering the life of another, or at least for homicide as a principal (*Abbott v. The Queen*, [1977] A.C. 755 (P.C.)). The crucial question is whether it can ever be reasonable to sacrifice one life to save others. The most famous case raising this issue is *The Queen v. Dudley and Stephens* (14 Q.B.D. 273 (Q.B. 1884)). Following a storm, Dudley, Stephens, Brooks, and a teenager were at sea in an open lifeboat. After twenty days and the food supplies gone, Dudley and Stephens killed the then helpless teenager. The surviors ate the teenager's body to stay alive, and four days later they were rescued. Dudley and Stephens raised a defense of necessity to a charge of murder. Can lesser evils (including necessity and duress) ever justify killing another?

One might argue that lesser evils cannot justify homicide, because at best the evils are balanced – one life for another. Moreover, as one cannot be certain that the anticipated harm will result, one would then be balancing a possible loss of life for a certain one. However, this argument overlooks the fact that many lives might be threatened (other arguments more blatantly ignore any such restriction, see Kilbrandon 1982, 191). It might well be a rational choice of lesser evils to sacrifice the certainty of one or a few deaths to avoid a high probability of the loss of many. Just such a situation arose in *United States v. Holmes* (26 Fed. Cas. 360 (C.C.E.D. Pa. 1842) (No. 15,383)). There, a seaman in an overcrowded lifeboat in a storm ordered some passengers thrown overboard to keep the ship seaworthy. Although Holmes was convicted, the judge suggested that forcing some persons overboard might have been justifiable had lots been chosen.

This suggests that lesser evils can justify killing if reasonable and fair procedures are used to determine who should die. In *Dudley and Stephens*, the teenager was not consulted about the matter. Had he been consulted and consented, then it would have been permissible. A rationale based on security and control over one's life plausibly supports this view. If other people are permitted to make such choices concerning one's life or bodily integrity, given the possibility of even reasonable mistakes, one runs a significant risk of unnecessary death or injury. Also, the control over one's life and body is surrendered to others. If one is involved in the decision that a sacrifice must be made and agrees to take the risk of dying, say, by drawing lots, then one retains control over one's life. However, this rationale will not cover all cases, because an opportunity for choice might not exist, for example, if a person at the wheel of a car out of control steers toward one person to avoid hitting several others. The rationale is even less likely to be available for duress.

Two other arguments against permitting the defense to homicide also seem to assume that more lives might be taken than saved. Anthony Kenny argues that while to resist duress or necessity might require heroism, in extraordinary circumstances heroism might be required and punishment for less than heroic conduct only enforces minimum standards of morality (Kenny 1982, 203). However, this argument assumes that it is wrong to take one life to save more, but that is the issue in question. Of course, heroism would still be required in cases of threats to one's life unless another one is taken. The other argument is that as the law operates as a system of threats, it cannot remove the threat when faced by a greater; if anything, on pure deterrence grounds, the threat should be increased (Kenny 1982, 204). If one appeals to humanity for not punishing, the reply is that humanity is also owed to the innocent victims. Again, however, with a requirement that the harm caused be less than that threatened, the greater humanity lies in saving the most innocent lives.

The upshot is that there is no reason to prohibit lesser evils including necessity and duress as a defense to homicide regardless of the consent or participation of the victim (see also Richards 1979, 1439). However, as the killing must be the lesser harm, more lives must be saved. Moreover, killing must be the least drastic alternative. Fewer people will die, and given an equal chance of being any of the persons involved (actor, victim, or rescued innocents), one's security is enhanced if the defense is allowed. However, before such a defense is acceptabale, two other conditions are required. These conditions raise some general issues about justifications.

One can approach the issue by considering the possibility of a killing in the erroneous belief that it was the lesser of evils. There are two approaches to justifications; one views them as privileges to breach norms, and the other as refined definitions of offenses (Robinson 1984, § 122(e)). On the latter approach, conduct is justified if the objective circumstances for a justification exist, whether or not the actor believed they did (Robinson 1984, § 122(f)). Thus, if a person subject to duress unreasonably believes that more lives will be saved by killing, but the belief turns out to be true, the person has a defense. If the person reasonably but mistakenly believes that lesser evils justifies an action, the person has a defense (Robinson 1984, § 184(a)(1)). On the norm-privilege view, the actor must have a reasonable belief that the justifying circumstances exist and act with a purpose of avoiding the greater harm.

If justifications are exceptions to the law, then there are two reasons for following the latter view. First, an actor is substituting his or her judgment for that of the legislature, contending that the legislative purposes do not support liability for the act. In substituting his or her judgment for the general judgment of the legislature, the person's judgment should be reasonable. Moreover, the principle of culpability should apply in an inverted form; one must have the proper mental state – act purposely to avoid the greater harm. It is objected that it is not clear to what extent a person must have the purpose – it be the only purpose, the dominant purpose, or what (Robinson 1984, § 122(b)(2). However, the answer is fairly clear; that purpose should have been sufficient for the person to so act.

Second, the law, especially the criminal law, is to guide people's conduct. To do so, it should be presented from the perspective of a person at the time of acting. One wants to encourage action based on reasonable beliefs for the purpose of avoiding greater harms. One has no reason to encourage action on unreasonable beliefs, perhaps in the hope that luckily one will have been correct anyway, or actions constituting offenses other than for the purpose of avoiding a greater harm. Moreover, the evidence must be very clear and convincing. One would not want to be a victim simply because someone unreasonably thought killing might be a good way to save others. Security is enhanced by restricting the exception to instances in which people act on reasonable beliefs for the purpose of minimizing harm.

Consequently, one has a good reason to accept a defense of lesser evils even for homicide and regardless of whether the danger is from human threats or nature, provided all the restrictions discussed above are met. *(6-16) The principle of lesser evils: persons should not be criminally liable if (a) they reasonably believed that (i) their conduct might effectively avoid a greater harm, and (ii) no less drastic alternative was available; and (b) they acted to avoid the greater harm.* This defense will not absolve people of any earlier offense getting them into the situation. As we note in the next section, sometimes the act is really part of one larger piece of criminal conduct, and so the defense does not apply.

One further point must be considered. The defenses of choice of evils and necessity are usually taken to be 'justifications'; that is, they show that in the particular circumstances the conduct was not wrong. The defense of duress is usually taken to be an 'excuse'; that is, although the conduct is wrong, the defendant is not appropriately liable because not responsible. But the same rationale underlies all three defenses as we have presented them, so it seems that all must be excuses or all justifications. If duress is treated as a justification, then it seems wrong for anyone to prevent or interfere with the person. Indeed, those who coerced the person to act might not be accessories to a crime, since the defendant would not have committed a wrongful act (Fletcher 1978, 830). Consequently, duress, it seems, must be an excuse, and so must necessity and choice of evils.

However, the argument that duress as a lesser evils defense would prevent interference and conviction of those creating the threats is unsound. First, the lesser evils defense only shows that the conduct is permissible (does not violate a duty of criminal law), and it is not necessarily wrong to interfere with conduct that is permissible as opposed to required (Bickenbach 1983, 95-96). Moreover, others would be wrong knowingly to interfere in a duress or lesser evils situation if they did not have a reasonable prospect of removing the threat, for otherwise they unduly risk bringing about the greater of the two evils.

Second, in duress, others have brought about the situation providing the defense. They knowingly caused a "choice of evils" to be made, and had it not been for their conduct, no evil need have occurred. The actor's conduct is merely the instrument through which they act, just as if they had physically compelled the person's behavior. Thus, they should be liable as principals, not accessories, for the harm done. They coerced, forced, and made the person act rather than aided, abetted, or helped the person to act (cf. Williams 1982, 737-38). The same, however, applies to anyone who knowingly creates a situation requiring a choice of evils. The Model Penal Code contains an offense of causing criminal conduct by an "innocent or irresponsible person" (§ 2.06(2)(a); see Robinson 1982, 281-83). If no one knowingly brought about the situation, which is usually the case in choice of evils and necessity cases, it makes no difference how the defense is classified.

There are other versions of duress emphasizing the inability of the average person to control conduct due to anticipated harm creating fear that a person of reasonable firmness could not resist (see M.P.C. § 2.09; Robinson 1982, 235; Robinson 1984, § 177(c)(1)). Again, the source of the threat – human or natural – should be irrelevant to such a defense. However, it is not clear that such a version should be allowed, since it excuses conduct even when it is not the lesser evil (Robinson 1984, § 177(c)(1)). Arguably, a person of reasonable firmness would resist unless the harm threatened is greater than that to be brought about. Nonetheless, it is conceivable that by a process of terrorizing one could in effect lose control – be unable to effectively resist. If so, the principle of reasonable opportunity would support such a defense, and it would be an excuse. The person is not responsible.

6.3.5. *Defense of persons.* In this section and the next, we consider two justifications that are basically specifications of lesser evils. One might wonder why the more specific defenses are needed. Historically, they were recognized before a generalization was made to lesser evils. Normatively, to guide people's conduct better, it is useful to have implications for frequent situations specified more precisely. Consequently, when applicable, the specific defenses control as providing more detailed legal determinations (see Robinson 1984, § 121(f)).

Self-defense is usually taken as a paradigm of a justification rather than an excuse. That is, the use of force in self-defense is considered an exception to the rules prohibiting assault, battery, and homicide, so the conduct is not wrong. However, one line of thought treats self-defense as an excuse negating the actor's responsibility. The underlying notion is that one cannot reasonably refrain from the use of force; it is a natural human response. The view of self-defense as a justification better accords with security. If the state via law enforcement cannot provide security, then one can do so oneself. One has a good reason to reject a law that prevents one defending oneself when necessary.

With some explanations and a minor modification, the principle of lesser evils supports the defense of self-defense (see also Richards 1979, 1437). Viewing self-defense from the perspective of a recipient of defensive force helps show the limitations on the justification. First, the use of force must be necessary. One would not accept force being used when there was no threat of immediate harm and a peaceable resolution of the matter might be achieved, for there would then be a less drastic alternative. Generally, this consideration suggests that a defender retreat or withdraw if he or she can do so safely, at least before using deadly force. However, there might be special situations in which retreat is not required. Must one retreat from one's own home? Perhaps in this situation, the excuse version of self-defense also applies; it is too much to expect persons to abandon their homes. But even on the justification view, since one desires security of both person and property, and the property in question is self-expressive or identifying (see 3.1.3), a requirement that one retreat would not be a less drastic alternative. Moreover, the amount of force used must also be necessary, for otherwise there would be a less drastic alternative.

Second, the amount of force must be proportional to the likely harm, for otherwise it will not be a lesser harm. If a person is threatened with only a face slap, shooting the attacker greatly outweighs the likely harm. As one might be either party, one could not accept self-defense in this situation. Consequently, deadly force should be restricted to situations in which death or serious bodily harm is threatened. The basic requirements, then, are that the use of force be necessary and proportional to the threatened harm (Robinson 1984, § 131(a)).

Two further possible limitations are more disputable. Third, must the defender's belief that force is necessary be reasonable? The Model Penal Code claims that if a defender is reckless in believing that self-defense is necessary, the person can be convicted of crimes requiring only reckless-ness (§ 3.09(2); see also Robinson 1984, § 62(b)). However, the concept of being reckless in acquiring or failing to acquire beliefs is nonsense. Re-cklessness is the conscious disregard of a risk; if the person does not believe that a circumstance exists or consequence is likely, that person cannot consciously disregard it. To be aware of a substantial risk is to believe that a substantial risk exists, otherwise one is only aware that others might think a substantial risk exists but not believe it. At best, the point must be that the person consciously disregards a substantial risk that his or her belief that no substantial risk exists is incorrect. At this point, any law is becoming too complex to serve people as a guide. The principle of certainty suggests one must either require the belief to be reasonable or not.

As discussed in the previous section, the rationale of the principle of lesser evils requires the belief to be reasonable. The use of force in self-defense is an exception to the prohibition of the use of force. A plausible claim that one's situation falls within the exception requires that the belief be reasonable. Thus, justifications require reasonable beliefs, whereas defenses showing lack of mens rea do not. The former apply to responsible conduct making particular exceptions to general legal judgments, so the decision must be reasonably supportable; whereas the latter show lack of responsibility. Moreover, one must balance the possible harm from being a victim of unreasonable force in self-defense with the possible harm of being punished for using unreasonable force in self-defense. One can avoid punishment by being reasonable, and one has no reason to subject oneself to unreasonable force.

A fourth possible limitation pertains to the culpability of the person against whom force is used. One ordinarily thinks of self-defense as the response of an innocent person to a culpable attack. As a potential victim of force used in self-defense, one could not accept its use if one's behavior was legally proper. There are two types of situations in which the innocence of the defender and the culpability of the attacker might not hold. In one, the attacker might have an excuse, such as mistake or insanity. In this type of situation, security concerns prevail. Given the above limitations, one has no reason to allow oneself to be assaulted or killed by mistaken or mentally abnormal persons. Thus, the defense must be against force or the threat of it that would be unlawful if the attacker were responsible for it (see Robinson 1982, 273-77).

The second type of situation requires a minor limitation to the principle of lesser evils. In these situations, the defender provoked or started the assault. In the previous section, we argued that the principle of lesser evils applies even if one was responsible for the situation requiring that choice, although one might be liable for some separate offense in creating the situation. Here that does not really apply, because there is one continuing course of conduct. For example, in *State v. Pride* (567 S.W.2d 426 (Mo. Ct.

App. 1978)), the defendants had robbed Ms. Stewart in a washroom at an interstate highway rest area. As they were getting into their car, a trucker with a pistol approached to stop them. One of the defendants fired at him with a rifle, and the trucker fired back. At their trial for robbery and assault, the defendants unsuccessfully pleaded self-defense to the assault charge. Although they were not using or threatening force at the time of the shooting, it was part of their wrongful course of conduct. Similar considerations apply if a person starts an argument and is attacked. However, if one breaks off the dispute and the other person is aware of it, then self-defense should apply. Consequently, the principle of lesser evils does not apply if one's culpable conduct creating the choice is part of one criminal activity (excluding conspiracy).

As the principle of lesser evils is not restricted to avoiding harm to oneself, the same considerations that apply to self-defense should apply to defense of others, simply requiring that one reasonably believe that the other person is in a position that justifies such a response. Security would be greatly enhanced were people encouraged to help protect one another. To positively punish people for aiding others would be contrary to security. However, the Law Reform Commission of Canada, following some U.S. jurisdictions, has recommended a significant limitation on the defense of others, namely, that it extend only to those under one's protection – usually family members (1982, 101-2). The only possible reason for so limiting a defense of others would be the likelihood of mistakes, but the requirement of a reasonable belief significantly limits that reason.

The unfortunate aspects of limiting defense of others are exemplified by *People v. Young* (11 N.Y.2d 274, 229 N.Y.S.2d 1, 183 N.E.2d 319 (1962)). The defendant saw two older men apparently attacking an eighteen year old male on a New York City street. He rushed to the young man's aid, and in the ensuing scuffle fell on one of the "assailants" injuring the person's knee-cap. As it turned out, the assailants were New York's finest in street clothes attempting to arrest the young man. The young man's defender was convicted of assault. The court reasoned that the young man could not have claimed self-defense, since he knew the men were policemen; consequently, his defender's justification could not have been any greater. In a city known for people standing by and watching a young woman raped and murdered without even telephoning the police, such a decision provides the wrong encouragement and is unacceptable. The test should be whether the actor reasonably believes the defense conditions obtain. Limiting the defense of others to people in one's care would also deprive the defender of a justification, because he was not responsible for the young man, and it is just as unacceptable a limitation. It would simply increase insecurity and encourage people not to be concerned for others.

6.3.6. *Defense of property*. With a few modifications required by the nature of property, the same considerations grounded in the principle of lesser evils that apply to defense of persons also apply to defense of property. The use and amount of force must be necessary. The force must be proportional to the threatened harm, and because property is of less value than human life, deadly force is no more permissible to defend property than it is to defend against minor assaults. The Law Reform Commission of Canada has proposed that force likely to cause serious bodily injury not be justifiable in defense of property (1982, 107-10). Whether this limitation is reasonable depends on whether the harm to property is a lesser evil than serious bodily injury, which in turn depends on what constitutes serious bodily injury. Theft threatens the stability of property generally as well as the particular loss, so some risk of personal injury in its defense would involve a lesser evil (see Robinson 1984, § 24(a)). Security of personal property, especially self-expressive property, seems sufficient to justify hitting a burglar with a baseball bat without warning (at least provided one does not smash the head). Although burglars are not usually violent, it is too much to ask people to turn on the light, warn the burglar not to take property, and then use force if the burglar does so. This sort of doctrine pushes the limits of excuse (one lacks the capacity to restrain oneself), let alone justification.

Another special limitation is that one must have possession of the property, be it goods or land, and the other person not have a legal right to it (but see Robinson 1984, § 131(e)(2)). If one knows that the other person is entitled to the property, then one should surrender it. One is not opposing unlawful force. The situation is more complex if both the possessor and the other person claim to be entitled to possession. Such disputes should be settled in courts of law. Consequently, the person who does not have possession should use legal means to acquire it, and it is plausible to hold that person guilty of a crime unless he or she has a reasonable belief that the disputed property will be destroyed unless possession is immediately acquired. However, even if the person trying to take possession is guilty of a crime, it does not necessarily follow that the present possessor is justified in using force to retain possession. The question is one of harm and less drastic alternatives. If the property is land, it will not disappear, so recourse to the courts is a less drastic alternative that can be safely pursued. If the property is personal, then recourse to the courts might not be a safe alternative; it might be removed. Force is also acceptable if the other person plans immediately to destroy buildings and so forth.

This last consideration leads to a respect in which defense of property is a broader justification than self-defense. The moveability of personal property implies that one need not always withdraw, because one cannot do so safely – the property might be removed. Similarly, reasonable pursuit can be justified for the same reason. If one has just had something taken from one's hands or catches a burglar escaping with something from one's home, one should be able to pursue the person and use force to recover one's property. Otherwise, once thieves or burglars had property in their hands, one would be compelled to stand by and let them abscond with it.

PUNISHMENT

6.4.0. *Introduction.* Throughout this chapter, we have assumed that conviction of a criminal offense would lead to punishment including the possibility of imprisonment. Many legal and moral problems surround penology – living conditions in prisons, parole, community corrections, and so on. Our topic is limited to principles to guide judges as opposed to corrections officers and so on. Thus, we primarily focus on the appropriate sentence. One must remember, however, that people are sent to prison as punishment, not for punishment, and the principle of reform can have significant implications for corrections programs. North American prisons often serve to train people for criminal careers rather than noncriminal ones, so considerable room exists for changes to further the aim of reform.

6.4.1. *The concept.* Although we have assumed that the criminal law remedy is punishment, we have not defined 'punishment'. As what is and is not punishment is not always clear, a definition is needed. A widely accepted philosophical definition of punishment has five elements (Hart 1968, 4-6; Flew 1969, 85-87). First, punishment involves an evil or deprivation. Second, it is for an offense against rules. Third, it is (or is supposed to be) of an offender for his or her offense. Fourth, it is imposed by human beings (is not a natural consequence of conduct). Fifth, those persons administering it are authorized to do so by the system of rules against which the offense was committed. This definition applies to punishment of football players by the National Football League as much as to legal punishment. Legal punishment is distinguished by the system of rules in conditions two and five being that of the criminal law.

It is difficult to distinguish punishment from treatment. When the U.S. Supreme Court held that conviction and punishment for being an addict constitutes unconstitutional cruel and unusual punishment, it suggested that compulsory treatment would be constitutionally permissible (*Robinson v. California*, 370 U.S. 660 (1962)). Defendants might see little difference between being imprisoned (punished) and being confined to a hospital. Indeed, defendants who successfully plead not guilty by reason of insanity are often automatically committed to psychiatric institutions until cured (*Jones v. United States*, 463 U.S. 354 (1983)). This discourages many defendants from pleading insanity, since they prefer a prison sentence with a fixed maximum to commitment without any guarantee of ever being released. As a character in a television drama once said, "I may be crazy, but I'm not that crazy." Thus, one might wonder why imprisonment of an addict or legally insane person for a fixed period would be cruel and unusual but indefinite commitment might not be.

Several features of punishment distinguish it from treatment. The requirement of an offense (the second defining condition) and the principle of a voluntary act are central to punishment. Punishment is for a discrete item of behavior, an act, whereas treatment is for a state of being or status. Although a discrete item of behavior is often part of the grounds for treatment, it is as a symptom or evidence of the status that is to be changed. Treatment could be justified without the discrete behavior were there other grounds for inferring the status. Other elements of the definition of punishment also help distinguish it from treatment. Punishment involves the intentional infliction of an evil (the first and fourth conditions). Were it not perceived by the recipient as evil or undesirable, it would constitute a reward rather than punishment. Although treatment can involve evil or an undesirable element, it does not intentionally do so. Treatment's purpose is to change a person's state of being, and if possible, pleasant means will be used. Moreover, punishment is for an offense, conduct for which offenders are responsible because they could avoid it. This concept of responsibility is not important in treatment. Usually people are not responsible for their status, for example, being mentally ill.

Treatment is not an appropriate criminal law sanction or remedy; that is, it is not something that should be imposed *because* of conviction. The denunciatory aspect of criminal conviction is usually inappropriate for treatment, because people are not usually culpable for their status. Directly to sentence persons to treatment is to confuse punishment for culpable and responsible acts with treatment for statuses irrespective of culpability and responsibility. Treatment can and should be available to convictees who need it. One has no reason to accept a criminal law system in which punishment is a bar to treatment. Although a convicted person presumably acted culpably, a status could still have been a contributing factor. Thus, treatment of the status might help ensure that the person not repeat the offense. A judge may suspend a sentence conditional on a person entering a treatment program, but a judge should not be able to sentence to treatment. Compulsory treatment should be based on a civil finding, although special considerations might apply to persons who are not responsible for dangerous criminal behavior (A.B.A. 1984, Standards 7-7.3 to 7-7.11). The usual argument for a separation is that one who is mad should not be thought bad, but in practice, the public, mental health workers, and the persons themselves usually view them as both mad and bad (Morris 1982, 74). Rather, the point here is to block the inference that because someone is bad, that person is also mad. It is far too easy to make such an invalid inference, and abolition of the insanity defense might encourage it.

6.4.2. *Amounts.* In 6.1.2, we accepted a principle of proportionality on preventive grounds. That principle requires the severity of punishments to be in proportion to the seriousness of crimes. As punishment usually consists of imprisonment, it is easy to rank punishment by length of time incarcerated. There is, however, a discrete gap, the in-out choice between those who are incarcerated and those who are not but given probation, suspended sentence, or whatever.

It is less clear how one ranks crimes. Two irreducible and incommensurable factors appear to be involved in determining the seriousness of criminal conduct: the harm and the mental element. Mental states can be ranked in declining order as purposely, knowingly, recklessly, negligently, and none of them (strict liability). Although we have rejected negligence and strict liability offenses, they are included here for completeness since many jurisdictions do have such offenses. The ranking of mental states, from least to greatest culpability, is illustrated by the following examples of automobile driving resulting in death. Strict liability: Grigg is carefully driving down the road, just having had his car repaired and safety inspected, when a pot hole covered by snow causes a nondefective tire to blow causing the car to slide uncontrollably into and killing a pedestrian walking along the edge of the highway. Negligently: Grigg forgets to have a safety inspection and his brakes fail at a traffic light resulting in his running down a pedestrian crossing with the light. Recklessly: Grigg knew his brakes were defective and drove anyway, resulting in a fatal accident as for negligence. Knowingly: Grigg is driving away from a bank robbery when a police officer steps into the road, and Grigg runs the officer down without any attempt to avoid doing so. (Reckless drivers do attempt to avoid hitting people when the risk materializes.) Purposely: as in television detective shows, Grigg swerves onto the sidewalk to run down his worst enemy. As one goes fiom strict liability to purposefulness, Grigg poses more of a threat to security – from doing everything possible to avoid harm to deliberately causing it.

The ranking of harms is not as easy. Death of a person is worse than loss of a hundred dollars, but is it worse than a violent rape not resulting in death? The U.S. Supreme Court thinks it clearly is (*Coker v. Georgia*, 433 U.S. 584 (1977)), but many people would disagree. Perhaps more difficult is distinguishing harms in crimes like bribery, theft, wiretapping, and false imprisonment. It is not feasible to give each harm a separate and distinct place on the scale. Instead, a 'partial ordering' dividing harms into groups ranked in order of seriousness is the best possible. It is unlikely that one would arrive at more than about ten groups, as in a Pennsylvania sentencing proposal although the classification was not solely by harms (Bedau 1985, 95). The Model Penal Code arrived at only three degrees of felonies plus two of misdemeanors (§§ 6.01(1) and 6.08).

To rank crimes by seriousness, one must use the culpability or harm rankings alone or combine them in some way. Using either alone is implausible. A ranking solely by mental elements implies that purposely stealing ten dollars is worse than knowingly causing death. A ranking by harms alone is more plausible, but recklessly causing slight bodily injury is not clearly worse than purposely swindling elderly people out of their life's savings, yet physical injury is plausibly worse than loss of money. A reasonably acceptable system is to use the ranking by harms as a base. Purposely causing a harm is the top category for that harm. Lesser culpability puts the crime at the next lower level. For example, purposeful killing is assigned to the category of worst crimes. Knowingly killing is then in the next worst category, and reckless killing is one category below that. In many cases, one might not distinguish between purposely and knowingly causing the harm. Thus, the primary ranking is by harm with culpability used to distinguish offenses involving the same harm.

This procedure does not correlate the ranking of criminal conduct with that of the severity of punishments. That is, it does not indicate whether the punishment for the most serious crimes should be capital punishment, life imprisonment without parole, or some fixed number of years. Nor does it indicate what the gaps should be between the different punishments. Moreover, as we rejected the strong retributivist claims to some form of equivalency of crime and punishment (6.1.2), it cannot be used. Nor is there any reason to assume that the most serious crime should receive the greatest punishment on the list (Davis 1985, 136, makes this assumption). Any correlation must thus rest on preventive or other considerations.

One can establish at least theoretical maximum and minimum punishments for each crime. The harm principle sets an upper limit to the amount of punishment appropriate. In no case should the expectable harm of punishment (severity times the number of offenders) be greater than the net harm prevented. (Actually, one should compare the harm of enforcement, not punishment, to that prevented; because enforcement involves other harms or costs than punishment, the justifiable severity of punishment is less than that equal to the harm prevented.) However, as the harm of punishment depends on both the severity of the punishment and the number of persons punished, the acceptable severity varies with the frequency of punishment. One could thus give greater punishment but discover and convict fewer violators, which would save enforcement costs (see Posner 1985, 1213)

Nonetheless, two considerations limit this approach of punishing a few severely. General deterrence is probably more dependent on certainty of punishment than severity, so doubling the arrest and conviction rate will probably have more deterrent effect than doubling the punishment. This difference in deterrence might be due to persons discounting future incarceration (see Posner 1985, 1213-14). Also, too high a penalty makes it difficult significantly to distinguish between categories of crimes (see Davis 1984, 97-101); increasing punishment for one category requires similar increases in all those above it.

Of course, as determining the upper limit depends on predictions of crimes and conviction rates which are interdependent, it is not practically and perhaps not theoretically possible (Davis 1985, 125-31) to apply the upper limit to individual categories of crimes. Instead, one can probably only apply it to the top. The idea underlying the principles of the least drastic alternative and of lesser evils implies that one should impose the least punishment that is effective (see Morris 1982, 155, 157-59, and passim (parsimony in punishment); Mackey 1984 (cruel and unusual punishment as not least restrictive alternative)). If a maximum punishment of, say, twenty-five years results in a tolerable level of crime, then there is little reason to increase penalties across the board.

It is more practical to set the minimum punishment for individual crimes. If the benefits of a crime are such that many people would prefer them with the punishment to not having them, then the punishment is too small. This point underlies our earlier criticism (6.1.2) of equivalence of punishment as equal harm. If the punishment is no more than what one would gain, it provides no rational deterrent and the principle of effectiveness would no longer support criminalizing the conduct.

It is appropriate to have ranges of possible punishment for each category of crime rather than one fixed amount. If one does not, then one must sacrifice considerations of specific deterrence, incapacitation, and reform. Not all instances of assault and battery are alike; they can differ by the amount of harm inflicted and other circumstances, such as a barroom brawl versus a random vicious assault. *(6-17) The principle of individualization of punishment: laws should permit, and judges should impose, individualized punishment within maximum and minimum limits for each crime.* Thus, the average sentence should be less than the maximum permissible to allow for aggravating and mitigating considerations. As a possible convictee, one would want and accept attention to mitigating features of one's case. Nor could one rationally object to a greater than average punishment based on aggravating factors so long as the punishment was no more than the maximum permissible. As a general member of society, one can accept this principle. The minimum amount of punishment helps ensure that prevention is not unduly weakened. Criminals are unlikely to take such variations into account in deciding to commit a crime (see Morris 1982, 154-55). We do not here consider the mitigating and aggravating factors that should be used (see generally Morris 1982, chs. 4-5).

Three categories of offenders or offenses raise an important questions of the appropriate range of punishment – habitual offenders, accomplices, and inchoate offenses. With habitual offenders, the issue is an increased range of punishment, while with accessories and inchoate offenses, the issue is one of a lesser range of punishment than for the principal offense. Habitual offender statutes permit or require greater punishment for persons having prior (usually three) convictions (see, for example, M.P.C. §§ 6.07 and

7.03). Repeat offenders pose a greater threat of future crime than first time offenders, because "[t]he best predictor of future criminality is past criminality (Morris 1982, 163). Also, apparently being more inclined to crime than average persons, a greater punishment is needed to deter them (see Posner 1985, 1216). Thus, the preventive aim, especially incapacitation, supports punishing repeat offenders more severely.

Nonetheless, different categories of permissible punishment for habitual offenders are unacceptable. Mandatory increases can cause severe disproportion. Consider *Rummel v. Estelle* (445 U.S. 263 (1980)). Because it was his third felony, in 1973 the defendant was sentenced to life imprisonment for obtaining $120.75 by false pretenses. His two previous convictions had been in 1964 for fraudulent use of a credit card to obtain $80 worth of goods and in 1969 for passing a forged check for $28.36. A majority of the Court could find no unconstitutional cruel and unusual punishment in the disproportion between the crime and the punishment. However, a few years later a majority did find life imprisonment for a seventh conviction of a nonviolent crime disproportional and cruel and unusual punishment (*Solem v. Helm*, 436 U.S. 227 (1983)). This illustrates the difficulty of using alleged intuitions of the proportionality between punishment and desert.

The principles of individualization of punishment, harm, and denunciation support another conclusion than in *Rummel*. Life imprisonment is clearly not proportional to the seriousness of the actual crime; theft of that amount is not as serious as homicide and kidnapping. Such punishment might decrease conformity to the law by bringing it into disrespect. Moreover, the harm and mental element are no worse the third time a crime is committed than the first. The extra punishment is for the state of being, the disposition to commit offenses. An increased category of punishment for being an habitual offender violates the voluntary act requirement, as such states of being are not properly crimes.

Nevertheless, it is still possible to punish repeat offenders more than first time offenders. Within permissible ranges of punishment for a crime, such as one to five years, the average should not be the maximum. Consequently, judges can sentence habitual offenders towards the higher limit, which is only to take incapacitation seriously. Thus, if the higher and lower amounts are within an appropriate range for a crime, sentencing guidelines might recommend greater punishment for repeat offenders (cf. Pennsylvania proposal discussed in Bedau 1985, 93-95). Persons charged with multiple offenses can also have their sentences run consecutively rather than concurrently.

Punishment for accessories should be one category below the principal offense. Accessories are not as great a threat to security as principal offenders, because acting alone they do not pose a threat. Unlike habitual offenders, here the difference in dangerousness is part of the definition of the criminal act – aiding and abetting – rather than the status of the offender. Consequently, a category difference in the punishment is appropriate. Nonetheless, the different categories of permissible punishment are likely to overlap, such as one to five years and four to eight years. So, a person sentenced for a lower category crime can receive a greater punishment than some people sentenced for a higher category.

The issue of lesser punishment for inchoate offenses is a difficult one. For each inchoate offense, the requisite mental element is purposefulness (6.2.4). Thus both the harm sought and the mental state are as serious as for the substantive offense. Were retribution the aim of the criminal law, there would be no reason to punish less, for the perpetrator of an inchoate offense evinces as wrongful an intent and disposition as a perpetrator of the substantive offense. However, retribution is not an acceptable aim of the criminal law.

The following discussion focuses on attempt, because more problems arise with it than with solicitation and conspiracy. One can distinguish between 'interrupted attempts' in which the person has not done enough to produce the harm in any circumstances, and 'completed attempts' in which the actor has done everything that he or she might have done in a successful crime but did not, for some fortuitous reason, succeed. For example, an assassin might be caught by police before being able to shoot at the victim (an interrupted attempt) or simply shoot and miss because a car drove in the way (a completed attempt). All attempts of crimes in which the conduct constitutes the harm, as in rape, are interrupted attempts. There can be completed attempts only in 'resultant-harm' crimes, where, as in homicide, the harm is causally separated from the actor's bodily movements.

One reason often given for punishing interrupted attempts less than successful crimes is to encourage criminals to desist. If the punishment for the successful crime is no more than for the attempt, a person has no reason to desist. Thus, security might be increased by lesser punishment of interrupted attempts, because fewer actual harms might result. Similar reasoning applies to solicitation and conspiracy. However, critics contend that some crimes allow little or no time for thought and reconsideration, and in any case, criminals have already considered and were undeterred by the likelihood of punishment for the successful crime. This reply, at least as concerns time for reconsideration, is not persuasive for solicitation and most conspiracies, because the act is further removed temporally from the completed crime than in attempts. Moreover, it has not been empirically established that lesser punishment is not as effective. So the principle of least drastic alternative, as modified to apply to punishment, supports the lesser punishment. Also, in interrupted attempts, one can never be certain the person would not desist. If a person would have desisted, then he or she has a less firm purpose and poses less of a threat to security. Moreover, as the act is further removed from the harm, erroneous convictions are more likely. Lesser punishments would reduce error costs (Posner 1985, 1217) Consequently, a lesser punishment for solicitation, conspiracy, and interrupted attempts is justifiable.

Our analysis has assumed that punishment for conspiracy and solicitation is based on the substantive crime. Conspiracy is usually, and solicitation can be, defined as a separate crime with a distinct punishment. If this is done, then they should be placed in the lowest category. Otherwise, if there are mandatory minimum punishments, some offenders will be punished more than appropriate. For example, if conspiracy is in the next lowest category, a person who conspires to commit a crime in the lowest category would be punished more than one who committed the crime. By placing conspiracy and solicitation in the lowest category, some offenders will receive less than were they one category lower than the substantive crime. This does not violate the above reasoning, for our argument is only that the punishment should be less than for the substantive crime, not that it must be one and only one category less. If punishment is based on the substantive crime, then punishment for a conspiracy to commit multiple crimes should be one category below that for the most serious crime the person conspired to commit.

This still leaves the issue of punishment for completed attempts. It has been suggested that the conduct in completed attempts exhibits the same dangerousness as successful crimes and so merits the same punishment; indeed, laws might be rewritten to define criminal conduct by the degree of dangerousness regardless of whether the harm actually results (Gross 1979, 430-37). Unless it was overtly impossible for the harm to result, it is claimed, these attempts should be punished equally with successful crimes. The challenge posed by this view is to show the relevance of the fact that "by chance" the harm did not occur.

Several reasons might lead one to prefer a lesser punishment even for completed attempts. First, suppose that at the very last instant Howe could not bring herself to murder her husband, and she shifted her aim in firing a gun so as to miss. Howe is less of a threat than she would be had she missed due to a car getting in the way, but she would have a very difficult time proving that she had a last minute change of heart. Second, the preventive reasoning behind the principle of proportionality applies. If people attempt murder and fail, then if they are already liable to the same punishment as for murder, they have little reason not to try again unless they might be convicted of two crimes. Third, the intended victims have benefited from luck; there is no apparent reason to deny the attempters the benefit of the luck as well. Granted, attempters do not deserve the luck, but luck is not a matter of desert; it is neither deserved nor undeserved. Consequently, one has good reason to assign even completed attempts to a lesser category of punishment than successful crimes (for a more complete discussion, see Bayles 1982b). Except for capital crimes, the permissible punishments for a successful crime and a completed attempt might overlap; some attempters can receive greater punishment than others guilty of the successful crime.

The conclusions of the arguments concerning accessories and inchoate offenses are summarized in the following principle. *(6-18) The principle of lesser punishments: persons convicted as accessories or of inchoate offenses should receive lesser punishments than they would as principals for the substantive offenses.* The principle does not imply that all attempters should receive punishment less than anyone convicted of the substantive offense. Instead, it is that they should receive lesser punishments than they themselves would have for the substantive offenses, that is, had they been successful. Normally, this can be achieved by placing them at the same point between maximum and minimum punishment in a lesser category. However, the principle permits putting consiracy in the lowest category.

6.4.3. *Other issues.* Many other issues arise concerning punishment, only a few of which are briefly commented on here. Full arguments are not developed; the point is merely to indicate how they can be accommodated or approached within our framework. The first pertains to judicial discretion in setting punishment within the limits for each category of crime. Unless standards exist to guide judges, signficant discrepancies in sentences are likely from judge to judge and from one part of a country to another. One has no reason to accept a system in which the punishment for similar perpetrators of similar crimes can vary by great amounts. In such a system, some people are probably receiving sentences greater than appropriate. Consequently, one has a good reason to prefer a system with standards to ensure a relatively uniform sentencing. This is not to deny that mercy or randomized parsimony of punishment is not acceptable (see Morris 1982, ch. 5); indeed, one has good reason to accept the latter – randomly letting some have less punishment than permissible if it is not needed for preventive purposes.

A second issue concerns 'indeterminate sentences', that is, providing a minimum and maximum sentence with release depending on the judgment of correctional authorities. Prisoners object to this practice, because it provides correctional authorities considerable power over them by threatening bad reports to parole boards. However, one purpose of indeterminate sentences is to provide correctional authorities just such power so they can better control prisoners. The other main purposes of indeterminate sentences are to protect society by retaining persons likely to commit further crimes and to avoid unnecessary punishment by releasing those who are not thought to pose a threat. One must ask whether the benefits of security and lesser punishment from this practice outweigh the harms. The answer depends on the reliability of predictions of recidivism and whether the power is abused. It also depends on whether determinate sentences result in retaining longer than necessary persons who could be released. Because these matters are not clear, one might reasonably decide either way. With indeterminate sentences, one would want reasonable precautions to limit abuses. One would also probably favor relatively small differences between the minimum and maximum period of imprisonment. A sentence of six to eight years might be acceptable, whereas one of two to twenty years would not be.

A third issue concerns the use of parole, community corrections, and probation. Although there are differences between these correctional methods, they all involve supervision of offenders in the community and present the same normative issue. The arguments in their favor are that they are at least as effective as imprisonment in reducing recidivism, are cheaper, and help the transition from prison to life in the community. If these claims are correct, then there is no sound reason to oppose them. Some people object that these methods result in criminals not receiving the punishment they deserve. However, this objection rests on a strong retributive aim of criminal law. It assumes that there is some appropriate minimum punish-

ment based on considerations other than those we have suggested for
determining minimum sentences. Others contend that such "easy" correctional methods will cease to deter. This consideration has some weight
if it pertains to the general deterrent effect of the law. Otherwise, it simply
challenges the empirical claims about recidivism without detracting from
the normative point that if the above claims are true, then such programs
are acceptable.

Some people claim that the extant criminal law ignores victims; it does
nothing to make victims of crimes better off. In one sense, this is true. The
criminal law itself does not restore victims of crime to the position they
were in before the crime was committed. Sometimes stolen property is
recovered and returned, but that is not frequent. In another sense, the
charge is false. The aim of criminal law is to prevent people being victims,
and from being victims again and again. Protection of potential victims is
the main concern of the criminal law system. One can still contend that
more should be done for crime victims. Often they must take off from work
and wait hours to appear as witnesses, only to be subject to humiliating
cross examinations by defense counsel and to see the defendant released.
Thus, some programs of victim compensation, restitution, and offender-
victim reconciliation have developed. These programs pose somewhat
different issues.

Victim compensation raises a normative issue of state responsibility. The
criminal law is to provide security of persons and property and is a function
of the state. When it fails to achieve its purpose, an individual often suffers
harm. (The effect on an individual might be minimal in an offense involving
public harm.) The question is whether security would be increased by a
system that provided compensation from state funds. Is the cost of a
government compensation program worth the gains? Much depends on the
existence of other programs. A comprehensive personal injury and property insurance scheme, as we have suggested (5.5.2), would make such a
program unnecessary. If, as in every developed country except the United
States, a government health insurance system already provides medical
care for any injuries and there is widespread private insurance against
property loss, then the compensation will be less worthwhile than did these
not exist. From this insurance perspective, it is an open question whether
such a program is worthwhile.

However, when one adds the fact that the state (people collectively) has
undertaken to provide security thereby inducing a minimal reliance and has
failed, the harm that befalls victims is a social responsibility. The justifi-

cation stems from a combination of the principles of compensation (5-3) and reliance (4-5). The costs can be spread, and the harm results from a failure of the activity of providing security. Although one might claim that the offender is the causally responsible agent, the state has undertaken to prevent such harm. One can reasonably rely on the state for protection, although it would be unreasonable to expect complete protection. In the absence of other adequate programs, these considerations tip the scales in favor of a victim compensation system.

Finally, restitution and reconciliation programs are certainly permissible so long as they do not usurp the preventive aim of criminal law. If the state is to operate a compensation program, it is appropriate that offenders provide as much of the compensation as possible. After all, they are the ones directly responsible for the victims' losses. The state is only secondarily responsible for not preventing their conduct. Victim-offender reconciliation might promote a better feeling of people towards one another and help reduce criminal conduct. Consequently, insofar as these programs have these effects, they are desirable. However, the programs are secondary to the aim of helping to ensure that fewer rather than more criminal acts occur, and should they detract from that purpose, they are unacceptable. The chief aim of the criminal law is to increase security of person and property by preventing criminal acts.

CHAPTER 7

VALUES IN THE LAW

INTRODUCTION

7.0. The aim of this book is to fill a gap between general jurisprudential theories applicable to all legal systems and detailed analyses of particular fields of law. We have developed normative principles for common-law fields that would be acceptable to rational persons. At this point one might find the number of principles and topics discussed blocking any overall view. Consequently, we should step back and briefly review certain themes running through the more detailed analyses.

Three general themes pervade our previous discussion. One is the method used to analyze legal problems. A second is the institutional nature of courts and the effect of it and legal procedure on substantive law. A third is the role of interests and values in the substantive law. The next section discusses the first two themes. The next three sections discuss the values of freedom, responsibility, and equality in the legal fields. The final section then considers the limits to these fields of law achieving all values, in particular, the social good.

A NONTHEORY?

7.1. One might complain that while we have provided an overview of basic common-law fields, no unifying theory of law has been presented. Three more specific points might be made. First, there is no methodological unity to the discussion as provided by an economic analysis or a social contract theory. Second, large and increasingly important parts of the law – constitutional, statutory, and administrative law – have been omitted. Consequently, at best, only a part of law, and that an increasingly less important part, has been considered. Third, there is no normative coherence. The argument does not proceed from any fundamental normative principle such as the utilitarian principle of maximizing happiness. Consequently, the discussion constitutes a nontheory of part of law.

These are strong objections and raise matters of legitimate concern. Undoubtedly, it is not possible to satisfy everyone on these points, besides which, in some respects there is some truth in them. However, they partly ask for something that was not attempted and that is otherwise inappropriate to seek. Moral theorists have often sought a theory based on one or two principles, such as the principle of utility or the categorical imperative in ethics, and a *Grundnorm* or rule of recognition in law, from which the whole of a system can be deduced. That conception of normative theory does not underlie this work, but a critique of it would lead too far astray (see Bayles 1984b; Bayles 1984c).

Nonetheless, there is a methodological unity in our analysis. For each topic, our question has been "What principles would rational persons accept on their merits for courts to use to decide the issues?" Often, asking the right question is the most important step in getting the right answer. Asking this question rather than some other, such as what would one do if one owned both pieces of property affected, makes a significant difference in the answer one will give (see 3.3.6). That a principle must be acceptable to a person in the position of either party to a dispute has other important implications, for example, in setting the limits of jurisdiction. The requirement that one be rational also affects the positions taken, for example, ruling out vengeance as a basis for the criminal law (6.1.2). Consequently, the very stating of the issue provides some unity and affects the answers that are accepted. It does not, however, provide an algorithm for reaching answers, for example, by calculating the most efficient rule or determining whether any of a short list of rights has been violated.

Another aspect of our question also provides a unity, albeit at the expense of not covering all of law. This is the aspect of limiting discussion to what principles judges should use to adjudicate cases brought to them. This institutional setting of the issues is another unifying and limiting factor throughout the work. We have not sought to provide an analysis of the whole of law, only the major fields of traditional common law, excepting family law. Consequently, no normative theory of the whole of law is provided, but none was intended. Indeed, the main purpose of discussing the limits of tort law as a method for accident compensation was to show the importance of the institutional constraints of adjudication (5.5). One of the reasons for the decline of the fields of law considered in comparison to other fields, such as administrative law, is recognition of the institutional inadequacy of adjudication (and legislation) as a method for achieving many governmental purposes.

Perhaps the primary source of the objection that we have presented a nontheory stems from the lack of a simple substantive unity. Our approach

has not been based on a single normative principle such as wealth maximization (Posner 1983; Posner 1977), equality of concern and respect (Dworkin 1977; Dworkin 1985), or a natural right to property (Epstein 1985).
Indeed, a constant theme in each main chapter is that rational persons will
have a multiplicity of aims or purposes for the legal field considered.
Consequently, no simple (minded?) normative unity based on one value or
norm runs through our analysis. Yet, a normative unity exists to the extent
rational persons have a consistent and limited set of normative aims. Many
of our more specific principles are justified by the principles stating these
aims, and some of the others, such as the principles of offers (4-8), acceptances (4-9), conditions and warranties (4-10), and inchoate offenses (6-12)
are largely definitional, although resting on or implying normative considerations. However, as none of the aims always overrides others no matter
the situation, we have had to settle for various principles that incorporate
these aims to different degrees and that must be weighed and balanced
against one another. The process of weighing and balancing is not deductive; it does not always provide one clear answer, so rational people can
disagree. However, it reflects how rational people decide matters when not
in a study seeking a false, deductive, theoretical unity.

Nevertheless, certain types of normative aims run through our discussion. We characterized rational persons (1.2) as having desires for or
interests in bodily and mental integrity, reputation, wealth, and security.
We have usually argued for principles on the grounds that they protect or
further those basic desires or interests. Tort law provides compensation
for, and some deterrence to, injury to person, reputation, property, and
privacy. Both property and contract law further one's interest in wealth,
and criminal law provides security of person and property. And economic
costs (wealth) were a significant concern in procedural law. There is no
point in reviewing these matters further.

We also mentioned some fundamental values that rational persons
would hold – freedom, responsibility, and equality. A critic might complain
that such values have not been sufficiently emphasized and that a normative legal theory should give prominence to fundamental values. Consequently, in the following three sections, we review the place of these
fundamental values in the common-law fields and how our principles
support them. The focus is not the extant law where that differs from what
the acceptable principles imply, but a legal system that instantiated our
principles. To the extent such a system incorporates these values, further
normative support is provided for the principles.

FREEDOM

7.2. The value of freedom, being free from some limit to do something, is recognized in each of the fields we have considered. Although freedom is less central than some other values in procedural law, it still has a role there. The principle of voluntariness (2-4) clearly recognizes the freedom to bring a lawsuit in civil cases. The principle of participation (2-5) supports the freedom to present one's reasons and arguments in legal cases. The principle of repose (2-9) also contributes to freedom by bringing disputes to an end so that one is free to go about one's affairs without the worry, bother, inconvenience, and cost of an unending legal action. For example, on the day I first wrote this, a newspaper carried a story about the U. S. Justice Department filing a brief in a case urging the Supreme Court to resolve a fourteen year old private antitrust lawsuit ("U.S. Urges" 1985). The cloud of possible liability hanging over firms can greatly restrict their freedom to allocate resources to new enterprises, and the same applies to individuals. Insofar as the principle of stale claims (3-16) is a specification of the principle of repose, it has the same effect.

The principle of freedom (3-8) establishes one aim of property law as avoiding legal limits to one's freedom to use property. Thus, in discussing use of property, we assumed freedom and focused on justifiable limits (3.3.2 through 3.3.4). The freedom to acquire property is another major element of property law. The principles of first possession (3-5) and labor (3-6) leave one free to acquire property by possession or labor. Similarly, freedom to dispose of property is central in the principle of transferability (3-3), which supports voluntary transfers and prohibits involuntary (unfree) ones. The principles of gratuitous disposition (3-17) and succession (3-18) specifically support freedom to give one's property away during life or after death.

Similar points can be made about freedom and contract law. The principles of freedom and transferability were incorporated as principles of contract law (4.1.4). Other principles protect one's freedom from internal and external limits. The principle of mistake (4-13) protects one from disadvantageous decisions that are less than fully rational due to ignorance. The principle of contractual incapacity (4-14) protects one from such choices due to immaturity or mental abnormality. Other principles help protect one from disadvantageous contracts due to external limits on one's freedom. Thus, the principle of required conditions (4-12) protects one when external circumstances prevent a reasonable choice between alternatives. Likewise, the principle of good faith (4-17) protects one from choices that are less free due to duress or undue influence. In general, only contracts freely entered are enforceable against a person.

We have already noted that the ability to make contracts increases one's freedom (4.1.1). Thus, all the principles specifying enforceable commitments contribute to freedom (see Fried 1981, 13-14). For example, the principle of gratuitous commitments (4-6) recognizes and supports the freedom to commit oneself to give property in the future, just as the principle of gratuitous disposition supports one's doing so in the present. These principles increase the freedom of promisees, for they can accept and hold promisors to commitments. They can plan and act free from fear of not obtaining the expected benefit of the interaction due to promisors' not performing. Promisors are enabled to act in ways that are otherwise usually not available. They can exchange a commitment of a future performance for a present or future performance.

But, it might be objected, what benefit is the ability to exchange commitments if, when the time for performance arrives, one regrets one's commitment because a bad bargain was made. This objection confuses the satisfaction of desires with freedom. Freedom is increased if limits to actions are removed, so it is increased when the number of possible alternative courses of action is increased. Unfortuitous exercises of freedom, for example, purchasing stock the price of which then falls, do not imply that one was not free. The freedom to purchase stock on a market gives one an opportunity to risk loss for possible significant gains. Freedom is not the only thing desired; wealth is also desired. If one loses money in the stock market, one does not regret the freedom to buy stock, but the particular exercise of that freedom because of the detriment that resulted to one's wealth.

The recognition of freedom in tort law centers around the principle of consent (5-11). Its recognition of freedom as a value is most clear in intentional torts. Many of the interests protected are not to have something occur without one's consent. This recognizes one's freedom to have something occur or not. If one did not consent, one is to be compensated. Of course, freedom is also directly protected by the tort of false imprisonment. Being able to assume risks can also increase one's freedom. For example, operators of ski jump contests might not let people participate, or even hold the contests, unless participants could relieve them of liability by assuming risks. In a sense, all tort defenses increase the freedom of defendants from liability, but that assumes a baseline of tort liability. It is better to view tort law as limiting freedom by imposing duties and liability; defenses are exceptions to these limits.

Criminal law is even more of a limit to one's freedom, for the usual punishment is imprisonment – external physical constraint of many actions. Yet, criminal law recognizes freedom as a fundamental value in the restrictions on its scope. The significance of the loss of freedom by incarceration is central to the arguments for stricter standards for liability in criminal than tort law, for example, the arguments against strict liability and negligence (6.2.2). The principles of certainty (6-9) and reasonable opportunity (6-13) also recognize the importance of freedom by limiting criminal liability to situations in which one could avoid it. From the perspective of a potential crime victim, one aim of the criminal law is to protect freedom by preventing kidnapping, murder, assault, and other such conduct. One is more free to engage in various activities without fear of such events. In many urban areas, elderly people are afraid to venture out at night for fear of being assaulted. The failure to prevent criminal acts thus decreases their freedom.

RESPONSIBILITY

7.3. The two central senses of 'responsibility' for the fields of law we considered are capacity-responsibility and causal-responsibility. Recognition of capacity-responsibility is part of respect as a rational person. All the fields of law presume that adults have capacity-responsibility. Procedural law assumes that people are capable of participating in trials. People are presumed capable of owning property and making contracts. Tort law assumes that they have capacity to avoid harms. Criminal law presumes that people are sane, and we noted how punishment as opposed to treatment presupposes that one is a responsible person (6.4.1).

The primary exceptions to presumed capacity-responsibility are minors and mentally abnormal persons. For minors, age is often used as the criterion of capacity-responsibility. However, in discussing the principle of contractual incapacity (4-14) in 4.3.4, we suggested that it might be better to recognize variable levels of capacity-responsibility as the law does in other areas. One can lack the capacity for some decisions but not others. Recognition of variable capacity (or incapacity) would accord respect as a rational person insofar as it is appropriate. These considerations apply to property ownership, contracts, and torts (where it is recognized in

356 CHAPTER 7

consent to medical treatment). We did stick to a minimum age requirement for criminal liability, although recognizing variable capacity above that age (6.3.0). The moral cost of convicting the innocent, which includes those persons lacking capacity-responsibility, provides a reason for a stricter requirement.

The primary concern is whether legal principles exempt people from liability or other requirements when they lack causal- or capacity-responsibility. Although procedural principles respect people as responsible, people are rarely exempted for lack of capacity-responsibility. The principle of voluntariness (2-4) recognizes people as capable of deciding to initiate lawsuits. The principles of participation (2-5) and intelligibility (2-7) also recognize people as capable of contributing to and understanding the proceedings. Trials and proceedings are often postponed if people are physically incapable of participating. But except for criminal cases, mental abnormality is rarely a basis for not having a trial. One is incompetent to stand trial for a criminal offense if one lacks sufficient mental capacity to contribute rationally to one's defense and to understand the proceedings (LaFave and Scott 1972, 297; A.B.A. 1984, Standard 7-4.1(b)). There are problems with defendants who might never be capable of so participating, and perhaps in such cases one should hold the trial anyway (Morris 1982, 35-53). Outside of the criminal law, the primary reasons for not recognizing lack of capacity-responsibility in procedure are that this might thwart the aims of the substantive law, that legal counsel can often defend one's interests anyway, and that sometimes the proceedings are prompted by the incapacity (civil commitment or guardianship).

Many legal defenses are based on a lack of capacity-responsibility, yet there are many situations in which people are held liable without capacity-responsibility. It is often said that contractual liability is a form of strict liability, for one is liable even if one's failure to perform is neither intentional nor negligent. However, this contention ignores several crucial features of contract law that recognize capacity-responsibility. Perhaps the central feature is the assumption of risk. If one has capacity-responsibility when making a contract, then one should be aware that events might prevent one's performance. One assumes the risk of certain uncontrollable events preventing one's performance and rendering one liable. In discussing the principle of mistake (4-13) in 4.3.3, we noted that the price might indicate which party assumed the risk of an uncontrollable event.

Nonetheless, one cannot rationally assume unforeseeable risks. In part, the doctrine of contract frustration (4.4.1) recognizes this point. If an unforeseeable event occurs that frustrates the contract's purpose and neither party has assumed its risk, then neither should be held to the contract. Neither party "took responsibility" for the risk. A similar consideration lies under the doctrine of impossibility. However, most events that occur are foreseeable and thus assumed, simply because they are of a type that frequently occurs. Moreover, the principle of contract damages (4-19) limits damages to foreseeable losses resulting from failure to fulfill commitments. Not only is assumption of the risk involved, but causal-responsibility is implied by the losses resulting from nonperformance. Limitation of liability to foreseeable losses resulting from nonperformance and the assumption of risks ground contract liability in causal and capacity-responsibility.

Tort liability clearly requires causal-responsibility. The principle of causation (5-12) applies to all torts. The only exception is vicarious liability, which is discussed below. The problem is that tort law appears to impose liability without capacity-responsibility. There are three main areas where this is so. First, children and mentally abnormal persons are held liable. Second, the objective standard of negligence imposes liability on some people who lack the capacity to conform to the law. Third, the various forms of strict liability hold people liable even if they cannot conform to the law.

More than any other field, tort law does hold people liable when they lack capacity-responsibility. Nonetheless, capacity-responsibility is still a value recognized by tort law, and the departures from requiring capacity-responsibility are acceptable. That the departures are acceptable need not be discussed, because that was shown in justifying principles that do depart. However, how the importance of capacity-responsibility is recognized requires further explication. First, although we have not emphasized it, tort liability requires a voluntary act. If during an epileptic seizure Anderson strikes Baker, she will not be liable for battery. This requirement also applies even in the strict liability area. The capacity for a voluntary act is thus required for all torts. Second, the reasonable person standard of negligence is modified for a person's physical conditions and experience. Children are judged by the standard of care expectable for people of a similar age and experience. Third, liability is restricted to foreseeable harms. If a reasonable person would have lacked the capacity to foresee harms, one cannot be negligent with respect to them. We also considered in some detail (5.2.7) how foreseeability underlies products liability. In short, one is not held liable if one lacked the capacity for a voluntary act, people with one's physical conditions and experience would have lacked capacity, or the risks of harm were not foreseeable so a reasonable person would have lacked capacity to avoid the harm.

It might be objectèd that even these elements are lacking in vicarious liability. A person held vicariously liable does not act. Thus, the voluntary act and causal-responsibility requirements do not apply. Moreover, the person's physical conditions and experience are not relevant, and the harms need not be foreseeable by a reasonable person in the defendant's position. Note, however, that although these charges are correct as applied to the person held vicariously liable, they often do not apply to the employee or other person for whose conduct a person is held vicariously liable. In short, capacity- and causal-responsibility are usually required for there to be tort liability, but they are less frequently conditions of the person who has to pay.

This point suggests a better way to view vicarious liability that makes it much like contractual liability. By our principle (5-8), one should be vicariously liable for another's conduct only if it is in furtherance of one's activities. As in contract, one stands to gain and has some choice about the activity. One can foresee that harms might result from the activity. Thus, one might be said to assume the risk much as one does in some contracts. The primary justification for vicarious liability is to help ensure compensation to victims, and the vicariously liable person in effect has the role of an insurer. Viewed in this perspective, people who are vicariously liable have as much capacity-responsibility as writers of liability insurance.

The criminal law recognizes the value of responsibility more than any other field. First, causal-responsibility underlies all crimes. Completed crimes either involve causing a condition deemed harmful or the act itself constitutes harm. Accomplice liability involves helping or trying to help another cause harm. The inchoate crimes of attempt, solicitation, and conspiracy involve the risk and purpose of bringing about harms. Second, one is not criminally liable if one lacks capacity-responsibility. A number of principles develop the requirement of capacity-responsibility: those of innocence (6-1), voluntary conduct (6-6), culpability (6-8), reasonable opportunity (6-13), and mental abnormality (6-14). Moreover, children are exempt from criminal liability. Our only weakening of the requirement of capacity-responsibility was in not extending the principle of intoxication (6-15) beyond negating a voluntary act or mens rea.

There are two main reasons why the value of responsibility receives greatest recognition in criminal law. First, the usual sanction – deprivation of freedom – is normally more severe than in other fields, although in specific cases payment of damages can have a more detrimental effect on a defendant's life than a short period of imprisonment. The second reason stems from the denunciatory aspect of punishment. Contractual and tort liability do not have the condemnatory connotation associated with criminal liability. A lawyer once told me that he had trouble settling a contract dispute, because his client refused to admit that he had "defaulted" on the contract. The client insisted that he had never defaulted on a contract. Finally, the lawyer explained that 'default' meant only that he 'had not done what he promised', that he had not delivered on time. The client immediately agreed that he had not and settled. This client thought that 'default' implies moral wrongdoing; he wanted to protect his reputation as a fair and honest businessman, the late delivery being due to factors beyond his control. This condemnatory connotation is not a normal part of contractual or even tort liability, but it is of criminal liability. Consequently, one would not accept being held criminally liable unless one had capacity-responsibility.

EQUALITY AND FAIRNESS

7.4. We analyzed equality and fairness as involving two factors – a fair distribution of burdens and equality of opportunity (1.3). Although equality of burdens and opportunity are presumed, they can be overridden by considerations indicating that a difference in treatment is appropriate. Our method of analysis largely guarantees recognition of equality in the acceptable principles. As principles are to be used in all cases to which they are relevant (1.4), they cannot be biased for particular situations or persons. More importantly, as we assumed that one might be either party to a case and used the general probability of being one or the other party (1.2), equal consideration has been given to all the persons involved. Nonetheless, it is worthwhile briefly noting particular features of principles expressing and promoting equality and fairness.

In procedural law, the principle of fairness (2-6) directly addresses unfair opportunities or burdens. It includes particular elements essential to equality of opportunity – a neutral judge, a hearing in which both sides can present evidence, and an opportunity to know and respond to the other's presentation. The principle of discovery (2-14) is designed to provide equal opportunities to obtain information and to avoid unfair surprise. The principle of burden of proof (2-16) recognizes unfairness as a basis for shifting the burden of production and unfair burdens (moral costs) as a reason for a higher standard of persuasion. The principle of jurisdiction (2-10(b)(ii)) explicitly limits jurisdiction if it would impose an unfair burden. The principle of notice (2-11) provides an essential factor for an equal opportunity to be heard. Finally, the principle of legal assistance (2-12) helps provide an equal opportunity to present one's position, at least in cases importantly affecting one.

In property law, the fair distribution of burdens is explicitly recognized in the principle of social burdens (3-7). It is also expressed in the principle of takings (3-15), which supports compensation to the extent people have been singled out for burdens. Equality of opportunity is indirectly recognized in principles for acquiring property; no restrictions are placed on who can obtain property by these means. The principles of labor (3-6) and intellectual property (3-10) respect the fruitful efforts of everyone. Similarly, the principle of first possession (3-5) recognizes equality. "First come, first served" is a commonsense principle providing equal opportunity; it denies privileges based on social rank or wealth. First possession was also prominent in our analysis of lost property (3.4.1). The only exceptions arise for the rights of owners of land on which property is found, but we carefully limited their claims to situations in which a finder had at least implicitly agreed to these rights by employment or was criminally on the property. In the latter case, the culpability of the criminal trespasser supports a difference in treatment.

Perhaps the most important principle recognizing the equality of persons in contract law is that of good faith (4-17). It broadly prohibits taking unfair advantage of others or depriving them of fair opportunities. An element of equality of opportunity is imported by the principle of required conditions (4-12). It prevents taking unfair advantage of another's lack of opportunities by requiring those minimal conditions that a party that had other opportunities would demand. It does not require that the opportunities be equal, for then there would be no reason to prefer one offer over another. The principle of rescission (4-18(b)) allocates any net losses equally between parties. An alternative is to let losses lie where they fall, but this would arbitrarily impose burdens on one party. Finally, the principle of illegal contracts (4-16(c)) requires distribution of losses on the basis of culpability; it does not let losses of illegal contracts unfairly fall on innocent parties as opposed to culpable ones.

Two principles particularly express equality and fairness in tort law. The abolition of immunities (5-15) denies special advantages to certain tortfeasors. All actors are equally liable for their torts. Similarly, the principle of apportionment (5-13) places all parties on an equal footing and fairly distributes burdens on the basis of culpability. By abolishing contributory negligence, it prevents an unjustifiable burden being placed on one party.

In criminal law, three principles help prevent an unfair distribution of burdens. The principle of innocence (6-1) is perhaps the most fundamental legal principle against unfair burdens. Admittedly, some innocent persons have been and will be punished, but the aim is to avoid this. Similarly, the principles of proportionality (6-3) and individualization of punishment (6-17), like the principle of apportionment, are designed to treat people differently on the basis of differences in culpability, the wrong done, and other mitigating and aggravating factors. Two principles of criminal law also especially provide equality of opportunity to avoid the burdens of punishment. The principle of reasonable opportunity (6-13) is directly concerned with this. The principle of certainty (6-9) also helps each person to know what conduct is prohibited and thus to have an equal opportunity to avoid criminal acts and punishment.

Social Good

7.5. An objection might be raised to the foregoing account of freedom, responsibility, and equality in the legal fields we have considered. In its most general form, the objection is that our normative principles and the extant law are individualistically oriented. They ignore the social, common, or collective good. The equality we have discussed is largely formal. Even with procedural equality, wealthier parties have many advantages over poorer ones (see 2.2). Although the principle of legal assistance (2-12) is of some benefit, the entire scheme gives too little consideration to the poor and the social good. Similarly, the analysis of freedom ignores the importance of extra-legal social conditions; unless one has property, the freedom to dispose of one's property is of little value. The legal fields developed along with individualism in Western thought, so it is not surprising to see a strong individualistic emphasis in them. Nevertheless, an historical explanation does not normatively justify them.

In part, this objection is misdirected against these common-law fields and our principles for them. It asks of the courts, especially in those fields, something they are institutionally incapable of providing. As we have explained in various places (1.4 and 2.3.9), courts are institutionally constrained. They do not have the powers of legislatures to raise funds and to create sweeping administrative schemes. They are limited to disputes brought to them by parties. To ask them to abolish poverty and to promote social equality is to ask something they lack the general authority and means to do (see also Levin and McDowell 1983, 77 (limit to contract law)). The institutional contraints of adjudication generally prevent it being a powerful engine for such social reform.

Property, contract, and tort law are not the primary legal fields in which to address these problems. Instead, social welfare legislation is needed – social security, job training, unemployment insurance, low cost housing, and anti-pollution, anti-discrimination, and antitrust laws. Once such legislation is in place, courts can often effectively enforce it. But the fields of law involved are then administrative law, environmental law, and so on. We recognized these concerns for the social good implicitly and the limits of the common-law fields explicitly in considering the inadequacies of tort law in providing compensation and preventing injury (5.5.1).

Nonetheless, the historical common law failed to consider the social good even to the limited extent it might have. Some recent developments in law and some of our principles provide a greater recognition of the social good. The principle of notice (2-11) can be of considerable assistance to poor people in defending against unjust repossession of goods bought on time, although as we have seen (2.3.2), the U. S. Supreme Court has not clearly developed an acceptable principle for such cases. The principle of legal assistance (2-12) would provide some help to poor persons. The implied warranties of habitability and workmanlike construction incorporated in our principle of leases (3-12) address the problems of the poor. Similarly, the principle of required conditions (4-12) addresses problems of unconscionability and contracts of adhesion that probably affect the poor more than the middle and upper classes. Likewise, the development of products liability (5-10) and the aims of economic deterrence (5-2) and compensation (5-3) address prevention of, and compensation for, injury. Many people become poor as a result of disability resulting from injury. The aim of preventing criminal acts (6-2) can benefit the poor and deprived. Even though people imprisoned in the United States are disproportionately poor and black, so are the victims of many kinds of crime. "Crime in the streets" is greater in poor neighborhoods than middle class ones.

Yet, one might say, poverty is not the only element of the social good. There are various other matters. Again, however, many of these are not directly matters for the legal fields we have considered or effectively addressed in the first instance by adjudication. Even so, a few principles have addressed them or made room for other principles and laws that do. The principle of public limits on property (3-14) restricts the rights of individual property owners for public purposes – the social good. The principle of takings (3-15) assists in two different ways. First, it implicitly permits the taking of property for public purposes. Second, it requires that compensation be given to those most seriously harmed. In the construction of freeways, housing projects, and dams, the persons whose property is taken are often poor. In contract law, the principle of the collective good (4-2) directly limits enforcement of contracts by policies for the collective or social good. An important recognition of this aim is in the principle of illegal contracts (4-16). Many cases that come under this principle involve contracts that violate laws and regulations designed for the social good, such as minimum wage and antitrust laws.

Thus, it is not true that the major common-law fields or our principles ignore the social good. They do recognize that value, but the recognition is limited by the institutional nature of courts and adjudication. These institutional constraints require that justification of principles for these fields must largely rest on individualistic considerations. In this respect, in light of the arguments presented for them and their relation to the values of freedom, responsibility, equality, and even social good, the principles adumbrated merit one's rational acceptance.

APPENDIX:
SUMMARY OF PRINCIPLES

PROCEDURE

2–1.   The principle of economic costs: one should minimize the economic costs of legal procedures.

2–2.   The principle of moral costs: one should minimize the moral costs of legal procedures.

2–3.   The principle of peacefulness: procedures should be peaceful.

2–4.   The principle of voluntariness: people should be able voluntarily to have their disputes legally resolved.

2–5.   The principle of participation: parties should be able to participate meaningfully in the legal resolution of disputes.

2–6.   The principle of fairness: procedures should be fair – treat the parties equally.

2–7.   The principle of intelligibility: procedures should be intelligible to the parties.

2–8.   The principle of timeliness: procedures should provide timely decisions.

2–9.   The principle of repose: a final resolution of the dispute should be made.

2–10. The principle of jurisdiction: persons should be capable of being sued (a) where they are or normally reside; (b) where they conduct ongoing activity if (i) the event or transaction in question occurred there and was related to the activity or (ii) the activity is so extensive that defense there would not be an unfair burden; and (c) where the event or transaction occurred if the plaintiff resides there.

2–11. The principle of notice: defendants should personally receive a statement of the complaint with adequate time to prepare a reply and make an appearance.

2–12. The principle of legal assistance: persons should be allowed legal counsel, and persons who cannot afford to pay should be provided legal counsel at public expense for important legal problems.

2–13. The principle of case scope: insofar as feasible, all claims and parties involving the same questions of fact or law should be considered in one case, and other claims involving the same parties should be permitted.

2–14. The principle of discovery: discovery of all matters directly related to claims and defenses in the case, except for privileged and private matters not admissible at trial, should be allowed.

2–15. The principle of evidence: evidence should be excluded if, and only if, it would be misleading or waste time.

2–16. The principle of the burden of proof: (a) the burden of production should rest on the party that raises an issue unless it would be unfair because of another party's special access to and control of the evidence, and (b) the burden of persuasion should rest on the same party and be the preponderance of the evidence unless a higher standard is needed to avoid greater moral error costs by decisions adverse to the other party in such cases.

2–17. The principle of jury trial: a right of jury trial with unanimous verdicts for conviction should exist in criminal cases.

2–18. The principle of stare decisis: courts should follow precedents.

2–19. The principle of appeals: appeals as of right should be available in criminal cases, and unless appellate courts have access to facts comparable to that of the trier, reversal on factual grounds should be limited to clearly erroneous findings.

PROPERTY

3–1. The principle of universality: all resources should be owned by determinate persons or it should be clear how determinate persons can acquire ownership of them.

3–2. The principle of exclusivity: ownership should be exclusive to the extent compatible with similar exclusivity of others' property.

3–3. The principle of transferability: (a) property should be voluntarily transferable from one person to another, and (b) involuntary transfers should not be allowed.

3–4. The principle of stability: legal ownership and possession should be stable.

3–5. The principle of first possession: ownership should be that of the first possessor of unpossessed property.

3–6. The principle of labor: people should be entitled to a significant proportion of property that, without obligation to others, they produce, make, or create.

3–7. The principle of social burdens: no grossly unequal burden should be imposed on a person for the production of collective benefits.

3–8. The principle of freedom: persons should be presumed to be free, compatible with a like freedom of others, to use, retain, and dispose of their property as they desire, the presumption being stronger the more property is self-expressive or identifying.

3–9. The principle of legal titles: the forms of legal title to land should be few in number and make transfer easy.

3–10. The principle of intellectual property: one should have ownership for a limited time of new processes and results produced by the use of laws of science and logic but not to the laws themselves.

3–11. The principle of the good faith purchaser: a bona fide purchaser for value without notice should be entitled to property against all previous owners.

3–12. The principle of leases: leases and contracts for construction of buildings should be treated like other contemporary contracts.

3–13. The principle of private limits: easements and covenants for private purposes should be construed to include only what is necessary for their purpose and should be implied or taken to run with the land only where necessary for the reasonable use of property.

3–14. The principle of public limits: reasonable restrictions to preserve or promote public purposes including ambience are acceptable provided alternatives are reasonably available.

3–15. The principle of takings: whether compensation is due depends on the extent to which individual property is singled out, owners had no reason to expect limitations when the property was acquired, and property rights are curtailed.

3–16. The principle of stale claims: after a reasonable time, claims of title against a possessor or user of property should be void, unless proper notice is given of the continuance of the claim.

3–17. The principle of present gratuitous disposition: people should be able, without a return benefit, presently to dispose of property voluntarily to anyone or no one as the owner and recipient (if any) desire, subject only to conditions necessary to establish that it was such.

3–18. The principle of succession: except for adequate provision for dependent children, people should be able by clear writing to dispose of their property to others after death as they desire; and if no such disposition is made, it should pass as the average person would desire.

CONTRACT

4–1. The principle of enforceable commitments: commitments to future transfers of property or services should be supported and enforced (a) in mutually expected beneficial plus sum interactions, and (b) in zero sum interactions if (i) it is necessary to prevent loss due to reasonable reliance by intended beneficiaries or (ii) donors indicate they are enforceable.

4–2. The principle of collective good: enforcement of commitments should be limited by social policies for the collective good.

4–3. The principle of consideration: consideration should be treated as evidence that an interaction is mutually expected to be beneficial and thus as providing a reason to enforce a commitment.

4–4. The principle of past benefits: a commitment made in recognition of a previously received benefit should be enforceable unless a reasonable person in the promisor's position could not view it as reciprocity for the benefit.

4–5. The principle of reliance: a commitment should be enforceable to the extent necessary to prevent loss due to foreseeable reliance.

4–6. The principle of gratuitous commitments: a written and notarized commitment, stating that it is to be legally binding, should be enforceable, without consideration, past benefit, or reliance, to the extent appropriate in view of any changed circumstances.

4–7. The principle of modifications: good faith modifications of contracts regardless of consideration, past benefit, or reliance should be enforceable.

4–8. The principle of offers: offers should involve the communication of a reasonably definite commitment in return for a reasonably definite act or commitment.

4–9. The principle of acceptances: acceptances should take effect when sent to offerors provided that if they are expressly conditional on changes, (a) the changes are reasonable and (b) offerors have a reasonable time to object to them.

4–10.   The principle of conditions and warranties: if a reasonable person in the promisee's position at the time of contracting would not have agreed to fulfill duties rather than adjust them if a given term was not fulfilled, then it should be a condition; otherwise it should be a warranty.

4–11.   The principle of implied terms: in the absence of clear evidence parties intended otherwise, if necessary to settle a case, terms to which reasonable people in the parties' positions would agree should be implied.

4–12.   The principle of required conditions: if one party has no reasonable opportunity to choose, the minimal contractual conditions to which rational persons would agree were there reasonable alternatives should be required by law and the parties prohibited from changing them unless they can show that it is to the advantage of both to do so.

4–13.   The principle of mistake: a contract should not be enforceable against a party who has made an innocent and substantial mistake of fact if either (a) that party has not assumed the risk of the mistake or (b) the other party knew or should have known of the mistake.

4–14.   The principle of contractual incapacity: a contract should not be enforceable against a person who, at the time of contracting, lacked capacity to make a reasonable choice to contract.

4–15.   The principle of a written memorandum: a written memorandum of a contract authenticated by the party against whom it is enforced may be required for contracts of significant value.

4–16.   The principle of illegal contracts: if a purported contract or its performance is contrary to a law, regulation, or judicially recognized public policy necessary for a collective good, then (a) it should be modified so as not to be contrary to the policy; (b) if that is not possible, the parties should be restored to their positions prior to the contract; and (c) if (b) is not possible, any losses from nonenforcement of the contract should be divided between them in proportion to their respective culpability.

4–17.   The principle of good faith: contract law should require conduct necessary for the minimal trust rational people need to interact with a reasonable prospect of it being mutually beneficial.

4–18.   The principle of rescission: when contracts are void, voided, or rescinded, (a) parties should be restored to the position they were in prior to the interaction; and (b) if there is a net loss not allocable on the basis of other principles, it should be split between them.

4–19. The principle of contract damages: if the contractual commitments of a party are not fulfilled, that party should place the other party in the position he or she would have been in had the contract been fully performed insofar as the other party's failure to be in that position is the foreseeable result of the commitments' nonfulfillment.

4–20. The principle of specific performance: specific performance should not be ordered unless damages would be inadequate and courts can easily supervise performance.

TORT

5–1. The principle of civil retribution: ethically culpable wrongdoers should make reparations to their victims.

5–2. The principle of economic deterrence: uneconomical harm should be deterred by imposing liability on the cheapest risk avoiders.

5–3. The principle of compensation: people should be compensated for their losses by those whose activities produced the harms and who either could have conducted the activities without producing them or are able to spread the costs.

5–4. The principle of intentional torts: persons should be liable for intentional invasions of others' interests in (a) their person, including bodily integrity, freedom, and emotional tranquility; (b) property, including economic loss by deceit and legal actions not in good faith; (c) privacy; and (d) reputation.

5–5. The principle of care: persons should exercise the care that reasonable, prudent persons of their age, experience, and physical characteristics would exercise in the circumstances.

5–6. The principle of foreseeability: the duty of care should extend to, and only to, harms from foreseeable kinds of causes to foreseeable persons.

5–7. The principle of interests protected from negligence: the duty of care should primarily extend to interests in (a) physical and mental integrity; and (b) property, including economic loss resulting from reasonable reliance on a person's undertaking, special skill, or special knowledge.

5–8.   The principle of vicarious liability: persons should be liable for the torts committed in furtherance of their activities by their employees and agents, and by people engaged with them in joint enterprises.

5–9.   The principle of abnormally dangerous activities: persons should be strictly liable for physical harm if it results from a type of cause making their activities abnormally dangerous.

5–10.   The principle of products liability: persons who manufacture or modify and sell defective products should be liable for physical harm from the foreseeable reasonable use of the products caused by the defects.

5–11.   The principle of consent: persons should not be liable for harms caused to people who knowingly and voluntarily consent to the risks of the harms.

5–12.   The principle of causation: persons should be liable for all foreseeable harm that occurred because an aspect of their conduct contrary to duty was a necessary element of a set of conditions jointly sufficient to bring about the harm.

5–13.   The principle of apportionment: parties should ultimately be liable for damages in proportion to their responsibility for the harm.

5–14.   The principle of occupiers: for purposes of assessing their liability to entrants on their land, occupiers of real property should be treated the same as other actors.

5–15.   The principle of immunities: no general immunity should be recognized.

5–16.   The principle of tort damages: damages should include all a party's actual losses that constitute foreseeable harm.

5–17.   The principle of injunctions: injunctions should be granted whenever they can stop tortious conduct.

CRIMINAL

6–1.   The principle of innocence: a person innocent of a criminal act should not be punished for it.

6–2.   The principle of prevention: criminal acts should be prevented.

6–3.   The principle of proportionality: the severity of punishments should be proportional to the seriousness of crimes.

6–4.   The principle of reform: reform of offenders should be sought in sentencing and correctional programs.

6-5.. The principle of denunciation: a denunciatory effect in preventing criminal acts should be fostered.

6-6. The principle of voluntary conduct: only voluntary conduct should be criminal.

6-7. The principle of the least drastic alternative: if the net benefits of noncriminal control of conduct are equal to or greater than those of criminal control, then the noncriminal method should be used.

6-8. The principle of culpability: only purposeful, knowing, and reckless conduct should be criminal.

6-9. The principle of certainty: criminal laws should be simple, clear, and precise.

6-10. The principle of harm: criminal law should primarily prohibit conduct in which the risk and gravity of harm to others is greater than the harm (loss of liberty, privacy, and so on) of enforcement.

6-11. The principle of effectiveness: a criminal law should deal effectively with the problem.

6-12. The principle of inchoate offenses: inchoate offenses should involve the purpose to commit a substantive crime and should not be compounded.

6-13. The principle of reasonable opportunity: persons should not be criminally liable for acts if at the time of acting they lack a reasonable opportunity to conform to the law.

6-14. The principle of mental abnormality: persons should not be criminally liable if, at the time of acting, due to mental disease or defect, they lack the capacity to appreciate the wrongfulness of their conduct or to conform to the law.

6-15. The principle of intoxication: persons should not be criminally liable by reason of intoxication if, and only if, at the time of acting, intoxication negates a voluntary act or a mental element of the offense.

6-16. The principle of lesser evils: persons should not be criminally liable if (a) they reasonably believed that (i) their conduct might effectively avoid a greater harm, and (ii) no less drastic alternative was available; and (b) they acted to avoid the greater harm.

6-17. The principle of individualization of punishment: laws should permit, and judges should impose, individualized punishment within maximum and minimum limits for each crime.

6-18. The principle of lesser punishments: persons convicted as accessories or of inchoate offenses should receive lesser punishments than they would as principals for the substantive offenses.

WORKS CITED

Abraham, Henry J.: 1975. *The Judicial Process*. 3rd edn. New York: Oxford University Press.

Alexander, Lawrence: 1980. "The Doomsday Machine: Proportionality, Punishment and Prevention." *The Monist* 63: 65–93.

American Bar Association, Standing Committee on Association Standards for Criminal Justice: 1983. "Recommendations on the Insanity Defense." *Mental Disability Law Reporter* 7: 136–41.

—: 1984. *Proposed Criminal Justice Mental Health Standards*. Chicago: American Bar Association. The Standards but not the Commentary have been approved for incorporation and citation as Chapter 7, *ABA Standards for Criminal Justice* (2d Ed. 1980).

American Law Institute: 1962. *Model Penal Code: Proposed Official Draft*. Philadelphia: American Law Institute.

American Psychiatric Association: 1983. "Report on the Insanity Defense." *Mental Disability Law Reporter* 7: 141–47, 210–11.

Atiyah, P. S.: 1979. *The Rise and Fall of Freedom of Contract*. Oxford: Clarendon Press.

—: 1980. "No Fault Compensation: A Question That Will Not Go Away." *Tulane Law Review* 54: 271–93.

—: 1981a. *An Introduction to the Law of Contract*. 3rd edn. Oxford: Clarendon Press.

—. 1981b. *Promises, Morals, and Law*. Oxford: Clarendon Press.

—. 1983. *Law and Modern Society*. Oxford: Oxford University Press.

Bartlet, J. V., ed.: 1922. *Property: Its Duties and Rights*. 2d edn. New York: Macmillan Co.

Barton, John H.: 1979. "The Economic Basis of Damages for Breach of Contract." In *The Economics of Contract Law*, 154–67. See Kronman and Posner 1979.

Bayles, Michael D.: 1978. *Principles of Legislation*. Detroit: Wayne State University Press.

—: 1980. *Morality and Population Policy*. University, Ala.: University of Alabama Press.

—: 1981. *Professional Ethics*. Belmont, Calif.: Wadsworth Publishing Co.

—: 1982a. "Character, Purpose, and Criminal Responsibility." *Law and Philosophy* 1: 5–20.

—: 1982b. "Punishment for Attempts." *Social Theory and Practice* 8: 19–29.

—: 1984a. *Reproductive Ethics*. Englewood Cliffs, N.J.: Prentice-Hall.

—: 1984b. "Moral Theory and Application." *Social Theory and Practice* 10: 97–120.

—: 1984c. "Ethical Theory in the Twenty-First Century." *Southern Journal of Philosophy* 22: 439–51.

—: 1986. "Mid-Level Principles and Justification." In *Justification: Nomos XXVII*, ed. by J. Roland Pennock and John W. Chapman, 49–67. New York: New York University Press.

Bayles, Michael D., and Bruce Chapman, eds.: 1983. *Justice, Rights, and Tort Law*. Dordrecht: D. Reidel Publishing Co.

Bazelon, David L.: 1984. "The Dilemma of Criminal Responsibility." *Kentucky Law Journal* 72: 263–77.

Becker, Lawrence C.: 1977. *Property Rights*. Boston: Routledge & Kegan Paul.

—: 1980. "The Moral Basis of Property Rights." In *Property: Nomos XXII*, 187–220. *See* Pennock and Chapman 1980.

Bedau, Hugo Adam: 1985. "Classification-Based Sentencing: Some Conceptual and Ethical Problems." In *Criminal Justice: Nomos XXVII*, 89–118. *See* Pennock and Chapman 1985.

Benditt, Theodore M.: 1983. "Liability for Failing to Rescue." In *Justice, Rights, and Tort Law*, 211–38. See Bayles and Chapman 1983.

Bickenbach, Jerome E.: 1983. "In Defence of Necessity." *Canadian Journal of Philosophy* 13: 79–100.

Blum, Walter J., and Harry Kalven, Jr.: 1965. *Public Law Perspectives on a Private Law Problem*. Boston: Little, Brown and Co.

—: "Auto Accidents and General Deterrence." 1970. In *Law and Philosophy*, 224–53. *See* Kent 1970.

Bohlen, Francis H.: 1926. "Incomplete Privilege to Inflict Intentional Invasions of Interests of Property and Personality." *Harvard Law Review* 40: 307–24.

Brandt, Richard B.: 1979. *A Theory of the Good and the Right*. Oxford: Clarendon Press.

—: 1985. "A Motivational Theory of Excuses in the Criminal Law." In *Criminal Justice: Nomos XXVII*, 165–98. *See* Pennock and Chapman 1985.

Bronaugh, Richard N., ed.: 1978. *Philosophical Law*. Westport, Conn.: Greenwood Press.

—: 1983. "A Secret Paradox in the Law." *Law and Philosophy* 2: 193–232.

Calabresi, Guido: 1970a. *The Costs of Accidents*. New Haven: Yale University Press.

—: 1970b. "Fault, Accidents and the Wonderful World of Blum and Kalven." In *Law and Philosophy*, 204–23. *See* Kent 1970.

Calabresi, Guido, and A. Douglas Melamed: 1983. "Property Rules, Liability Rules, and Inalienability: One View of the Cathedral." In *Law, Economics, and Philosophy*, ed. by Mark Kuperberg and Charles Beitz, 41–80. Totowa, N.J.: Rowman & Allenheld.

Calamari, John D., and Joseph M. Perillo: 1977. *The Law of Contracts*. 2d edn. St. Paul, Minn.: West Publishing Co.

Canada: 1982. *The Criminal Law in Canadian Society*. Ottawa: Government of Canada.

Cane, Peter: 1982. "Justice and Justifications for Tort Liability." *Oxford Journal of Legal Studies* 2: 30–62.

Carrington, Paul D., and Barbara Allen Babcock: 1983. *Civil Procedure*. 3rd edn. Boston: Little, Brown and Co.

Casner, A. James, and W. Barton Leach: 1969. *Cases and Text on Property*. 2d edn. Boston: Little, Brown and Co.

Chapman, Bruce: 1983. "Ethical Issues in the Law of Tort." In *Justice, Rights, and Tort Law*, 13–43. See Bayles and Chapman 1983.

Chase, Edward, and E. Hunter Taylor, Jr.: 1985. "Landlord and Tenant: A Study in Property and Contract." *Villanova Law Review* 30: 571–699.

Chayes, Abram: 1979. "The Role of the Judge in Public Law Litigation." In *The Structure of Procedure*, 492–505. See Cover and Fiss 1979.

Chitty, Joseph: 1983. *Chitty on Contracts*. 2 vols. 25th edn. London: Sweet & Maxwell.

Christie, George C.: 1983. *Cases and Materials on the Law of Torts*. St. Paul, Minn.: West Publishing Co.

Clerk, John Frederic, and W. H. B. Lindsell: 1982. *Clerk & Lindsell on Torts*. Ed. R. W. M. Dias. London: Sweet & Maxwell.

374   WORKS CITED

Coleman, Jules L. 1975. "Justice and the Argument for No-Fault." *Social Theory and Practice* 3: 161–80.
—: 1983. "Moral Theories of Torts: Their Scope and Limits." Parts 1 and 2. In *Justice, Rights, and Tort Law*, 45–96. See Bayles and Chapman 1983.
Coons, John E.: 1979. "Compromise as Justice." In *Compromise in Ethics, Law, and Politics: Nomos XXI*, ed. J. Roland Pennock and John W. Chapman, 190–204. New York: New York University Press.
Cooter, Robert, and Melvin Aron Eisenberg: 1985. "Damages for Breach of Contract." *California Law Review* 73: 1432–81.
Corbin, Arthur Linton: 1952. *Corbin on Contracts*. One vol. edn. St. Paul, Minn.: West Publishing Co.
"Courts: A Major Battleground of Social Upheaval." 1984. *U.S. News & World Report*, 28 January, 48–50.
Cover, Robert M., and Owen M. Fiss, eds.: 1979. *The Structure of Procedure*. Mineola, N.Y.: Foundation Press.
Cribbet, John E., and Corwin W. Johnson: 1984. *Cases and Materials on Property*. 5th edn. Mineola, N.Y.: Foundation Press.
Cunningham, Robert A., William B. Stoebuck, and Dale A. Whitman: 1984. *The Law of Property*. St. Paul, Minn.: West Publishing Co.
Damaška, Mirjan: 1979. "Structures of Authority and Comparative Criminal Procedure." In *The Structure of Procedure*, 292–306. See Cover and Fiss 1979.
Davies, F. R.: 1977. *Contract*. 3rd edn. London: Sweet & Maxwell.
Davis, Michael: 1984. "Setting Penalties: What Does Rape Deserve?" *Law and Philosophy* 3: 61–110.
—: 1985. "How to Make the Punishment Fit the Crime." In *Criminal Justice: Nomos XXVII*, 119–55. See Pennock and Chapman 1985.
Donahue, Charles, Jr.: 1980. "The Future of the Concept of Property Predicted from Its Past." In *Property: Nomos XXII*, 28–68. See Pennock and Chapman 1980.
"Drunken Driving Laws Are Made Stricter." 1986. *Gainesville Sun*, 20 June, 3C.
Dworkin, Ronald: 1977. *Taking Rights Seriously*. Cambridge: Harvard University Press.
—: 1985. *A Matter of Principle*. Cambridge: Harvard University Press.
Eisenberg, Melvin A.: 1979. "Donative Promises." *University of Chicago Law Review* 47: 1–33.
—: 1982. "The Principles of Consideration." *Cornell Law Review* 67: 640–65.
Epstein, Richard A. 1979a. "Possession as the Root of Title." *Georgia Law Review* 13: 1221–43.
—: 1979b. "Unconscionability: A Critical Appraisal." In *The Economics of Contract Law*, 93–100. See Kronman and Posner 1979.
—: 1980a. *A Theory of Strict Liability*. San Francisco: Cato Institute.
—: 1980b. "Automobile No-Fault Plans: A Second Look at First Principles." *Creighton Law Review* 13: 769–93.
—: 1982. "Private Property and the Public Domain: The Case of Antitrust." In *Ethics, Economics, and the Law*, 48–82. See Pennock and Chapman 1982.
—: 1985. *Takings*. Cambridge: Harvard University Press.
Feinberg, Joel: 1973. *Social Philosophy*. Englewood Cliffs, N. J.: Prentice-Hall, Inc.
—: 1984. *Harm to Others*. Vol. 1, *The Moral Limits of the Criminal Law*. New York: Oxford University Press.
—: 1985. *Offense to Others*. Vol. 2, *The Moral Limits of the Criminal Law*. New York: Oxford University Press.

—: 1986. "Sua Culpa." In *Philosophy of Law*, 512–27. *See* Feinberg and Gross.

Feinberg, Joel, and Hyman Gross, eds.: 1986. *Philosophy of Law*. 3rd edn. Belmont, Calif.: Wadsworth Publishing Co.

Fentiman, Linda C.: 1985. "'Guilty But Mentally Ill': The Real Verdict Is Guilty." *Boston College Law Review* 26: 601–53.

Fingarette, Herbert: 1972. *The Meaning of Criminal Insanity*. Berkeley and Los Angeles: University of California Press.

—, and Ann Fingarette Hassee: 1979. *Mental Disabilities and Criminal Responsibility*. Berkeley and Los Angeles: University of California Press.

Fleming, John G.: 1968. *An Introduction to the Law of Torts*. Oxford: Clarendon Press.

Fletcher, George P.: 1978. *Rethinking Criminal Law*. Boston: Little, Brown and Co.

—: 1983. "The Search for Synthesis in Tort Theory." In *Justice, Rights, and Tort Law*, 97–122. *See* Bayles and Chapman 1983.

Flew, Antony: 1969. "The Justification of Punishment." In *The Philosophy of Punishment*, ed. H. B. Acton, 83–104. London: Macmillan and Co.

Frankel, Marvin E.: 1977. "The Search for Truth: An Umpireal View." In *1977 National Conference on Teaching Professional Responsibility*, ed. Stuart C. Goldberg, 177–205. Detroit: University of Detroit School of Law.

—: 1980. *Partisan Justice*. New York: Hill and Wang.

Fridman, G. H.: 1976. *The Law of Contract in Canada*. Toronto: Carswell Company Ltd.

—: 1978. *Introduction to the Law of Torts*. Toronto: Butterworths.

—: 1983. "On the Nature of Contract." *Valparaiso University Law Review* 17: 627–54.

Fried, Charles: 1981. *Contract as Promise*. Cambridge: Harvard University Press.

Frey, R. G., ed.: 1984. *Utility and Rights*. Minneapolis: University of Minnesota Press.

Fuller, Lon L.: 1941. "Consideration and Form." *Columbia Law Review* 41: 799–824.

—: 1978. "The Forms and Limits of Adjudication." *Harvard Law Review* 92: 353–409.

Fuller, Lon L., and Melvin A. Eisenberg: 1981. *Basic Contract Law*. 4th edn. St. Paul, Minn.: West Publishing Co.

Fuller, Lon L., and William R. Perdue, Jr.: 1936–37. "The Reliance Interest in Contract Damages." Parts 1 and 2. *Yale Law Journal* 46: 52–96, 373–420.

Galanter, Marc: 1979. "Why the 'Haves' Come Out Ahead." In *The Structure of Procedure*, 199–211. *See* Cover and Fiss 1979.

Galligan, D. J.: 1981. "The Return to Retribution in Penal Theory." In *Crime, Proof and Punishment*, 144–71. *See* Tapper 1981.

Gelin, Jacques B., and David W. Miller: 1982. *The Federal Law of Eminent Domain*. Charlottesville, Va.: Michie Co.

Gilmore, Grant. 1974. *The Death of Contract*. Columbus, Ohio: Ohio State University Press.

Glasbeek, H. J., and R. A. Hasson: 1977. "Fault – the Great Hoax." In *Studies in Canadian Tort Law*, 395–424. *See* Klar 1980.

Goetz, Charles J., and Robert E. Scott: 1979. "Liquidated Damages, Penalties and the Just Compensation Principle: Some Notes on an Enforcement Model and a Theory of Efficient Breach." In *The Economics of Contract Law*, 194–207. *See* Kronman and Posner 1979.

—: 1980. "Enforcing Promises: An Examination of the Basis of Contract." *Yale Law Journal* 89: 1261–1322.

Golding, Martin P.: 1975. *Philosophy of Law*. Englewood Cliffs, N.J.: Prentice-Hall, 1975.

—: 1978. "On the Adversary System and Justice." In *Philosophical Law*, 98–121. *See* Bronaugh 1978.

Goldman, Alan H.: 1979. "The Paradox of Punishment." *Philosophy & Public Affairs* 9: 42–58.

Gorsky, Morley R.: 1978. "The Adversary System." In *Philosophical Law*, 127–38. *See* Bronaugh 1978.

Great Britain, Royal Commission on Civil Liability and Compensation for Personal Injury: 1978. *Report*. 3 vols. London: Her Majesty's Stationery Office.

Gross, Hyman: 1979. *A Theory of Criminal Justice*. New York: Oxford University Press.

Guest, A. G., ed.: 1961. *Oxford Essays in Jurisprudence (First Series)*. Oxford: Clarendon Press.

Hall, Jerome: 1960. *General Principles of Criminal Law*. 2d edn. Indianapolis: Bobbs-Merrill Co. '

Hardin, Garrett: 1976. "The Tragedy of the Commons." In *Ethics and Population*, ed. Michael D. Bayles, 3–18. Cambridge, Mass.: Schenkman Publishing Co.

Harris, D. R.: 1961. "The Concept of Possession in English Law." In *Oxford Essays in Jurisprudence (First Series)*, 69–106. *See* Guest 1961.

Harris, D. R., Anthony Ogus, and Jennifer Phillips: 1979. "Contract Remedies and the Consumer Surplus." *Law Quarterly Review* 95: 581–91.

Hart, H. L. A.: 1968. *Punishment and Responsibility*. Oxford: Clarendon Press.

—: 1983. *Essays in Jurisprudence and Philosophy*. Oxford: Clarendon Press.

Haslett, D. W.: 1986. "Is Inheritance Justified?" *Philosophy & Public Affairs* 15: 122–55.

Henderson, Stanley D.: 1971. "Promises Grounded in the Past: The Idea of Unjust Enrichment and the Law of Contracts." *Virginia Law Review* 57: 1115–84.

Hillman, Robert A.: 1982. "Contract Modification Under the Restatement (Second) of Contracts." *Cornell Law Review* 67: 680–703.

Hobhouse, L. T.: 1922. "The Historical Evolution of Property, in Fact and in Idea." In *Property: Its Duties and Rights*, 1–33. *See* Bartlet 1922.

Hohfeld, Wesley Newcomb: 1946. *Fundamental Legal Conceptions as Applied in Judicial Reasoning*. Ed. Walter Wheeler Cook. New Haven: Yale University Press.

Holmes, Oliver Wendell: 1963. *The Common Law*. Ed. Mark DeWolfe Howe. Original edn. 1881. Boston: Little, Brown and Co.

"Home Razing Fulfils Wish of Spinster." 1984. *The London Free Press* (Canada), 10 August, C3.

Honoré, A. M.: 1961. "Ownership." In *Oxford Essays in Jurisprudence (First Series)*, 107–47. *See* Guest 1961.

Jones, David A.: 1981. *The Law of Criminal Procedure*. Boston: Little, Brown and Co.

Kalven, Harry, Jr., and Hans Zeisel: 1971. *The American Jury*. Chicago: University of Chicago Press.

Kant, Immanuel: 1965. *The Metaphysical Elements of Justice*. Trans. by John Ladd. Original German edn. 1797. Indianapolis: Bobbs-Merrill Co.

Keeton, Robert E.: 1959. "Conditional Fault in the Law of Torts." *Harvard Law Review* 72: 401–44.

—: 1986. "The Basic Rule of Legal Cause in Negligence." In *Philosophy of Law*, 496–503. *See* Feinberg and Gross 1986.

Keeton, W. Page, Dan B. Dobbs, Robert E. Keeton, and David G. Owen: 1984. *Prosser and Keeton on the Law of Torts*. Ed. by W. Page Keeton. 5th edn. St. Paul, Minn.: West Publishing Co.

Keeton, W. Page, and Robert E. Keeton: 1971. *Cases and Materials on the Law of Torts*. St. Paul, Minn.: West Publishing Co.

Kennedy, Duncan: 1982. "Distributive and Paternalist Motives in Contract and Tort Law, with Special Reference to Compulsory Terms and Unequal Bargaining Power." *Maryland Law Review* 41: 563–658.

Kenny, Anthony: 1982. "Duress *per Minas* as a Defence to Crime: II." *Law and Philosophy* 1: 197–205.

Kent, Edward Allen, ed.: 1970. *Law and Philosophy*. New York: Appleton-Century-Crofts.

Kilbrandon, Lord: 1982. "Duress *per Minas* as a Defence to Crime: I." *Law and Philosophy* 1: 185–95.

Klar, Lewis N., ed.: 1977. *Studies in Canadian Tort Law*. Toronto: Butterworths.

Kronman, Anthony T.: 1978a. "Mistake, Disclosure, Information, and the Law of Contracts." *Journal of Legal Studies* 7: 1–34.

—: 1978b. "Specific Performance." *University of Chicago Law Review* 45: 351–75.

—: 1980. Contract Law and Distributive Justice." *Yale Law Journal* 89: 472–511.

Kronman, Anthony T., and Richard A. Posner, eds.: 1979. *The Economics of Contract Law*. Boston: Little, Brown and Co.

LaFave, Wayne R., and Austin W. Scott: 1972. *Handbook on Criminal Law*. St. Paul, Minn.: West Publishing Co.

"Lawmakers Pass Budget, Agree on Liability Package." 1986. *Gainesville Sun*, 7 June, 1A, 16A.

Law Reform Commission of Canada: 1974. "The Meaning of Guilt." In *Studies in Strict Liability*. Ottawa: Information Canada.

—: 1977. *Criminal Law: Theft and Fraud*. Working Paper 19. Ottawa: Law Reform Commission of Canada.

—: 1979a. *Our Criminal Law*. Ottawa: Law Reform Commission of Canada.

—: 1979b. *Report: Theft and Fraud*. Ottawa: Law Reform Commission of Canada.

—: 1980. *The Jury in Criminal Trials*. Working Paper 27. Ottawa: Law Reform Commission of Canada.

—: 1982. *Criminal Law, the General Part*. Working Paper 29. Ottawa: Law Reform Commission of Canada.

—: 1984. *Homicide*. Working Paper 33. Ottawa: Law Reform Commission of Canada.

Lawson, F. H.: 1958. *Introduction to the Law of Property*. Oxford: Clarendon Press.

Leach, W. Barton: 1952. "Perpetuities in Perspective: Ending the Rule's Reign of Terror." *Harvard Law Review* 65: 721–49.

Leff, Arthur: 1967. "Unconscionability and the Code – the Emperor's New Clause." *University of Pennsylvania Law Review* 115: 485–559.

Levin, Joel, and Banks McDowell: 1983. "The Balance Theory of Contracts: Seeking Justice in Voluntary Obligations." *McGill Law Journal* 29: 24–87.

Linden, Allen M.: 1977a. *Canadian Tort Law*. Toronto: Butterworths.

—: 1977b. "Whatever Happened to Rylands v. Fletcher?" In *Studies in Canadian Tort Law*, 325–41. *See* Klar 1977.

Lindsay, A. D.: 1922. "The Principle of Private Property." In *Property: Its Duties and Rights*. *See* Bartlet 1922.

Luntz, Harold: 1975. *Compensation and Rehabilitation*. Melbourne: Butterworths.

Lyons, David: 1973. "On Formal Justice." *Cornell Law Review* 58: 833–61.

—: 1985. "Formal Justice and Judicial Precedent." *Vanderbilt Law Review* 38: 495–512.

Mackey, David S.: 1984. "Rationality Versus Proportionality: Reconsidering the Constitutional Limits on Criminal Sanctions." *Tennessee Law Review* 51: 623–79.

Macneil, Ian R.: 1980. *The New Social Contract*. New Haven and London: Yale University Press.

Mashaw, Jerry L.: 1981. "Administrative Due Process: The Quest for a Dignitary Theory." *Boston University Law Review* 61: 885–931.

Megarry, Robert, and H. W. R. Wade: 1975. *The Law of Real Property*. 4th edn. London: Stevens & Sons.

Mermin, Samuel: 1973. *Law and the Legal System – An Introduction*. Boston: Little, Brown and Co.

Michelman, Frank I.: 1967. "Property, Utility, and Fairness: Comments on the Ethical Foundations of 'Just Compensation' Law." *Harvard Law Review* 80: 1165–1258.

—: 1982. "Ethics, Economics, and the Law of Property." In *Ethics, Economics, and the Law: Nomos XXIV*, 3–40. See Pennock and Chapman 1982.

Morris, J. H. C., and W. Barton Leach: 1962. *The Rule Against Perpetuities*. 2d edn. London: Stevens & Sons.

Morris, Norval: 1982. *Madness and the Criminal Law*. Chicago: University of Chigao Press.

National Commission on the Insanity Defense: 1983. *Myths and Realities*. Arlington, Va.: National Mental Health Association.

New Zealand, Royal Commission of Inquiry: 1967. *Compensation for Personal Injury in New Zealand*. Wellington: R. E. Owen, Government Printer.

Nocenti, David M.: 1983. "Complex Jury Trials, Due Process, and the Doctrine of Unconstitutional Complexity." *Columbia Journal of Law and Social Problems* 18: 1–38.

Note: 1983. "Guilty But Mentally Ill: A Critical Analysis." *Rutgers Law Journal* 14: 453–77.

Packer, Herbert L.: 1968. *The Limits of the Criminal Sanction*. Standord, Calif.: Stanford University Press.

Paton, George Whitecross: 1964. *A Text-Book of Jurisprudence*. 3rd edn. Ed. David P. Derham. Oxford: Clarendon Press.

Pennock, J. Roland, and John Chapman, eds.: 1980. *Property: Nomos XXII*. New York: New York University Press.

—: 1982. *Ethics, Economics, and the Law: Nomos XXIV*. New York: New York University Press.

—: 1985. *Criminal Justice: Nomos XXVII*. New York: New York University Press.

Posner, Richard A.: 1973. "An Economic Approach to Legal Procedure and Judicial Administration." *Journal of Legal Studies* 2: 399–458.

—: 1977. *Economic Analysis of Law*. 2d edn. Boston: Little, Brown and Co.

—: 1983. *The Economics of Justice*. Cambridge: Harvard University Press.

—: 1985. "An Economic Theory of the Criminal Law." *Columbia Law Review* 85: 1193–1231.

Posner, Richard A., and Andrew M. Rosenfield: 1977. "Impossibility and Related Doctrines in Contract Law: An Economic Analysis." *Journal of Legal Studies* 6: 83–118.

Prichard, J. Robert S., and Alan Brudner: 1983. "Tort Liability for Breach of Statute." In *Justice, Rights, and Tort Law*, 149–77. See Bayles and Chapman 1983.

Rabin, Robert L.: 1985. "Tort Recovery for Negligently Inflicted Economic Loss: A Reassessment." *Stanford Law Review* 37: 1513–38.

Radin, Margaret Jane: 1982. "Property and Personhood." *Stanford Law Review* 34: 957–1015.

Rashdall, Hastings: 1922. "The Philosophical Theory of Property." In *Property: Its Duties and Rights*, 35–68. *See* Bartlet 1922.

Rawls, John: 1971. *A Theory of Justice*. Cambridge: Harvard University Press.

Raz, Joseph: 1972. "Legal Principles and the Limits of Law." *Yale Law Journal* 81: 823–54.

"Reagan Proposal Makes Products Liability Suits Tougher." 1986. *Gainesville Sun*, 21 April, 13A.

Reich, Charles A.: 1984. "The New Property." In *Property: Cases, Concepts, Critiques*, ed. Lawrence C. Becker and Kenneth Kipnis, 102–15. Englewood Cliffs, N.J.: Prentice–Hall.

Reiter, Barry J.: 1980. "Contracts, Torts, Relations and Reliance." In *Studies in Contract Law*, 235–311. *See* Reiter and Swan 1980.

—: 1983. "Good Faith in Contract." *Valparaiso University Law Review* 17: 705–34.

Reiter, Barry J., and John Swan, eds.: 1980. *Studies in Contract Law*. Toronto: Butterworths.

Richards, David A. J.: 1979. "Human Rights and the Moral Foundations of the Substantive Criminal Law." *Georgia Law Review* 13: 1395–1446.

Robinson, Paul H.: 1982. "Criminal Law Defenses: A Systematic Analysis." *Columbia Law Review* 82: 199–291.

—: 1984. *Criminal Law Defenses*. 2 vols. St. Paul, Minn.: West Publishing Co.

Ryan, Alan: 1984. "Utility and Ownership." In *Utility and Rights*, 175–95. *See* Frey 1984.

Sales, Bruce D., and Thomas Hafemeister: 1984. "Empiricism and Legal Policy on the Insanity Defense." In *Mental Health and Criminal Justice*, ed. Linda A. Teplin, 253–78. Beverly Hills, Calif.: Sage Publications.

Sartorius, Rolf: 1984. "Persons and Property." In *Utility and Rights*, 196–214. *See* Frey 1984.

Sax, Joseph L.: 1971. "Takings, Private Property and Public Rights." *Yale Law Journal* 81: 149–86.

Schwartz, Alan: 1979. "The Case for Specific Performance." *Yale Law Journal* 89: 271–306.

Seavey, Warren A.: 1927. "Negligence – Subjective or Objective?" *Harvard Law Review* 41: 1–28.

—: 1942. "Principles of Torts." *Harvard Law Review* 56: 72–98.

Simon, William H.: 1978. "The Ideology of Advocacy: Procedural Justice and Professional Ethics." *Wisconsin Law Review*, 29–144.

Slobogin, Christopher: 1985. "The Guilty But Mentally Ill Verdict: An Idea Whose Time Should Not Have Come." *George Washington Law Review* 53: 494–527.

Smith, Chester H., and Ralph E. Boyer: 1971. *Survey of the Law of Property*. 2d edn. St. Paul, Minn.: West Publishing Co.

Smith, J. C.: 1981. "Secondary Participation and Inchoate Offenses." In *Crime, Proof and Punishment*, 21–44. *See* Tapper 1981.

Smith, J. C.: 1984. "Economic Loss and the Common Law Marriage of Contracts and Torts." *University of British Columbia Law Review* 18: 95–126.

Solomon, Robert, and Bruce Feldthusen: 1977. "Recovery for Pure Economic Loss: The Exclusionary Rule." In *Studies in Canadian Tort Law*, 167–88. *See* Klar 1977.

Stening, Anders: 1985. "Evidence and Statistics in Legal Reasoning." In *Man, Law and Modern Forms of Life*, ed. by Eugenio Bulygin, Jean-Louis Gardies, and Ilkka Niiniluoto, 241–49. Dordrecht: D. Reidel Publishing Co.

380 WORKS CITED

Summers, Robert S.: 1968. "'Good Faith' in General Contract Law and the Sales Provisions of the Uniform Commercial Code." *Virginia Law Review* 54: 195–267.
—: 1974. "Evaluating and Improving legal Processes – A Plea for 'Process Values'." *Cornell Law Review* 60: 1–52.
—: 1978. "Comment: 'On The Adversary System and Justice'." In *Philosophical Law*, 122–26. *See* Bronaugh 1978.
Swan, John: 1980. "The Allocation of Risk in the Analysis of Mistake and Frustration." In *Studies in Contract Law*, 181–233. *See* Reiter and Swan 1980.
Swinton, Katherine: 1980. "Foreseeability: Where Should the Award of Contract Damages Cease?" In *Studies in Contract Law*, pp. 61–91. *See* Reiter and Swan 1980.
Tapper, C. F. H., ed.: 1981. *Crime, Proof and Punishment*. London: Butterworths.
Thibaut, John, and Laurens Walker: 1975. *Procedural Justice*. Hillsdale, N. J.: Laurence Erlblaum Associates.
Thomson, Judith Jarvis: 1984. "Remarks on Causation and Liability." *Philosophy & Public Affairs* 11: 101–33.
Michael J.: 1980. "An Economic Approach to the Doctrine of Unconscionability." In *Studies in Contract Law*, 379–421. *See* Reiter and Swan 1980.
Treitel, G. H.: 1979. *The Law of Contract*. 5th edn. London: Stevens & Sons.
—: 1981. "Contract and Crime." In *Crime, Proof and Punishment*, 81–108. See Tapper 1981.
Tullock, Gordon: 1980. *Trials on Trial*. New York: Columbia University Press.
United States, Tort Policy Working Group on the Causes, Extent and Policy Implications of the Current Crisis in Insurance Availability and Affordability: 1986. *Report*. Washington, D.C.: Government Printing Office.
"U.S. Urges the Supreme Court to End Antitrust Suit Against Japanese Firms." 1985. *Wall Street Journal*, 24 January.
Van den Haag, Ernest: 1986. "The Neoclassical Theory of Crime Control." *Criminal Justice Policy Review* 1: 91–109.
Waddams, S. M.: 1980. "Restitution for the Part Performer." In *Studies in Contract Law*, 151–79. *See* Reiter and Swan 1980.
Walker, N. D.: 1981. "The Ultimate Justification: Varieties of the Expressive Theory of Punishment." In *Crime, Proof and Punishment*, 109–26. See Tapper 1981.
Weinrib, Ernest J.: 1983. "Toward a Moral Theory of Negligence Law." In *Justice, Rights, and Tort Law*, 123–48. *See* Bayles and Chapman 1983.
Wexler, David B.: 1985. "Redefining the Insanity Problem." *George Washington Law Review* 53: 528–61.
"When Nightmare of False Arrest Comes True." 1984. *U.S. News & World Report*, 17 December, 45–47.
Williams, Glanville: 1951. "The Aims of the Law of Tort." *Current Legal Problems* 4: 137–76.
—: 1961. *Criminal Law: The General Part*. 2d edn. London: Stevens & Sons.
—: 1965. *The Mental Element in Crime*. Jerusalem: Magnes Press, The Hebrew University.
—: 1978. *Textbook of Criminal Law*. London: Stevens & Sons.
—: 1982. "The Theory of Excuses." *Criminal Law Review*, 732–42.
Williams, Glanville, and B. A. Hepple: 1976. *Foundations of the Law of Tort*. London: Butterworths.
Winston, Kenneth I.: 1974. "On Treating Like Cases Alike." *California Law Review* 62: 1–39.
Wright, Charles Alan: 1983. *The Law of Federal Courts*. 4th edn. St. Paul, Minn.: West Publishing Co.

TABLE OF CASES

381

INDEX

Note: technical terms are often defined and principles are stated at the first reference unless otherwise noted.

387

396INDEX